PLANNING THE PACIFIC NORTHWEST

PLANNING THE PACIFIC NORTHWEST

Edited by Jill Sterrett, FAICP; Connie Ozawa;
Dennis Ryan; Ethan Seltzer; and Jan Whittington

Routledge
Taylor & Francis Group
LONDON AND NEW YORK

Also available in this series
Planning Los Angeles, David C. Sloane, ed.
Planning Chicago, J. Bradford Hunt and Jon B. DeVries, AICP
Planning Atlanta, Harley F. Etienne and Barbara Faga, eds.

First published 2015 by the American Planning Association

Published 2017 by Routledge
2 Park Square, Milton Park, Abingdon, Oxon OX14 4RN
711 Third Avenue, New York, NY 10017, USA

Routledge is an imprint of the Taylor & Francis Group, an informa business

ISBN: 9781611901283 (pbk)

Library of Congress Control Number: 2015930550

CONTENTS

ACKNOWLEDGMENTS

This book is in your hands because of the hard work of a lot of people. We are incredibly grateful to our authors who enthusiastically contributed their chapters and cheerfully dealt with our requests for changes. Many thanks, too, to the Oregon and Washington Chapters of APA for sponsoring this project, and to the staff at APA Planners Press, particularly Sylvia Lewis and Camille Fink, who steered the process. Finally, a huge vote of thanks to my fellow editors (Connie Ozawa, Dennis Ryan, and Jan Whittington) and to Jill Sterrett who, more than anyone, made this a labor of love and insisted on getting it right, and without whom this would have never come to be.

—*Ethan Seltzer*

FOREWORD

Landscape, Culture, and Planning in the Pacific Northwest

The Pacific Northwest is home to misty forests (OK, rainy forests), rocky coastlines, cascade peaks, and high deserts. Appreciation of this landscape, and the desire to protect the natural resources that drive our economies, helped to create statewide growth management programs that are the envy of planners throughout the country. Our growth management history is rooted as much in the landscape and the natural resources that grew our economies as in the culture of those who settled the Pacific Northwest.

Historical settlement patterns continue to influence our planning today. It is this convergence of place and people that defines our region and how we plan for its future. But today the Pacific Northwest is a changing place. New people arrive every day, as much for the diversity of our cities and the cultures harbored and nurtured here, as for the beauty of the place. People still visit to see the natural wonders but many more are now visiting to experience our culture of coffee, beer, food, and bikes and the progressive tolerance of Seattle and Portland.

The Washington and Oregon Chapters of APA have a long history of working together. Building on past successes, we enjoy sharing our experiences and lessons learned. But planning is not static—we are making meaningful changes to our programs, exploring regionalism and the possibility of new frameworks, and considering ecosystems, equity, and the triple-bottom-line goal of sustainability. Like many regions, our demographics are changing, bringing new opportunities and challenges such as declining infrastructure, climate impacts, and social inequities.

Our two chapters come together to explore new issues, celebrate what makes us unique, and yes, to explore our rivalries. Competition between the two states has been and remains fierce . . . and friendly. We began in competition for West Coast primacy through rail termini and shipping ports. Today the rivalry is a bit more tame but no less meaningful. Whether it is who makes the better cup of coffee (Starbucks or Stumptown), who has the best soccer team (Sounders or Timbers), which city has the better transit (the Arial Tram or the Water Taxi), who has the better music scene (grunge and Jimi Hendricks or indie folk), which port you should park your business at, and certainly who makes the best beer, exploring these rivalries makes a trip to the Northwest interesting and worthwhile!

It is our hope that your visit to the Pacific Northwest, through the pages of this book, will provide a better understanding of how our growth management programs came to be and how they have evolved. We also hope that our love for this landscape, our struggles to evolve our planning systems in the face of new demographic and political realities, our commitment to collaboration—and yes—our friendly rivalry shine through.

Welcome and enjoy your visit to the Pacific Northwest!

Ivan W. Miller, AICP
APA Washington
Chapter President

Jason Franklin, AICP
APA Oregon
Chapter President

INTRODUCTION

A Glimmer in the Eye: Planning for a New Northwest

Ethan Seltzer

What makes a region? For the last 100 years, the idea of "region" has taken several turns. To some, regions are distinguished from one another by those features that make them different and separate from all other regions. For others, regions are best defined by what they contribute to something larger, that "whole" of which they are a "region." And for others still, regions are simply defined by the ways in which a large number of characteristics—including ecological, landscape, meteorological, economic, political, infrastructural, historical, cultural—overlap in particular places. We use the term in all kinds of ways.

In 2015, the American Planning Association is meeting in Seattle, in the region known by many as the Pacific Northwest, by others as Cascadia, by some as the northern temperate rainforest, and by others still as Salmon Nation. And that does not even begin to scratch the surface of how this part of North America has been dissected, bounded, described, and defined since it was once known by the fledgling United States simply as the "Oregon Territory."

However, even these definitions fail to reflect other elements of this territory, namely that it is one of the oldest continually inhabited places on the continent. There is a record of human inhabitation here that goes back 12,000 years or more. Whatever we know as the Pacific Northwest is built on what the First Peoples of this place discovered over millennia of living here, trying things, failing, succeeding, and trying new things.

In the 19th century, settlers coming to what is now Oregon's Willamette River Valley believed that these grassy bottomlands had been prepared for them by God. Today we know that the Native American practice of burning the bottomlands to concentrate game in forest edges produced the Edenic landscape encountered by those early Anglo settlers.

So keep your eyes open as you read this book, and you will find examples of many of these region-defining principles at work in the Pacific Northwest today. History, economics, politics, culture, and landscape combine and recombine to present this place as distinct, connected, and more than the sum of the parts. In this regard, we are no different than any other corner of North America.

However, among our distinguishing characteristics is that we plan. This is a region born of planning, when planning was a great national endeavor. Just over 200 years ago, Lewis and Clark took their epic walk, their journey of discovery. The prevailing sense of the region at that time was that after cresting the Rockies, Lewis and Clark would encounter a gradual slope leading off to the shores of the Pacific. Not for the first time, grand plans hatched at a distance had to change drastically.

The use and development of the Columbia River itself spawned another ambitious, nation-scale planning effort as a means for lifting the region, then regarded as a dependent natural resource supplier for the humming economy emanating from eastern metropolises, out of the Great Depression. That planning led to capturing the energy of the Columbia, cumulatively equal to 40 percent of the total hydropower capacity of the nation in this one river system, for rural and urban electrification and the creation of new industries.

Although the lights went on and those new industries were established, as Lewis Mumford famously remarked in 1939, " . . . neither Portland nor Seattle show, from the standpoint of planning, more than metropolitan ambitions that have over-reached themselves. The melancholy plan to increase Portland's population from 300,000 to three million succeeded in disordering and unfocusing its growth: but it did little to give it the benefit of modern city planning practice . . . ."

Despite the use of park plans by the Olmsted brothers in both cities, and occasional grasps for urban greatness, it was slow to arrive in the region. Although planning, as collective intentionality, was part of the development of the region from its start, it was not until the emergence of growth management and the environmental movement that this became a region that was looked to as a leader for planning and planning innovation.These stories and more are all reflected in the chapters that follow.

We undertook the production of this book with a desire to explore the regional roots for the planning here. We asked, "What, if anything, makes planning and its practice distinctive in the Pacific Northwest?" In essence, could we provide our audience of practicing planners, visiting this region on the occasion of the American Planning Association's 2015 National Planning Conference, with

Cascadia Region Context & Challenges

The Cascade Mountains provide extensive natural resources & recreational opportunities–but they also are a "Cascade Curtain," separating progressive & urban "coasties" from more conservative & rural eastern communities.

Thriving Vancouver B.C., Seattle/Tacoma & Portland metropolitan regions along the Cascade corridor, each with the challenges of addressing rapid growth & change.

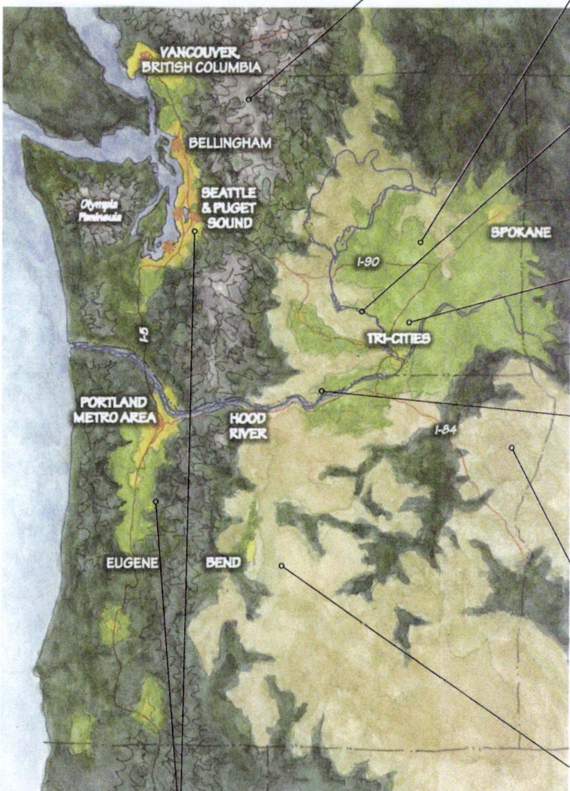

Irrigation from Columbia River has made the area a breadbasket, providing fruit, wheat & wine.

Extensive wind turbines along with 14 hydroelectric dams on the Columbia River provide low cost alternative energy.

Nuclear cleanup at Hanford currently provides an economic base.

The mighty Columbia River runs 1,243 miles from its headwaters in Canada to the Pacific Ocean, forming the boundary between WA & OR

Significant areas of Oregon's basin shrub-steppe ecosystems east of the Cascades have been preserved after 20th century resource extraction pressure.

Central Oregon communities experience growth pressure from recreation-based economic boom.

7 major volcanic peaks, including Mt. St. Helens & Mt. Hood, provide recreational uses & dramatic scenic beauty.

Federal land management has a strong presence in the region, including 14 national forests.

Puget Sound/ Willamette Valley ecosystems are under continuous development pressure - driven by strong I-5 & metro area economies.

Significant earthquake & tsunami threats along Pacific Coast create major planning challenges.

Loss of farmland has been slowed in Oregon but not in Washington.

Coast, southern & eastern areas in both states have high unemployment & few economic development opportunities.

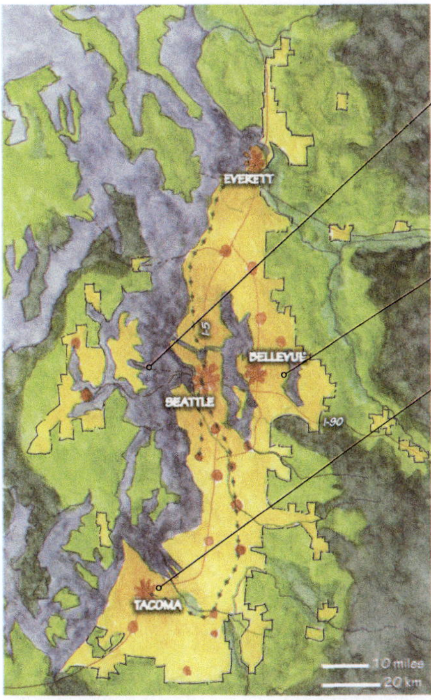

Puget Sound Regional Council provides planning direction for the 4 county region.

Disparate urban counties are connected by floating bridges & ferries.

The region's historic economic base, shipping & timber products, is still reflected in the strength of the maritime activities, e.g., Ports, Navy, ship building.

High tech industries (e.g., Amazon, Microsoft) have gravitated to Downtown Seattle & the Bellevue-Redmond Corridor.

Puget Sound's industrial base (e.g., Boeing, shipping) is spread throughout the region.

The Cascade & Puget Sound region provides extensive & highly accessible outdoor recreation opportunities.

Link light rail & bus rapid transit systems are beginning to connect the region.

- Metropolitan centers
- Urban centers
- Urbanized areas
- Rural areas
- Agricultural lands
- Forest lands
- Major highways
- Rail transit
- Urban growth boundaries (UGB)

Vancouver WA–historically a bedroom community–is now developing a stronger economic base.

Older Portland neighborhoods are vibrant, mixed-use & pedestrian friendly, served by streetcar & frequent bus service.

Extensive & growing light rail transit system.

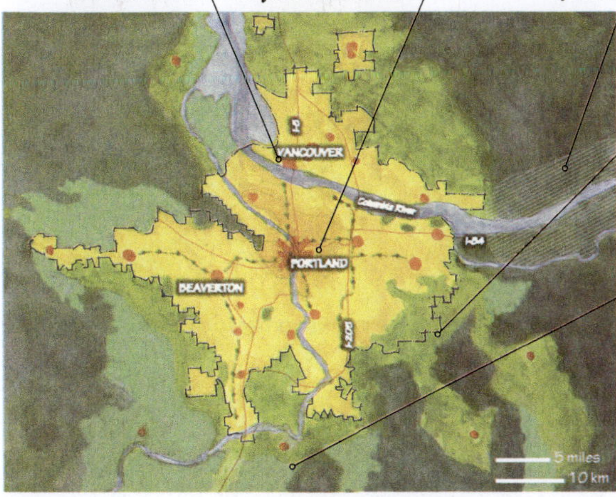

Coordinated bi-state & national planning protects the Columbia Gorge National Scenic Area

Urban & rural reserves provide areas for 50-year urban expansion & farm/forest protection.

Willamette River Valley is a productive agricultural region.

Metro Regional Government provides growth & development controls for cities & counties within UGB.

a portrait of planning in the Pacific Northwest that illuminated the connections between what was seen, what was done, and the landscape it took place in?

Perhaps the fact that we, a group of planners, both practicing and academic, asked these questions is illuminating enough. After all, we ask about connections between landscape and planning because landscape means a lot to this region and the people who have chosen to make it their home. This is an abundant place in a diverse setting. Mountains, rivers, valleys, deserts, and ocean beaches, and yes, cities and suburbs and sprawl all characterize the place. You can take a day trip to the wilderness from an urban center here, and we work hard to make sure that that will always be the case.

We also think about the climate and our weather a lot. Like the number of words that the Eskimos have for "snow," so, too, are we blessed with a lengthy list of words for "rain." Get us started and it is hard to stop: drizzle, sunbreaks, rain, showers, mist, heavy fog, pineapple express, downpour, continuous precipitation, snow level, La Niña, El Niño, and the list goes on. Our planning occurs, rain or shine, conscious of the conditions outside. In this modern era, there is a place at the table here for the natural world, and the landscape keeps us honest.

There is also a place for the public. In Oregon, Goal One of the Statewide Planning Program is, intentionally, Citizen Involvement. In both Seattle and Portland, citizens expect to be involved, so much so that some believe that the process takes on a relentless life of its own. However, the fundamental notion that those affected by the planning ought to be actively engaged in making the plans is accepted. We assume, and often demand, access.

Planning theorists may propose that, on the one hand, planning is a process of social learning, and planners are engaged in ensuring the full and free flow of information and decisions. On the other, others would propose that planning is less about process, and more about outcomes.

Here in the Pacific Northwest, planning practice embraces both points of view. We are here to engage in a social learning process that collaboratively creates plans that we live by, and those plans are expected to improve the fit between people and the landscape and advance conditions of justice and sustainability in our society. It is both, not one or the other, and that, too, should be evident in what you read in the coming pages.

Finally, we expect to make change. We expect planning to make change. Planners, architects, landscape architects, and urban designers have all been deeply engaged in the major social movements of this region in the last 50 years. We are optimistic about what tomorrow will bring, a classic "western" perspective—born of the pioneer movement where moving west held the promise of a better life. We also like to believe that this optimism is born of pragmatism. As one of our regional Fortune 500 corporations likes to say, "Just Do It!" We believe that we should, we must, and we will.

All that said, we will be the first to tell you that you will have a tough time finding the definitive proof that planning in this region is different than planning in other regions. We tried to find it, but planning practice is both so contextual and, at the same time, borrows so heavily from practice in other places that the dividing line between what is authentically regional, and what is not, is hard to discern.

This book arose from a request made to planning practitioners and academics in the region to contribute articles that exemplified the art, practice, and outcomes of planning in Oregon and Washington. The chapters here emerged from that call for participation. However, know that there are more facets to planning in our region than are present here. We did not separately seek to fill gaps in the contents.

As a result, not all important planning work is captured by these articles. There is a dearth of social policy and equity work in this collection, and only a light mention of health-related planning. Planners in the Pacific Northwest are also working on pressing issues associated with urbanization and change, particularly with shifting demographics among youth, the elderly, immigrant communities, and growing diversity generally.

We face huge challenges in this region with public finance and the ability of local communities to meet basic service needs, quite apart from investing in the implementation of plans. New issues surrounding coal exports and oil trains, along with ocean planning and species recovery, make environmental planning an ongoing focal point for planner activity.

The collection does not illustrate any of the region's planning exports: involvement in the global arena—particularly urbanization in the Pacific Rim—which constitutes a loop of new intelligence and experiences that come back to influence policies and practices at home. Similarly, this is a collection with a profoundly urban and westward tilt: There are important and specific issues associated with the dry side of the Cascade Mountains, with planning on tribal lands, and with public lands that keep planners busy.

Consequently, although we set out to address broad questions about the nature of planning here, we worked with what we received and did not attempt to achieve a comprehensive, encyclopedic recitation of activity. That said, we still think this collection works well for our purposes.

Think of it like this. Looking for regional differences in planning styles is much like birding: You have to relax and look for the movement out of the corner of your eye to actually find what you're looking for. The chapters here are like birds flitting through the forest. Keep your eyes open and you will find plenty.

Here in the upper left edge of the continent, we're kind of beverage-crazy. Beer, wine, coffee, cider, boutique spirits . . . we do them all. Our advice: Grab your favorite beverage, read these chapters, and then draw your conclusions, just as we have.

In fact, view this book as a bit of a map to that unmapped part of the continent that Lewis and Clark visited. We've organized your trip here using three distinct lenses: past, present, and future. In the first section, we trace the link between planning and the transition in this region from its historic timber and agricultural past to its high-tech and creative class present. In the second section, we present a series of chapters that help to explain our interest in being green, and more than that, our commitment to serving that green drive behind much of what we do.

In the third section we look to the future. What's next? Where will we see it first? How will it tackle the "wicked problems" we have left behind for the next generation of planners, activists, and decision makers?

We are proud to call ourselves planners and to be able to bring you this volume. We are committed to the art and practice, craft and profession, and vital role that planning is and plays in this region we believe in.

As some have proposed, planning is the "collective organization of hope." Planning is fundamentally a hopeful enterprise. We do it together, on behalf of real places with pressing needs and valuable, legitimate aspirations. Frankly, it's a privilege to be a planner in this region, and to be entrusted with working with our communities, big and little, toward these ends. We hope you, too, enjoy the journey.

SECTION 1:
PLANNING RETROSPECTIVE: FROM TIMBER TO TECHNOLOGY

Introduction

Connie Ozawa

The Pacific Northwest has changed dramatically over the past half century. Population growth has far exceeded the national pace. Between 1950 and 2010, the population of Oregon increased by 152 percent and Washington's population grew by 182 percent, compared to 104 percent for the country as a whole. The region's three major cities, Portland, Seattle, and Vancouver, British Columbia, have grown steadily during this period, with a minor dip in the 1970s, and nearly explosive, double-digit growth since the 1990s. Historically, the region's economy was based on the land and sea's rich natural resources, with timber, agriculture, fisheries, and shipping playing strong roles. Today, although timber and agriculture remain important, Washington is home to eight Fortune 500 companies, and five of these are notably not resource-based: Microsoft, Amazon, Starbucks, Costco, and Nordstrom Department Stores. Oregon hosts two Fortune 500 companies: Nike, producing sports shoes and apparel, and Precision Cast Parts, a manufacturer in the aerospace and defense industry. Intel, although not a Fortune 500 company, is Oregon's largest private employer. The firms mentioned here evoke popular images associated with the Pacific Northwest but they represent a distinct shift from the region's historical economic base. How has the region accommodated such change?

Consider hometowns across North America. Many of today's urbanites, who grew up on farms or in small cities in the 1960s or 1970s, return to see

Puget Sound on the Pacific Coast, *1870. Albert Bierstadt's paintings have defined the country's image of the Pacific Northwest for over a century.*

subdivisions sprawling out across former wheat fields and rangelands, downtowns that are boarded up as big box stores conveniently located just off the interstate highways draw in yesterday's Main Street shoppers. The landscapes of our cities, metropolitan areas, small towns, and the spaces in between are our collective creations. As planners, what is our role in these transitions?

Planning Does Not Occur on a Blank Canvas

As Ethan Seltzer pointed out in the Introduction to this volume, while the landscape of the Pacific Northwest had been shaped by First Nations peoples for thousands of years, the institutions affecting planning as we know it in this region, specifically the legal and state-level resource administration, have a much, much briefer history. The Pacific Northwest bears many similarities across the jurisdictional boundaries of the states of Oregon and Washington, and its Canadian neighbor, British Columbia, but institutions that have developed over the past five decades are distinct and have created particular, though perhaps subtle, differences.

What is common about planning in the Pacific Northwest is first, that we do it—and we do it statewide. Oregon was among the pioneers in state-level land-use planning, putting laws and institutions in place in the 1960s, 1970s, and 1980s to compel localities to undertake comprehensive plan making to protect the state's natural resources for its resource-based economy. Washington started state-level land and coastal areas management slightly later, with an arguably less top-down approach and with a stronger eye toward containing and managing growth. It is clear that the institutions in both states reflect an awareness of the precious nature of natural resources, riding along with the national awakening of the environmental movement of the 1960s and 1970s, but, in an important distinction from the other parts of the country, also acting on it.

In the chapters that follow, the authors provide a primer to key legislation as well as land and natural resource management strategies at the state and local levels in Washington and Oregon, a sense of how their implementation looks on the ground, and the effectiveness of these major efforts.

But, also as Seltzer notes, the history of planning in the Pacific Northwest is not encrypted only in relatively prescribed outcomes, state planning goals, and urban growth boundaries, but also in process. The "uncommon level of civil engagement" in Portland observed by sociologists Putnam and Feldstein (2003, 268) and the mandate for citizen participation in the Oregon state land-use law suggest attention to the changeable nature of culture and values, and the need for a mechanism to allow for change. This commitment to broaden the bandwidth of information and perspectives through public outreach and participation is also evident in Washington, especially in the Seattle region.

Interestingly, those who have commented on the cultural characters of different regions across North America demarcate differences between Oregon and Washington. Perhaps best known is political scientist Daniel Elazar's identification of three political cultures: individualist, moralistic, and traditionalistic (Elazar 1972). In his work of nearly half a century ago, Elazar described Washington as a blend of moral and individualistic political cultures, whereas he saw Oregon as decidedly moralistic, suggesting a stronger commitment to collective needs and community benefits as contrasted to the privileging of private gains. Was Elazar's assessment accurate? Can we see the influence of divergent political cultures in state institutions and in our cities today? Or have the political cultures moved toward convergence?

The chapters that follow provide insights into these questions and others. We assume the table of contents is a sufficient road map for readers to navigate this section, so rather than preview each chapter, we simply invite you to move at your own pace across these pages. Those less familiar with the Pacific Northwest will enjoy Sheila Martin's introduction to the region. More than simply the observations of an "astute visitor," Martin hints about the commonalities and the differences that distinguish Portland, Seattle, and Vancouver, British Columbia. Tovar and McCormick, Eber, and Adler review critical elements of the legal frameworks that mark the region and the primary actors and political tensions that created and recreated pivotal institutions. Daniels et al. provide a rigorous scientific assessment of the effectiveness of Oregon and Washington land-use policies in protecting working farms and forest lands. Other chapters (here, but also in Part Two) illuminate the degree to which the state systems have influenced local planning in a variety of cities across Oregon and Washington. The section ends with a vignette about what we imagine is a critical element of good planning: a planner's rediscovered recognition of the passion and love she feels for place—in her case, Seattle and the Pacific Northwest.

Places have unique pasts, but our histories hold a reservoir of alternative models that can spark new ideas and adapt old ones. We hope that by sharing knowledge about the foundations of planning in the Pacific Northwest, we will ignite a wider dialogue about the importance of institutions and laws and the role of the various publics and professionals in our planning efforts. After all, cultures and values are constantly changing, and today's action is tomorrow's history.

CHAPTER 1

Eclectic Cascadia

Sheila Martin

A visitor to the Pacific Northwest might discover its multiple personalities by boarding an Amtrak train in Eugene, Oregon, and riding it north to Vancouver, British Columbia. The slow ride north offers an opportunity to read Cascadia's history, absorb its present, and contemplate its future while surveying the landscapes, the character of the cities and towns, and the people who inhabit them. Join me in a quick journey through this unique place via the narrative of one person's view. During our journey, we might ask, "What weaves these diverse people and places into the tapestry that we call Cascadia?" (Figure 1.1).

As we board the train in Eugene, we consider the characteristics of urban life and rural landscapes that unite Cascadia. The region's economic history is tied to its forests, mountains, seas, rivers, and valleys. The southern start of the Amtrak Cascades route is also the south end of the Willamette Valley. Defined by the river that emerges from the Calapooya Mountains near Eugene and flows to its confluence with the Columbia River, the Willamette Valley contains more than two-thirds of Oregon's population and nine of its 10 largest cities. The river feeds the fertile valley that sustained native peoples for over 10,000 years and attracted the early, mostly white, settlers of the 19th century. The mouth of the Columbia River was the site at which the Lewis and Clark Corps of Discovery sighted their destination, the Pacific Ocean, in 1805.

Today, the valley's agriculture includes the dominant grass seed and nursery industry, and the smaller growers that feed the region's foodie reputation. As we travel through the valley we find patches of berries, orchards of nuts and small fruits, fields of hops and vegetables, poultry and dairy farms, and many vineyards. Oregon's fruits and vegetables are grown on relatively small farms—quite different from the massive tracts of wheat, silage corn, and soybeans of the Midwest. With a strong appreciation for this agricultural diversity and legacy, Oregon's planning system has played a key role in preventing the rapid loss of farmland that has occurred in many other urbanizing places (Farmland Information Center 2014).

Arriving in Portland at Union Station, we emerge at the center of a region that has experienced a radical transformation since the 1980s: growth, prosperity, and redevelopment reshaped the city and the region from a backwater timber town to an edgy, progressive, and prosperous metropolis that attracts the young creative class from the Midwest and East, retiring baby boomers from California, and immigrants from all over to the technology businesses in the central city and the suburbs. While these groups are attracted by different amenities, they all experience a place that looks different from where they came. And they may understand that planning has a lot to do with it.

With a 2013 population of 592,000 (Population Research Center 2013), Portland is part of a seven-county metropolitan area of just over 2.2 million. Growing, thriving regions have long attracted young, smart people to begin their careers. Despite an economy subject to steep downturns and slow recoveries, Portland's ability to draw and retain young creatives has exceeded expectations. (Jurjevich and Schrock 2012) These in-migrants have transformed parts of inner northeast and southeast Portland into enclaves of high educational attainment and income in neighborhoods that once were considered blighted. As we look around at the pubs, restaurants, unique retail, reliable transit, and bike lanes we understand the appeal.

Hop off at Union station and you can take light rail across the river to the east side of the city or off to its western suburbs, into downtown, or walk a short way into the Pearl District. The transformation of the district's warehouses and a former 140-acre switching yard into a pedestrian-friendly area with upscale restaurants, bars, and retail, the nation's largest independent bookstore, and a mix of upscale housing alongside affordable units demonstrates the power of urban renewal.

From the Pearl, you can grab the streetcar through a downtown that re-emerged earlier than many others in the United States. Short city blocks, bike lanes, transit options, a beautiful riverfront, food carts, coffee and bike shops, and tax-free shopping define downtown. Portland State University anchors the south end and serves the city as a source of knowledge, entertainment, and art. After a little downtown exploring of the south end, you hop on the Max Yellow or Green Line back to Union Station, ready to continue the Cascadia journey.

Cross the Columbia River and enter Vancouver, Washington, a Portland suburb with a distinct identity stemming from a different tax system, planning system, and a "we aren't Portland" attitude that offers an alternative to the hipster lifestyle across the river. Washington State is bigger, richer, and more famous than Oregon. With almost seven million in population, its economy includes big hitters like Boeing, Microsoft, and Amazon. Its planning system is less top-down than Oregon's, but the variation in its landscape and the contrasts between its urban and rural areas are similarly stark.

Following the Columbia

Traveling into northern Clark County, Washington, you're following the Columbia River that separates Oregon and Washington through a landscape that begins to feel rugged as Mount St. Helens—which lost 1,300 feet of height in its 1980 eruption—comes into view on the right, followed by Mount Rainer. While Washington has less total forestland than Oregon, its 21 million acres of forests represent about 50 percent of its land area. With a temperate rain forest and one of the mainland United States' highest peaks, Washington has a lot to protect.

The train stops near Olympia, Washington's capital, at the south end of Puget Sound, where the state legislature debates changes in planning and environmental laws that attempt to protect the state's many natural jewels. The state's Growth Management Act, State Environmental Protection Act, and Shoreline Management Act comprise a trio of policies enacted over the years to preserve the state's environment and guide its growth.

As we approach Seattle, we begin to notice a difference from the city we left behind in Portland. Seattle seems bigger, faster, and richer, with a more dramatic landscape. When the clouds lift, you can see the tall peaks of the Cascades as well as the shorter, but dramatic, Olympics range, surrounded on three sides by water.

This faster, bigger, richer feel is backed up by the data. The Seattle metropolitan area population outranks Portland's by 1.3 million, and it has 680,000 more workers (U.S. Bureau of Labor Statistics 2014). The Seattle metropolitan economy added almost 147,000 jobs from 2003 to 2012—an increase of 9.5 percent. By contrast, Portland's job growth during the same period was a slower eight percent. And Seattle area wages average about $10,000 per year higher than those in the Portland region. Both states have minimum wages higher than that set by the federal government. But Washington's, at $9.32 is 22 cents higher than Oregon's. And as a sign of the region's progressive politics, the municipality of SeaTac voted in November 2013 to give their workers $15.00 minimum (Johnson 2013).

The train pulls into Seattle at the King Street Station near Pioneer Square. Walk east, and you're in the International District, emblematic of one of the key differences between Portland and Seattle: ethnic diversity. With just over 600,000 people, the city of Seattle is not much larger than Portland, but Census 2010 tells us that ethnic minorities comprise a larger share of its population, although both cities are less diverse than the United States overall (U.S. Census Bureau 2010a).

Like Portland, Seattle residents are proud of their sustainability ethic, and they show it in how they get to work. Residents of both of these Cascadian cities are less likely to drive alone to work than the residents of many other U.S. cities. Across the United States, about 76 percent of commuters drive alone to work compared to 59 percent in the city of Portland and 49 percent in Seattle. In Portland, 11 percent of workers choose public transit while 20 percent of Seattle workers do; compared to the national average of five percent (U.S. Census Bureau 2012). Despite their more sustainable commuting habits, the population of the Seattle region overall spends more miles on the road—23 percent more vehicle miles traveled on a per capita basis than people living in the Portland region (Schrank, Eisele, and Lomax 2012).

We catch the Number 40 bus and head north to the South Lake Union area. Once an industrial center, South Lake Union is now a symbol of Seattle's new economy. It is home to the headquarters of Amazon and includes a heavy presence by Microsoft and a number of tech startups. Microsoft cofounder Paul Allen understood that starting a technology company is lonely work, and that success might depend upon one's ability to meet with and talk to others doing the same thing. So he created a place where smart people can work, live, and hang out—and share their ideas.

And smart they are. Among Seattle adults almost 58 percent have at least a bachelor's degree, while only 45 percent of their Portland counterparts do. This probably goes a long way toward explaining the difference in per capita income and wages. While Portland's per capita income is about 95 percent of the national metropolitan average, Seattle is over-performing the nation's metro average by 18 percent (U.S. Bureau of Economic Analysis 2013). The region's economy includes a mix of mature and emerging industries, including aerospace, information technology, transportation and logistics, and life sciences. These industries offer plenty of high-paid, high-skilled jobs and the region also nurtures a growing clean-tech industry.

We head down to Pike Place Market to visit the longest continuously running farmers market in the United States and one of Cascadia's most visited tourist attractions. Here we get a glimpse of the variety of seafood and produce available in Washington and a view of the waterfront that once was the center of Seattle maritime trade. When the Alaskan Way Viaduct is taken down in 2016, after the completion of a new tunnel, this beautiful waterfront will be visible from many parts of the city.

As we head back to the King Street Station to reboard the train, we notice that it has started to rain. That rainy, cloudy environment unites Seattle, Portland, and Vancouver, all within the northern temperate rainforest on the west side of the Cascade Mountains.

The train takes us up through the northern suburbs of the Salish Sea (formerly known as Puget Sound) region and we enter the Skagit Valley. Defined

Sister Cities of the Northwest

CATEGORY	VANCOUVER	SEATTLE	PORTLAND
YEAR FOUNDED & ECONOMIC ORIGINS	1886 - Central government direction	1869 - Lumber boom, Yukon gold rush	1845 - Farming, Oregon Trail
ECONOMY	International trade, regional service	Robust high tech & high skill economy	Intel, Nike, clothing designers, artisans
CULTURE	International cosmopolitan	Geek hip w/ a leftover hint of grunge	Mellow, woodsy with full hipster cred
NICKNAME	Terminal City	The Emerald City	Stumptown
COOL NEW PLANNED DISTRICT	False Creek Olympic Village	South Lake Union	Pearl District
"EVEN-COOLER" DISTRICT	Mount Pleasant	Capitol Hill	Northwest 23rd
REGIONAL PLANNING	Intentionally compact with dense livable centers	Not as organized as Portland, but Regional Council is trying	Strongest Metro governance in the country, HoooYAAAH!
MEDIA EXPOSURE	2010 Winter Olympics, X-files	Sleepless in Seattle, 2013 SUPERBOWL, Frasier	Portlandia
TRANSIT	Driverless SkyTrain	Late on rail, yet lowest SOV use	"MAX" Rail transit, streetcars, excellent TOD
BICYCLING	Separated bike lanes into downtown & along waterfronts	Regional trails & commuters pedaling up "impossible" hills	10 times the national average of greenways,
FAVORITE DRINK	Afternoon tea with Mum, Molson's with a hockey game	Coffee, coffee, coffee, beer, coffee, coffee, wine, coffee	Beer - consumed within ¼ mile of the brewery
GREEN CRED	Greenpeace birthplace, plans to be world's "Greenest" by 2020	Salmon recovery, shoreline restoration Sustainable Seattle	Grey to Green program, Climate Action Plan, home of the Bottle Bill
LANDMARK	Whistler, pencil towers	Mt Rainier, Space Needle	Mt Hood, bridges
PARKS	Stanley Park & False Creek, run by a rare elected parks board	Great system built on Olmsted legacy & "Forward Thrust"	5,000-acre Forest Park, skateparks, urban parks, regional trails
SIGNATURE ATTRACTION	Granville Island & a really great Chinatown	Pike Place Market, Waterfront	Powell's Books Riverwalk
SIGNATURE FOOD	Dim sum in the morning sushi at night	Thrown salmon, local celebrity chefs' specials	Donuts, food carts, freegans

Figure 1.1. Sister cities of the Pacific Northwest: Three shades of gray

by the Skagit River that flows westward from the Cascades, the Skagit Valley, famous for its tulips and daffodils, is one of the most important agricultural valleys remaining and contains one of the region's strongest remaining salmon runs (Canty, Martinsons, and Kumar 2012). It is, however, under increasing development pressure; the state's Office of Financial Management predicts that more than 45,000 people will move to Skagit county by 2040—a 40 percent increase in its population.

As we leave the Skagit Valley and near Bellingham, Washington, Mount Baker looms toward the east, and we are reminded that Cascadia is part of the Ring of Fire—and that all of our cities lie within the Cascade Subduction Zone.

We cross the border at Blaine and soon we are in Vancouver, a city with about the same number of people as Seattle (Statistics Canada 2014), but a very different feel. As we emerge from the train, we hear many languages—only about half of the city's residents speak English as their first language. With more than 100,000 people speaking either Cantonese or another Chinese language, the city has a decidedly Asian feel.

Vancouver is also geographically much smaller than either Portland or Seattle at about 114 square kilometers or about 44 square miles, fitting Seattle's population into less than one-third of the space. Like the cities to the south, Metro Vancouver's population is growing. The region added about 197,000 residents from 2006 to 2011, and the greatest share of that growth was in the suburban city of Surry (Statistics Canada 2014b).

The economy of metro Vancouver appears to be recovering from the recession. With a 7.1 percent unemployment rate, it is one of the lowest in Canada, but still higher than the current rates in both Seattle and Portland. The city boasts job growth in many new economy sectors, including digital media, information and communications technology, life sciences, and sustainable industries. But the region's economy continues to rely heavily on the mining industry, an important part of the economy since the gold rushes of the mid-1800s. It is strongly linked to the region's transportation and logistics sector which benefits from its close geographic and cultural ties to Asia.

Rural Cascadia

After returning to Seattle from Vancouver, we choose the train east from Seattle to Spokane, ride through the pass and enter the dry landscapes of Eastern Washington. Eastern Cascadia seems a different world than the wet west. Rural counties in Oregon and Washington feel economically distant from the technology and sustainability driven world of urban Cascadia.

Much of our journey through eastern Washington follows the mighty Columbia River. As the Columbia flows on its 1,200 mile course, it covers territory in seven states and the Canadian province of British Columbia, dividing Washington and Oregon through the scenic Columbia Gorge. The Columbia

River provided passage for the Lewis and Clark Corps of Discovery and it was at the mouth of the Columbia River, northwest of Portland, that they finally reached their destination, the Pacific Ocean. Hundreds of dams on the Columbia provide low-cost power that supports irrigation of this dry land. Passing wheat fields, apple orchards, vineyards, and rangeland dotted with wind turbines, we realize that the rural areas of Cascadia are vital to the survival of its cities and the economy of the region. The energy, water, and food provided by rural Cascadia to its cities are essential to their sustainability. As we plan the future of our states we realize that it depends in equal measure on the thriving cities and the people, towns, and landscapes that fall between them.

Perhaps it is this common fate that provides the thread that stitches together Cascadia's tapestry of cities, forests, mountains, farms, orchards and wide-open spaces. Perhaps our common appreciation of these diverse treasures keeps us asking, "How do we enhance and protect our human and natural assets?" As the train returns to Portland and we step into its thriving downtown, I realize that this question connects Cascadia's past with future, its north and south, and its rural and urban people.

CHAPTER 2

The Evolution of Washington State's Growth Management Law

Joseph Tovar, FAICP, and
Michael J. McCormick, FAICP

Among Western states, Washington has a relatively large population (its 6.9 million is second only to California) and yet it is geographically among the smallest (only Hawaii is smaller). Forestry, fisheries, and mining were the state's economic base during its first century (1889 to 1989), but as these industries declined Washington's economy shifted to other sectors. The state's diverse physical and evolving economic regions have shaped its political geography, which in turn has shaped state laws, institutions, and the practice of planning.

Agriculture has remained a mainstay of Washington's economy, focused in the rural counties throughout the much of the state (Figure 2.1). In contrast, the Seattle Metro region's four counties and 82 cities are home to 60 percent of the state's population and almost 70 percent of its jobs, all in less than 10 percent of the state's land mass. It is also home to aerospace, high-tech, and biotech industries, and was identified in a 2013 study at the University of Toronto as one of the planet's peak performing economic centers. The tension between rural/agricultural Washington and urban Washington has been a major factor in the structure and application of our state's Growth Management Act (GMA), resulting in a number of features to respect and reflect regional diversity.

This chapter provides a brief overview of Washington laws and institutions designed to address the tensions, frictions, and conflicts inherent in planning; a summary of the first 25 years of planning under the GMA; challenges for the next 25 years; and potential lessons for other states and their community of planners.

Washington's Land-Use Law Trifecta: SEPA, SMA, and GMA

Washington's legislature adopted planning enabling statutes beginning in the 1930s, but it was not until the 1970s that the first two pieces of the state's modern land-use law trifecta emerged. In 1971, the legislature adopted the State Environmental Policy Act (SEPA), and the Shoreline Management Act (SMA). Both laws were passed a year after the first Earth Day, and reflect a strong environmental protection bias. SEPA's purpose was to "prevent or eliminate damage to the environment and biosphere" while the SMA's purpose was "to prevent the inherent harm in an uncoordinated and piecemeal development of the state's shorelines." Both these statutes have continued in force since then, but were inadequate to address the escalating growth challenges that emerged in the 1980s.

That decade saw a dramatic 18 percent increase in the state's population, from 4.13 million to 4.87 million. Although most of the growth, impacts, and political turmoil were concentrated in the greater Seattle region, other parts of the state also experienced growth pains. The majority of state residents did not live in cities in 1989, but in unincorporated urban areas. The dominant pattern of new growth and development in the 1980s was neither truly urban nor truly rural. It was a landscape of suburban sprawl—a low-density development pattern with inadequate infrastructure, marginal services, fragmented governmental accountability, local government competition and conflict, degraded environmental quality, and a visual environment that was anonymous at best, unsightly at worst.

By the end of the decade, a "perfect storm" of political forces converged. There was a public outcry about escalating property taxes, housing costs, traffic congestion, environmental degradation, and the continued loss of farm and forest lands to urbanization. In 1989 three key events happened.

First, over the summer, a series of articles by urban critic Neal Peirce was featured in the *Seattle Times*, illuminating the state's broken land-use decision-making process. Second, a longtime conservative councilman from a rural district in King County (the state's most populous county), was defeated in the Republican primary by a slow-growth advocate, prompting the state Republican Party to recognize that growth management was a potent political issue.

Third, a report issued by the state associations of city and county planning directors, "Toward a Growth Strategy for Washington," detailed the specific shortcomings of Washington's prior land-use laws and offered recommendations for a new approach. Printed in the *Seattle Times*, their report was broadly circulated to state, county, and city elected officials and provided input to the Growth Strategies Commission (GSC), which was chartered in 1989 by the governor and the legislature. The GSC developed a comprehensive set of recommendations, incorporating much of the planning directors' work, to serve as the basis of the 1990 legislation.

Urban and rural counties in Washington State

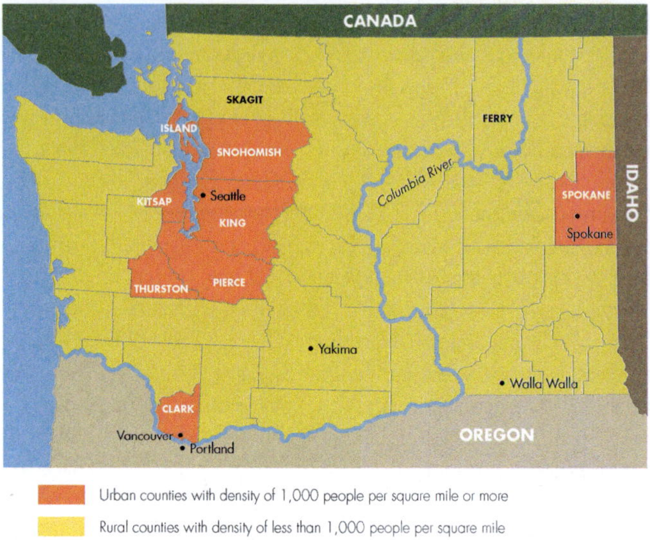

Figure 2.1. Seventy-three percent of Washington's population is concentrated in eight urban counties, with six in the greater Seattle region along Puget Sound.

State leaders responded to this rising tide of discontent. Gov. Booth Gardner, Democratic House Speaker Joe King, and Republican Senate Majority Leader Jeanette Hayner led the legislature to adopt House Bill 2929 in the winter of 1990, phase I of the GMA. Believing this first phase was too weak, an environmental coalition put Initiative 547 on the fall ballot of 1990. Their initiative would have replaced the GMA with a more top-down, centralized system, with a much stronger state role in many respects similar to the Oregon model.

Development interests, editorial boards across the state, and the Washington Chapter of the American Planning Association (APA) opposed I-547. State legislative leaders of both parties promised to strengthen the GMA if I-547 was defeated. When the voters rejected the initiative by a wide margin, the legislators adopted House Bill 1025 in the 1991 legislative session. This legislation strengthened the GMA by creating a state appellate body, the Growth Management Hearings Board, and incorporated many of the recommendations of the governor's Growth Strategies Commission. The new planning regime, with the GMA as its foundation, was established.

Foundational Principles

The GMA is the product of the political process—an intent explicitly noted at the time of the statute's creation in 1990. Much of the debate on the initial bills was the role of the state verses the role of local elected officials. The political decision was to defer to local decision making within the broad (and sometimes ambiguous) language found in the Act. This principle and four others resolving such conflicting views illuminate the underpinnings of the GMA.

Compelling State Interests versus Local Autonomy

Land-use, transportation, and environmental planning in Washington occur primarily at the local level. However, local planning takes place within a statutory framework that includes the GMA, the SMA, and SEPA (Figure 2.2).

In considering a new statutory framework, the laws in Florida, New Jersey, Georgia, and Oregon were surveyed. The balance between the roles of the state government and local government was a key part of that inquiry. The GMA was an attempt to create an updated framework for land-use decision making that is proactive rather than reactive, comprehensive rather than piecemeal, and compels cooperation and coordination among local govern-

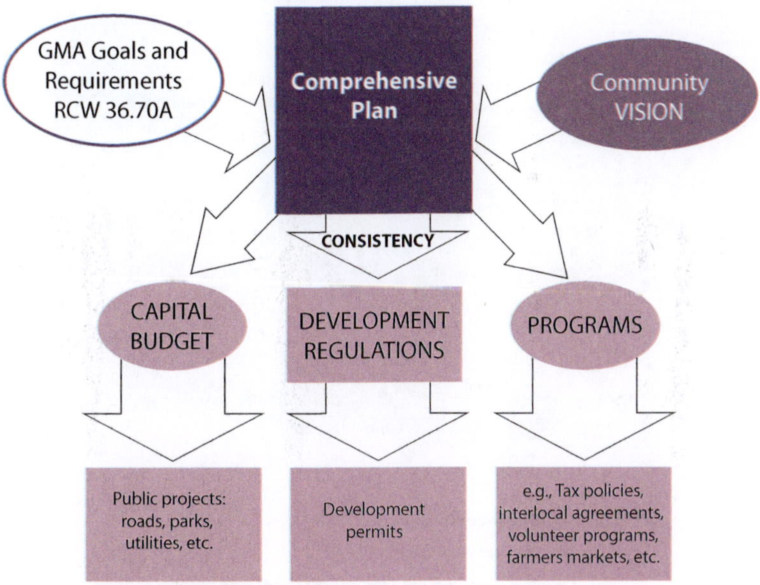

Figure 2.2. The Growth Management Act requires that local comprehensive plans comply with state goals and requirements and that local development regulations, capital budgets, and programs be consistent with the local comprehensive plan.

ments rather than perpetuate a history of competition and conflict. It reformed prior laws and institutions that had made managing growth difficult, contentious, confusing, and ineffective.

Rather than require local government plans and regulations to first receive state approval before becoming effective, Washington's legislature instead decided that the plans and regulations adopted by cities and counties are to be presumed valid upon adoption. Such local actions may only be reversed if appealed by a party with standing, and found by the state growth management hearings board to be "clearly erroneous," which is a relatively high standard of proof.

When appeals do occur, they travel different paths in Washington than Oregon. Rather than the Oregon model of a single appellate institution with jurisdiction throughout the state, the GMA created three independent growth hearings boards to adjudicate appeals: one for cities and counties in the Seattle metropolitan region, one for every other Western Washington county and city outside the Seattle region, and one for those east of the Cascade Mountain Range. This bow to regional differences reflected the political reality that legislators from more conservative parts of the state that did not want to have a centralized, top-down appellate process. Similarly, the legislature decided to require only the largest

Figure 2.3. Of Washington's counties, 29 are under the authority of the Growth Management Act and include 95 percent of the state's population.

appellate process. Similarly, the legislature decided to require only the largest and fastest-growing counties to be subject to all of the GMA's provisions (Figure 2.3). Although later consolidated into a single board for administrative purposes, the structure of three regional review panels was retained.

The "bottom-up" component of the GMA delegated to local governments the need to balance the goals of the GMA and make local choices within the framework of GMA requirements. Each goal of the Act is clear enough when viewed alone (e.g., Goal 11, "protect the environment," or Goal 6, "protect private property rights"). But the tension among the goals becomes apparent when viewed together. These tensions ultimately have to be resolved at the local level by the city and county elected officials who adopt comprehensive plans and regulations.

Some point to the defeat of I-547 to argue that Washington's GMA is a "bottom-up" system rather than a "top-down" system. It has elements of both. Local governments have broad discretion to make policy choices (the bottom-up part); however, those choices are bound by the goals and requirements of the Act and are subject to appeal to the Growth Management Hearings Board (the top-down part). This balance of top down (state) and bottom up (local) was finally clarified by the 2007 Washington State Supreme Court ruling:

> The Growth Management Hearings Board is charged with determining compliance with the GMA and, when necessary, invalidating noncomplying comprehensive plans and development regulations. Although RCW 36.70A.3201 requires the Board to give deference to a [city or county], those [local] actions must be consistent with the goals and requirements of the GMA (*Swinomish Indian Tribal Community v. WW-GMHB*, 61 Wn.2d 415, 423-24, 166 P.3d 1198 (2007)).

The flexibility that the GMA assigned to local governments created a major unintended consequence for local elected officials. The elections of 1992 and 1994 saw a dramatic turnover at the county level, particularly in more conservative rural counties. In some cases, incumbents chose to retire quietly; in others they were turned out by more conservative candidates. It is too simplistic to blame all of it on the GMA, but votes on critical area ordinances and resource lands regulations did contribute to a large turnover of county officials in the 1990s.

Initially, the state's role was seen as a source of financing and technical assistance. The enactments relegated to the state the role of responding to local plans and being subject to the consistency requirement. The Department of Commerce continues to play an important role in providing technical assistance and advice to local governments. Unfortunately, many other state agencies view the GMA as just another statute, and less important than other statutes that gave them a more dominant role. This view of the GMA by some state agencies has made integration of the GMA with the SMA and SEPA difficult, as shown in the three case studies below.

SEPA and GMA

One of the products of the Regulatory Reform Act of 1995 was direction to integrate SEPA and the GMA. The theoretical construct was to have SEPA analysis provide needed environmental information to support planning under the GMA. Early demonstration projects helped sort out how integration could be done at the level of comprehensive plan adoption to enable the reduction (or elimination) of need for further environmental review at the permit level.

In 2012 the legislature initiated a stakeholder group to study ways to reform SEPA, such as increasing the threshold for exemptions of projects from environmental review, provided sufficient analysis had been performed at the level of the plan or regulations. Resistance from environmental groups, tribes, and some state agencies has limited the success of these efforts at reform.

SMA and GMA

While SMA and GMA were nominally integrated by legislative fiat in 1995, several major philosophical conflicts stood in the way of functional integration, and continue to do so. In contrast to the GMA, the SMA has a stronger state role, which includes broad authority to accept or reject both local plans and project permits.

A hearings board decision in 2002, which attempted to interpret the meaning to the 1995 statute, evoked a strong pushback from both local governments and state agencies. The legislature took the unprecedented step of unanimously reversing the hearing board decision, in effect undoing its own prior intent to "integrate" these two laws. This led to several years of appellate litigation and further legislative action before the dust finally settled. To date, meaningful integration of the SMA and the GMA remains elusive.

Watershed Planning and the GMA

The need to deal with water issues has long been a hotly contested issue. Who gets the water—and for what—is the single most important factor in where and how growth occurs. The federal listing of salmon in Puget Sound as a threatened species spawned more than a decade of state, regional, and local government effort, studies, plans, controversy, and litigation.

The planning for salmon protection and recovery was deliberately designed and imposed from above as a process parallel to, but disconnected from, the planning, regulation, and capital improvement budgeting under the GMA. Local governments, in turn, have refused to accept any further encroachment on their land-use prerogatives for the sake of improving water quality and the health of the Puget Sound ecosystem. It is not clear how the ultimate need to protect the environment and regulate growth and development will be reconciled.

Institutional Dysfunction Among Pre-GMA Local Governments—Blurred Roles

Local governance (the authorities and roles of city, county, and special district governments) was a major pre-GMA source of confusion, competition, friction, and conflict. These shortcomings, and some of their land-use consequences, were documented in a study commission report to the state legislature titled *The Quiet Crisis in Local Governance* (Washington State Local Governance Study Commission 1988). The report identified the archaic, fragmented, and dysfunctional system of local governance in Washington. The report explained that the proliferation of special purpose districts and the rise of counties as urban-services providers sapped the economic vitality from cities as focal points for new growth. This resulted in a burgeoning pattern of rapidly urbanizing and poorly served suburbia. By the late 1980s over half the state's residents did not live in an incorporated city.

Counties competed with cities for residents and tax base while city annexations frequently "cherry-picked" tax-rich lands. Each locality defined how much of the region's growth it would accept and under what circumstances (if any) it would accommodate regionally needed, but locally unpopular, facilities. This blurring of city and county roles contributed to a blurring of the physical landscape. Absent a mandate to use land efficiently, many cities indulged in large-lot zoning and underinvested in infrastructure, thereby "ruralizing" the cityscape. Lacking a mandate to protect rural character, many counties suburbanized the countryside.

The GMA, at RCW 36.70A.210(1), provided concise but clear direction about the different roles contemplated for cities and counties: "The legislature recognizes that counties are regional governments within their boundaries, and cities are primary providers of urban governmental services within urban growth areas." The Growth Hearings Board interpreted this language to mean that counties were to assume the regional roles of drawing urban growth area boundaries and allocating population and employment targets to cities, but should cease to compete with cities as the providers of urban governmental services (*Snoqualmie v. King County,* Central Puget Sound Growth Hearings Board Case No. 92-4.2304c (1994)).

Several urban counties that have designated "Potential Annexation Areas" have explicitly embraced the GMA vision of city governance of urban growth areas. Likewise, the voters who incorporated 14 new cities statewide since 1990 have embraced the GMA vision of cities as the "primary providers of urban governmental services."

Another measure of the magnitude of the impact of this GMA vision is the pronounced increase in the percentage of population in cities from 1990 to 2009. Over the first two decades of planning under the GMA, the percentage of statewide population in cities has jumped from 49 percent to 64 percent. Within the Seattle metropolitan region, the city percentage has jumped from 54 percent to 66 percent, and within the most populous county in the state (King), it has increased from 66 percent to 84 percent.

Sprawl versus Concentrated Growth: The Well-Tempered Landscape

Prior to the GMA, there was no clear indication of how far into the countryside a city could propose to annex and there was no countywide or regional policy guiding such decisions. Consequently, annexations were largely driven by desires to enhance tax base rather than broader objectives for efficient urban service delivery or protection of agricultural or environmentally sensitive lands. That changed with the GMA.

The GMA required the designation of all lands as one of three mutually exclusive types: urban, rural, and resource lands (forestry, agricultural, and mineral). The organizing concept for this "three-tiered differentiated landscape" is that urban areas should look and function like cities, rural areas should look and function like a traditional countryside, and agricultural, forestry, and mineral industries should be conserved on working landscapes.

In April 2008, the 86 city and county government members of the Puget Sound Regional Council (PSRC) voted resoundingly to adopt Vision 2040, the Regional Growth Strategy, which included a specific multicounty planning policy that essentially "froze" the Seattle metropolitan urban growth boundary for 30 years. Under this Regional Plan, only about 15 percent of the region is committed to urban growth, 25 percent is rural, and 60 percent is agricultural or forestry resource land. Repeated attempts to expand the urban growth area in King County, even in small increments, have been rebuffed. To many city and county legislators in King County, the "green line" is a permanent line.

Another "sprawl-busting" action that occurred in 2009 was the passage of an amendment to the GMA to prohibit the expansion of urban growth areas into the floodplains of Western Washington Rivers. APA Washington drafted and lobbied heavily for ESHB 1967, pointing out that there was sufficient unconstrained land within urban growth areas to accommodate the forecasted growth without locating it in river floodplains. This action also helped protect agriculture from urban conversion because much of the cropland west of the Cascade Mountains is located in fertile floodplains.

Regional Planning

Regional coordination has prospered most in the area of transportation planning. The tradition of regional transportation planning existed prior to the GMA through regional and metropolitan planning organizations or as a result of federal legislation. But under the GMA, state, regional, and local transportation plans had to fit together. Funding priorities were established from local governments through their regions to the state. Money followed the priorities, including local and state funding as well as federal transportation funds.

The Regional Transportation Planning Organizations (RTPOs) were created as part of the GMA; 14 now cover the state. The PSRC serves the Central Puget Sound region. Under GMA authority, the PSRC "certifies" that local plans are consistent with state and regional plans and this certification is required to receive state or federal transportation funding. This provides a tremendous incentive for compliance, cooperation, and rational regional decision making.

Property Rights versus Community Rights

Like Oregon's 2004 experience with Measure 37, Washington dealt with a property rights ballot measure in 2006. The same "pay to enforce regulations or waive them" argument was presented to Washington voters. Although fronted by the Washington Farm Bureau, most of the funding for the Initiative 933 campaign was provided by wealthy out-of-state groups who pushed similar measures in other Western states. APA Washington joined with many good-government and environmental groups to urge "NO on I-933." The chapter and its members contributed funds to the NO campaign, wrote a critical analysis of the likely consequences of the proposed law, wrote letters to newspapers across the state, and lobbied their editorial boards, which unanimously wrote editorials in opposition to I-933.

Washington was aware from Oregon's experience that the populist "pay or waive" argument was very potent, as attested by the fact that Measure 37 passed even in the Portland Metro region. After focus group reviews and other polling, it became clear that what resonated with people was the need to protect their environment, their neighborhoods, and their homes from irresponsible development. Stories from Oregon were very useful in illustrating that no claim was too preposterous, and that cash-strapped local governments, given a fiscal dagger at their throats, would be obliged to waive those protections.

I-933 was defeated by a 60 percent margin; the strongest no vote came from the urban counties west of the Cascade Mountain range, and the eastern Washington counties of Spokane and Whitman. (See Fig. 1.) Interestingly, the county that most strongly opposed I-933 was Skagit, a primarily agricultural county north of Seattle. While part may be attributed to people who commute to Seattle, a significant part of the vote was from progressive farmers in the Skagit Valley, who have banded together as Skagitonians to Preserve Farmland.

Looking Back: The GMA After 25 Years

Recently, the Washington Chapter of APA has urged the state legislature to commission a comprehensive, objective, and fact-based review of the success of the GMA in achieving its original legislative intent and its 13 planning goals. Although several legislators and a number of stakeholder groups have agreed with the need for such a review, it has not yet been funded. This is likely to remain a legislative priority for the chapter in the coming years.

In many ways, the GMA has been a qualified success, providing a coherent and effective framework for local government planning and implementation. A 2011 review of the largest, fastest-growing urban counties showed that the percentage of new residential development occurring inside designated urban growth areas was 96 percent. This was a significant increase compared to 2001, when the percentage was 85 percent.

The clarification of the respective roles of counties and cities has eliminated much of their competition, redundancy, and conflict. The enhanced role of counties in making regional policies and cities as the most efficient mechanism for delivery of urban governmental services has enabled each to do what it does best.

Most of Washington's citizens now have their urban governmental services provided by cities (64 percent) rather than counties and special districts, which is a strong contrast from pre-GMA (49 percent).

The GMA has protected essential regional facilities, such as wastewater treatment plants, high-capacity transit lines, and the expansion of SeaTac International Airport. These large projects were enabled to come online in years rather than the decades that would have been required without the GMA.

Environmentally "critical areas" such as wetlands, shorelines, and unstable slopes have been protected and agricultural and forestry lands conserved statewide, and the floodplains of Western Washington rivers have been protected from encroachment by Urban Growth Areas.

Planning for and accommodating growth remain controversial and contentious issues both at the local level and in the legislature. However, the GMA and comprehensive planning have become mainstream within Washington's political culture. Voters rejected by large margins (60 percent) two direct ballot challenges to the GMA (Referendum 48 in 1996 and Initiative 933 in 2006). Likewise, the legislature has rejected periodic bills to repeal the GMA.

The state Department of Commerce estimates that 99.2 percent of local actions in recent years comply with the GMA, meaning that actions were not appealed to the Growth Hearings Board, or if appealed, were not found out of compliance. The requirement that local comprehensive plans and regulations be updated every eight years has generated some grumbling, but no serious pushback. The first round of updates is under way and due for completion by mid-2015.

Washington's Next 25 Years

State demographers project that by the year 2040, Washington's population of 6.7 million could swell to a high of 10.7 million. The Puget Sound Regional Council projects that up to half of the statewide increase will locate in the four counties and 82 cities in the Seattle metropolitan region, together with 1.4 million additional jobs. This will present tremendous challenges to planners in this part of the state to accommodate that growth while retaining the region's prized environmental quality.

Many challenges remain. In a 2013 survey, APA Washington members identified climate change as the number one challenge facing the state. Although the legislature has adopted numeric targets for statewide reduction of greenhouse gas emissions, there is no mechanism in place to connect those targets to regional transportation planning or local land-use planning.

APA Washington's legislative committee has worked to add climate change mitigation and adaptation as a GMA planning goal, or as an element of comprehensive plans, but thus far the legislature has declined to do so. Because transportation and new building construction are two of the greatest sources of greenhouse gas emissions in our state, the chapter's efforts may shift to strengthen climate change considerations in regional transportation planning and best practices in development and building codes.

Another major challenge will be to identify funding sources to make up for decades of neglect of urban infrastructure. This problem will become more acute in areas expecting robust growth. APA Washington has advocated that the legislature authorize local option financing tools like tax increment financing (TIF). This is an area where Washington could benefit from learning from other states not only what infrastructure improvement opportunities TIF can create, but also what procedural or structural pitfalls to avoid in the enabling legislation.

Learning from the Washington Experience

Looking back over 25 years with the GMA, there are lessons to be shared with planners in other states. First, recognize that the root of all public policy, including land-use policy, is politics. State and local laws, capital and operating budgets, plans, and regulations are all adopted by elected decision makers who operate within a political environment. Two examples of APA Washington's appropriate and successful engagement in the political process are the efforts of our legislative committee to advocate for improvements to our state's planning laws and the active participation of our chapter board and members in defeating Initiative 933, the antiplanning property rights ballot measure.

Second, to successfully advocate for good planning, it is important to cultivate relationships not only with key state legislators, but also with stakeholder groups such as associations of local governments, builders, environmentalists, business, and labor. As an APA chapter, our credibility is founded on our broad and deep collective expertise and our professional commitment to serve the public interest above other interests. Legislators know that our legislative committee can be counted on to provide technically sound help in drafting legislation, testimony at legislative hearings, and networking to build support for or against key bills.

Third, when considering statewide legislation, recognize the importance of regional diversity. While some things are important statewide, other things may be less so. For example, prohibiting the expansion of urban growth areas into river floodplains was more important in Washington's high-growth urban counties than in rural ones experiencing very little development. Our law reflects that. Most states have such east-west or upstate-downstate diversity that must be respected.

Fourth, borrow good ideas where you can, but be careful to apply it to your state's unique situation. In our case, Washington clearly borrowed the "urban growth area" concept from Oregon, but there were other parts of the Oregon system that were not appropriate for Washington.

Fifth, recognize that while land-use regulation is an important tool in the plan implementation, it is just one. A broad range of capital projects (e.g., roads, parks, utilities, etc.) and programs (e.g., tax policies, public education, intergovernmental agreements) can be as important, or more important, in achieving good results. Ideally, all three tools will be used to implement comprehensive plans.

Sixth, it is important that planners become advocates for "well-tempered" regulations—sensible regulations needed to achieve important outcomes that the market alone will not, while guarding against regulations that overreach. Since most Americans are uneasy with the word "regulation," take the time to convey that "regulations" can be the means to ends that citizens do value—fundamental fairness, environmental and neighborhood protection.

Finally, recognize that not every problem requires a legislative solution. Some of the problems that your communities or your state encounter may more appropriately and effectively be addressed by identifying and supporting best practices at the regional or local level.

Washington's experience with growth management has enhanced the livability of our state for nearly 25 years. With new challenges upon us, there is more work to be done, but we can build on that strong foundation.

CHAPTER 3

Taming the 'Shameless Threat': Farmland Protection and Corralling Sprawl in Oregon

Ronald Eber and Ed Sullivan

Governor Tom McCall warned that the "ravenous rampage of suburbia in the Willamette Valley" was a "shameless threat to the environment" and the primary push behind Oregon's statewide land-use planning program in 1973. But the concern for the loss of Oregon's farmland is long-standing. Oregon developed state and local techniques to protect its agricultural economy and farmland from urban development in the early 1960s. These efforts utilized a combined strategy of tax incentives and development restrictions that were incorporated into the state's new comprehensive planning system. Together these have been used to prevent scattered rural development and to reinforce compact urban growth to protect farmland.

By 1980, the National Agricultural Lands Study recognized Oregon's farmland protection program as "the most fully integrated and comprehensive in the country" (Coughlin, Keene, and Esseks 1981). Oregon's farmland protection program is part of a broader planning effort designed to contain sprawl and provide for needed housing and the efficient provision of public services and facilities. The overall program is legally sound and on the ground it is effective. (See Lettman et al., Chapter 5.) Politically, it is constantly challenged and has been continuously updated to address changing conditions, situations, and public sentiment.

Oregon's Land-Use Planning Elements

In 1973, the desire to preserve farmland and contain urban development, particularly in the Willamette Valley, led to the adoption of Senate Bill 100, which established the current land-use program, including the creation of the Land

Conservation and Development Commission (LCDC) (seven citizens appointed by the governor) to supervise its staff in the Department of Land Conservation and Development. LCDC's primary task was development of Statewide Planning Goals with which every city and county comprehensive plan and zoning and implementing regulation must comply. Plans and regulations were generally completed and acknowledged as meeting the goals by 1986. The state provided more than $25 million in direct grants to local governments to develop or update these required plans.

Also in 1973, the legislature enacted SB 101 (now ORS Chapter 215), a comprehensive rewrite and update of the exclusive farm use (EFU) zone first adopted in 1963. Most significantly, SB 101 enacted the Agricultural Land Use Policy (ORS 215.243), which recognized the vital natural and economic value of farmland to justify its special protection, expanded the list of permitted nonfarm uses, and continued an earlier linkage of land-use regulation to preferential farm use assessment.

The enactment of SB 100 and 101 marked the transition from a voluntary incentive-based system to one that required zoning restrictions to protect agricultural lands with reciprocal tax benefits. Together, their passage enabled the establishment of a comprehensive program for the protection of agricultural land as well as the containment of urban development that would emerge as Statewide Goals 3 (Agricultural Lands) and 14 (Urbanization) in 1974.

Goal 3 and the Policies That Support It

Oregon's efforts to protect agricultural land and contain urban development have always been driven by the economic importance of agriculture to the Oregon economy. The Oregon Department of Agriculture calculates that in 2010 the total direct and indirect contribution of agriculture and the food processing industry to Oregon's economy was $29 billion. This contribution was 10.6 percent of the total sales for all Oregon goods and more than 12 percent of all Oregon jobs. To protect this vital industry, Oregon provided farmland property owners tax reductions of more than $3.8 billion in property taxes between 1974 and 2004 (Richmond and Houchen 2007).

Goal 3 requires: (1) an inventory and designation of agricultural land; (2) use of the statutory EFU provisions to restrict zoned land to farm uses and other nonfarm uses; and (3) a standard for any minimum lot sizes in EFU zones less than set by the state law. LCDC made these land-use and tax provisions mandatory by requiring the use of the statutory EFU zone because of the legislatively approved list of farm and nonfarm uses and its provision of tax benefits to property owners.

These EFU zoning provisions have evolved from a system where general discretionary standards that did not adequately protect farmland or limit urban development were replaced with clear and objective standards that were effective.

Goal 3 includes several distinct elements that, when applied by either a city, county, or state agency, can establish a comprehensive and successful program to protect agricultural lands, including:

- Policies on the economic, social, and environmental value of agricultural lands;
- A clear, measurable definition of the agricultural lands to inventory and protect;
- Specific farm and nonfarm uses (including dwellings) permitted on these lands;
- Standards for review of land divisions and minimum lot sizes;
- Complementary tax and regulatory policies; and
- Containment of urban and rural development.

Containing Urban and Rural Development in Non-Farm Areas

Statewide Goal 14 (urbanization) prohibits urban uses outside an urban growth boundary (UGB). Every city is required to establish a site-specific UGB that includes sufficient land to satisfy the community's housing, commercial, industrial, and other urban land needs for 20 years. Goal 14 encourages efficient use of urban land in order to minimize sprawl and promote livable communities. State law sets priorities for lands eligible for expansion of UGBs; more productive farm and forest lands are generally the lowest priority for inclusion and cities are discouraged from bringing these lands inside the UGB until other options are exhausted. Perhaps more important, urban facilities such as sewer service and city streets are generally prohibited outside UGBs, reducing the growth-inducing influence of expensive public works projects on resource lands.

The general rule is that urban uses are confined to UGBs and only allowed outside that boundary by express legislative sanction, by UGB changes in unincorporated communities, or by an "exceptions process." More recently, in 2013, the legislature "streamlined" the UGB amendment process to give more flexibility on the location of UGB changes once a "need" is established. Nevertheless, agricultural land is the least preferred land for urban expansion. Alternatively, the LCDC Unincorporated Communities Rule allows for limited development within areas already committed to urban or quasi-urban uses.

Thus, Oregon has strong land-use policies to contain urban and rural development that support and complement its efforts to protect agricultural land. If development is to be effectively limited on agricultural land, it must be accommodated and encouraged elsewhere. Oregon's planning program puts a great emphasis on meeting future housing and development needs inside urban growth boundaries, on lands already committed to rural development, or on non-resource lands.

Only 33 percent of the land added to UGBs since 1987 was zoned EFU (18,166 acres) or less than one percent of all the land zoned EFU (15.5 million acres). Over 15 years, the total acreage of all lands added to UGBs statewide represented a two percent increase in the total land area within UGBs (782,000 acres). It is likely that fewer options for expansion onto farmland will be available to cities in the future.

Rural development (including industrial, commercial, and residential development outside a UGB) has also been restricted to existing unincorporated communities and centers, non-resource lands or land where development is recognized through an *exception* to the goals. An exception is a limited process available to designate land for rural development outside UGBs. To do this, the exception must set forth the reasons why Goals 3 and 4 should not apply and the proposed use should be allowed, including the amount of land needed and why the use requires a location on resource land.

Rural residential development is strictly limited and the reasons used to justify a new area cannot be based on the market demand for housing, assumed continuation of past urban and rural population distributions, or housing types and cost characteristics. A jurisdiction can only support an exception for rural residential development by demonstrating that the rural location of the proposed residences is necessary to satisfy the need for housing generated by existing or planned rural industrial, commercial, or other economic activity in the area.

Final Thoughts

Overall, Oregon has had an effective program to protect agricultural lands and contain urban development. However, land-use planning is controversial. It is primarily driven by popular desires and perceptions about the relative value of resource lands as well as growth and development, as was highlighted by recent citizen initiatives that reasserted the perceived loss of "property rights" and the development opportunities of certain property owners. Also, American land-use planning has tended to focus on the development of cities, rather than recognizing, evaluating, or promoting the value of resource lands. Planners planned for development (i.e., housing, industry, and shopping centers) and leftover lands were labeled Agriculture or Open Space and were intended as holding zones to accommodate future growth and development.

The Oregon program has tried to protect agricultural lands and contain sprawl using the traditional land-use planning approach. However, agricultural land is the irreplaceable foundation for crops and livestock and a resource in its own right. Looking to the future, the protection of agricultural land must have equal footing with plans for industrial parks, commercial centers, and single-family residential neighborhoods and be an integral part of our efforts to establish livable communities and sustainable environments. The protection of farmland and the source of our food supply cannot only be a rural planning issue solely for lands beyond the urban area. Agriculture must be an integral part of our urban areas with the promotion of urban farms, community gardens, and farmers markets. Public education and understanding of all these rural and urban issues is essential if any program to protect agricultural lands and contain sprawl is to succeed.

How we face these issues will affect whether or not we succeed in the complementary objectives to protect agricultural lands and contain sprawl. Protecting agricultural land and containing urban development are policy choices between an individual's use of land versus the long-term preservation of productive lands and the efficient use of urban lands for the common good. Our choice will decide how successful we are at protecting our important farmlands and creating livable communities.

CHAPTER 4

A Historical Perspective on the Metropolitan Portland Urban Growth Boundary

Sy Adler

This chapter sketches the history of the original Portland metropolitan area urban growth boundary (UGB), which has become a cultural icon as well as an income-producing asset; planners, local government officials, journalists, and others come from around the world to study it. Planning and implementing the UGB was a major milestone in the history of growth management in the United States, and it won't come as a surprise that the original UGB was the product of a complex, lengthy, and very contentious process.

In brief, the arc of the story in this space-constrained chapter begins with a description of innovative state laws that were enacted and governmental agencies that were established in Oregon during the 1960s and 1970s. Those laws and agencies, and the requirements they articulated—including a requirement that a boundary be drawn—created a context within which a growing community of local, regional, and state level professional planners worked. The planners were actively watchdogged by land-use and environmental advocacy and industry groups, and they struggled to craft a boundary that met legal requirements, was in line with emerging professional norms about growth management, and was politically feasible. Planners debated several long-standing theoretical and practical issues along the way, including optimal regional forms and functions, the possibilities and limits of long-range planning to reduce uncertainty, and the dynamics of managing adaptively in the face of changing political and economic circumstances. They continued to confront many of the same challenges following implementation of the original boundary, and a hybrid approach to addressing those issues based on an institutionalized learning process has emerged.

Institutional Innovations

In the early 1960s the Oregon legislature linked the designation of exclusive farm use zones by county governments to property tax breaks for owners of farmland in those zones. The zones had to be consistent with county land-use plans. Many legislators worried about the urbanization of farmland, especially in the highly productive Willamette Valley; agriculture was one of the most important economic sectors in the state, and the legislators wanted to protect resource lands for commercial production. However, very few counties were willing to embrace planning and zoning at that time, so relatively few acres were designated.

Leaning heavily on leaders in the professional planning community for the substantive elements of a bill, as well as on the farm sector, a leading statewide industry organization, and an emerging environmental movement for political support, the legislature passed a law in 1969 that was aimed at stemming the loss of farmland. SB 10 required every city and county government to comprehensively plan and zone its jurisdiction by the end of 1971, and authorized the governor's office to take over planning and zoning if a local government failed to comply. The law included a set of goals that were intended to guide the governor's office in the event it intervened; "an orderly and efficient transition from rural to urban land use" was among those goals (Oregon 1969, 579).

Most local governments missed the deadline, in large part because the state did not provide any funding to local governments to plan and zone, and there wasn't a state-level agency designated to assess the quality of those plans that local governments did produce. In the context of continuing concern about the loss of farmland, and political action by strongly supportive environmental and other public interest advocates, the legislature enacted SB 100 in 1973. That law, an American Planning Association-designated National Planning Landmark, created a new state agency, the Land Conservation and Development Commission (LCDC), charged it to adopt statewide land-use planning goals by the end of 1974, gave it the power to review city and county comprehensive land-use plans and implementing ordinances for compliance with adopted statewide goals, and authorized it to take over local planning and zoning in the event a local government failed to comply. Given the resolutely local orientation of land-use planning in the United States, the willingness of the Oregon legislature to authorize state-level takeovers was remarkable.

Building on the transition from rural to urban land-use goal in the 1969 law, the LCDC adopted Goal 14 (Urbanization), which required every city in the state to have an urban growth boundary. SB 100 required county governments to coordinate boundary-related planning within their jurisdictions. However, in the Portland metropolitan area, another 1973 law—SB 769—gave the boundary coordination responsibility to a regional planning district, the Columbia Region Association of Governments (CRAG). Transforming an existing regional association of governments whose plans at the time were advisory, the new regional entity was another substantial institutional innovation, one able on paper—in conjunction with statewide goals regulating land use beyond growth boundaries—to more effectively counter sprawling tendencies than efforts under way in any other metropolitan area in the country. In a manner parallel with LCDC, CRAG was authorized to formulate goals, prepare a comprehensive regional plan, review local plans for compliance with its regional goals, and to require local governments to change their plans to bring them into compliance. SB 769 also authorized CRAG to designate regionally significant areas and activities and regulate them. CRAG was governed by a board of directors composed of city and county elected officials, though, who found it very challenging to agree on distinctly regional goals. CRAG finally approved a growth boundary just before it was abolished at the end of 1978 (Figure 4.1).

Another major institutional innovation—and still the nation's only directly elected regional government—superseded CRAG in 1979. The Metropolitan Service District (MSD)—subsequently renamed Metro—was governed by council members elected from districts that cut across city and county boundaries. The hope was that council members elected this way would be more easily able than local government officials to formulate and implement a regionwide perspective. MSD inherited many, but not all, of CRAG's authorities and responsibilities. MSD would not, for example, prepare and adopt a comprehensive regional plan. MSD's jurisdiction was smaller than CRAG's had been. CRAG encompassed all of the three Oregon counties comprising the Portland metropolitan area at the time; much rural land in those counties remained outside of MSD's jurisdiction. MSD would be dependent, though, as CRAG had been, on local government funding for its operations. The state legislature passed a law in 1979 that clearly assigned CRAG's growth boundary planning responsibility to MSD. Adopting a growth boundary and getting it acknowledged was as important for the new regional government as it was for LCDC.

Planning For and Inside the Boundary

Building on work that had been done by a predecessor regional planning agency during the mid-1960s, three alternative regional development forms were debated throughout the 1970s by CRAG and local government planners, land development-related industry representatives, and public interest land-use and environmental advocates.

A Regional Cities approach supported individual community identities, required expanded freeway and arterial road networks, and protected open space between cities. A Radial Corridors configuration would strengthen the role of the central city in the region, encourage high-density multifamily

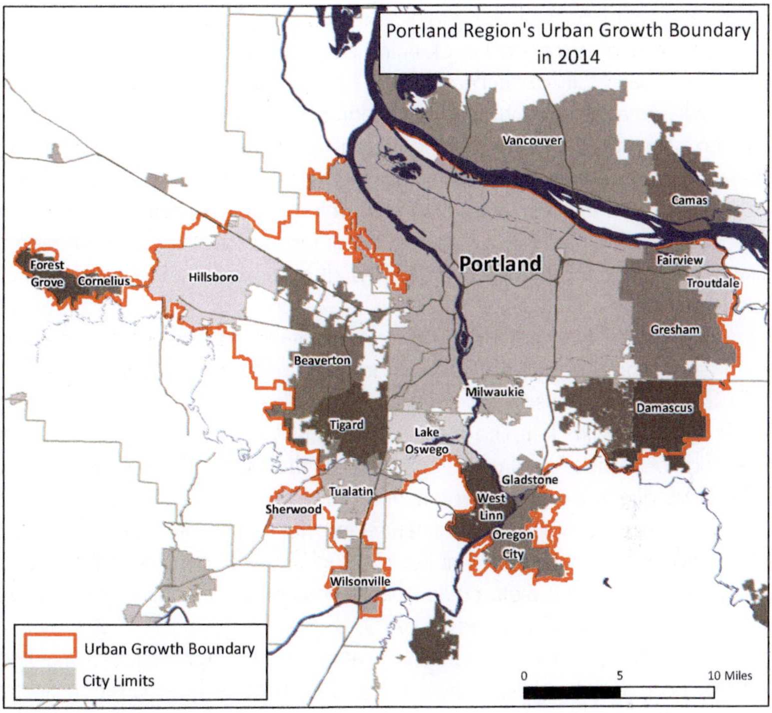

Figure 4.1. There are 25 cities and portions of three counties within Metro's jurisdiction. Metro is required to review the Urban Growth Boundary every five years. There are several cities within the portions of the counties that are outside Metro's jurisdiction that have their own growth boundaries.

residential development, make high-speed rapid transit feasible and service provision efficient, and enable easy access to open space, but would require "rigid" land controls to maintain the form. Trend City was based on assembling the land-use plans that had been done by city and county governments. It would be the easiest form to achieve because it would require the least amount of change in current behaviors. Land requirements would be high, the auto-highway system would be dominant, services would be costly to provide, and supplying effective mass transit would be particularly problematic; the position of the central city would continue to weaken (Metropolitan Planning Commission 1996).

An Interim Regional Plan map, which was adopted by CRAG in 1970 and designated the first explicit urban growth boundary, was firmly anchored in Trend City. The CRAG staff noted that creating a composite of existing city and county plans took "advantage of a common ground between jurisdictions, recognizes political and practical realities, and permits local viewpoints which have been expressed in planning programs to be included in regional planning." Trend City assumptions about housing types and densities, and the extremely generous amount of industrial land designated by each of the cities and counties in order to compete for taxpaying businesses, led the staff to acknowledge the Interim Plan's potential downsides: "The main disadvantages of the approach are that it does not purport to provide a compelling vision of a new environment greatly different from our present one, and that a regional viewpoint may be only partially attained" (Columbia Region Association of Governments 1970, n.p.).

Shortly thereafter the CRAG executive director, a former city manager, received a paper approved by 33 practicing planners that harshly criticized CRAG planning efforts to date, especially the Interim Plan. CRAG planners were charged with "keeping the waters calm by actively promoting present development trends," and avoiding "any real effort to determine and evaluate alternative directions for development." The signatories expressed frustration that the composite nature of the Interim Plan "represents one option, the one that would result if CRAG did not exist; it only shows how the Portland area will develop without a metropolitan plan, without metropolitan goals, without metropolitan direction" (Cannady 1970, 3–4).

The CRAG executive director observed about the signatories: "Only two occupy positions of responsibility to the degree that they have to reconcile the theories of planning with the practical world of implementation. . . . [T]heir criticisms of CRAG . . . reflect a real ignorance of the world of politics" (Chandler 1970, 2). This was the first instance of conflict within the community of professional planners about the balance between political feasibility and professional norms of practice, and the critique supported efforts by CRAG planners to place alternatives to Trend City on the regional planning agenda.

Trying to Transcend Trend City

Based on their experience producing the Interim Regional Plan, and on their studies of academic planning-related literature, CRAG planners compared and contrasted two different types of planning environments: hierarchically organized, as in a corporate planning situation; and an "Association or Federation," which they identified as "The Regional Planning Environment." Unlike the corporate context, the regional planning environment was decentralized. There was shared decision making by a frequently changing cast of participants, which led to changes in goals, values, and procedures. A pluralistic situation was associated with less stable, more uncertain settings, and less direct, more flexible and exploratory approaches to decision making.

The CRAG staff concluded that planning within an associational context would necessitate allocating as many resources as possible to communications-related activities and a clearinghouse role, devoting a great deal of time to negotiating differences, and working with and through advisory groups as much as possible so that all issues were considered. The "plan" that emerges in such a context, CRAG staff thought, "is a recording of . . . agreements and commitments . . . by elected and appointed officials (and the private sector) at any point in time . . . to immediate next steps to be taken," and "progress cannot be accurately predicted in advance." The regional planners also noted, though, that the times were changing, and a new relationship between regional and local governments regarding land use was becoming both necessary and possible. In 1972 they wrote, "[P]hotographs of the earth taken from the moon have created a new awareness that resources may not be infinite, that there may be limits to growth. . . . [T]here has been a sharp increase in public concern about urban congestion, pollution, environmental degradation and other ills associated with burgeoning growth. . . . Land use zoning ordinances have not been able to withstand the pressures of land speculation and outward sprawl beyond the urban fringe. Economic forces and trends seem to be dictating the continuing absorption of prime agricultural land for urban uses" (Columbia Region Association of Governments 1972, 98, 135–144).

A blue-ribbon committee appointed by the CRAG board of directors proposed transforming the structure of intergovernmental relations (Mays 1972, 2): "CRAG must make the transition from an advisory voluntary association to a planning organization. As such, its central authority should be to review plans and implementation programs developed at <u>any</u> level of government—local, state, and federal—that have a significant impact on the region. Such authority should include the right to approve, disapprove and modify plans and programs as they affect the region." SB 769 in 1973 embodied those proposals.

The CRAG board struggled to decide whether to analyze regional cities, radial corridors, or both regional form alternatives to Trend City in order to develop a comprehensive plan. Regional cities were favored by Washington County, the county within the metropolitan area that was growing most rapidly in population and economic activity, and particularly by the cities in the western part of the county, farthest from Portland. Those local governments wanted to promote autonomous economic development, rather than remain as primarily bedroom communities for the central city. Creating and sustaining distinct identities, and maintaining green spaces between each other and the regional core, were top priorities for Washington County planners. The city of Portland favored radial corridors, which emphasized moderately dense, compact development focused around a limited number of high-speed, high-capacity transit lines that would link downtown Portland with outlying communities. An initial decision was made to focus on a regional cities approach. The Portland mayor then persuaded a slim majority to prioritize the radial corridors configuration. In light of the conflict, staff was directed to analyze both.

CRAG planners released a draft Regional Land Use Framework Plan in December 1975. It drew fire from 1000 Friends of Oregon, the public interest law firm established to watchdog the implementation of the statewide land-use planning program. 1000 Friends told CRAG planners that they were violating the procedural and substantive requirements of LCDC's Urbanization goal. The first of the seven factors that the goal required planners to consider when establishing growth boundaries is: "Demonstrated need to accommodate long-range urban population growth requirements consistent with LCDC goals" (Oregon Land Conservation and Development Commission 1974, 38). 1000 Friends noted that CRAG planners had concluded, "Because future population projections of the region are not agreed upon, use of such projections should be limited to a rough evaluation as to whether the areas identified for further urban and rural development are ample." 1000 Friends argued, "CRAG has chosen to simply accommodate the highest hypothetical projection," and was, as a result, refusing to justify its proposed boundary "in terms of a 'demonstrated need' for the amount of land taken" for future urban development. 1000 Friends was extremely worried that a great deal of urbanizable land would be incorporated within CRAG's proposed boundary, facilitating a continuation of sprawling Trend City development; far more productive farmland would be urbanized as a result than would be necessary (Stacey 1976, 2).

The revised Land Use Framework Element that the CRAG board of directors adopted in December 1976 set forth the following guiding policy: "Adopted regional growth and development goals being achievable by a cooperative regional management effort, resort to no-growth or fixed population philosophies is unnecessary and is rejected" (Columbia Region Association of Governments 1976, 1). In line with its earlier statements about the character of regional planning, CRAG planners proposed to adaptively manage regional development based on a monitoring system that would measure and compare the demand for urban residential land and the development capacity of land in urban areas over time, rather than take a long-range planning approach shaped by predetermined objectives and targets. CRAG decided not to implement the more hierarchical approach that SB 769 enabled it to take.

The adopted Framework Element was "to be implemented without substantial adverse effect on the housing industry's ability to provide housing within the income levels of the region's existing and future populations" (Columbia Region Association of Governments 1976, 2). The potential negative impact of a UGB on the supply of affordable housing had been discussed at length during LCDC's 1974 goal development process. One outcome of that discussion was the inclusion of a housing goal sought by home builders, realtors, and affordable housing advocates that placed affirmative responsibilities on local governments to zone land to accommodate diverse types of housing affordable to households with varying incomes. The CRAG policy reflected the continuing efforts of industry groups at the regional level to secure a supply of urbanizable land that would not put upward pressure on land prices and would maintain their ability to obtain land for single-family home construction on relatively large lots. In addition, CRAG contemplated preserving options for a "rural way of life" within the growth boundary (Columbia Region Association of Governments 1976, 2). Local government flexibility to zone land for industrial development was also accommodated. Those policies were anathema to 1000 Friends, which wanted a relatively tight boundary that would promote compact, higher density development, including a larger share of multiunit development, in order to reduce pressure on agricultural land.

In the end, CRAG planners were unable to stray very far from Trend City; they incorporated housing density and type assumptions that reflected what were in individual local government plans and zoning ordinances. They did include, though, interim urban growth boundaries, although there were many cases where they were unable to reach agreement with local governments about precisely where those boundaries should be locate. Those areas were to be studied, and development would be rigorously regulated in them until final boundary determinations were reached.

1000 Friends appealed the Framework Element to LCDC in early 1977. The attorneys charged that the adopted element didn't explicitly assess the "need" for the amount of land required to accommodate a population forecast, and they also charged that CRAG hadn't adequately reported the "results" of its consideration of all seven of the Goal 14 factors it was required to take into account. Based on an analysis that 1000 Friends attorney Bob Stacey had done that utilized the approach contained in the Real Estate Research Corporation's very influential study, *The Costs of Sprawl* (1974), he argued that CRAG had included a great deal of urbanizable land that wouldn't likely be needed to accommodate a reasonable year 2000 population forecast, and that it would require a great deal of unnecessary money to service the population that would settle in the Trend City pattern that CRAG's boundary would yield (Stacey 1977).

This was likely the first time in the United States that a land-use plan was legally challenged because justifications for recommended courses of action were missing and/or inadequate. The hearings officer employed by LCDC to advise it in that case agreed with 1000 Friends, and told the commission that the CRAG-adopted boundary should be invalidated because it failed to comply with the goal's procedural requirements. CRAG was told that its interim boundaries could be implemented immediately, but the boundary in its adopted Framework Element had to be revisited (Oregon Land Conservation and Development Commission 1977).

Rather than undertake a substantial revision process, CRAG invented a surplus land figure that it claimed would be necessary to prevent land market prices from rising so much that choice and variety in the housing market would be unacceptably reduced. CRAG planners adopted required findings to justify their surplus land figure. The political commitments that CRAG officials had made to local governments and to the housing industry constrained what planners could do (Columbia Region Association of Governments 1978). 1000 Friends' characterization of the "political" nature of the CRAG response figured prominently in media stories during 1979 about the very slightly revised boundary that CRAG adopted at the end of 1978. Power exerted by local governments and the housing industry shaped the technical analysis deployed by planners to justify a course of action (Alesko 1979; *Oregonian* Editorial Board 1979).

Adopting the growth boundary at the end of 1978 was CRAG's last act. MSD adopted the CRAG-approved boundary as its own and sent it to LCDC for acknowledgment. 1000 Friends once again challenged the boundary, and the LCDC planners reviewing the plan for compliance with the statewide planning goals also thought it was inadequate. Both 1000 Friends and the state planners harshly criticized the market-factor argument (Oregon Department of Land Conservation and Development 1979). However, LCDC was highly motivated to acknowledge the most important urban growth boundary in the state in order to show progress toward achieving its farmland protection goal. That goal stipulated that rural lands outside urban growth boundaries that fell into higher quality soil classifications be zoned exclusively for farm use; a process to except rural areas that were committed to current or likely future urban uses from the Agricultural Lands goal requirements was available.

Regional officials were loath to revisit the framework plan that had been adopted by the local elected officials on the CRAG board, and were loath to ask the planners to redo the work they had done. While 1000 Friends continued to challenge the UGB, state planners focused attention on an interim boundary that could be enforced while additional monitoring and evaluation beyond the interim line took place.

LCDC voted to acknowledge the boundary, although the commissioners stated that "a market factor or surplus factor alone is not sufficient justification for establishment or expansion of an urban growth boundary which includes more lands than needed using the criteria set forth in factors 1 and 2, Goal 14." They allowed though, that the situation in the Portland metropolitan area was unique, that "there is a compelling need for early establishment of an urban growth boundary," and that Metro (as MSD is now called) promised to manage development within the acknowledged boundary adaptively. LCDC pointed out that it would be reviewing the plans and zoning ordinances adopted by the cities and counties in the metropolitan area, including county territory outside Metro's jurisdiction, and it would act to ensure effective implementation was occurring (Oregon Land Conservation and Development Commission 1980).

LCDC's acknowledgment of the UGB was, arguably, the most important single decision the agency has ever made, and a singular moment in the history of American land-use planning.

A hybrid approach to growth management emerged in the Portland metropolitan area during the course of conflict and compromise among a growing, diverse community of planners, one that combined, in theory, elements of long-range planning and shorter-range management of regional change. An interim growth boundary was in place during the early to mid-1980s while MSD finalized the larger regional growth boundary, and later in the 1980s the regional government began to develop a Regional Land Information System to provide the capacity to monitor development and relate it to the supply of urbanizable land. The integrated implementation of LCDC's Urbanization and Agricultural Lands goals positioned MSD and the metropolitan area counties to more effectively constrain sprawling development and preserve land for commercial agricultural production than anywhere else in the country (Figure 4.2).

After UGB Acknowledgment

Institutional innovation at both state and regional levels continued during the 1980s and 1990s. LCDC turned its attention to the patterns of development inside urban growth boundaries. Key manifestations of that turn in the Portland

Figure 4.2. *The metropolitan urban growth boundary at the edge of the city of Tigard in Washington County, the county with the most rapidly growing population in the state*

Figure 4.3. The Bethany area in northwest Washington County, where the UGB was expanded

region were the Metropolitan Housing Rule and the Transportation Planning Rule. Rule-making by LCDC evolved into a process during which the large and diverse community of planners addressed issues of concern that emerged as a result of implementing the statewide planning goals amid changing land-use-related conditions; it became an institutionalized learning process. The Housing Rule, adopted in 1981, clarified needed housing types that local government plans within the Portland region had to accommodate and set density minimums for residential zones to prevent sprawl inside boundaries. The Transportation Planning Rule (TPR), adopted in 1991, required the regional government to prioritize reducing principal reliance on the automobile within its jurisdiction and to revisit land-use plans and ordinances in order to facilitate significant increases in bicycle, pedestrian, and transit modes of travel, and established long-range reduction targets per capita for vehicle miles traveled and parking spaces. 1000 Friends played a particularly important role in pushing the envelope to integrate of transportation and land use planning. While MSD initially resisted the requirement to revisit land-use plans and ordinances, over time the regional government came to embrace it.

In 1995 the state legislature passed a law that required Metro to review the UGB every five years to determine whether or not there was a sufficient supply of land within it to accommodate a 20-year forecast of growth in residential demand, a law that codified the earlier CRAG proposal to adaptively manage the boundary based on a land monitoring system. However, the technical, political, and financial demands of analyzing and deciding on a continuing basis persuaded the legislature to permit Metro and the counties to designate up to 50 years' worth of urban and rural reserves, thereby building in a long-range planning dimension to the adaptive management process (Figure 4.3).

MSD itself implemented several very significant institutional changes during the 1990s. Enabled by the state legislature to adopt a home-rule charter contingent on approval by the regional electorate, the regional government did so in 1992, and declared urban growth management to be its primary responsibility. In the context of the TPR and a review of the UGB, a reconfigured Metro took up planning-related tasks that CRAG had been authorized to do during the 1970s, including articulating Regional Urban Growth Goals and Objectives and adopting a Region 2040 Growth Concept (1994) and a Regional Framework Plan (1997) to achieve them. The Growth Concept and Framework Plan reflected a hybrid of the Regional Cities and Radial Corridor regional form concepts with which CRAG had wrestled. Implementing the CRAG authority to designate areas and activities of regional significance and set standards for them, Metro adopted Urban Growth Management Functional Plan elements beginning in the mid-1990s dealing with, for example, parking policy, water quality and floodplains, industrial and employment areas, housing, centers, corridors, station communities, and main streets, and planning for new urban areas when the boundary is expanded. As the federally designated metropolitan planning organization, Metro periodically adopts regional transportation plans, and in 1992 adopted a Metropolitan Greenspaces Master Plan.

Metro is subject to many of the same political and technical challenges that were present during the 1960s and 1970s regarding urban growth management. The continuing willingness of state legislative majorities to enable the region to innovate institutionally, and the creativity that has emerged from the diverse community of planners working within and outside those institutions, has sustained growth boundary planning and implementation in metropolitan Portland, and keeps the regionalist project that emerged then moving forward.

CHAPTER 5

Protecting Working Farm and Forest Landscapes: How Do Oregon and Washington Compare?

Gary Lettman, Katherine Daniels, AICP, and Tim Trohimovich, AICP

Those of us who call the Pacific Northwest home like to think of our region as a national forerunner in natural resources protection through land-use planning. But is this true? Is there more than anecdotal evidence to support this thought? New information from the Oregon Department of Forestry shows that both Oregon and Washington have protected their working farm and forest landscapes, each in its own distinctive way, although Oregon has been more protective.

These states' traditional farm and forest sectors continue to contribute significantly to the economic well-being and quality of life of the region. Oregon just celebrated the 40th anniversary of its statewide land-use planning program, focused on farm and forest land protection, while Washington has more general state standards that give its counties more discretion in protecting these working landscapes. How effective have these contrasting approaches been? This chapter compares nonfederal land-use change between the two states over time, drawing conclusions about the comparative effectiveness of these contrasting statewide approaches to protecting farms and forests of commercial significance.

Two Approaches

Oregon

Oregon's program, adopted as Senate Bill 100 in 1973, required all counties and cities to adopt comprehensive land-use plans and implementing ordinances in accordance with 19 statewide planning goals. Farm and forest land protection are at the heart of the program, which also features urban growth boundaries to direct most growth into urban areas. The bill created a new commission, the Land Conservation and Development Commission, and an agency to staff it, the Department of Land Conservation and Development, or DLCD.

DLCD has the authority to "acknowledge"—or officially approve—comprehensive plans and implementing ordinances for all counties and cities in Oregon. Early generalized review standards resulted in significant litigation, which in turn was the impetus behind the creation of the Land Use Board of Appeals in 1979 that since then has handled most land-use disputes involving local governments. This specialized body has particular expertise in land-use issues that ordinary trial courts in other states often lack.

Goal 3 (Agricultural Land), Goal 4 (Forest Land), and related laws and regulations that have evolved over four decades require that nonfederal lands meeting broad state definitions of farm and forest land be zoned to enforce large minimum parcel sizes and strictly limit development to be consistent with resource land protection goals. Counties use a state-mandated minimum parcel size of 80 acres for forest and farmland divisions and 160 acres for rangeland divisions, with some exceptions. Approximately 96 percent of nonfederal lands in Oregon are in farm or forest zoning.

Permitted dwellings and other uses in these areas are limited and subject to specific review criteria. Dwellings in forest zones are allowed on existing parcels where there is a pattern of parcelization and development in a prescribed "template" area. Up to two dwellings on new parcels are permitted in farm zones on soils that are unsuitable for farm or forest use. Dwellings are allowed on parcels of 160 acres or greater in farm and forest zones. Dwellings for farm operators and farm help are also permissible on farms that have grossed $80,000 annually on high-value farmland or $40,000 on other farmland. There are other limited provisions for temporary family health hardship dwellings, and dwellings on certain parcels owned by the current owner prior to 1985. Finally, voter-approved Measure 49 in 2007 authorized close to 5,000 dwellings in farm and forest zones on properties that predated the land-use program. The program has been adjusted regularly over the years to increase specificity as a trade-off for added flexibility.

Washington

Washington's Growth Management Act (GMA) was adopted in 1990. All counties and cities are required to adopt criteria and maps identifying agricultural lands, forest lands, and mineral resource lands with long-term commercial significance. Counties with larger and faster-growing populations, or that opted into the planning program—referred to as fully planning counties—must adopt development regulations including zoning. These regulations must conserve designated resource lands and ensure that the use of adjacent lands does not interfere with their continued use for the production of agricultural products, forest products, or minerals. The Washington State Department of Commerce adopts and periodically updates guidelines for designating and conserving natural resource lands. Currently, 27 of the state's 37 counties and the cities in those counties fully plan under the GMA.

Participants in the planning process may appeal the adoption of plans, development regulations, and amendments to the Growth Management Hearings Board, a state agency, to determine if they comply with the goals and requirements of the GMA. State agencies must obtain the governor's approval to appeal. Comprehensive plans and development regulations must be updated to comply with the GMA every eight to 10 years. No state agency is responsible for approving comprehensive plans or development regulations.

In Washington, development regulations for agricultural lands typically require minimum lot sizes or densities of one dwelling unit per five, 10, 20, 40, or, less frequently, 120 acres. Development regulations for forest lands typically require minimum parcel sizes or densities of one dwelling unit per 10, 20, 40, or, less frequently, 80 acres. In most counties residences at these densities are permitted outright. Washington has early vesting that allows development applications to retain a "vested right" to develop under preexisting zoning for many years after new regulations are adopted, sometimes in perpetuity. In contrast, preexisting parcels in Oregon are not automatically entitled to a dwelling but rather are subject to the current zoning regulations in effect.

As an adjunct to development regulations, an increasing number of counties and cities are adopting transfer of development rights (TDR) programs to protect natural resource lands. Washington State provides incentives for counties and cities in the Central Puget Sound region to participate in regional TDR programs. Some counties also have purchase of development rights programs funded by taxes and state and federal grants. Tens of thousands of acres of forest and agricultural lands have been conserved under these programs.

Measuring Land-Use Change

The Oregon Department of Forestry, in partnership with the Forest Inventory and Analysis Program of the U.S. Forest Service Pacific Northwest Research Station, collected land-use data going back to 1974 for Oregon and 1976 for Washington. The data were collected from aerial photos, by interpreters from these two organizations, using consistent data definitions and locations for 81,557 sample points on nonfederal lands on a systematic-random grid that covers both states. The photos were taken in Oregon in 1974, 1984, 1994, 2000, 2005, and 2009; and in Washington, in 1976, 1994, and 2006.

For each date, interpreters assigned each sample point into one of eight land-use classes based on land cover, density and pattern of development, and road density. The number of structures was counted in 80-acre circles around each nonurban point. Each point was also classified by ownership: forest industry, other (nonindustrial) private, or other (nonfederal) public. The

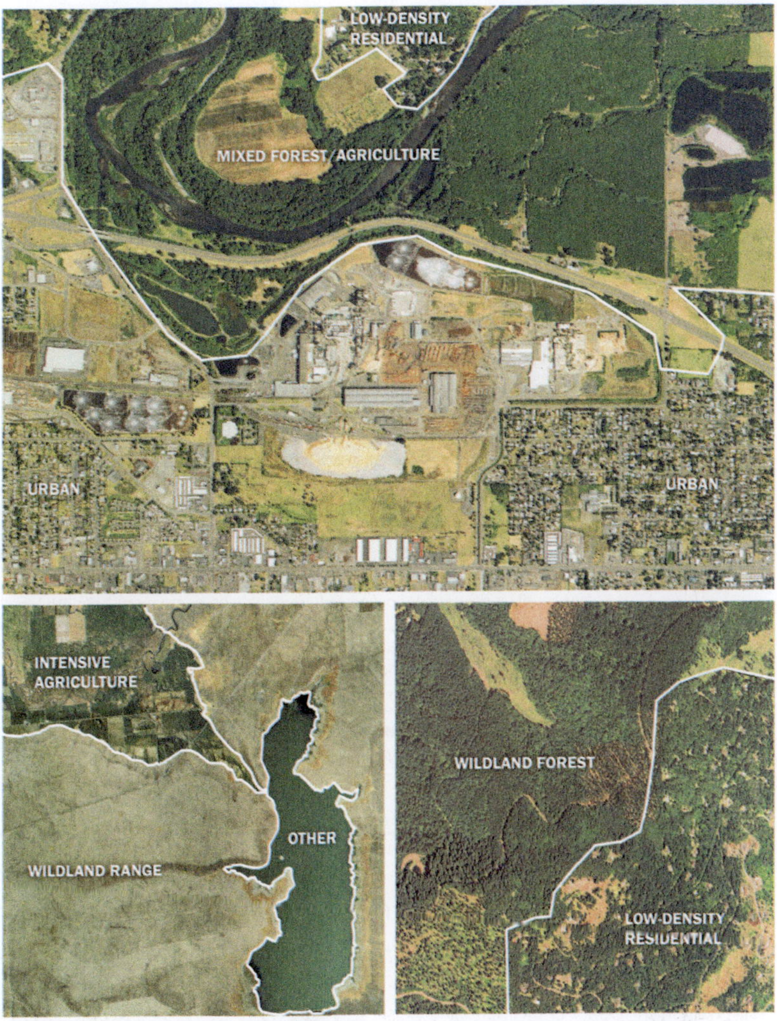

Figure 5.1. Aerial photographs of land uses

eight land-use classes referred to here were designed to correlate to resource land zoning standards under Oregon's statewide land-use planning program, and are the same as those used in the Oregon land-use studies (Lettman et al. 2011). Figure 5.1 displays examples of the land-use classes and Table 5.1 describes each in more detail.

Figure 5.2 shows the spatial pattern of the eight land-use classes across Oregon and Washington in 2009 and 2006, respectively, the most recent

TABLE 5.1.	Land-Use Classes
Wildland Forest	Contiguous tracts one square mile or larger with more than 80% of the area forested and fewer than five structures per square mile.
Wildland Range	Contiguous tracts one square mile or larger with fewer than five structures per square mile, where forest land is less than 51% of the area, agricultural land less than 20% and the remaining area is undeveloped rangeland. This classification is used only east of the crest of the Cascade Mountains.
Mixed Forest/ Agriculture	Contiguous tracts one square mile or larger with fewer than nine structures per square mile. Between 20 and 80% of the area is agricultural, while forest land is 50% or more of the remainder.
Mixed Range/ Agriculture	Contiguous tracts one square mile or larger with fewer than nine structures per square mile. Between 20 and 80% of the area is agricultural, while range land is 50% or more of the remainder. This classification is used only east of the crest of the Cascade Mountains.
Intensive Agriculture	Contiguous tracts one square mile or larger with fewer than nine non-farm-related structures per square mile and with more than 80% of the area in agricultural use.
Low Density Residential/ Commercial	A tract of any size, usually larger than one acre, in rural residential or low-density residential or commercial uses with nine or more structures per square mile.
Urban	A tract of 40 or more acres, consisting of commercial, service or residential areas with city road patterns and closely spaced buildings.
Other	A contiguous tract of 640 or more acres of lava, sand, reservoirs, lakes, mountain-top rock, snow, or ice.

Source: Oregon Department of Forestry and the USDA Forest Service, Forest Inventory and Analysis Program, Pacific Northwest Research Station

years for which data are available. The figure also delineates the boundary between the eastern and western Oregon and Washington substate regions used in this analysis.

The study periods that are the basis for the key findings below are 1974 to 2009 for Oregon and 1976 to 2006 for Washington. Some of the findings relate to nonfederal lands, which include private, tribal, state, and local government lands, while other findings relate to private lands only. Land-use plans were largely implemented by 1984 for Oregon and by 1994 for Washington. Resource land includes land in wildland forest, wildland range, mixed forest/agriculture, mixed range/agriculture, and intensive agricultural uses; developed land includes land in low-density residential and urban uses. References to conversion indicate a loss of resource land to low-density residential or urban development.

Oregon and Washington are comparable in many ways. The states are similar in size and both have large areas of land in federal ownership—53

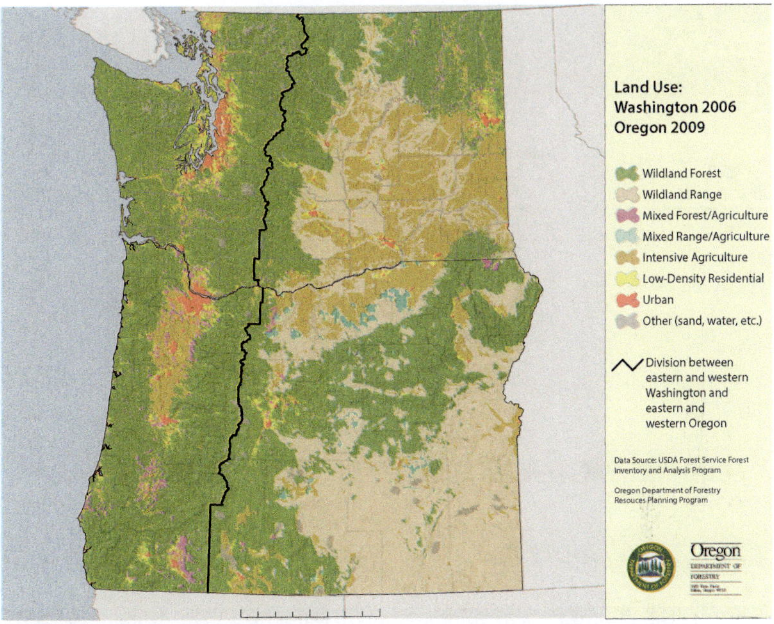

Figure 5.2. Spatial patterns of eight land-use classes in Oregon and Washington

percent in Oregon and 29 percent in Washington. Much of Washington's federal land ownership is close to developed areas, thus exercising a constraining effect on additional development. Both states have experienced substantial population growth. During the study period, the population of Washington increased by 77 percent, for a gain of 2,785,000 people, while Oregon's population grew by 67 percent, increasing by 1,531,000 people. The populations of both states are concentrated west of the Cascade Mountains, along the Interstate 5 corridor.

Key Findings

Resource Land Loss

There are similarities and major differences in resource land loss and conversion patterns in Washington and Oregon over the study period. In both states, the fastest percentage rate of conversion of nonfederal resource to developed lands was on mixed forest/agricultural lands—9.6 percent in Oregon and 22.3 percent in Washington. These mixed use lands were mostly close to already developed areas. In Oregon, the largest area loss of land in a specific resource land-use class was a decrease of 229,000 acres that shifted from wildland range use (Table 5.2). In Washington, the largest area loss was the 649,000

TABLE 5.2. Area of Nonfederal Land in Oregon and Washington, by Land-Use Class and Year

Oregon: land-use class	1974	1984	1994	2000	2005	2009	Change in area, 1974 to 2009
	Thousand acres						
Wildland forest	10,697	10,580	10,531	10,520	10,504	10,496	-200
Wildland range	9,320	9,187	9,139	9,112	9,096	9,091	-229
Mixed forest/ agriculture	947	895	873	871	864	856	-91
Mixed range/ agriculture	640	646	648	660	663	663	23
Intensive agriculture	5,849	5,795	5,779	5,751	5,741	5,730	-119
Resource Land Area	**27,453**	**27,103**	**26,970**	**26,914**	**26,868**	**26,836**	**-616**
Low-density residential	791	1,064	1,159	1,184	1,201	1,225	434
Urban	378	454	491	523	551	560	182
Developed Land Area	**1,169**	**1,518**	**1,650**	**1,707**	**1,752**	**1,785**	**616**
Other	85	85	85	85	85	84	0
Total area	**28,706**	**28,706**	**28,706**	**28,706**	**28,706**	**28,706**	**0**

Washington: land-use class	1976	1994	2006	Change in area, 1976 to 2006
	Thousand acres			
Wildland forest	13,713	13,298	13,064	-649
Wildland range	6,081	6,035	5,945	-136
Mixed forest/ agriculture	547	475	425	-122
Mixed range/ agriculture	64	64	64	0
Intensive agriculture	9,025	8,859	8,770	-255
Resource Land Area	**29,430**	**28,731**	**28,268**	**-1,162**
Low-density residential	1,302	1,834	2,137	835
Urban	612	776	934	322
Developed Land Area	**1,914**	**2,610**	**3,071**	**1,157**
Other	255	259	261	6
Total area	**31,600**	**31,600**	**31,600**	**0**

Source: Oregon Department of Forestry and the USDA Forest Service, Forest Inventory and Analysis Program, Pacific Northwest Research Station

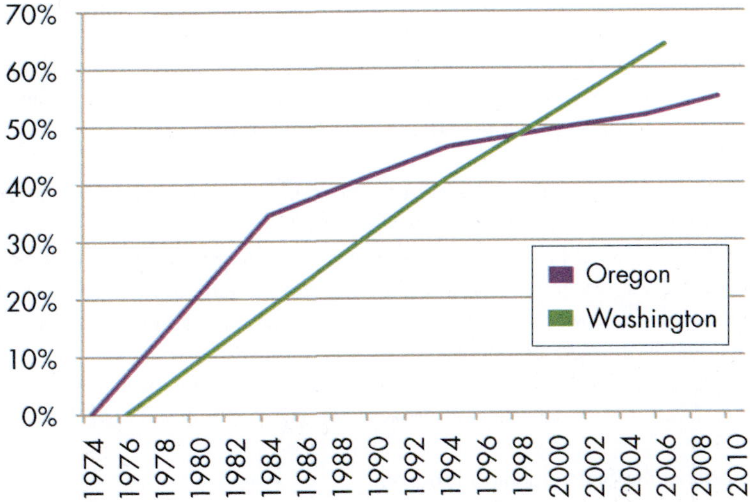

Figure 5.3. Percent change in area of low-density residential land during study period

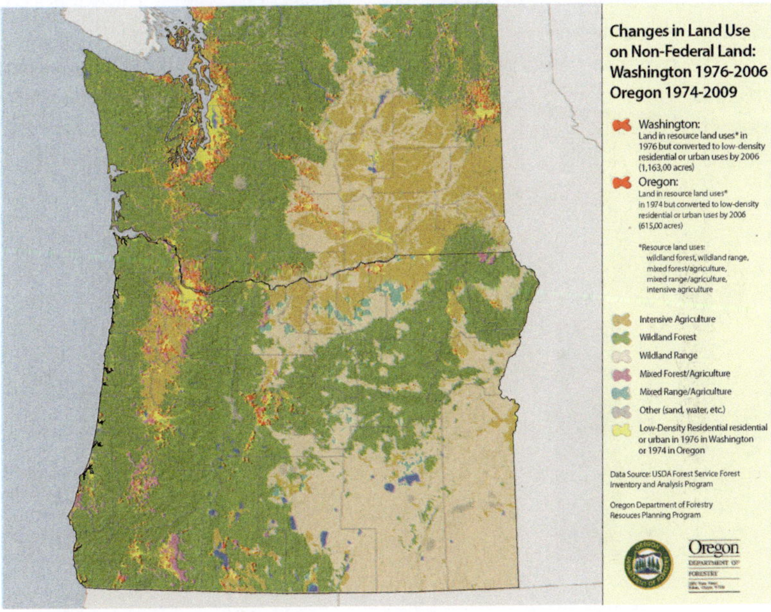

Figure 5.4. Changes in land use

acres that shifted from wildland forest use. Oregon experienced more shifting of land uses among resource classifications than did Washington in the study period. Notably, in eastern Oregon, 75,000 acres changed from wildland range to intensive agriculture. Figure 5.4 on the previous page shows changes in land use between 1974 and 2009 in Oregon and between 1976 and 2006 in Washington.

The conversion of nonfederal resource land uses to low-density residential or urban uses accounted for 70 percent of all net area change in land uses in Oregon. The comparable figure for Washington was 81 percent. In both states, the largest single gain in area for a specific land use during the study period was for low-density residential use—55 percent of the converted land for Oregon and 64 percent for Washington. However, while the rate of increase for this land use in Washington has remained steady over time, the rate of increase for Oregon has noticeably slowed (Figure 5.3 and Figure 5.4).

Impact of the State Planning Programs

A key difference between the two states is that while the rate of conversion of resource land to accommodate population growth was comparable for the two states at the beginning of the study period, by the end of the study period and after the implementation of the two state planning programs, conversion rates were notably different.

The average acreage converted per net new resident from nonfederal resource to low-density or urban uses decreased for both states over the study period, dramatically so for Oregon from 0.91 to 0.23 acres per new resident but only slightly so for Washington from 0.42 to 0.41 acres per new

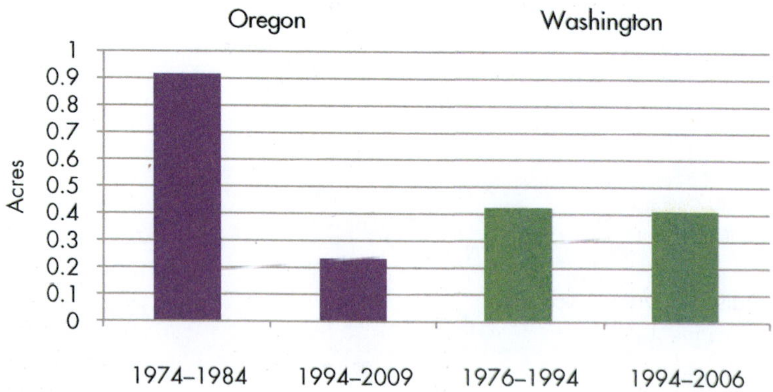

Figure 5.5. Average acres per net new resident of land converted to low-density residential or urban uses before and after the implementation of state land-use plans

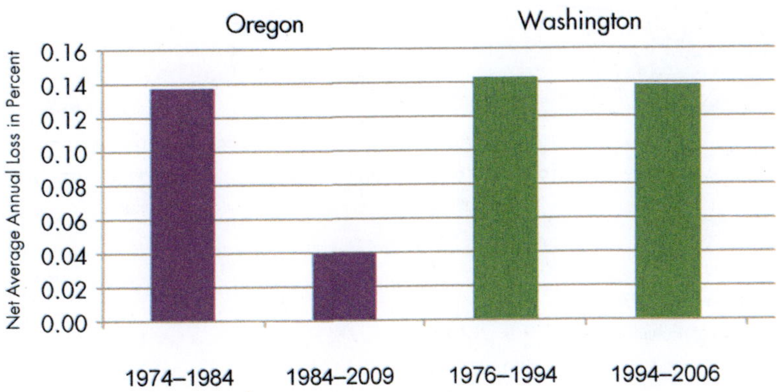

Figure 5.6. Net average annual loss of private resource land converted to low-density residential or urban uses before and after the implementation of state land-use plans

resident, reflecting policies in effect before and after implementation of the two state planning programs (Figure 5.5). Less land area developed per new resident means a higher density of population on land in low-density residential and urban areas and less development on resource lands.

Almost all development in both states occurs on private land and the conversion of private land in resource zones to low-density or urban land uses slowed dramatically in Oregon, but only a little in Washington, after the two state land-use planning programs were implemented. In Oregon, the net average annual loss in private resource land to conversion dropped steeply from 0.138 percent annually to 0.041 percent, while the rate of decline in Washington changed from 0.143 percent to just 0.138 percent (Figure 5.6).

The conversion of private land in resource land uses in the western portions of Oregon and Washington occurred more rapidly than in the eastern portions of Oregon and Washington (Table 5.3). Approximately 90 percent of the development of private land in western Oregon and western Washington occurred within 30 miles of Interstate 5. Notably, the development of resource lands in western Oregon after land-use plans were implemented declined by 89 percent.

Threats to Private Wildland Forest

As documented in Table 5.3, in Washington more land was converted from wildland forest than any other natural resource category, with the wildland forest loss making up 56 percent of the converted natural resource land. In Oregon, wildland forest loss was 32 percent of converted resource land. The land area in wildland forest use owned by the forest

TABLE 5.3. Area and Average Annual Change in Area of Private Land in Oregon and Washington Before and After the Implementation of Land-Use Plans by Size of State and Land-Use Class*

Oregon: Land-use class	1974	1984	2009	Average annual change in area 1974–1984	1984–2009	1974–2009
	Acres (thousand)			% change		
Western Oregon						
Wildland forest	6,264	6,172	6,114	-0.2	0.0	-0.1
Mixed forest/agriculture	762	721	691	-0.6	-0.2	-0.3
Intensive agriculture	1,949	1,843	1,778	-0.6	-0.1	-0.3
Low-density residential	486	669	743	3.6	0.4	1.2
Urban	263	320	397	2.3	0.8	1.2
Eastern Oregon						
Wildland forest	2,947	2,927	2,904	-0.1	0.0	0.0
Wildland range	8,281	8,184	8,090	-0.1	0.0	-0.1
Mixed forest/agriculture	127	120	112	-0.6	-0.3	-0.4
Mixed range/agriculture	625	624	641	0.0	0.1	0.1
Intensive agriculture	3,639	3,669	3,677	0.1	0.0	0.0
Low-density residential	239	321	400	2.8	0.9	1.5
Urban	52	65	86	2.1	1.1	1.5

Washington: Land-use class	1976	1994	2006	Average annual change in area 1976–1994	1994–2006	1976–2006
	Acres (thousand)			% change		
Western Washington						
Wildland forest	5,937	5,640	5,464	-0.3	-0.2	-0.3
Mixed forest/agriculture	334	284	243	-1.0	-1.2	-1.1
Intensive agriculture	811	712	650	-0.8	-0.7	-0.7
Low-density residential	854	1,178	1,345	2.0	0.9	1.5
Urban	331	450	562	2.0	1.6	1.8
Eastern Washington						
Wildland forest	4,735	4,635	4,587	-0.1	-0.1	-0.1
Wildland range	5,770	5,725	5,635	0.0	-0.1	-0.1
Mixed forest/agriculture	173	156	147	-0.6	-0.5	-0.5
Mixed range/agriculture	63	63	63	0.0	0.0	0.0
Intensive agriculture	8,123	8,061	8,037	0.0	0.0	0.0
Low-density residential	377	571	703	2.3	2.0	2.2
Urban	225	256	295	0.7	1.3	0.9

**Land-use plans were largely implemented by 1984 for Oregon and by 1994 for Washington. 0.0% = less than 0.05%*

Source: Oregon Department of Forestry and the USDA Forest Service, Forest Inventory and Analysis Program, Pacific Northwest Research Station

TABLE 5.4. Change in the Area of Nonfederal Land Classified in Wildland Forest Use in Oregon (1974–2009) and Washington (1976–2006) by Size of State and Owner Class

	Forest industry	Other private	Other public	All nonfederal owners
		% change		
Oregon	**0**	**-6**	**-1**	**-2**
Western Oregon	0	-8	-1	-2
Eastern Oregon	0	-3	0	-1
Washington	**-1**	**-10**	**-1**	**-5**
Western Washington	-1	-23	-1	-6
Eastern Washington	-1	-4	-1	-3

Source: Oregon Department of Forestry and the USDA Forest Service, Forest Inventory and Analysis Program, Pacific Northwest Research Station

industry and by other public (nonfederal) forest land owners was nearly constant in both states over the study period. However, land in wildland forest use owned by other private (nonindustrial) owners declined six percent (179,000 acres) in Oregon and 10 percent (575,000 acres) in Washington. Notably, between 1976 and 2006, the area of land in wildland forest use on other private ownerships in Western Washington declined by 23 percent (Table 5.4).

Other private (nonindustrial) owners are more likely to develop their wildland forest than are other owners. Recent forest land ownership changes may accelerate development of private wildland forest. TIMOs (Timber Investment Management Organizations) and REITs (Real Estate Investment Trusts) have recently purchased large areas of land in wildland forest use in both states that were previously owned by forest industrial owners, potentially leading to land division and development of forest lands. The acquisition of these properties, which had previously been owned by forest industrial owners, could impact efforts to minimize fragmentation and development within forested landscapes. Whether these TIMOs and REITs will retain this land in wildland forest use for a long time, develop it, or sell it to other private (nonindustrial) owners with a higher propensity to develop is an open question that should be addressed in future land-use studies.

Conclusions

The evidence is clear: Land-use planning and regulation can protect forest and agricultural land. Oregon's mandatory state standards, state agency, and enforcement authority have resulted in a significant reduction in the conversion of resource lands to more developed uses and in the rate and number of dwellings approved on resource lands over the years, whereas Washington's approach, using more local discretion, has not had as much of an impact on reducing farm and forest land conversion.

Washington's standards for designating agricultural and forest land of long-term commercial significance are general and subject to modification by counties and cities, providing for highly variable designation of these lands. Similarly, the standards for permissible uses and densities to protect these lands are also general, thus the level of protection varies from county to county.

In the next 30 years, Oregon's population is projected to increase by 37 percent and Washington's population by 31 percent. Given current land uses and rates of conversion of resource land together with current land-use policies, we can project changes in land use into the future. Without continued protection of commercially viable resource lands in Oregon and increased protections in Washington, an additional three million acres of resource land are projected to be developed in the two states over the next 30 years.

Many states have effective strategies to plan for growth in urban areas, but lack a cohesive strategy for directing growth away from agricultural and forest lands. As population and development increase, states will need innovative strategies to protect forests, rangeland, and farms from ever-increasing conversion pressures. They will also need to begin to methodically collect and analyze land-use change data to provide a solid base of information on which to base future policy choices.

CHAPTER 6

Implementing State, Regional, and Local Housing Diversity Policy through Master Planning

Daniel Pauly, AICP, and Chris Neamtzu, AICP

Wilsonville, Oregon, on Interstate 5 between Portland and Salem, is a vibrant suburban city with over 21,000 residents and 17,000 jobs (Wilsonville 2014). Through the implementation of master planned developments over the last 40 years, Wilsonville's built environment reflects a range of state and regional policies seeking a diversity of housing types, preservation of farmland and open spaces, and the coordination of land-use and transportation plans and actions. Wilsonville's experience shows planning on a large scale through master planning can support successful implementation of state, regional, and local policies.

Oregon Statewide Planning Goal 10 (Housing) requires cities and counties to plan for and accommodate a diversity of needed housing types, such as multifamily and manufactured housing. It requires each city to inventory its buildable residential lands, project future needs for such lands, and plan and zone enough buildable land to meet diverse housing needs of the community over a 20-year planning horizon (Oregon 2012c).

In the Portland metropolitan region, the Metropolitan Housing Rule is used to measure local plan compliance with Goal 10. The rule specifies the housing mix and minimum densities expected of jurisdictions within the Portland region's urban growth boundary (UGB). For Wilsonville, the rule requires the city to plan for 50 percent or more of all new residential units to be attached single-family or multifamily units (Oregon 2012a), and for new "needed" housing development to be planned to occur at a density of no less than eight dwelling units per net buildable acre (Oregon 2012b). Metro's regional Urban Growth Management Functional Plan also encourages the development of affordable housing (Metro 2012).

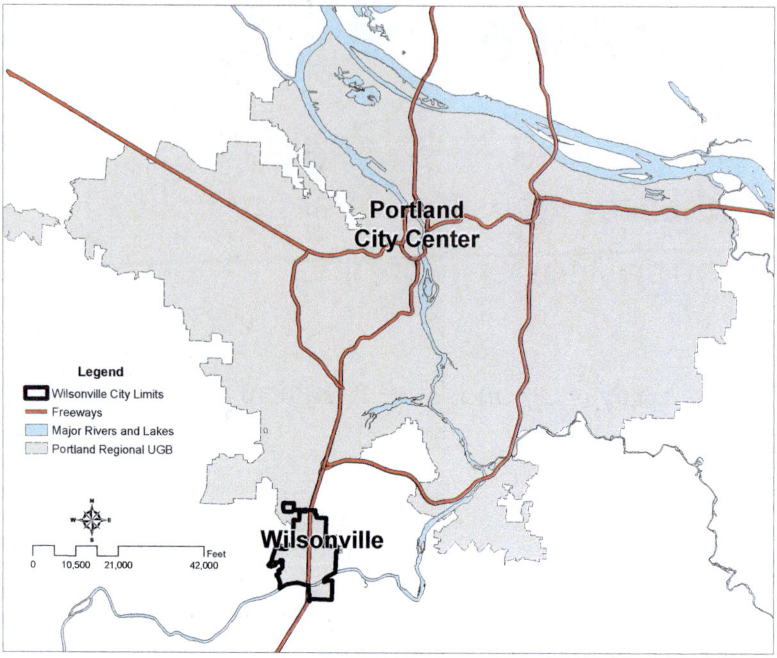

Figure 6.1. Wilsonville's location in the Portland region (Source: Data from City of Wilsonville and Metro Data; map by Daniel Pauly, AICP)

Wilsonville meets those requirements by using master planned development. The city's Comprehensive Plan contains an implementation measure stating "Establish residential areas that are safe, convenient, healthful and attractive places to live while encouraging variety through the use of planned developments and clusters." It further states, "Encourage the construction of diverse housing types, but maintain a general balance according to housing type and geographic distribution." (Wilsonville 2013a, D-15).

In the Portland region, Metro, the regional government, is responsible for establishing and managing a UGB for all cities and counties in its jurisdiction, including Wilsonville. Due to Wilsonville's location at the southern boundary of the regional UGB, separated from other municipalities and surrounded by farmland, the regional process has resulted in a number of large-tract UGB expansions for Wilsonville (Figure 6.1).

The addition of large UGB areas to Wilsonville fits well with the city's focus on master planning and helps shape the development process within the city. Rezoning can occur only if it isconsistent with a master plan. All development requests involving land more than two acres in size, except public facilities, must go through a multistage planned development process (Wil-

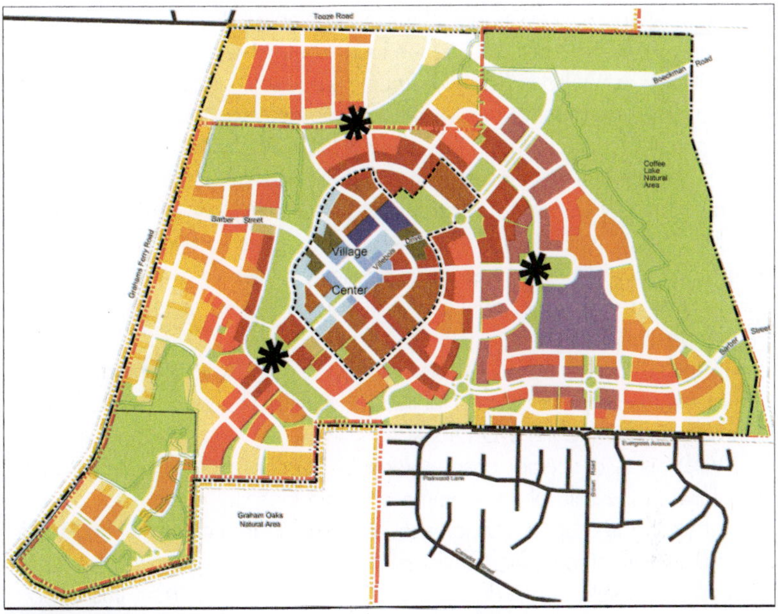

Land Use	Density (Net)	Units	Acres
Speciality Condos	50	127	2.0
Mixed Use Condos	40	104	2.3
Urban Apartments	35	90	2.4
Condos	30	124	3.9
Village Apartments	30	411	13.1
Neighborhood Apartments	22	31	2.2
Rowhouses	16	314	24.3
Small Lot Attached	12	205	14.9
Small Lot Single Family	10	604	36.0
Medium Lot Single Family	10	343	34.0
Standard Lot Single Family	6	138	31.8
Large Lot Single Family	5	132	22.7
Estate Lot Single Family	3	22	7.2
Residential Unit Totals	**13**	**2645**	**196.8**
School Site (Excludes 3 ac of community park)			7.0
Open Space (Excludes Detention Pond F)			158.9
Area in R.O.W. (Includes detention ponds)			118.9
Planning Area Total			481.6

Figure 6.2. Villebois land uses (Source: Wilsonville 2013)

sonville 2013b). Further, master plans must comply with state land-use goals, mandatory regional policies, and the local comprehensive plan.

Villebois is Wilsonville's most recent large-scale master plan and provides a good example of master planning to achieve housing diversity. The combination of land added to the regional Urban Growth Boundary in 1998 and the campus of the closed Dammasch State Mental Hospital created a planning area of about 480 acres. The Villebois Village Master Plan identifies 13 different residential land-use types ranging from condos, urban apartments, and row homes to large-lot single-family homes for a total of more than 2,600 units and a net residential density for the development of 13.44 units per residentially zoned acre (Figure 6.2) (Wilsonville 2013c). Construction of Villebois began in 2003. Approximately 1,000 dwelling units have been completed to date, including 11 of the 13 identified housing types. Two types of urban condos are the exceptions.

Villebois is a special case. When the Oregon Legislature passed the bill allowing the sale of the Dammasch State Hospital campus for development they required up to 10 acres to be set aside for community housing for individuals with chronic mental illness. In addition, the legislature designated the bulk of the sale proceeds to be put in a community housing trust account (Oregon 2013a). By leveraging the statutory requirements and scale of the Villebois master plan, the Villebois project has integrated a variety of community housing, including for those with limited incomes, into the diverse fabric of the new neighborhood. Community housing constructed in Villebois for individuals with chronic mental illness includes limited-access apartments and

Figure 6.3. Community housing in Villebois for individuals with chronic mental illness

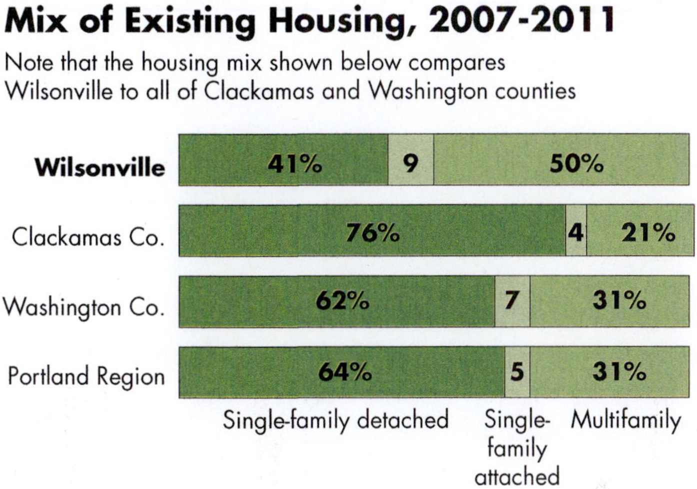

Figure 6.4. Wilsonville mix of existing housing compared to counties and Portland region (Source: Wilsonville 2014)

low-income apartments near the village center, as well as group homes set among the larger-lot single-family neighborhoods (Figure 6.3).

As represented by a higher percentage of multifamily housing (50 percent compared to 31 percent for the region) and single-family attached housing units (nine percent compared to five percent for the region), Wilsonville has realized a level of housing diversity greater than the region as a whole (FIgure 6.4) (Wilsonville 2014). Master planned developments make up a vast majority of the housing. However, in smaller master plans ranging from 50 to 200 acres, the variety of unit types and related sale and rent prices are not as diverse as the larger Villebois Master Plan. A number of smaller master plans offer only garden apartments and front-loaded single-family units. Others include only four or five unit types, such as single-family home, town homes, condo flats, and garden apartments. Also, regulations and processes built for master planning of larger tracts has been difficult to apply to smaller infill projects of two to three acre. While this to some extent encourages property consolidation, no requirement exists for such consolidation, though smaller infill projects do tend to struggle to meet city requirements.

The Wilsonville master planning experience, especially in Villebois, shows successful implementation of housing policy in larger master plans that is otherwise difficult at smaller scales. Establishing the local policy, zoning, and development framework to encourage planning and development on a broader scale, especially in new urban areas, creates opportunities within the city to better implement a range of state, regional, and local policies, especially housing diversity.

CHAPTER 7

Implementing Oregon's Transportation Planning Rule

Terra Lingley, AICP

Oregon's Transportation Planning Rule (TPR) provides a framework for logically and systematically approaching transportation planning within the state (Oregon 2014d). It includes requirements for public involvement, multimodal transportation considerations, transportation, and land-use requirements, as well as coordination among all affected jurisdictions including cities, transit organizations, Oregon Department of Transportation (ODOT), and metropolitan planning organizations (MPOs).

While several states require transportation planners to consider local interests in future land uses and comprehensive plans, Oregon's statewide legal requirements for entwining the transportation planning with local land-use and zoning decisions is unique. Local ordinances and transportation system plans—including plans for state highway improvements—are required to be consistent throughout all levels of government (local, regional, and state) and include provisions for considering the relationship between transportation and future land-use or zoning changes. This legal framework ensures that future plans are supported by the force of law, as well as local and state transportation infrastructure investments.

This chapter illustrates how the TPR governed three state transportation planning projects. In Seaside, a multimodal plan looking at alternative mobility standards shifted visitor and resident travel away from the highway and resolved conflicting visions for the state highway. Bend's metropolitan area incorporated the community's vision for city and regional growth into its transportation plan. Vernonia improved resiliency by relocating vital transportation connections outside the flood zone.

The Transportation Planning Rule

Oregon's 19 Statewide Planning Goals, adopted in 1973, provide the basis for all planning in the state (Oregon 2010b). These goals also introduced the requirement of urban growth boundaries for cities and metropolitan regions, as a way to protect prime farmland from development. Goal 12 addresses transportation: "To provide and encourage a safe, convenient, and economic transportation system" (Oregon 2010b, 39). Although Goal 12 was adopted at the policy level in 1973, it wasn't until 1991 that the Oregon Department of Land Conservation and Development Commission provided direction on how to implement it with the enactment of the TPR (OAR 660-012).

As suggested in the following cases, the requirement of coordination and consistency forces community leaders to think about the choices and trade-offs for transportation facilities and how people currently—and will someday—use the transportation system.

he requirements for public involvement can lead to more appropriately scaled plans, reflective of community values, which are integrated with ideas and suggestions from the system's daily users. Community members are encouraged to get involved in the process by creating a vision for growth, the community's future character, transportation modes, and household and employment opportunities. The TPR requires transportation system plan updates if there are any significant land use changes; if an MPO updates a plan, member jurisdictions must also update their plans.

Local plans must also be consistent with state, county, and regional transportation system plans to ensure they accommodate regional and state transportation needs. Ideally, jurisdictions update their transportation system plans every five to 10 years to ensure the plans are still relevant, and to address changes as cities grow. These elements, and additional long-range planning details, are codified in Section 660-012-0020 of the TPR.

Before a jurisdiction can adopt a transportation system plan, the TPR requires documentation to ensure that the transportation system serves existing and anticipated future land uses. ODOT looks to long-range transportation system plans when making statewide transportation funding decisions. Once projects of statewide significance are in included in a plan they are more likely to be added to the Statewide Transportation Improvement Program and programmed for funding. It is highly unusual for projects to be built (at any funding level) if they are not included in the local, regional, or statewide transportation system plan.

Jurisdictions develop transportation system plans based on existing and planned land uses. Any future land-use changes must be compatible with the adopted transportation system plan to ensure consistency between plans and to protect the function of the transportation facilities (TPR Section 660-012-0045).

Seaside: A Coastal City Along a State Highway

Before Seaside (population 6,445) successfully adopted the 2011 transportation system plan, the city had gone through several transportation planning processes (Seaside 2011). A city-led plan in 1996, which addressed only local roadways, was put on hold due to an ODOT request to include a plan for US 101 (the state highway that runs through the city). ODOT had also led a planning process to address highway congestion from Pacific Way to Dooley Bridge (Pac-Dooley project), a plan that would widen it to five lanes through Seaside and create a couplet on US 101 at the south end of the city. Neither plan was adopted. The community believed the Pac-Dooley project was out of character for the city and had too many impacts, while ODOT wanted to meet highway mobility standards and address anticipated future congestion levels. As a result, the city and ODOT reached an impasse over the long-term vision for the highway.

In 2007, ODOT asked the city to prepare a transportation system plan to address all modes. In return, the city requested a more inclusive, flexible process to ensure that the resulting plan would be more in line with the community's values and vision, meaning that the city would not endorse the Pac-Dooley project as proposed. Both jurisdictions sent letters of commitment to each other to explore alternative mobility standards for the highway. ODOT needed the city's commitment to think about congestion on the highway; the city needed a plan to move forward with community-focused transportation projects.

Alternative Mobility Targets

The transportation system planning process allowed the city and ODOT to focus on a transportation network, beyond the highway, to provide travel options within Seaside. During the process, ODOT reviewed statewide mobility standard requirements and relaxed them to reflect the city's desire to minimize widening the highway. This process created a methodology for jurisdictions around the state to implement "alternative mobility targets" to recognize funding, as well as transportation facility construction constraints, when selecting a project.

The Seaside project management team (consultant, ODOT, and city staff) for their transportation system plan discovered that widening US 101 would not meet the existing mobility targets. These findings allowed the city and ODOT to explore alternatives to meet community transportation goals and minimize impacts. In particular, the team realized:

- Seaside's geography limits transportation options. The city is sandwiched between the Pacific Ocean to the west and extensive wetland systems and steep hillsides to the east, with two parallel river systems running through the middle of the city.
- Simply widening US 101 would not achieve mobility standards (and funding was uncertain).

- Congestion problems are seasonal, creating a major issue only on specific weekends (generally, in the summer).

The city and ODOT explored other ways of moving people around the community by accepting that US 101 would be fairly congested during specific times during the summer. The project team communicated these implications to the public and stakeholders. They also developed a package of improvements, policy statements, and analysis that supported the alternative standards and kept congestion at manageable levels for most of the year. This integrated approach created understanding and support throughout the community.

The alternative mobility targets are supported in the transportation system plan through:

- Investment in local streets and connections to provide alternate routes to US 101
- Investment in alternative modes (bicycle, pedestrian, and transit network) to make it easier for visitors and residents to reduce reliance on their vehicles
- Access management measures to improve safety and reduce congestion on US 101, through the use of development opportunities to relocate and consolidate driveways, as well as adding medians on the highway to restrict dangerous turning movements
- Consideration of land use and future development along the highway (The city implemented an overlay zone for land adjacent to US 101 to promote walking and bicycling uses and review requirements for vehicle-intense uses)

The Seaside planning process provided a framework for the city and ODOT to repair a strained relationship and come together to create a plan that was acceptable to both parties. According to the city, the process allowed the community to clarify priorities related to transportation: livability, preserving community character, and protecting local businesses and residences. Community members were supportive because they had the opportunity to provide input and consider fresh perspectives in the planning process, which resulted in locally appropriate options that were not cookie-cutter solutions.

Bend: A Metropolitan Plan for a Growing Region

The city of Bend (population 76,600) is an emerging and rapidly expanding metropolis in central Oregon that attracts tourism throughout the year for outdoor recreational activities. Because of the focus on tourism, the city is sensitive to the negative impacts of transportation systems on air quality, water quality, and personal health. As a result, the metropolitan transportation plan goals and objectives focused on balancing practical and convenient transportation with preserving environmental quality and livability.

The Metropolitan Transportation Planning process allowed the community and city to create a shared future vision for Bend, and the plan reflects these values (Bend 2014). In 2002, when the Bend was in the midst of this planning process, the region qualified as an MPO, expanding the scope of the plan to a regional level. Development of the plan took an extended amount of time as the region grappled with meeting the TPR requirements, particularly a state-adopted performance measure requiring MPOs to demonstrate that plans will reduce vehicle-miles traveled (Oregon 2006). A disconnect between the planners and community members resulted. The public perceived that the focus on this metric neglected nonmotorized modes such as bicycling and walking. The public involvement TPR requirement opened a dialogue between the public and policy makers, resulting in a plan that addressed citizen concerns and won a high level of community support.

According to city and regional planners, the level of detail provided has been the greatest value of the plan. The TPR requirements, although time-consuming and detailed, enabled the city to consider more extensive nonautomobile-oriented solutions. The resulting plan includes a robust bicycle and pedestrian plan, in-depth public transit plan, consideration for compact community design, efficient land-use organization, and a way for the region to reduce transportation demand. This focus has enabled planners to reduce implementation of larger, more expensive projects that are at odds with the community's values.

According to Rick Root, planner from the MPO, the organization enjoyed taking a "public facilities" approach to providing transportation for the community. It was easy to identify the needs and discuss capacity issues with the public, in much the same way that public conversations about providing water, sewer, or electricity facilities to new and growing areas can be straightforward and fruitful. Transportation projects differ from other public facilities when addressing need because of differing ideas regarding what is "adequate." Bend planners recognized that cars and roads were only one way to meet mobility standards, and there are a number of ways to identify and measure acceptable levels of service.

Outside of ODOT facilities, the MPO is responsible for establishing the acceptable level of service for transportation (and conversely, the acceptable level of congestion). The Bend community was interested in shifting the conversation from moving cars to moving people. The planning process facilitated discussions about the trade-offs among dense urban centers, walkable neighborhoods, and potentially congested transportation facilities. Bend planners were able to look at the entire system by utilizing the TPR requirement for adequate transportation facilities and to "right-size" those facilities with mobility standards that incorporated community interests and values.

Planners looked at a number of transportation aspects that they might not otherwise have considered. Public involvement led to a better understanding of transportation issues and policies for all involved: developers, businesses, community activists, and public organizations. The planning requirements allowed the city and region to bring local capital improvement programming and maintenance practices in line with the transportation system plan, ensuring the city would make progress toward community transportation goals. The planners credit the TPR requirements and planning process for guiding the city toward a more compact and efficient community design.

Vernonia: Planning in the Wake of a Flood

Development of a transportation system plan for the city of Vernonia (population 2,260), located in Oregon's coastal range west of the Portland metro area, came on the heels of two significant and devastating flood events in 1996 and 2007. Vernonia's economy and population has been declining since the lumber industry downturn of the 1950s. The city was in the process of moving toward a tourist-based economy and supporting the technology industry when flooding events impacted the downtown core. The devastation left in the wake of the 2007 floods resulted in widespread recognition that significant changes were needed to prevent future flooding.

The 2007 floods had impacted vital community facilities, including downtown retail and services, all three public schools, the electric substation, the senior center, food bank, and the only medical clinic. In response to the flooding, Oregon's governor issued an executive order to provide the city with the funds and expertise needed to recover and develop flood reduction plans (Oregon 2010a). This resulted in federal assistance, access to grant opportunities, streamlined zone changes, and money to relocate the schools and provide transportation access for Safe Routes to Schools. As part of this flurry of planning activity, the city extended the downtown zone with a new commercial area west of the core, which spurred development and increased resiliency by moving the facilities out of the flood zone.

The biggest issue addressed in the transportation system plan was relocating and providing safe routes to the schools outside of the flood zone. The plan focused on providing bicycle and pedestrian routes to the new schools, along with ensuring the existing streets would be adequate to serve the new school site (Vernonia 2011). The plan also supported downtown zoning changes by focusing on walkability and the redevelopment of a concentrated commercial district (through intersection improvements, pedestrian crossings on the highway, and new citywide road standards that included bicycle and pedestrian facilities).

The plan provided the framework to support economic development goals and formed the basis of the transportation chapter of the master capital program. According to the city, the plan led to thoughtful development of the downtown district and a gateway area. Focusing on alternate modes, with specific consideration of safe routes to schools, led to discussions about the road network and how to connect bike trail systems and other facilities to create a network for all modes.

Once Vernonia adopted the transportation system plan, the city was quick to seize the momentum, using the document to create a capital improvement program and pursue grants and other available funding sources. As a result of additional state and federal assistance, Vernonia has been able to quickly prioritize projects for implementation, especially those that meet economic development and flood recovery goals.

A Statewide Rule for Local Goals

The implementation of Oregon's TPR provides a regulated and systematic way to approach transportation planning, including a framework to consider alternative transportation modes and local community values while also coordinating across multiple agencies and jurisdictions. In the process, it is resulting in decisions that unite state highway system plans with local interests. The TPR requirement for coordination and consistency can strengthen and repair relationships between state agencies and cities, as in Seaside, or can be used as a process to bring together a number of agencies to help the community recover, as in Vernonia. Each of these plans created a vision and plan for transportation to help the cities address their unique needs, often using alternative transportation as in Bend, while providing direction for ODOT and city decision makers to prioritize and allocate funding.

CHAPTER 8

Seattle Neighborhood Planning

Roger Wagoner, FAICP, and Marty Curry, AICP

Seattle is known as a city of neighborhoods, each with a unique character resulting from its geography, transportation, open space (including Olmsted parks), and the growth of the city through successive annexations. By the 1960s, Seattle recognized at least 60 self-identified neighborhoods. Two neighborhood planning processes in the 1970s focused on neighborhoods that met criteria for Community Development Block Grant Funds and resulted in city-adopted plans for more than 10 neighborhoods. Projects from these neighborhood plans were implemented, but no further neighborhood specific planning took place through the 1980s.

Seattle formalized its commitment to strong neighborhoods with the formation of the Office of Neighborhoods in 1988, forming 13 district councils and the City Neighborhood Council to formalize city-neighborhood relations. This structure, with ongoing city support and limited authority over allocating some local improvement funds, has created a strong and respected voice for neighborhoods.

This chapter highlights the neighborhood planning program in the 1990s, shaped by the city's history with neighborhoods and Comprehensive Plan goals for managing expected growth and density while protecting and enhancing the unique identity of neighborhoods. As a result of a "revolt" among established single-family constituents who feared upzoning and "densification" from the 1994 Comprehensive Plan, the city committed to a broad neighborhood planning process for designated "urban villages."

This city-funded, four-year neighborhood planning process was "bottom-up," engaging and educating thousands of citizen volunteers and resulting in 38 neighborhood plans. In "Neighborhood-Planning as Collaborative Democratic

Design," Sirianni (2007) describes this program well. The remainder of this chapter examines the lessons learned from this "bottom-up" approach and highlights how planning at the neighborhood level has continued to evolve since then.

The Urban Village Strategy and Neighborhood Planning—a Brief Review

In Washington, the Comprehensive Plan is driven by the Growth Management Act, which seeks to concentrate growth in urban areas to protect Washington's natural resources from sprawl. Seattle plans for 20 years of new growth using population and employment forecasts based on state, regional, and county sources. Each urban center and village has new households and jobs targets based on current levels of development and potential for higher densities through redevelopment and infill. Other factors affecting targets include the introduction of high-capacity light-rail transit and other new public transportation such as streetcars and express buses.

The Comprehensive Plan's urban village strategy is a tool to guide new population and jobs growth into existing areas zoned for multifamily, commercial, and mixed use densities. These are the heart of neighborhoods and commercial centers. However, the challenge to this strategy is the fact that the majority of Seattle is zoned for single-family residential uses.

Between 1994 and 1999, 38 neighborhoods worked with the Neighborhood Planning Office and consultants to craft plans for their communities. The urban village plans included goals and policies for future growth and development and visions that expressed each neighborhood's unique character. The goals and policies were adopted into the Urban Village Element of the Seattle Comprehensive Plan. Specific implementation measures for development regulations, design guidelines, capital improvements, and other solutions for local needs were identified and formed "adoption and approval" matrices that were intended to be work plans for city departments' further analysis and action.

At the end of the planning process in 2000, neighborhood stewardship organizations were identified to maintain communication and coordination with appropriate city departments in moving forward recommended implementation projects and strategies. However, budget problems in the early part of the new millennium and administration changes inhibited staffing the stewardship program. Consequently, monitoring of the progress of the action plans was dependent on the dedication and capacity of the neighborhood stewardship groups.

Assessing the Success of Neighborhood Planning

Have Neighborhood Plans Been Implemented?

There is broad agreement that many of the priority projects and actions identified in the neighborhood plans have been accomplished, although not everything has been implemented. Some neighborhoods expected the city to act on every project and priority identified in their plan and the city's Adoption and Approval matrix. However, city staff had to determine project feasibility and the fit with other city priorities and commitments. As is so often quoted, "the devil is in the details," and this was the case with some priorities and projects that were broad and general, were inconsistent with city policies, or were simply too expensive to undertake. While this caused some disappointment, many neighborhood activists continue to view this bottom-up neighborhood planning approach as the best model for effective planning and for empowering citizens to direct the future for their neighborhoods.

Have Neighborhood Plans Had Lasting Value?

Most people recognize and applaud the lasting value of neighborhood plans, although in different ways. Both city staff and neighborhood activists identified the continuing importance of the visions and goals of the neighborhood plans. In most cases these broad goals and policies remain relevant today. The city references them as its departments set priorities and launch new initiatives. According to one city staffer, this has changed the way the city does business with neighborhoods, reflecting recognition and respect for these visions and goals.

A related result has been better coordination among city departments. Interdepartmental task forces or action teams have become more the norm in recent planning initiatives (station area planning, neighborhood plan updates). At the same time such coordinated efforts or all-at-once approaches sometimes "feels like drinking from a fire hose," as expressed by one neighborhood activist.

What Issues Have Been Identified by Neighborhoods?

A number of reviews and assessments of the first round of neighborhood plans have been conducted by the city, local universities, and neighborhood activists. The Seattle Planning Commission published reports documenting the neighborhood planning process and surveying stewardship groups soon after completion of the plans. They found most citizens hopeful about implementing key priorities, but struggling with community energy and resources to play a strong role in this implementation phase. The city also provided status reports for neighborhood plans in 2001 (Seattle 2001a, 2001b).

In 2008, the city council appointed 12 community leaders to the Neighborhood Planning Advisory Committee (NPAC). The committee carried out an intensive review of the plans and implementation progress, issuing more than a dozen reports summarizing their findings and recommendations for future planning. Some activists that were still concerned about the directions to be taken generated a number of minority reports on specific issues.

The committee emphasized several key points:

- Outreach and communication were lagging due to diminished funding.
- Web-based surveys did not adequately reach all sectors of the population.
- Movement of professional planning from consultants working for the neighborhoods into city hall created more of a "top-down" process.
- Growth targets for the villages should be vetted through the neighborhoods before adoption.
- Updated plans should maintain consistency with the Comprehensive Plan format "but should also address issues of unique or particular significance to each neighborhood."

The NPAC review revealed issues related to the implementation of neighborhood plans. The city council directed the planning commission in 2009 to prepare a status report on the plans and recommend how subsequent updates should be conducted. The commission's report was based on surveys and meetings for each of the nonindustrial area plans.

Council Resolution Guiding Current and Future Planning at the Neighborhood Level

The work of the NPAC, the planning commission, and the City Neighborhood Council generated a 2013 council resolution that reaffirms the city's commitment to neighborhood planning including a regular cycle of community engagement to address changing priorities, priority for neighborhoods with significant growth and change, and direction to the planning department, department of neighborhoods, and the planning commission to implement the resolution.

Seattle Neighborhood Planning—Today and in the Future

The 1990s bottom-up approach to neighborhood planning was the right model for the situation, but is not likely to be the model for the future in Seattle. The city is focusing new efforts on targeting larger subareas and specific areas that are or will experience significant growth and change, a more effective use of limited staff and financial resources for planning at the neighborhood level.

Planning Approaches

There are currently three overlapping planning processes under way in Seattle. These have varying intensities of community involvement and overarching city government intents.

Neighborhood Plan Updates

The Seattle Department of Development (DPD) is charged with updating the neighborhood (village) plans to work with urban villages that are expected to change dramatically due to transit improvements, recent growth and demographic changes. DPD staff work in collaboration with the city's department of neighborhoods, which provides trained Planning Outreach and Education Liaisons to reach and engage underrepresented groups. This has been more successful than any previous attempts to engage the significant immigrant populations in the city in planning efforts.

Urban Design Frameworks

DPD is also engaged in land-use and urban design "framework" planning for larger villages and centers, especially those with new transit facilities and significant growth potential. This process includes in-depth assessment of existing conditions, forecasts of future growth with market implications, and considerations for future zoning changes to accommodate emerging uses and increasing density at major locations within and beyond the urban village designations.

Economic Revitalization

Finally, the city's Office of Economic Development leads the "Only in Seattle" program, somewhat similar to the national Main Street Program. It focuses on neighborhood business districts "to allow small businesses to grow and flourish," "reflect the unique character of the neighborhoods," and "empower business owners to organize around a common vision and attract investment." This process involves organization, marketing, and promotion strategies as well as business organization development to improve the neighborhood's appearance and pedestrian use, and make the business districts clean and safe.

These initiatives draw on a broad palette of planning methods to support the positive evolution of urban villages (and their surroundings) while addressing the expected growth. A major challenge is to help community members distinguish among these different planning processes and to know how and when to be involved without being overwhelmed.

Some Final Observations for Planners

The 1990s neighborhood planning process was an important turning point in how Seattle envisioned and carried out neighborhood planning. It empowered citizens to plan for their neighborhoods and to work effectively with city staff and officials. Even today there are a number of citizens who believe that the bottom-up model for neighborhood planning should be the norm for future planning.

One of the most important legacies of the neighborhood planning process is a clear vision and goals for each of the 38 neighborhoods. These visions and goals also continue to provide a foundation for city staff and elected officials to work with neighborhoods in addressing new planning challenges and opportunities.

Neighborhood planning in the 1990s built healthy relationships between citizens and city staff and planners. Neighborhood participants developed more confidence in their own abilities and trusted that the city was listening to them as they identified their hopes and concerns. This reinforces the importance of inclusivity and transparency in local planning and a commitment to educate citizens and integrate their ideas and values into city policies.

Changes in how people live, work, and socialize in their communities requires broader thinking about engaging people in planning for the future. More people may be less connected to their physical neighborhood with more self-contained homes and greater use of social media. Today, many people put their energy into their nongeographic communities rather than investing time and energy in their immediate geographic community.

In many cities, including Seattle, there is a significant immigrant community that is continually evolving. Many people with different cultural traditions are not comfortable with our American practices of public meetings and workshops where people come and voice their opinions. Just as we are seriously taking on race and social justice issues, planners must also learn and practice innovative ways to interact with and engage people from different cultures and from different age groups in our communities to reflect and integrate all cultural assets. While technology is a great tool to reach out and engage people, face-to-face engagement is essential to learning from one another and to plan inclusively for our communities' futures.

CHAPTER 9

Designing Seattle: The Role of Urban Design in the City's Evolution—1970 to 2020

John Owen

Our story: Jenny, an urban planning grad student from back East, is visiting her Uncle Bob, an urban designer in Seattle. He has promised to show her around and tell her about how urban design activities since 1970 have helped to shape the city.

Jenny! Welcome to Seattle. I know your time is short, and for once it's not raining, so let's go see some of our urban design efforts.
But first let me give you a bit of background. I'm going to focus on events over the past 40 years, but much of Seattle's design character was framed up way before then. Of course, most prominent is our beautiful natural setting, which really dwarfs our human-built structures. In the late 19th and early 20th centuries, Seattleites did all they could to "tame" the land to make it more useful for settlement. R. H. Thompson, our most famous engineer, initiated a series of hill-leveling projects or "regrades" that sluiced about 50 million cubic yards of earth into Elliott Bay and created much of the current port area. This was great for commerce and street grids but not so good for the natural ecology or sense of place.

During the early 20th century, the city also hired the Olmsted Brothers to plan an ambitious park and boulevard system which remains the most intact Olmsted designed park system in the world. This confrontation, or dialog, between an engineering and development-driven pragmatism versus a more ecologically sensitive perspective is a recurring theme in the city's design character.

With a thriving collection of post-WWII industries, many of which supported the aerospace industry, Seattle grew as a mostly prosperous, self-satisfied town through the middle 20th century, sporting the freeways and shopping malls of typical American cities. The city hosted the 1962 World's Fair with the optimistic theme of *Century 21*. But, with the cancellation of Boeing's supersonic transport plane came the "Boeing bust," which decimated the company's work force and devastated the local economy. The city and its region were on the ropes.

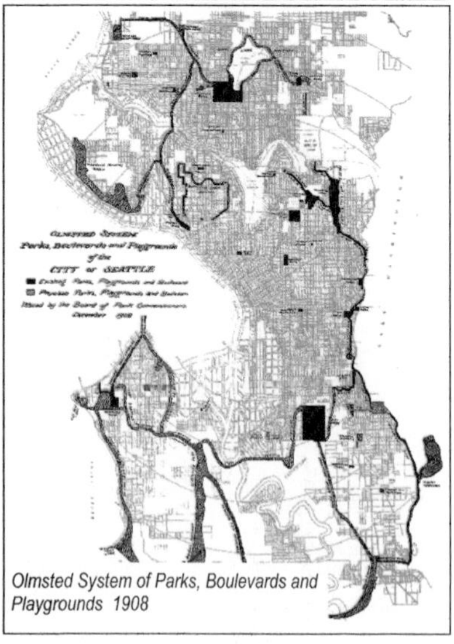

Olmsted System of Parks, Boulevards and Playgrounds 1908

Fortunately, just about this time, scads of ambitious young people (including your Uncle Bob), drawn by the unsurpassed natural environment, cheap housing, good universities, and opportunities for civic engagement, started migrating to this corner of the world. Several other forces aligned to make urban design an important part of the city's recent evolution. For one thing, University of Washington professors such as Myer Wolfe had built a strong urban design program and showed how the discipline could facilitate a rational, participatory public decision-making process.

URBAN DESIGN is the manipulation of the physical environment in a way that: serves multiple clients (including the general public), addresses a range of scales (not just the project limits), considers the sensory environment, supports larger comprehensive planning objectives, is conducted through an inclusive public decision-making process, and is accomplished through strategic implementation.

And UW Professor Victor Steinbrueck led a successful citizens' movement to "Save the Pike Place Market" from urban renewal. This elevated the value of historic preservation as a social objective and demonstrated that the public could play a significant role in public decisions.

A series of Forward Thrust bond measures in 1968 and 1970 provided over $400 million in funds for parks, roads, the Kingdome, community centers, sewer systems, and neighborhood improvements. This was an economic shot in the arm, and it provided a wealth of infrastructure that we enjoy today. Perhaps more importantly, the success of these investments let people see that their taxes produce valuable benefits and that their governments could be counted on to deliver the goods.

A number of civic activities indicate that the scales of public opinion were tipping toward environmental quality and neighbohood livability. For instance, nationwide, this was a time of freeway construction and urban renewal, of technocratic solutions to urban problems. But here in Seattle, citizens prevented the R. H. Thompson Freeway from cutting through neighborhoods and forced the funding of a lid over the I-90 freeway.

Context	1970s	1980s	1990s	2000s
Big Institutional Movements	**Boeing bust** **SEPA/NEPA** **Shoreline Management Act**	**Modest prosperity** **Interest in waterfronts**	**Growth Managment Act** **VISION 2020 regional plan** **Solid Growth**	**Tech boom - then bust** **Salmon recovery** **Environmental focus**
Downtown	1973 Downtown Plan Pike Place Market Pioneer Square	Westlake Park & Tunnel CAP initiative limits building heights	Convention Center Art Museum Building boom	Downtown Library Continued development
Frames (e.g., Denny Regrade)	Denny Regrade Plan	Second Avenue improvements and first wave of development in Denny Regrade	Continued Regrade and First Hill development. Seattle Commons	Major development in South Lake Union South Lake Union Park
Neighborhoods	"Main Street" improvements Bootstrap neighborhood efforts	Modest neighborhood improvements	Neighborhood planning to accommodate growth mandated by regional plan	Solid growth in neighborhood centers
Open Spaces and Green Infrastructure	Gas Works Park Freeway Park Waterfront Park	Fishermen's Terminal Port of Seattle shoreline restoration efforts start	New environmental regulations. Alki/Harbor/ Duwamish Corridor	Sculpture Park Growing Vine Street Waterfront Plan
Puget Sound Region	Forward Thrust parks and infrastructure Some farmland protection	Many shoreline access parks around Puget Sound	Rise of several town centers Urban design tools for growth management	Rail transit Emergence of Bellevue and Tacoma downtowns

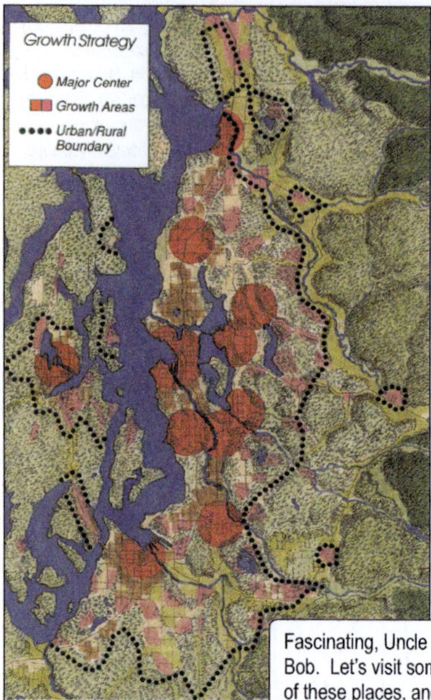

From Puget Sound Regional Council VISION 2020

Some of the places Jenny and her uncle will visit

A Downtown
B Pioneer Square
C Ballard
D Denny Regrade
E South Lake Union
F Alki/Harbor/ Duwamish Corridor
G Downtown Waterfront
H Olympic Sculpture Park and Vine Sreet
I Hiram Chittenden Locks

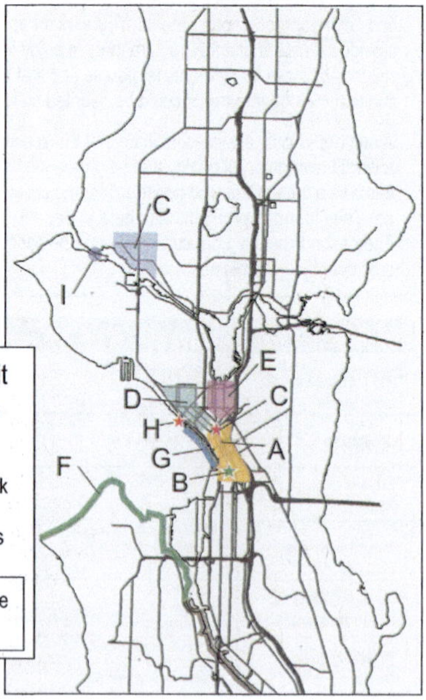

Seeing Seattle (1994) by Roger Sale is an excellent guide to Seattle's physical attractions.

The Neighborhoods

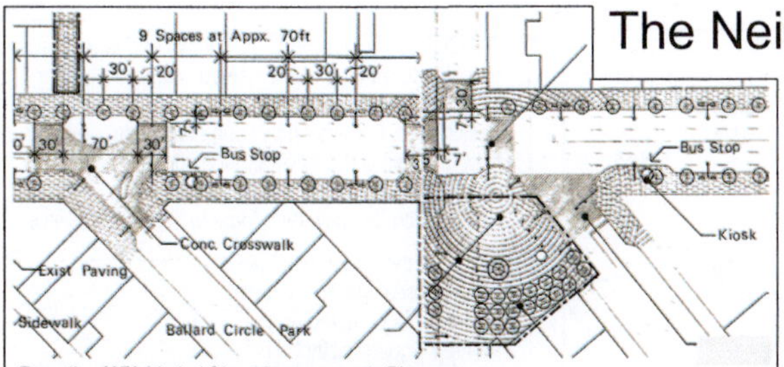

From the 1973 Market Street Improvements Plan

Seattle is truly a city of neighborhoods, and I could take you to any number lively 'hoods with vibrant commercial centers and unique identities. But Ballard, the old Scandinavian community, is a good example because it was the first neighborhood to get an urban design makeover. Back in the early 1970s, the neighborhood commercial districts were losing business to the malls, and families were moving to the suburbs. To combat neighborhood erosion, the city began sprucing up the neighborhood business districts with street improvements using a mix of federal, city, and property owners' funds. And it worked. In Ballard, retail sales went up 12 percent over inflation the first year.

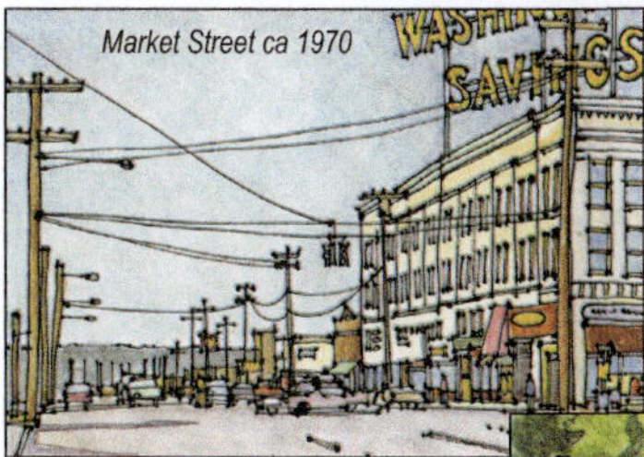

Market Street ca 1970

Market Street today

You mean that brick pavers, street trees, and fancy lights revitalized this neighborhood?

Well, it was more than physical improvements. Because the design was developed through a participatory public process, residents and property and business owners got involved. That led to other productive collaboration such as festivals and joint marketing; much like the Main Street Program which started a few years later.
There were also a lot of volunteer projects such as street tree planting in residential areas. These efforts led to stronger communities and modest private investments. Then, to accommodate growth mandated by GMA in the 1990s, the city undertook an ambitious neighborhood planning program. In Ballard, this led to a new Ballard Commons Park, surrounded by a library and lots of mixed use development.

I can see why someone would want to live here.

And, they've managed to retain local industry. People of all ages are moving in and keeping Ballard a full-spectrum community.

Downtown

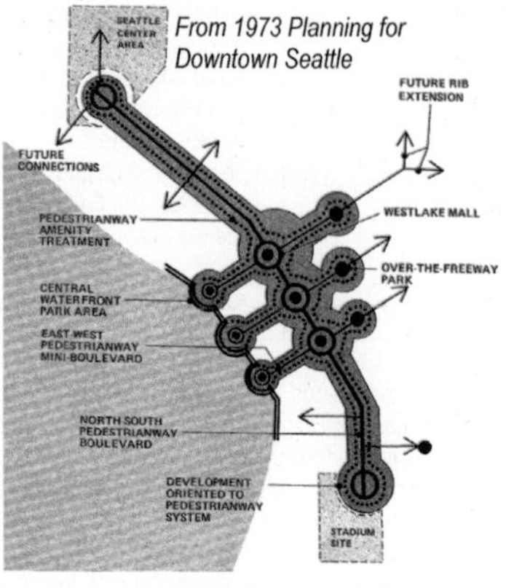

From 1973 Planning for Downtown Seattle

Seattle has long valued its downtown and taken steps to make sure that it has remained vital. In fact, the 1973 Downtown Concept Plan was our first real urban design plan. Developed by young urban designers, the plan featured a strong, integrated concept with focal points connected by a central pedestrian spine running from the new Kingdome to the Seattle Center.

But, after the Pike Place Market was restored, the real focus of design work centered on the Pioneer Square district. This effort combined historic preservation with parks and street improvements to create a lively setting that attracted start-up firms, artists, and entertainment venues.

In 1985, the city implemented many of the 1973 plan's concepts through new zoning, incentives, and other measures. And, over the years, the city gradually added important elements that have made Downtown the region's commercial, civic and cultural center. Westlake Park, built in 1988, is the city's civic gathering space. Other civic elements include the Freeway Park (1976), the Transit Tunnel (1988), the Convention and Trade Center (1988 and 2001), the Seattle Art Museum (1991), Benaroya Hall and the Garden of Remembrance (1998), a new City Hall (2003), and the flamboyant Seattle Public Library.

From 1973 Pioneer Square Plan

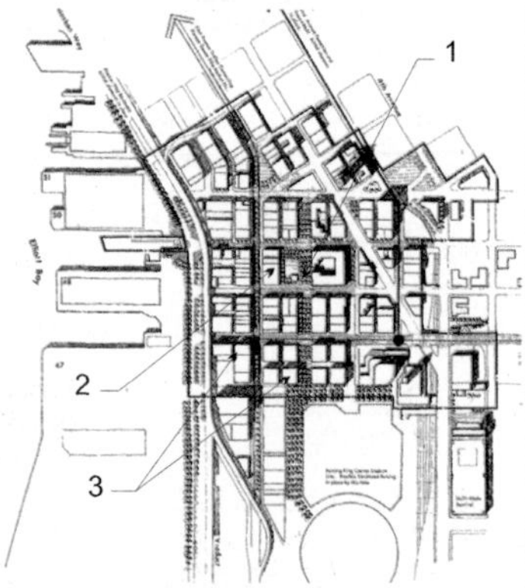

Pioneer Square Redevelopment Strategy

1. Street and public realm improvements
2. Pioneer developments in core
3. Larger, second-phase developments taking advantage of tax incentives

But, Uncle Bob, the way the different attractions are scattered around downtown seems kind of hodge-podge.

Well, I'd say it's "situationally incremental" rather than hodge-podge. But, yes, the features' locations have been determined more by politics, special opportunities and factors other than urban design concepts.

On the other hand, the grid of pleasant streetscapes makes it all work, and the city has achieved the 1973 plan's objectives, if not its geometry.

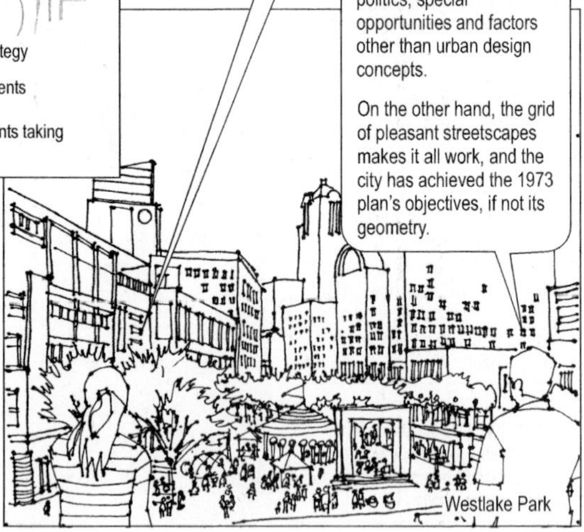

Note: To see a downtown in which the major features have been assembled according to a coherent plan, visit downtown Tacoma or the Pearl District in Portland.

For more on the downtown, see *Seattle Architecture: A Walking Guide to Downtown* (2007) by Maureen Elenga

Downtown Frame

From Denny Regrade Development Plan

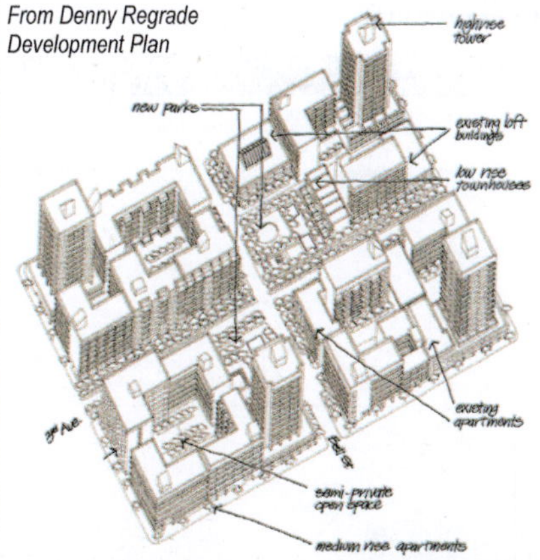

Downtown is surrounded by what I'd call "frame" areas that have historically supported the core with service and lower intensity uses. But as the downtown has grown in the past few decades and inner city living has become more popular, these frame areas are redeveloping. For example, the 1974 redevelopment plan for the Denny Regrade, just north of Downtown (remember the hills that R. H. Thompson's crews leveled?), envisioned a dense mixed use neighborhood. To many, this seemed improbable at the time, but today the Regrade seems to have grown pretty much according to plan.

Interestingly, it was three little actions taken a decade or so later that triggered the redevelopment: 1) some modest street improvements to enhance the area's residential character, 2) a zoning change reducing the maximum height from 20 stories to 6 to discourage property owners from sitting on their properties while waiting for the high-rise market to materialize, and 3) the changing of the building code to allow five stories of stick frame over one or two of concrete.

South Lake Union, a 300-acre district just north of Downtown, offers another example. In 1991, a group of designers and civic activists proposed a 61-acre park called the "Commons" to provide the city center with an expansive open space. It was a compelling idea but had a number of problems, and the public voted down a $111 million levy measure in 1996. Shortly after, developers moved in and over the past few decades have transformed the area into a mecca for high-tech companies. The developers also persuaded the city to build a streetcar line and widen the Mercer Street freeway connection. Then, the city initiated a public and volunteer effort to develop an "Urban Design Framework" which established goals and a vision for the area. Based on the framework, which provided design direction for the area, zoning was revised to allow much greater development intensity, along with incentives for affordable housing. This model for an urban design framework is now being applied to other districts in the city.

Yes, well, urban design is a process, especially in Seattle.

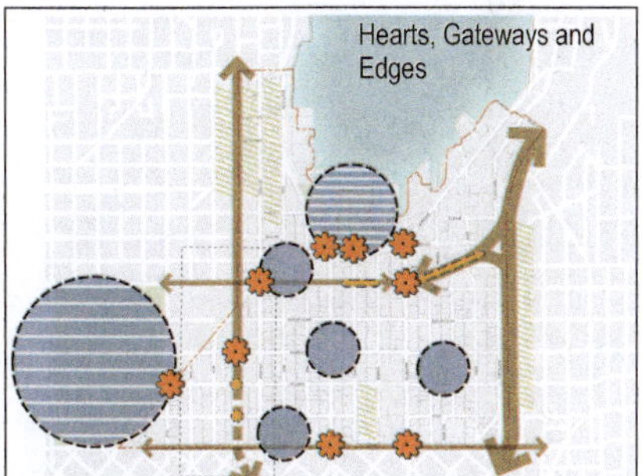

From South Lake Union Urban Design Framework

Neighboring Cities and Towns

Since the early 1990s, much of the most interesting urban design work has occurred in the cities and towns outside of Seattle. The state's GMA and the VISION 2020 regional growth strategy mandates that much of the region's growth be directed toward urban centers. This resulted in a number of implementation challenges as municipalities searched for ways to intensify local downtowns and new centers and to protect sensitive areas and rural lands. Urban designers were ready with a number of tools to address these challenges, such as those on this chart. The work resulted in a number of more livable, sustainable, pedestrian-oriented mixed use centers. For example, Downtown Bellevue has experienced substantial growth over the past couple of decades. Through an integrated set of zoning regulations, design guidelines, streetscape standards transit improvements, an expansive downtown park, and a pedestrian corridor, the downtown developed the form that you see here. Because the downtown was laid out in a mid-20th century superblock pattern, the city instituted a program to achieve an extensive system of mid-block pedestrian connections and open spaces that is starting to give the downtown a unique, park-like character.

GROWTH MANAGEMENT CHALLENGE	URBAN DESIGN SOLUTION OR TOOL
Connecting growth to transportation systems	• Transit-oriented development • Subarea planning • "Linear community" models
Greater density in urban centers	• Design review to ensure compatibility of new development • Design amenities for livability • New building prototypes
Multimodal transportation	• Pedestrian and bike systems • Pedestrian-oriented guidelines
Mix of uses in urban centers	• Form-based guidelines
Urban-rural transition	• Rural design strategies
Implementation	• Public-private joint development practices
Sensitive area protection and stormwater management	• Low-impact development standards • Green infrastructure solutions

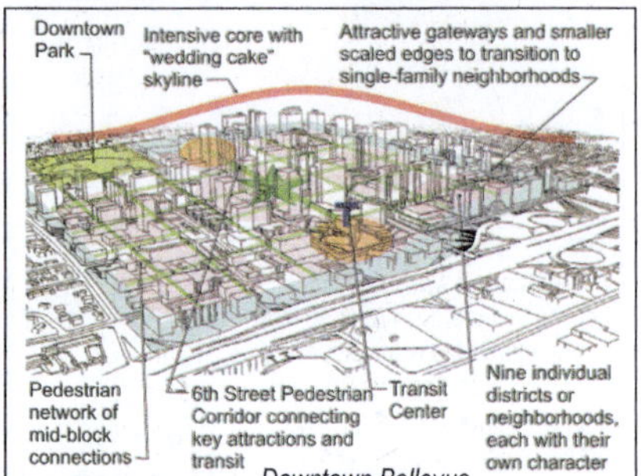

Downtown Bellevue

Even more ambitious is a set of urban centers being planned along the Bel-Red light rail segment which will connect downtown Bellevue to the neighboring city of Redmond and the emerging Overlake District (home of Microsoft and other major employers). Both cities employ a full spectrum of tools to make this corridor livable as well as economically preeminent. For example, Redmond is developing three new parks with green infrastructure, complete streets, new guidelines, and a pedestrian-bike freeway crossing at the Overlake Station.

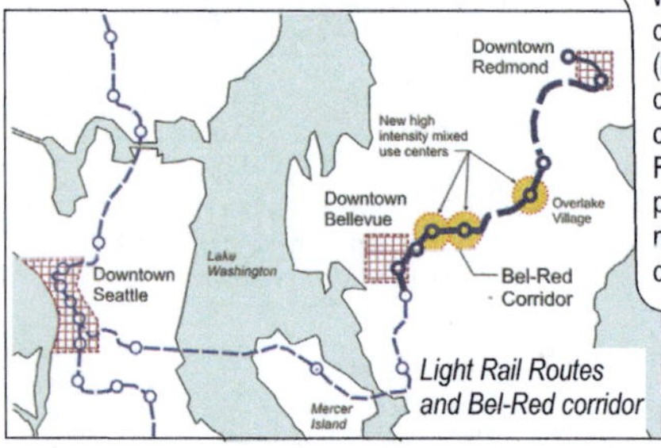

Light Rail Routes and Bel-Red corridor

That's impressive Uncle Bob—kind of like the station areas other cities such as Vancouver and Portland have been building for decades.

Uh, right. Voters here have been slow off the mark regarding light rail, but a Bel-Red linear metropolitan complex will change the whole region's development focus.

Overlake Village Final Phase Visualization

Sustainable Urban Design

Uncle Bob, we've heard a lot about what a green, sustainable city Seattle is. Can you tell me about that?

Sure! A lot of us urban designers around the country think we've been practicing "sustainable" design for decades by creating more compact, walkable, mixed use communities, and the GMA was a huge move in terms of sustainability. But in recent years there has been a greater focus on ecologically responsive solutions, and in the Northwest that means (besides energy conservation) protecting aquatic ecosystems and open space/resource conservation. Because stormwater management is critical to healthy aquatic habitats and our threatened salmon species, urban designers have explored "low impact development" (LID) techniques to reestablish natural drainage and water absorption patterns. The University of Washington's Green Futures Lab has developed a number of green infrastructure tools. One of the earliest and most interesting urban LID projects is "Growing Vine Street" in the Denny Regrade (also called Belltown) that incorporates artwork to celebrate the way the street's landscaping and engineering provide water absorption.

Vine Street

Shorelines are especially significant in the Northwest, and urban designers here have developed solutions to restore urban shorelines while accommodating the marine industry and improving public access. A good example of a comprehensive approach to this challenge is the Alki/Harbor/Duwamish Corridor Design Plan which integrated several Port of Seattle terminal development and shoreline restoration projects with parks, street and infrastructure improvements, and public art—all connected by a trail that runs back to Downtown and will extend ultimately over the Cascade Mountains.

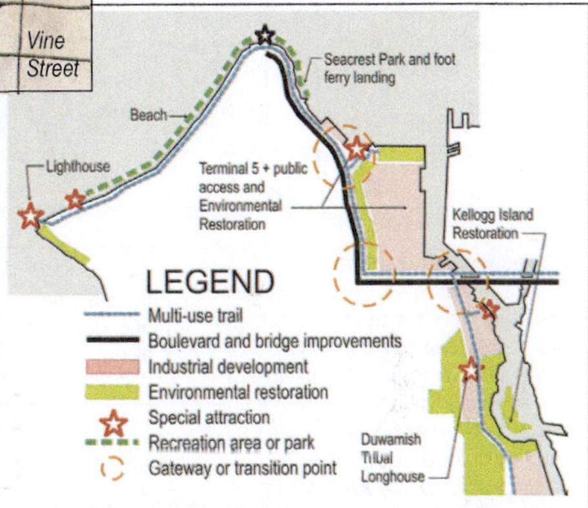

Alki/Harbor/Duwamish Corridor Concept

The most ambitious current urban design project is the central waterfront plan–a city-led effort with much public involvement that included business interests and philanthropic leaders. The project will rebuild the 100-year-old Elliott Bay Seawall and create 22 acres of new parks and public spaces, restore marine habitat, and introduce new civic and recreational spaces along a one-and-a-half-mile promenade. Alaskan Way will be transformed into a multimodal corridor, and there will be a major new pedestrian connection back to the Pike Place Market with public overlooks and amenities.

Central Waterfront Plan Vision - Looking south

Uncle Bob, I've noticed that both the Waterfront and South Lake Union plans are bisected by wide arterials accommodating heavy traffic. How will that work?

Well, we will just have to see. For me, one of the most interesting pieces is the replacement of the old seawall with a more natural beach area that promises to be a natural amenity and important refuge for migrating salmon.

Our new Olympic Sculpture Park includes a piece of beach restoration that shows how to "restore" an urban waterfront. A Seattle Art Museum/Trust for Public Land effort, the park opened in 2007 and includes dramatically structured forms and landscaped settings for the art pieces. It has become a much-loved jewel that anchors the north waterfront.

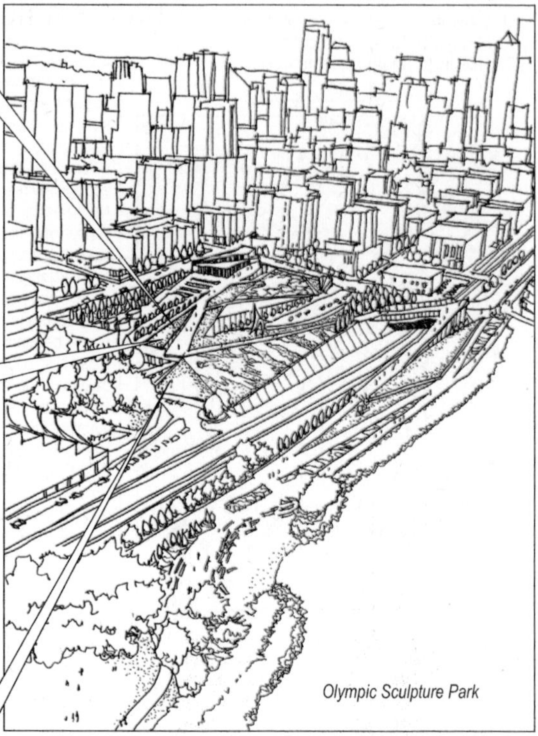

Olympic Sculpture Park

The artworks are impressive, but they seem dominated by the views of the water and the mountains–which are the real sculptures. You know, Uncle Bob, it's interesting to me that the park contrasts a hard engineered character with a more natural feel. It's as if the park balances both R. H. Thompson's and the Olmsteds' visions. I wonder what they would have to say about the project.

"I do not know of any place where the natural advantages for parks are better than here. They can be made very attractive and will be in time one of the things that will make Seattle known all over the world." (*Seattle Post Intelligencer*, May 1, 1903)

"To secure this increase in population and increase in trade, we have, since the founding of the city, provided (civic infrastructure) facilities for a highly civilized people. To assist in providing these facilities has been my life's work. . . . But the job of making Seattle the city I have always held it would be is not done; it will never be done as long as Seattle continues to grow." (*That Man Thompson*, 1950, 129)

If you want to see perhaps Seattle's best example of combining environmental, aesthetic and functional objectives, visit the Hiram M. Chittenden Locks completed in 1917. With its refined engineering structures, botanical gardens, fish passage ladder, varied marine traffic and excellent public access, it may be Seattle's quintessential piece of urban design. And for more on this topic, see *Emerald City: An Environmental History of Seattle* (2009) by Matthew Klingle.

The Bigger Picture

Summary of Factors Affecting Urban Design Activities in Seattle

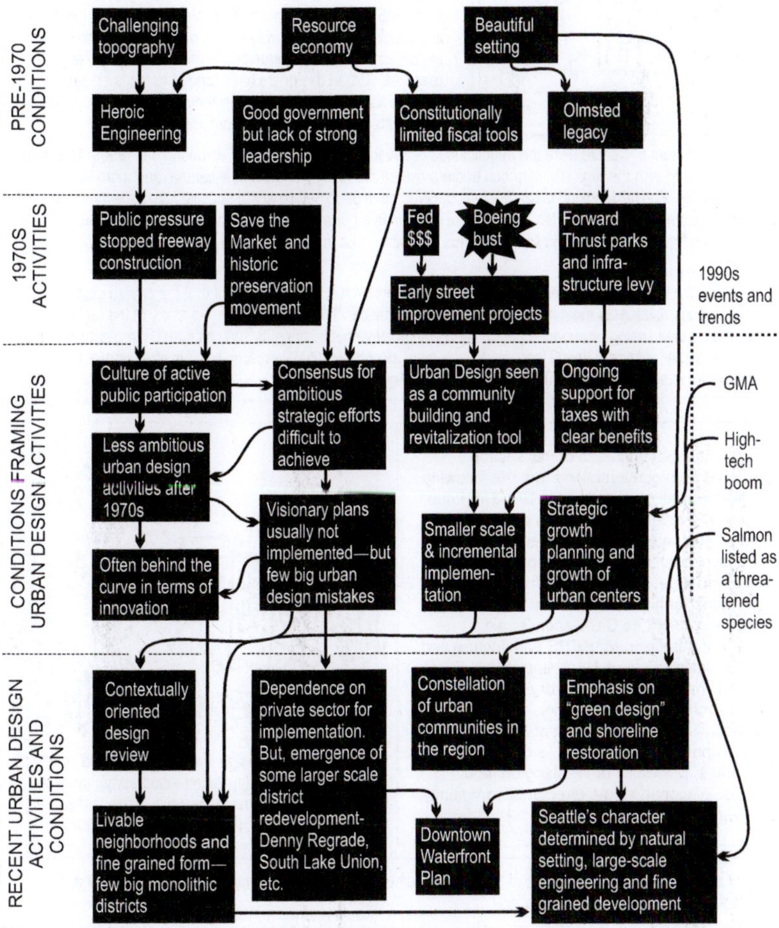

As mentioned earlier, the city's natural setting dominates its physical character, but it was also the basis for the region's resource-based economy and led to the need for the robust, large-scale engineering that allowed the city to grow. The city's political and social climate has also been an important factor. While the local populace has been generally progressive (although at times, not without deplorable racism), during the past half century there has not been a tradition of dynamic political leadership. Added to that, the state's constitution placing severe constraints on public activities related to private enterprise, means financing tools such as tax increment financing are not possible. And, ever since the successful public movements to save the Pike Place Market and halt invasive freeway construction, civic decision making in Seattle has emphasized public involvement so that any urban design measure requires a high level of public consensus. Just as urban design issues gave rise to Seattle's tradition of public activism, that activism now shapes urban design activities. Seattle's innovative design review process involves citizen design review boards and emphasizes directing new projects toward fitting into their urban design contexts. All of this means that, mostly, we do not do large scale, visionary projects. For example, the Seattle Commons and monorail proposals were defeated after years of effort, and it has been hard to build consensus for light rail.

Our civic attention span doesn't seem to be long enough to take on big projects that require sustained commitment. The lack of strong leadership and other constraints also means that our profession here has not had many chances for groundbreaking innovation. There are exceptions, such as the Seattle Center, Pioneer Square revitalization, and some very interesting parks like Gas Works and Freeway Parks, of course. But then again, we have had fewer opportunities to make big urban design mistakes. Urban designers have tended to focus on smaller, incremental measures that, when they have been properly coordinated, can have a significant impact.

Urban designers in Seattle were the beneficiaries of several fortunate occurrences during the 1990s. The state GMA, coupled with the region's high-tech boom provided the energy to build new centers and more livable communities. Forward-looking urban design concepts have been necessary to successfully implement our regional planning objectives. Also, the listing of salmon as a threatened species helped us to focus on integrating "green" urban design solutions. This is another area in which we have often been ahead of the curve.

However, the lack of public investment or political consensus has generally meant that the private sector initiates and implements most of the real city-building projects. The general pattern in many of the region's cities is to relax zoning or provide bonuses and then achieve public benefits such as street improvements, open spaces, and affordable housing through development incentives. That can work, but it is often harder to achieve an integrated, thoughtfully planned public realm.

Most of the observations of this section resulted from conversations with the following individuals, all of whom have played important roles in Seattle's urban design activities over the past decades: Knute Berger, columnist, *Crosscut.com*, an online newspaper and editor-at-large, *Seattle Magazine*; David Brewster, founder and editor-at- large, *Crosscut.com*; Lee Copeland; Gerald Hansmire, partner, MAKERS architecture and urban design; Dennis Haskell, principal, SRG; Mark Hinshaw, FAICP, director of urban design, LMN Architects; Dennis Meier, strategic advisor, Seattle Department of Planning and Development; Dennis Ryan, professor emeritus, University of Washington; and Roger Wagoner, FAICP, director of community design, BHC Consultants.

Seattle's urban design character is shaped largely by its natural setting (including topography), modest public realm improvements, context-sensitive regulatory regime, and neighborhood orientation.

For a witty and clear-eyed picture of the "Seattle culture" that gives rise to many of these phenomena, see *Pugetopolis,* (2008) by Knute Berger.

You make it sound like urban designers here are pretty constrained and often work in a reactive mode. That must be frustrating.

Not at all! There have been some truly great efforts. We've learned to work within the constraints, and they have helped us to focus on our assets. And people here care a lot about the quality of their environment. When the bunch of young professionals migrated to the region in the 1970s and 80s, many of us envisioned building a city with a world perspective and maybe even a global influence–but that was still livable and retained its natural assets. I'd like to think that urban design has been an important part of working toward that goal.

Sounds like it. What have you left for my generation to do?

Lots! My group of friends thinks that new multi-modal transportation systems such as bus rapid transit will provide plenty of opportunities for new solutions, such as creating "linear communities." It will take a lot of urban design work to implement our large new plans such as those for South Lake Union, the Central Waterfront, and the U District to make them livable and equitable, with affordable housing and a vibrant public realm. In the larger picture, there will be new quantitative modeling techniques that will help us better analyze a host of issues from ecosystem evaluation to the community benefits of multimodal transportation options. And, since urban design depends on a public decision-making process, we need to be better at communicating ideas and facilitating that process. Perhaps new cognitive science findings can help us in that regard. Many of our most difficult economic, ecological, infrastructure, and social equity challenges must be addressed at the regional as well as the local scale. We need to build a sense of regional community to address these challenges collectively–and urban design is a proven community building tool. Maybe you can find ways to apply urban design at the regional scale.

Finally, there will always be the need for well-executed, small-scale projects. City building is like gardening. You need to prepare the seed bed, and sow, cultivate, and nurture over a long period of time the things you want to grow.

What about fertilizer?

Oh, urban designers always have plenty of that to spread around.

Urban design concepts are being used successfully at the regional scale in such projects as PSRC's Regional Design Strategy (shown at right), the Mountains to Sound Greenway, and the University of Washington's Regional Open Space Strategy.

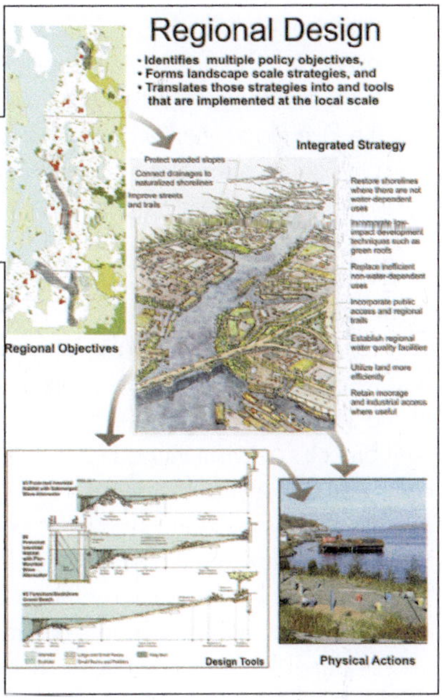

Acknowledgments

Thanks to: Lee Copeland for materials on the Denny Regrade Development Plan; Marshall Foster, city planning director, City of Seattle Department of Planning and Development, and Dave LaClergue, urban designer, City of Seattle Department of Planning and Development for materials on the Seattle Waterfront Plan and South Lake Union development activities; Brice Maryman, landscape architect, SvR Design Company for materials on Growing Vine Street; and Lori Peckol, AICP, policy planning manager, City of Redmond, Washington, and Jeff Churchill, AICP, senior planner, City of Redmond, Washington for materials related to the Bel-Red Corridor. Special thanks to Bob Bengford, AICP, partner, MAKERS architecture and urban design, and Jenny Farmer, production specialist, MAKERS architecture and urban design for serving as models for Uncle Bob and Jenny.

CHAPTER 10

Seattle's Past at Present: Local Approaches to Historic Preservation

Holly Taylor

During the first decade after the 1966 National Historic Preservation Act established a legal framework for conserving the built environment, Seattle achieved recognition for its community-based municipal preservation program. As a review of preservation in the late 1960s and early 1970s explained:

> Public policy which developed during this period received national attention for its vision, and Seattle became a model for its innovative local preservation efforts. For example, the ordinance which created the Pike Place Market Historic District sought to preserve not only the physical features of the district but the historic uses in the market and thus, its character and atmosphere. (Bean and Krafft 1988, 6)

Victor Steinbrueck, an architecture professor at the University of Washington, led the fight to protect Pike Place Market from the ravages of urban renewal. Steinbrueck also played a key role in preserving the Pioneer Square neighborhood, Seattle's first historic district (listed in 1970), and one of the largest districts in the country at the time. The populist character of Steinbrueck's activism infused his 1962 book *Seattle Cityscape*, an annotated collection of sketches focused not on high-style architecture, but on vernacular neighborhoods and territorial views encompassing both urban buildings and the natural setting that frames the city (Figure 10.1).

Steinbrueck's vision shaped the early preservation movement in Seattle, and that movement has expanded, professionalized, and become integrated into sustainable planning. Books such as *The National Trust Guide: Seattle*

Figure 10.1. Sketch of Pike Place Market by Victor Steinbrueck

by Walt Crowley (1998), *Made to Last* by Lawrence Kreisman (1999), and *Shaping Seattle Architecture*, edited by Jeffrey Karl Ochsner (2014), present overviews of local architecture history and preservation.

This chapter provides an introduction to historic preservation in Seattle, highlighting early activism (1960s and '70s), and examining two broad themes that characterize current local preservation approaches—sustainability initiatives and efforts to preserve traditional use along with built form. The properties discussed below are either designated City of Seattle Landmarks or listed on the National Register, or both.

Development History and the Early Preservation Movement

Seattle's history begins not with Europeans (Britain's Captain Vancouver explored Puget Sound in 1792), but with thousands of years of habitation by Chief Seattle's people, ancestors of today's Duwamish, Suquamish, and Muckleshoot Tribes, who spoke the Lushootseed language. These Puget Salish people's place names, archaeological sites, and traditional cultural properties such as nearby Snoqualmie Falls are part of the region's heritage as well as present-day preservation concerns, and tribes actively comanage cultural and natural resources in partnership with public agencies. (See Chapter 13, which discusses Coast Salish heritage).

Non-native settlers arrived in 1851, and the town of Seattle developed slowly until the mid-1880s, when transcontinental railroads spurred rapid

Figure 10.2. Pioneer Square

Figure 10.3. Ornamental terra cotta figures on Seattle's Arctic Building

growth. A catastrophic fire in 1889 destroyed the commercial core of Victorian masonry and rustic wood buildings. Reconstruction began immediately, and the subsequent building boom replaced destroyed structures with sturdier brick and stone edifices that comprise today's Pioneer Square Historic District, one of the nation's best surviving collections of late 19th century urban commercial architecture (Figure 10.2) (Farley 1977).

The Klondike Gold Rush in 1897 brought an infusion of wealth to Seattle, as the city proclaimed itself the "Gateway to Alaska." Emblematic of the continuing connection with Alaska are the Tlingit totem pole at Pioneer Place (First and Yesler), and the terra cotta-clad Arctic Building (Third and Cherry, now a hotel) (Figure 10.3), decorated not with gargoyles, but with ornamental walrus heads. This Alaska connection also inspired Seattle's first World's Fair, the 1909 Alaska-Yukon-Pacific Exposition (AYPE), held on a then undeveloped portion of the University of Washington campus. The AYPE showcased Seattle as a major Pacific port, and marked its transition on a national level from a frontier boomtown to an urban center.

By the early 20th century, most new commercial buildings were constructed outside of Pioneer Square as the city's business district expanded northward. Residential development extended along streetcar lines that served growing suburban communities. Bypassed by post-World War II development and damaged by a 1949 earthquake, Pioneer Square became known as Skid Road, after the settlement-era practice of skidding logs down the steep hillside to shoreline sawmills. The Skid Road moniker captured the neighborhood's "down-and-out" character which persisted until a handful of architects and urban visionaries began purchasing and rehabilitating historic buildings in the 1960s (Crowley 1998).

Seattle's hosting of the 1962 World's Fair sought to position the city as a forward-looking metropolis. Themed "Century 21," the fair symbolized the creation of modern Seattle, and also marked the origin of efforts to preserve the city's past (Crowley 1998, 13). By 1971, Seattle had two locally designated historic districts, Pike Place Market and Pioneer Square. The city hired one of the nation's first municipal historic preservation officers in 1973, following passage of a "strong" landmarks ordinance allowing designation without owner consent (Kreisman 1999). The Seattle-based nonprofit Washington Trust for Historic Preservation formed in 1976 as a statewide advocacy organization.

In addition to government and community models, the "Seattle approach" to preservation also includes public development authorities (PDAs), which are municipal corporations chartered under state law to provide public services. Historic Seattle PDA was created in 1974 to acquire and rehabilitate threatened historic properties citywide (surplus public properties or those sold by private owners), and either steward them as community assets or resell them with protective easements (Kreisman 1999). Historic Seattle also sponsors education and advocacy programs, but the real estate component of its mission distinguishes Historic Seattle and allows its use of business finance tools to achieve preservation goals.

A new era of preservation planning followed passage of the statewide Growth Management Act in 1990, which directed jurisdictions to "identify and encourage the preservation of land, sites and structures that have historical, cultural and archaeological significance" as a fundamental goal.

Adaptive Reuse and Sustainability

Adaptive reuse, an essential strategy of preservation and core principle of sustainability, involves rehabilitating historic properties and adapting them for new purposes. One prominent adaptive reuse project is Lake Union's Gas Works Park (1975), a pioneering approach to preserving industrial relics on a site adapted for recreation. State Historic Preservation Officer Allyson Brooks praised landscape architect Richard Haag's award-winning design that "conserved part of Seattle's industrial heritage along with introducing a groundbreaking experiment in bioremediation into urban life" (Berger 2013).

Preservationists have embraced the mantra "the greenest building is the one already built" (Elefante 2007) to align their field with the burgeoning sustainability movement. In 2009, the National Trust for Historic Preservation established the Preservation Green Lab (PGL) in Seattle, to foster 21st century preservation through innovative demonstration projects and public policy research. While the PGL also has staff elsewhere, it is based in Seattle in part because local preservation, development, and political leaders all demonstrated commitment to integrating sustainability and preservation.

Developer and founding PGL director Liz Dunn emphasized the program's goal of making the reuse of older buildings easier—not only landmarks and other historically significant buildings, but also a broad range of small-scale buildings that are typically overlooked by the current retrofit market (Levitt 2011). PGL generates and analyzes data to support preservation of the kind of "urban grain" buildings that Jane Jacobs (1992) had in mind when she said "new ideas must use old buildings."

High-profile reuse projects have extended the life of monumental public buildings through conversion to private uses, including Queen Anne High School (1908), adapted for housing in 1986, and the Lake Union Steam Plant (1914), rehabilitated for biotech offices in 1997.

Seattleites may be most proud of landmarks serving public purposes. The International District's East Kong Yick Building (1910), a former Chinese Family Association headquarters, became Wing Luke Asian Museum in 2008; the Central District's Colman School (1909) became Northwest African American Museum also in 2008; and South Lake Union's Naval Reserve Armory (1942) reopened as the Museum of History and Industry in 2012. These rehabilitated facilities created public spaces that have become centers of community life, reinforcing the idea that historic preservation is "one of the deliberate ways that culture is shaped in modern society" (Mason 2006, 30).

Preserving Traditional Uses

While adaptive reuse projects often generate broad acclaim, ongoing efforts to perpetuate traditional uses while still maintaining historic integrity are also noteworthy. Perhaps the best and most complicated local example of preserving traditional use is the Pike Place Market. Established in 1907, it is the oldest continuously operating public market in the country. During the 1910s, arcade buildings were constructed to allow shoppers to "meet the producer" and buy directly from Japanese, Italian, and other mostly immigrant farmers.

When an urban renewal scheme threatened the market with demolition, Seattle citizens voted in 1971 to establish the Pike Place Market Historical District. Following this success, preservationists developed regulations to guide not only conservation of the market's physical fabric, but also allocation of stalls to individual growers and craftspeople and leases to independently owned businesses. Historian Walt Crowley enthusiastically described this strategy as preservation of a social and economic anachronism, albeit one that is often called "the soul of Seattle."

Seattle preservationists rallied to protect historic theaters and support their ongoing use as performance venues after the 1991 demolition of the Spanish baroque Music Hall (1929). That loss spurred legislation to protect remaining theaters through transfer of development rights, grant-funded restorations, and creation of a Downtown Historic Theatre District.

Throughout the city, many landmarks retain their original function and some have been meticulously restored. Pioneer Square's King Street Station (1906), with its prominent clocktower patterned after St. Mark's Basilica in Venice, originally served the Great Northern Railroad. After decades of deterioration, a city-led restoration project concluded in 2013, and the station continues to serve as a rail hub.

Another landmark retaining its traditional use is the Panama Hotel (1910), a single-room-occupancy hotel in Seattle's Nihonmachi or Japantown, now individually recognized as a National Historic Landmark, and part of the Chinatown-International Special Review District. The Panama Hotel retains its tradition *sento*, or Japanese bathhouse, in the basement. Although the bathhouse no longer operates, the hotel and teahouse still welcome guests.

Architecture critic Vincent Canizaro (2007, 27) called authenticity "a quality of engagement between people and things or people and places . . . not a property inherent to things or places but a measure of our connection to them." These historic places, which retain both their form and their traditional use, may inspire the strongest sense of connection and authenticity.

Ongoing Challenges

Half a century ago, Victor Steinbrueck advocated preserving "the fabric of the city, particularly the older historic fabric, as an embodiment of the history, life, and culture of ordinary people" (Ochsner 2008, 123). Echoing this concern, preservationist Lawrence Kreisman observed:

> The buildings that are most endangered will continue to be unprotected, having slipped through the landmarks program. They are background buildings of terra cotta and brick—small and unassuming street walls of retail and office that are not considered individually significant but that collectively provide an important visual tie with the past traditions of city life. (Kreisman 1988, 15)

Journalist Knute Berger has lamented Seattle's tendency to tear down perfectly good old structures—albeit structures that did not meet the criteria for landmarking—and replace them with bland new ones at the expense of the character that makes mature cities attractive. Berger regards landmarks laws as important pieces of the city-shaping puzzle; however, "they resemble environmental rules that protect only the oldest and finest trees in the forest and not the forest itself" (Berger 2008).

To protect the forest of "character buildings," Berger urges an alternative development ethic that emphasizes recycling of older structures and a determination not to tear down sound buildings that are already part of the city's identity, saying that we need to "preserve use, character and affordability, not simply architectural significance" (Berger 2008). New incentives to encourage rehabilitation of existing buildings, and to discourage demolition, are needed in Seattle and many other cities.

Assessing the life cycles of buildings and using policy recommendations from the PGL can support preservation and reuse of all building stock, not just designated landmarks. Preservationists are also collaborating with environmental advocates to ensure that sustainability checklists prioritize reuse over demolition and redevelopment. Locally and nationally, planners can support preservation efforts through their willingness to explore creative regulations and incentives that go beyond just protecting outstanding landmarks to effectively conserve the character, scale, and identity of historic neighborhoods, whether or not such neighborhoods are formally designated as historic districts.

CHAPTER 11

The Emerald and the Rose: Open Space Planning in Metropolitan Seattle and Portland

Michael Houck, Nancy Rottle, and John Owen

It's no secret that Seattle and Portland are endowed with spectacular natural settings and legacies of excellent park planning and design. In 2012, Bloomberg *Businessweek* named Seattle #2 and Portland #5 in its ranking of "America's Best Cities," with heavy weighting given to leisure amenities and the proportion of park acreage to population (Konrad 2012). The Trust for Public Land (TPL) (2013) gave top-10 ParkScores to both cities, with their rankings based on park acreage, services, and access.

With inherent natural endowments and park planning by the Olmsted brothers over a century ago, both city-regions in recent decades have taken ambitious and innovative steps to build upon their assets:

- Both Seattle and Portland have built robust metropolitan systems using diverse strategies that have relied upon local leadership, committed civic constituencies, and regional as well as city-scale approaches to envision, plan and fund coherent, ecologically-based systems.
- Both municipalities operate under state growth management mandates which have propelled park and open space planning while posing challenges related to providing open space within compact urban forms.
- Both jurisdictions have made exemplary strides in pursuing a green infrastructure and green urbanism approach that requires interdisciplinary collaboration and interdepartmental efforts and communication.

This chapter focuses on the factors that have enabled these developments to take place. The chapter first tells the story of growing Portland's and the Portland-Vancouver metropolitan region's open space network, followed by an outline of the development of Seattle's and King County's park systems. It briefly examines and compares key parallel aspects of each city's Olmsted foundations, followed by recent regional approaches, connections to planning activities, civic involvement, "green infrastructure" innovations, and funding and implementation mechanisms, concluding with a summary and a table outlining "lessons learned."

The Rose: Open Space Planning in Portland, Oregon

Historically, the belief that the city is an entity apart from nature and even antithetical to it has dominated the way in which the city is perceived and continues to affect how it is built. Today's planners understand that the city must be recognized as part of nature and designed accordingly (Spirn 1984).

Foundations

The impetus for creating Portland's park system came largely from a trio of visionary park "nature lovers." Rev. Thomas Lamb Eliot, retired banker Colonel Lester Leander Hawkin, and architect Ion Lewis first convinced the Oregon legislature in 1899 to require any city of 3,000 or more to create a park commission. In 1900 they successfully advocated for the creation of the Portland Park Commission and shortly afterward recruited the famed Olmsted firm to produce a park master plan (Orloff 2004).

Portland park commissioner Colonel Hawkins related his intimate knowledge of Portland's landscapes with John Charles Olmsted from his horse-drawn carriage, Tally-Ho-Jupiter. Over a four-day period Hawkins shared his own vision for what features should be included in Portland's park system, most of which were featured prominently in Olmsted's master plan (Hawkins 2011). His 1903 *Report of the Park Board* was less a treatise on park design than it was a "land-use sermon" (Hockaday 2009, 17–18). To be sure, it was a blueprint for a comprehensive, interconnected park, boulevard, and parkway system. But it was also a "greenprint" for integrating natural landscapes into the city's urban fabric (Figure 11.1). For example, Olmsted presaged today's stream and watershed restoration efforts, when he counseled that:

> Marked economy may be effected by laying out parkways and parks so as to embrace streams that carry at times more water than can be taken care of by drain pipes of ordinary size. Thus brooks or little rivers which would otherwise become nuisances that would someday have to be put in large underground conduits at enormous expense, may be made the occasion for delightful local pleasure grounds or attractive parkways. (Olmsted et al. 1903, 20)

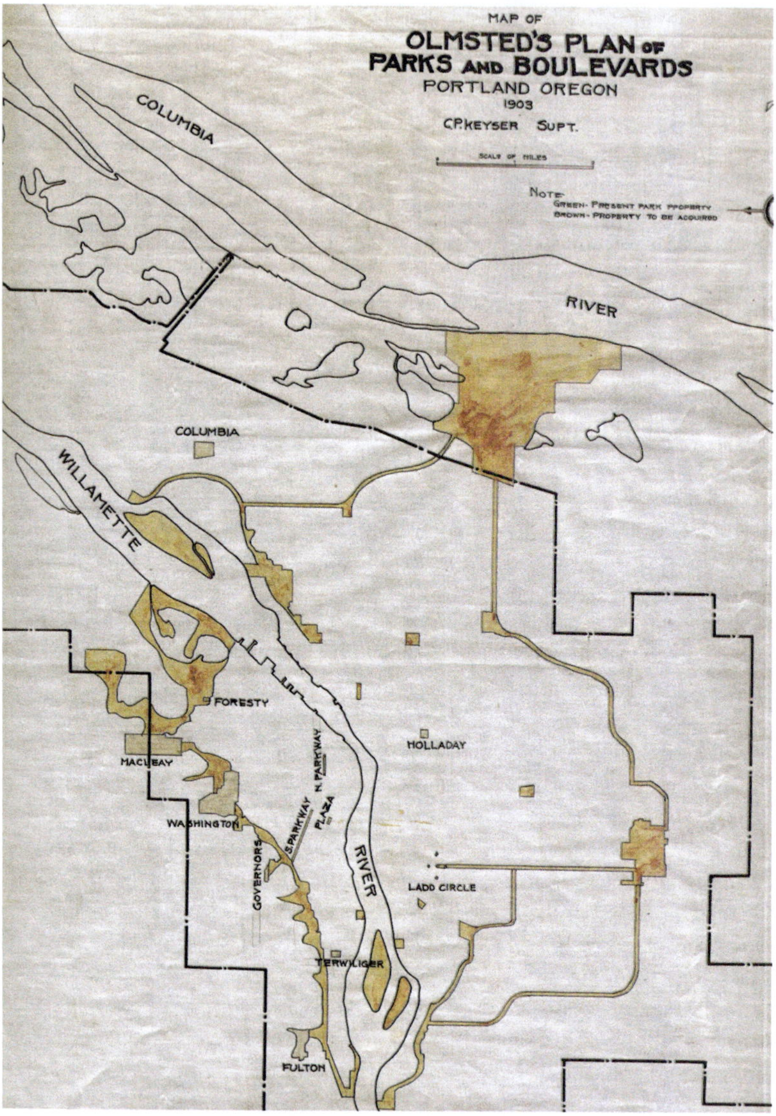

Figure 11.1. Map of 1903 Olmsted Plan of Parks and Boulevards for Portland

Olmsted observed that the city was "most fortunate, in comparison with the majority of American cities, in possessing such varied and wonderfully strong and interesting landscape features" (Olmsted et al. 1903, 34). His proposed "system of public squares, neighborhood parks, playgrounds, scenic reservations, rural or suburban parks, and boulevards and parkways" was built around many of the features that are today's iconic landscapes, including 5,200-acre Forest Park, Ross Island, and 2,000-acre Smith and Bybee Lakes.

Open Spaces and Greenspaces Era

Portland's park and open space planning from 1960 through most of the 1980s did little to further Olmsted's vision for "scenic reservations" and "rural parks" that were intended to provide "quiet contemplation of natural scenery" and "preserve notable landscape features." But in 1984, the creation of the 40-Mile Loop Land Trust resurrected the vision of an interconnected park system, which sparked in Portland an open-space renaissance based on Olmstedian principles. In 1988, the city council's adoption of the Oaks Bottom Wildlife Refuge Management Plan created the Portland's first urban wildlife refuge as an integral element of the park system and signaled another philosophical and programmatic shift toward ecologically significant open spaces.

Between 1980 and 2001 Portland added more than 900 acres to its natural areas portfolio, $300,000 for natural area maintenance to the bureau's budget, and new staff ecologists. In 2001, the city also adopted the Parks Vision 2020 Plan, which stated:

> The city's parks, natural areas and recreation programs are among the essential elements that create a livable, dynamic and economically vibrant city; Portland Parks will promote regional strategies to protect natural resource values of wildlife corridors. (Portland 2001b)

Thus, for the first time since the 1903 Olmsted Master Plan, natural resources and natural resource management enjoyed parity with recreational facilities and neighborhood and community parks. Today, three-quarters of the Portland park system's 10,000 acres of land assets are natural areas.

Green Infrastructure and Green Urbanism

With the 2005 adoption of Portland's Watershed Management Plan, the city's Bureau of Environmental Services evolved from what had been a single-purpose sewer bureau into a more holistic environmental and watershed health agency. Urban stormwater had become a valuable resource rather than waste to be carried off in pipes to the nearest body of water (Portland 2005). In 2008 the city's *Grey to Green* program earmarked $55 million over five years to implement green infrastructure projects including planting more than 30,000 street and yard trees that were projected to capture 18 million gallons of stormwater annually.

In addition to promoting more open space at the streetscape and neighborhood scale, the emphasis on green infrastructure led to one of the largest open space purchases in decades with the acquisition of Riverview Cemetery property in Portland's southwest hills. The purchase, brokered by The Trust for Public Land, brought together Metro, Portland Parks and Recreation, and the Bureau of Environmental Services. The 146-acre forest represents a shift from a silo-oriented single-agency, single-purpose approach to a collaborative, multiobjective strategy that leverages multiple funding sources and achieves multiple goals including providing recreational opportunities, adapting to climate change, improving water quality, and protecting the city's biodiversity.

Listing Chinook salmon and steelhead trout as threatened under the Endangered Species Act in 2003 catalyzed improved integration of parks, planning, and environmental services missions, and led to significant improvements in open space restoration and management. At the local level, Portland's newly updated Comprehensive Plan now recognizes "(the) importance of watershed health for its utilitarian, cultural, spiritual, and intrinsic value" and states: "Preserving ecological function and ecosystem services is wise because (they) support public health and safety, preserve the quality of life, and improve and maintain the well-being of Portland's residents" (Portland 2013a).

Regional Open Space Planning

Regionally based open space planning began in 1988 when a small, passionate group of park and open space planners and citizens from Portland Parks and Recreation, Tualatin Hills Park and Recreation, Clark County, and several nonprofits gathered at Metro to launch what would become the Metropolitan Greenspaces initiative. Taking lessons from London, New York City, the East Bay Regional Park District, and other open space initiatives around the country, Metro Council adopted a bistate Greenspaces Master Plan for the Portland-Vancouver (Washington) region in 1992.

With the Greenspaces Master Plan in hand and reinforced by the Region 2040 Growth Concept, Metro was able to secure passage for two regional bond measures in May 1995 ($135.6 million) and in 2006 ($227.4 million), to acquire natural areas and build a regional trail network. Taking a lesson from the East Bay Regional Park District, 75 percent of the bonds went to Metro and 25 percent to local park providers for their priority natural area and trail projects. To date Metro and local park providers have added more than 16,000 acres of natural areas and trails to the region's public open space system. Metro passed a third bond measure in 2013, raising $53 million for operations and management of its natural areas.

However, land-use planning for open space and natural resources in the metropolitan region has long been influenced by a bias against "too much" emphasis on open space and natural resource protection inside the Urban Growth Boundary (UGB). The region's UGB, it has been asserted, is to protect nature "out there," in the rural hinterlands. As a result, open space

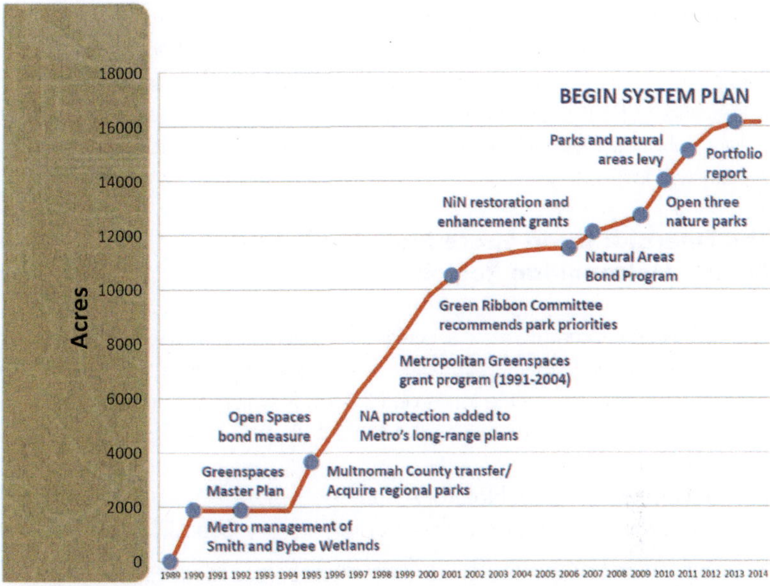

Figure 11.2. Regional accretion of public lands in the Portland region from 1989 to 2014

and natural resource protection lagged behind the other progressive planning initiatives, both within the city of Portland itself and regionally (Houck and Labbe 2006; Wiley 2001). Fortunately, by the early 1990s the canard that compact urban form meant open space had to be sacrificed was on the wane, largely because the public was demanding access to nature and open space as the city and region adopted policies to further densify within the region's UGB. Figure 11.2 shows the accretion of public lands in the region from the late 1980s to 2014.

Civic Organization and Cultural Attitudes

Citizen involvement in open space planning has not only continued since citizen park commissioners brought Olmsted to Portland, but has exploded over the past 30 years. The city is unique in its diverse, citizen-based nonprofit organizations dedicated to park, trail, and natural area issues. And while there is a natural tension between advocates and government agencies, a sense of common mission with regard to open space planning has evolved to the extent that they have become partners in an acceleration of park, trail, and natural resource planning that was largely nonexistent before the 1980s.

In 2011 a new nonprofit organization, the Intertwine Alliance, was spun off from Metro. More than 100 partners, including local and regional governments, nonprofits, corporations, and health providers, have joined the Alliance in what is a "collective impact" model of collaboration (Kania and Kramer 2011) to create a world-class, interconnected system of parks, trails, and natural areas in the Portland-Vancouver metropolitan region. It is John Charles Olmsted's vision for a comprehensive, interconnected park system writ large.

The Emerald: Open Space Planning in the Seattle Metropolitan Region

> Where the water flows, the positive benefits of open space are the clearest. If we follow this track in our open-space planning, we are at once securing the prime lands and the lands which give linkage and continuity—in a word, regional design. (Whyte 1968, 181)

Foundations: Building on Natural Assets

Swept up in the nationwide enthusiasm for the City Beautiful movement that grew out of the 1893 Chicago World's Fair, Seattle's civic leaders of the early 20th century decided that the time had come for the city to take on the trappings of the sophisticated cities back east. "Let Us Make a Beautiful City of Seattle" read a *Seattle Post-Intelligencer* article from that period. Taking action on this sentiment, Seattle Park Board Secretary Charles W. Saunders wrote to the Olmsted brothers in December 1902, inviting them to undertake a parks and boulevards plan for the city. On April 30, 1903, John Charles Olmsted arrived in Seattle.

Olmsted worked feverishly for the next two months and in June he submitted a transformative parks plan calling for an interconnected system of boulevards, greenswards, parks, and shorelines with maps and numerous sketch designs for specific parks (Figure 11.3). The city council accepted the plan in October 1903, and over the next 16 years he worked continuously for the plan's successful implementation, making 10 trips to Seattle and using all his powers of persuasion to achieve what he considered only a portion of his plan (Hockaday 2009).

By 1909 Seattle boasted nearly 700 acres of parks and boulevards. Within the next 18 years the city had 42 parks, nearly as many playgrounds, 10 bathing beaches, 24 miles of boulevards, four field houses and 62 "vest pocket" open spaces (Klingle 2007, 141). Equally important, the basic framework of the original 1903 plan was intact. In the words of Joan Hockaday, "Despite more than a dozen subsequent reports, sketches and drawings completed for the city between 1903 and 1911, John Charles' 1903 report remained Seattle's main blueprint for planning parks and parkways in a continuing professional manner" (Hockaday 2009, 43).

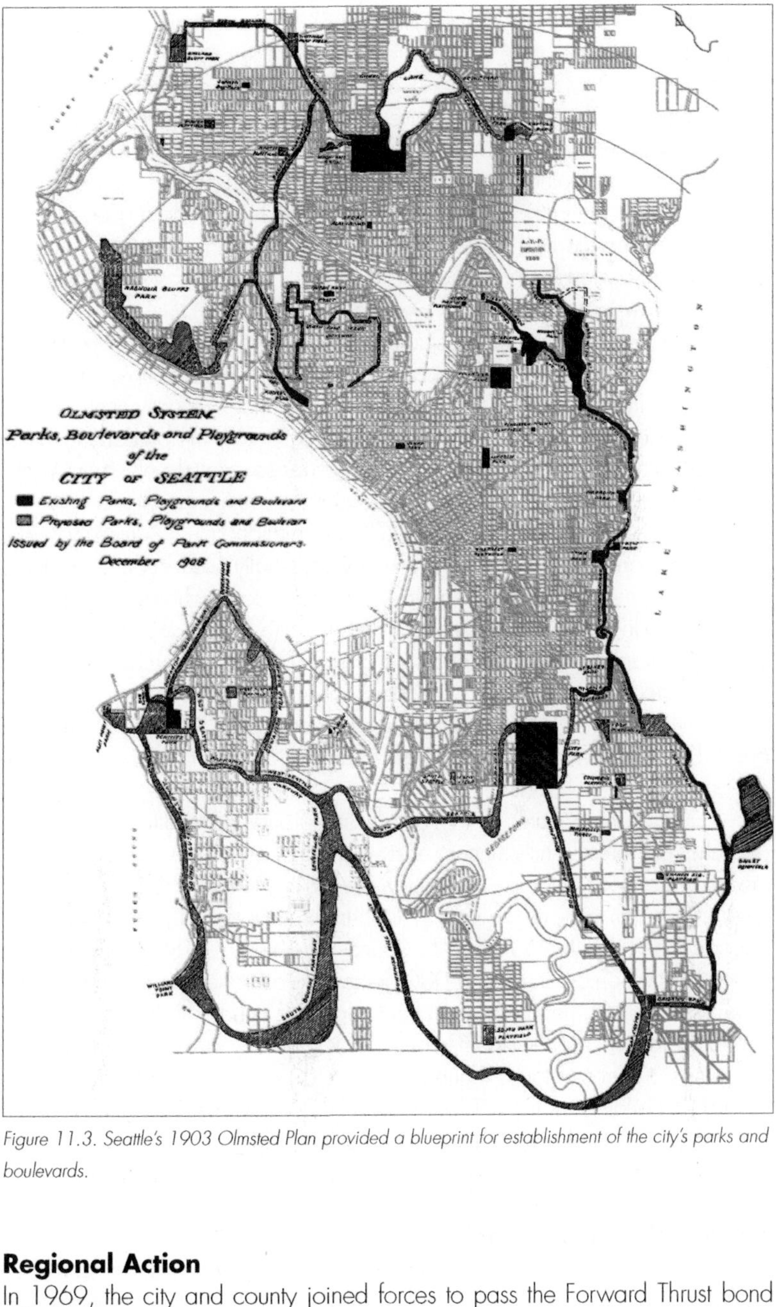

Figure 11.3. Seattle's 1903 Olmsted Plan provided a blueprint for establishment of the city's parks and boulevards.

Regional Action

In 1969, the city and county joined forces to pass the Forward Thrust bond measure for a host of much-needed infrastructure improvements, including $118 million for parks (Klingle 2008; Seattle 2004). Forward Thrust not only added numerous new parks, trails, and recreational facilities, its broad and county-wide scope for the first time produced what felt like an integrated regional system. Forward Thrust parks in Seattle currently comprise about 40 percent of the city's park system, and the new parks, constructed mostly between 1970 and 1980, often featured innovative designs and new design concepts. For example, in designing Gas Works Park (1971), Richard Haag argued successfully for retaining the old cracking towers as an industrial artifact and Angela Danadjieva's design for Freeway Park bridged I-5 with a cascading series of spaces and water features.

This growing regional appreciation for a greater spectrum of parks and open spaces led to further progressive action. Alarmed by the rapid disappearance of productive farmland in King County, in the late 1970s county leaders had convinced voters, on the third try, to approve a $50 million bond measure to protect high-value farmlands through voluntary sales of development rights, which ultimately preserved 13,000 acres of prime farmland in the county.

In 1982 King County adopted a Conservation Futures property tax to be used for landscape protection, which was initially used to purchase farmland development rights and gradually expanded to purchase open spaces, greenbelts, and parks in the county and its cities. In 1986, King County formally initiated an Open Space Program, and in 1988 issued a report that identified trail corridors, open space lands, and river and stream corridors with strategies for their acquisition and protection. Funding for the plan passed on a second try in 1989, eased by designating a third of the $117 million for the city of Seattle.

With this momentum, in 1990 a hiking group, advocating preservation of a chain of forested hills running eastward from Seattle, inaugurated a movement to create a 100-mile greenway paralleling Interstate 90. By bringing diverse government, nonprofit, and industry stakeholders together, in its first decade the nonprofit Mountains to Sound Greenway (MTSG) had brokered deals to transfer more than 125,000 acres of forests and farms to public ownership, sponsored the construction and repair of hundreds of miles of trails, supported cultural and environmental facilities, and stewarded the restoration of thousands of acres of lands in the corridor and its adjacent watersheds (Rottle 2005). Expanding on the MTSG, today's Regional Open Space Strategy for Central Puget Sound echoes Intertwine's Portland regional goals for a coalition to secure and steward a larger connected open space system.

Intergration with Planning

Passage of the state Growth Management Act (GMA) in 1990 bolstered MTSG's goals of supporting rural communities separated by green space, and mandated that Washington cities address parks and recreation within their established Urban Growth Boundaries. Building on a 1990 "Bands of Green" report detailing an expansionary plan for boulevards, trails, and linear parks based on Olmsted's original principles, in 1993 Seattle Parks produced a Complan as part of the city's response to the GMA requirement.

With both planning and funds in hand, during the 1990s Seattle substantially grew its open space system. Funding of $42 million from the county Open Space bond funds allowed the city to leverage state and other funds to purchase 531 acres of open space lands, almost doubling the number initially identified for acquisition. Public meetings to identify priority projects were held in nearly every neighborhood so that designated greenbelts, natural areas, and trails were distributed across the city.

King County's $14 million Waterway 2000 program, established in 1994, also supported acquisition of shorelines within the city boundaries, while passage of $60 million of additional county bonds paid by Conservation Futures funds provided $15 million for Seattle open space. Response to the severe pollution in the lower Duwamish River also brought port and mitigation funding to construct several park, trail, and restoration sites along the constructed waterway's mouth at Elliott Bay, creating a connected bicycle trail and ecological stepping stones through this inhospitable stretch of the river.

Civic Engagement: A Key Force

Environmental leadership and a public participation ethic from Seattle mayors Rice (1990–1998) and Schell (1998–2002) enabled robust citizen participation to contribute to the growth of the city's park and open space system. Local watershed groups such as the Thornton Creek Alliance, Ravenna Creek Alliance, and Carkeek Park Watershed Community Action Partnership formed to advocate for the health of individual stream watersheds. The Friends of Seattle's Olmsted Parks also were instrumental in advocating for both preservation of existing historic parks and continued realization of the Olmsted connected park vision.

Between 1995 and 1999, Seattle's Neighborhood Planning Office instituted a citywide Neighborhood Planning Program funding neighborhood councils to lead local processes to identify how predicted growth should occur in each of the 39 city districts. Many of the resulting plans identified need for green space, habitat, and parks. To fund these and other projects, in 1998 voters approved a $198 million lid-lift levy to fund acquisition, development, maintenance and operations of parks, trails, community gardens, forested hillsides, and creeks. The levy included an innovative Opportunity Fund to which citizens could apply for project support.

The role of NGOs grew significantly after the turn of the millennium. In 2000, the Seattle Parks Foundation was established, with a mission to advocate and raise funds "for community-led public space projects . . . to support a shared vision of a city connected through great parks, trails and natural areas" (Seattle 2014e). The foundation raised over $20 million to design and construct the new South Lake Union shoreline Park, which opened in 2010.

Green Infrastructure/Green Urbanism: An Ecological Perspective

In 1999, the U.S. Department of the Interior listed the Puget Sound Chinook salmon and bull trout as threatened under the Endangered Species Act, bringing more intense focus to salmon recovery efforts. Additionally, Mayor Paul Schell initiated the $16 million Millennium Urban Creek Legacy program to restore salmon habitat and public access on four miles of the city's largest urban creeks. Seattle's famed SEA Streets—which detain stormwater in vegetated streetside swales to prevent downstream scouring and pollutants in Piper's Creek—were inaugurated in 2001, constructed first on a long block and then followed in a several-block grid in the urban creekshed. In 2004, the city issued a science-based "Restore our Waters Strategy" focusing on urban drainage, creeks, and lakes, supporting Seattle Public Utilities' (SPU) expansion of the successful SEA Streets program into other creek watersheds.

The first decade of the new millennium saw significant growth in parks for Seattle, with an emphasis on active and passive recreation, largely as a result of the $196 million Pro Parks levy and guided by the 2000 Complan update. The Complan update had set park and open space standards for the city—such as "breathing room" of one acre per 100 residents, shoreline access every one-half mile, and parks within one-eighth to one-half mile of every resident. A GIS-based "gap analysis" identified which neighborhood areas were deficient in park space to help prioritize park levy expenditures.

With the 2003 Olmsted Plan centennial, the Cascade Land Conservancy (now Forterra) launched a regionwide set of conversations to envision the future of the coming century, with resulting recommendations that growth be channeled to cities in order to preserve the metropolitan region's little remaining farmland, forests, and open space. Seattle citizens followed with visioning processes for the city's open space future, to accommodate that growth while ensuring an ecological, connected urban open space system (Figure 11.4). Bolstered through these grassroots initiatives, Seattle voters passed a $146 million Parks and Green Spaces Levy in 2008, while King County passed three levies in a dozen years totaling over $660 million.

In the second decade of the millennium, urban attentions have turned to reclaiming gray and turning it green. The Alaskan Way viaduct will be removed, providing space for a new Central Waterfront park, and a new seawall with aquatic habitat features is under construction. SPU is removing pavement to install neighborhood raingardens to prevent combined sewer overflows in several city basins, and is collaborating with the Seattle Depart-

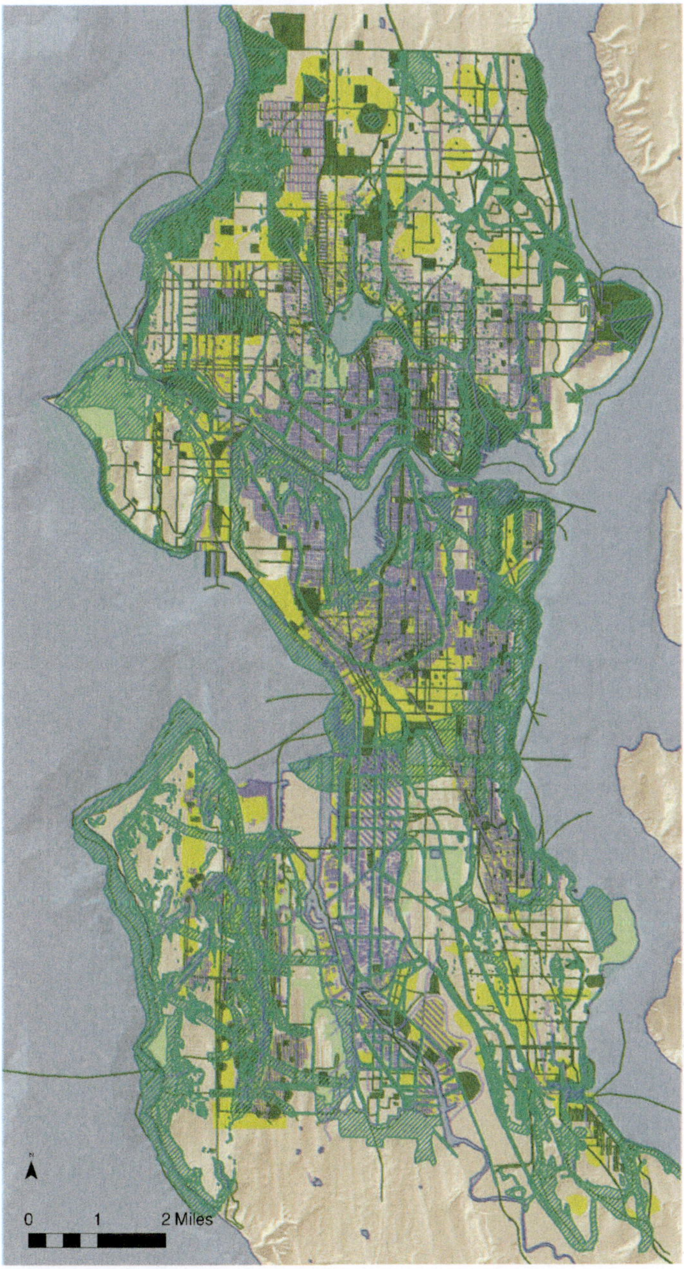

Figure 11.4. Participants in the 2006 Green Futures charrette envisioned Seattle's future open space system in the year 2100.

ment of Transportation and King County Metro to establish green stormwater streets hospitable to cycling and walking.

Summary

Several patterns emerge from a survey of the park and open space development in the two city-regions. First, John Charles Olmsted's plans for both systems provided visionary, multifaceted, and pragmatic foundations upon which future improvements were developed. Park development and improvement initiatives generally follow periods of rapid population growth, but they also seem to occur when the public perceives a critical social or environmental problem. Both park systems represent an amalgam of visionary and expansive efforts such as the Olmsted plans and Forward Thrust program, along with pragmatic, incremental steps such as park levy planning.

The open space systems in both cities have always been a subject for extensive public debate and civic pride, and decisions regarding parks have typically been influenced by political, economic, and equity-related concerns. What has often distinguished local and regional park development activities is the exuberance with which the populace and its leadership have thrown themselves into park building and natural area conservation.

Another key factor is a local conservation ethic and culture, influenced by the region's scenic beauty and prodigious resources. To be sure, there has always been a drive to overexploit and despoil the region's forests, fertile floodplains, salmon, water bodies, and other natural treasures. But there have always been voices that have provoked public action to try to remedy these mistakes. What is currently emerging is a holistic sense of how urban development fits within the larger environment, and a notion of what could be done to better integrate natural and human-made systems.

CHAPTER 12

There's No Place like Home

Salina Lyons, AICP

IL N'Y A QUE DEUX ENDROITS AU MONDE OÙ L'ON PUISSE VIVRE HEUREUX: CHEZ SOI ET À PARIS. (HEMINGWAY)

TRANSLATION: THERE ARE ONLY TWO PLACES IN THE WORLD WHERE WE CAN LIVE HAPPY: AT HOME AND IN PARIS.

Few people know about and even fewer understand what a city planner is responsible for day to day. We're a group of people that envision how the built environment can be shaped in ways that provide safe and healthy places to live, work, and play. Yet no planning course or conflict resolution scenario can prepare a planner for the moments when their professionalism is challenged or when politics override a "makes good planning sense" decision. These are hard lessons to learn. I know, because I learned them early in my career.

My career began in a small suburban city outside of Seattle. I was full of hope and promise. People and their places mattered to me and I was moving through the professional ranks, all the while holding the charge of the American Planning Association and Making Great Communities Happen. However, with a slight shift in government politics, I began facing challenges that cut me to the core. I went from loving everything about my profession to being a jaded and angry city planner. I began to question if I was in the right career and how long I could withstand politicians and emotionally charged public meetings.

After five years I was OVER IT! The politics, bureaucracy, and stream of policies and procedures that created barriers to change had become exhausting and seemed insurmountable. The young idealist in me desperately held onto the idea of being a city planner; however, if I was going to change the world, I was beginning to think I needed to find a way that didn't involve working with people.

In the mist of my personal crisis, I received a birthday card from a friend that read, "I promise your life will never be the same, and the world will never seem larger, after you've watched the sunrise on the other side of the world." It was settled. I wanted to be happy and home was pissing me off; so, with Hemingway's quote in the back of my mind I thought, "Why not give Paris a shot?"

My first stop was the Eiffel Tower. Exhausted from the flight, I struggled to wait in line for a lift so I could view the city from the top. Paris was vast and vibrant and each structure and person looked as if they had been perfectly placed. It was overwhelming and in that moment I became jealous of the city.

As the days went by I took in everything Paris had to offer. I soaked up the buzz of the people moving through the city, enjoying parks, lingering over drinks in cafes, and commuting on the Paris Métropolitain. But no matter how many ways I found to enjoy Paris, I began to feel lonely. In search of some familiarity, I attended an expats dinner where I had the great fortune to meet a man by the name of Schmid. Schmid was an environmental policy analyst for the United Nations and he and his wife were visiting Paris from Spain.

When Schmid asked me why I chose to visit Paris I think he was just being polite. I don't think he was prepared for me to unleash my frustrations about my home and my job. I told him how convinced I was that my profession was a hoax. The very nature of where and how people lived is politically driven, and at the end of the day, decisions are made by people with no professional experience in land-use planning. I was saddened that the great minds in city planning were not revered. Most people know the words of Hemingway, Fitzgerald, and Stein, but few know the words of Burnham, Olmsted, or Jacobs. I stepped higher up on my soapbox as I complained about how we don't teach planning to young people; we don't have a culture that truly understands the cost of infrastructure, energy, water, and where their taxes go; we don't value the public process; and we don't value our neighborhoods. Therefore, I wondered if we truly valued people.

It turned out that Schmid had lived in Seattle for two years. And I think he was delighted by the opportunity to mentor a young American girl. He said to me; "You, young lady, are lucky to live and work in region that believes in protecting the environment and has a political climate that has consistently values the integrity of its cities."

He reminded me to take pride in my profession and accept the obligation to be aware of the land, environment, and people. Our rules of conduct tell us that we have an obligation to promote our profession and preserve the integrity and heritage of the natural and built environment. As city planners it is our job to navigate the political environment and help the people who make decisions understand the value or consequences of their choices.

Schmid was delighted to talk with me about Seattle, praising it as one of his favorite cities. He loved the proximity to the mountains and ocean and the variety of neighborhoods to explore. He touched on everything that defines the region; the availability of fresh foods, great restaurants, the extremely friendly albeit closed-off people (aka Seattle Freeze), the influx of young people looking for their ideals, and everyone's desire to hike, bike, walk most everywhere, despite the city being wrapped in gray skies throughout the winter months. As he continued to share his stories with me, I officially became homesick for Seattle. I was ready to leave Paris.

It did take a trip to Paris to watch the sunrise on the other side of the world to remind me of why I love Seattle and the region. I needed to feel revived about the place I call home. I no longer take for granted the views of majestic, snow-topped mountain ranges, sparkling bodies of water, genuine Olmsted parks and green spaces and—when the gray skies clear—a sunset that shines a spotlight on it all. While it is difficult to beat the matured sophistication of Paris, I think Seattle is maturing with its own style and vibrancy. My hope that is that that when people view Seattle from atop the Space Needle it will evoke the same jealousy I felt that first day atop the Eiffel Tower over a perfectly placed city.

SECTION 2
PLANNING TODAY: GREEN TO THE EXTREME

Introduction

Jan Whittington

The natural environment of the Pacific Northwest is grand. The deep green of our forests, snow-capped mountain peaks, abundant river flows, and vast blue surfaces of our seas, lakes, and shorelines command our attention. As others have mentioned, we have an abundance of rain. Here, in the Olympics, Cascades, and western Rockies, rain is both measurable and musical, an essential part of the hydrologic cycle and the basis for life in our forests and fields. To plan for ourselves amidst towering conifers, oftentimes older than the structures we inhabit, is a humbling experience. Like the iconic species of our region—the salmon, orca, or bald eagle—the tall trees are constant, gentle reminders of the place we share in a natural order. In this landscape, the principles of our science textbooks and mythical tales of our origin both play out before us in ways that appear clear and present. In a place so green, it is difficult to imagine a plan for life in any other color.

And planning today in the Pacific Northwest is green to the extreme. Extreme—as in the tail of the bell curve, the thrill of a new sport, the frontier of the digital economy, and the long view of our changing global climate. In this section, if the sum of the parts is greater than the whole, it is because of the practices of local planners striving to reshape—as if in the broad strokes of paint on canvas—the uses of land. Planners in this part of the book write

Gravel Beach Skokomish River, 2007. *Northwest artist Robert Connell uses bold colors to create graphic, abstracted, striking images which celebrate both the natural and industrial beauty of the Seattle area. Connell's work is shown in the Davidson Galleries in Seattle.*

of their efforts or those of their colleagues to scrub away the wasteful remains of the industrial era (as in the contributions from Gerend and Ackley on restorative development by the Coastal Salish tribes and Nunley on the replacement of the Alaskan Way Viaduct); celebrate and preserve the spirit of social diversity within our urban form (as in the chapter from Chalana on the Pike/Pine neighborhood, and the piece from Creager and Peninger on affordable housing); realign urban form and function in closer harmony with nature (with contributions from several authors, touching on water, parks, wildlife, our scenic Columbia Gorge, transportation, energy, and the prevention of floods through urban design); and usher in the physical infrastructure of the online world (see Vitro and Whittington, on data center investments in the region).

As planners, the public interest is our interest and our vision for the public stretches farther across space and further in time than other disciplines care to go. The actions we take each day are like steps along a tightrope, taken with care and deliberation, knowing that the consequences of the decisions we support are likely to be significant in the eyes of many and so expensive as to be irreversible for the communities we advise. In preparation for this act, we train ourselves toward a spot on the horizon—a focal point for our attention—and draw upon the tools of our trade as if they formed a beam in our grip, here to give us the added sense of balance we may need, should we falter. Our plans, policies, organizational and institutional structures, literatures, skill sets, and communities of practice support us. We act today to motivate, persuade, and perhaps require others to become more conscious of the impact of their actions on the natural environment and our economy, or to illuminate a more socially responsible path.

The plans and planners described in this section may be said to span the divided visions of the future characterized just a few decades ago in *The Limits to Growth* (Meadows et al. 1972) and in *The Closing Circle* (Commoner 1971). Both seminal works either stated or assumed, correctly, that we are share one global ecosystem, where everything is connected to everything else; that, as part of nature, we live in a system which is inherently more efficient than the technologies we generate; and that the products and waste we produce continually convert useful into useless resources and generate harmful pollution. The futures depicted in these works diverge over the question of how population, society, and technology will address these limitations. Most of the models presented by the authors of *The Limits to Growth* depict a world overwhelmed by exponential population growth, pollution, and damaging rates of resource depletion. Commoner, on the other hand, imagines that technology and society will intervene, and bring about a gradual decline in population and consumption to sustainable levels.

The unwavering beauty of the Pacific Northwest landscape compels all but the most cynical resident to forge their practice in search of more environmentally sound and socially equitable outcomes. Will the population of this region, and its consumption of resources, speed toward collapse? In this part of the world, investments in software, the Internet backbone, low-carbon electricity, and a skilled labor force have grown to overshadow the heavy industries and timber extraction of years prior. Here you will read about planners intent on reviving salmon runs through stormwater and shoreline retrofits, reducing the impact of energy and transportation with more efficient alternatives, reusing and recycling the products of our economy, and establishing shared, more cohesive perspectives about the preservation of our cherished places. We do not know whether we will arrive at a place of equilibrium with nature, but we do know the direction we need to travel. We are heading in that direction, one step at a time.

CHAPTER 13

Native Currents and Coast Salish Planning

Jennifer Gerend, AICP, and Kristina Ackley

Native Americans have emerged as key players in the planning and development of communities in the Pacific Northwest. Their influence and authority over the region's landscapes has ebbed and flowed over the years, as 19th and 20th century federal and state legislation and policies dispossessed native nations of much of their land and undermined tribal nation sovereignty. Highly resilient, Native American tribal nations in the 21st century have seen an unprecedented revitalization of tribal economies and communities, allowing them to move into a phase of active growth for the first time in many years.

The Coast Salish tribes are linked by language, cultural traditions, and political alliances that predate settler colonialism. Coast Salish people have contributed to the regional makeup of British Columbia, Washington, and Oregon, but their presence and visibility has been obscured by the better-known Northwest Coast tribal people (with whom they share similar cultural traditions), as well as the overall rapid urbanization and dislocation of native people. Today, many Coast Salish people are members of federally recognized native nations that exercise self-governance over land that has been clearly defined by formal treaties. The geographic proximity of many Coast Salish tribes to Puget Sound, which is both environmentally threatened and highly urbanized, makes them essential partners in some of planners' greatest challenges in the region (Figure 13.1).

To conceptualize native nations' influence on land use in the Northwest in the early 21st century, this chapter approaches planning with a framework that is based on spatial relationships: local reservation-based planning and regional planning and collaboration around natural and cultural resources.

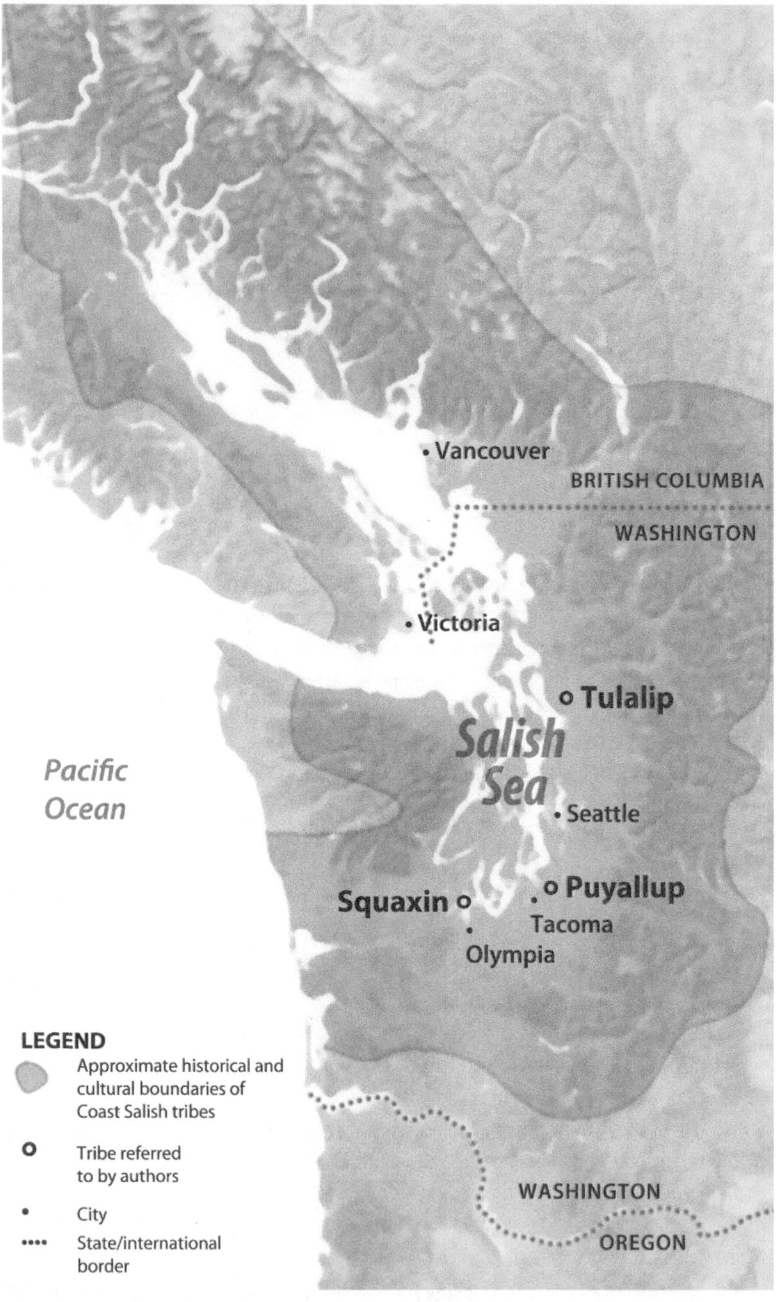

Figure 13.1. Map of Coast Salish tribal areas (Source: Data from Brotherton 2008)

Reservation-based planning issues are discussed through the economic development activities of the Tulalip and Puyallup tribes. For regional natural and cultural resource issues, the practice of comanagement between tribal nations and state agencies in Washington is described, as is the growth of events such as the Tribal Canoe Journeys, recently hosted in 2012 by the Squaxin Island Tribe. While providing a background on the historical context and unique political status of native nations, this analysis focuses on native nations and their planning concerns in the present. Contrary to "the vanishing Indian" stereotype (Deloria 2004; Thrush 2008), native nations of today are expanding their influence and managing growth and collaboration on their own terms, as evidenced through the region's tribal economic development and the preservation of culture.

Coast Salish People and Places

Modern native identity is multifaceted, from the simple declaration of census/demographic information to official tribal membership and to a larger informal Pacific Northwest Coast native experience. For the purposes of the census, native people may identify as native, alone or in combination with one or more races. According to the 2010 U.S. Census, 5.2 million people across the United States identified themselves this way, an increase of 39 percent since 2000. In Washington, the increase was 25 percent (U.S. Census Bureau 2010b).

Nationally, the federal government officially acknowledges (recognizes) 566 Native American tribes and Alaska Native villages (U.S. Bureau of Indian Affairs 2013). Federal acknowledgment of the trust relationship between the federal government toward a tribal community is one that must be legally recognized by both parties, a process often fraught with complications and controversy (Gonzales and Evans 2013). Historically, tribes were recognized through the process of signing a treaty with the U.S. government, often based on the tribe ceding larger parcels of lands (lands on which they sometimes were able to reserve certain rights) while maintaining authority over smaller areas of land reserved for regular use (reservations). In recent years, the federal government has created an extensive process for acknowledging additional tribes, including requiring a tribe to prove a continual presence in a geographic location and a functioning tribal government, which can be difficult given that at different points in history a tribe may have been forcibly removed from their homelands. There are 29 federally recognized tribes in Washington State. The population of Native Americans living on reservations or trust lands in Washington State was 32,246 in 2010, or 16 percent of the state's population of native persons (U.S. Census Bureau 2010b).

The term Coast Salish recognizes the common culture of native nations related by language, culture, politics, economics, and geography. Coast Salish people can be distinguished from the more familiar art and culture of the northern Haida, Tlingit, and Tshimshian nations, whose totem poles, button blankets, and formline designs have shaped typical conceptions of Northwest native identity. Cedar, woven textiles made from goat's wool, and welcome figures are some of the ways Coast Salish people distinguish themselves from their more northern neighbors (Brotherton 2008). In recent years, Coast Salish people have been active in reclaiming space and place, including the renaming of places to relate to the native people, an effort sometimes referred to as "decolonizing" practices in the Native American studies literature. The most visible official renaming is that of the "Salish Sea," to complement Juan de Fuca Strait, the Strait of Georgia, and Puget Sound (all names associated with settler colonialism). First coined in 1988, the name was approved by the U.S. Board of Geographic Names in 2010 (Berger 2012).

Native in the City: Reservation-Based Planning and Economic Development

Native Americans in Washington reside mainly in urban areas (74 percent), a product both of the mobility of a population that moves often between reservation areas and other places for a variety of reasons (including participation in the labor force, schooling, and military service), as well as the lingering impacts of federal relocation legislation. In 1952, the federal government initiated a policy of relocation designed to encourage reservation dwellers to seek employment in several major urban cities. Relocation, coupled with legislation that terminated federal recognition of several tribes, further weakened many reservation economies and contributed to the urbanization of native people nationwide. One should note, however, that many Native Americans who moved to major U.S. urban cities from the 1950s to 1980s arrived to find conditions that many white middle-class Americans were abandoning in favor of the suburbs. In addition, a number of Washington State reservations are located in close proximity to major urban centers. Thus, the contemporary story of Native American people in the Northwest (and nationally) is largely an urban one, as further exemplified by a look at local tribal economic development in the Puyallup and Tulalip reservations.

The Puyallup Tribal Terminal

In south Puget Sound, the Puyallup Tribe is planning a new 200-acre container port terminal in cooperation with the Port of Tacoma and SSA Marine. In 2008, a complex three-way deal among these parties was finalized, encompassing shipping and on-land storage areas; agreements for real estate, infrastructure, and operations including cooperative land exchanges, berth and land leases; and the widening of the Blair Waterway (Dibenedetto 2008, 22). The roots of this deal illustrate how federal legislation and policies, treaties, and legal settlements play an essential role in understanding the contemporary planning context with tribal entities.

In the 1854 Treaty of Medicine Creek, the Puyallup and other area tribes ceded approximately 2.24 million acres of land to the U.S. federal government in exchange for $32,500, designated reservation lands of 1,280 acres, and the permanent right of access to traditional hunting and fishing grounds, an act that effectively enabled the further white settlement of the area and would be heavily disputed for many years (Puyallup Tribe of Indians 2014). Subsequent presidential orders established the formal Puyallup reservation boundaries at the mouth of the Puyallup River leading into Commencement Bay. Like many tribal reservations, the Puyallup's land holdings were later reduced as a result of the General Allotment Act of 1887 (U.S. Congress 1887). It shifted reservation lands from federal lands held in trust for the tribe as a whole to individual ownership by tribal members to be held in fee simple. These lands then often passed into nonnative ownership through individual sales—when the new native owners were unable to pay taxes—or outright fraud (McDonnell 1991). Today, these allotment policies continue to complicate planning and jurisdiction for contemporary tribes as trust lands, fee lands, and lands owned by tribes, individual Indians and non-Indians are mixed together within the reservation, creating a checkerboard pattern of jurisdictional management. Indeed, the size of the Puyallup reservation has fluctuated by thousands of acres over the years. During much of the 1980s the Puyallup Tribe pursued a legal claim to regain some of their lost tidal land along Commencement Bay, a prime industrial area today (albeit complicated by past contamination and ongoing remediation).

A major shift in interjurisdictional relations came at the end of the 1980s in Washington. A settlement for the Puyallup Tribe (Puyallup Tribe of Indians Settlement Act of 1989) was reached the same year as the 1989 Washington State Centennial Accord between the 26 federally recognized tribes (today there are 29) and the state of Washington. It provides a framework for government to government relationships among sovereign governments with the intent of helping them achieve mutual goals.

For the Puyallup Tribe, the 1989 settlement constituted the foundation for their current marine terminal work in several important ways. They received more than 900 acres of land, financial contributions for social services and economic development projects, environmental decontamination of the port area, and a fund for widening and deepening the Blair Waterway (U.S. Congress 1989). The tribe was also granted the ability to engage in foreign trade (Nelson 1994). In light of this settlement, the Puyallup created an economic development arm called Marine View Ventures (MVV) in 1989 to further their terminal project and other economic development endeavors. MVV manages approximately 300 acres of commercial real estate, industrial/port real estate, marinas, gas stations, and billboards under a master lease agreement with the Puyallup Tribe of Indians (Marine View Ventures 2014). As of 2014, the Puyallup Tribal Terminal has received the necessary permits and development will occur as lease agreements are reached. The agreements ensure that the entire property will be held in a tribal trust, and the port will use union labor (Steinberg 2013).

The Tulalip Casino and Seattle Premium Outlet Center

The Tulalup reservation sits 35 miles north of Seattle, between Puget Sound on the west and Interstate 5 (I-5) on the east. Similar to the Puyallup reservation, the land ownership exhibits a checkerboard pattern of lands held in trust status and fee-simple title. With a long history of planning for reservation lands, the Tulalip tribes completed the reservation's first comprehensive plan in 1972. Their current plan identifies the Tulalip Bay area "as the focus of Tribal life; to be owned and enjoyed by the Tulalip people, where Tulalip's heritage can be shared and passed on to future generations" (Tulalip Tribes 2009, 4). Over the last decades, population growth in the surrounding Snohomish County has increased substantially, so the Tulalip reservation now sits in the midst of a growing region. The Tulalip's 2,000-acre frontage along I-5 presented a highly visible opportunity for development.

The tribes' Master Plan from the early 1980s guided development along I-5 with an initial 460 acres as its Business Park in 1998 (Quil Ceda Village 2014). Basic infrastructure was put in place, and the tribes secured leases with major national retailers, including Wal Mart and Home Depot. In 2003, the tribes developed a tribally owned 34,000-square-foot retail center adjacent to the two anchor tenants and the 227,000-square-foot Tulalip Casino.

Furthering their retail plans, the tribes negotiated with Chelsea Property Group, a large national retail outlet center corporation, and constructed the 370,000-square-foot Seattle Premium Outlet Center (now owned by Simon) with 125 outlet stores such as Banana Republic and J.Crew. Cabela's, a giant outdoor recreation retailer, is a notable anchor with a 110,000-square-foot store. Together, these developments on tribal land represent one of the largest retail agglomerations in the Northwest.

Planning On- and Off-Reservation Spaces: Comanagement of Resources and the Tribal Canoe Journeys

Because a large proportion of Native Americans in Washington reside apart from reservation and trust lands (or regularly move between the reservation and other places), intertribal art and cultural events create mobile hubs of activity that contribute to the livability of off-reservation spaces. With the increasing role of native people in off-reservation issues, there is great potential for policy relationships between the tribal and state agencies as they forge new directions in comanaging shared environmental and infrastructure resources.

Comanagement of Resources in Washington State

Following litigation in the mid- to late-20th century that secured many tribally reserved fishing and hunting rights, comanagement of resources emerged as a viable policy and process representing a significant shift in tribal-state relations. Prior to the 1980s, the Washington Department of Fish and Wildlife was among the most recalcitrant of state agencies to recognize tribal sovereignty (American Friends Service Committee 1972; Wilkinson 2006). In fact, it took several years for the state of Washington to fully implement the 1974 *U.S. v. Washington* decision (also known as the "Boldt Decision").

In contrast, the 1989 Centennial Accord acknowledged a new formal relationship between the state and federally recognized tribes that was further solidified by the 1999 New Millennium Agreement (Institutionalizing the Government-to-Government Relationship in Preparation for the New Millennium) (Washington 1999). Taken together, this signifies a substantive commitment at the state level to consult with and engage native nations in partnerships. This can be witnessed in the collaborative stewardship of Washington's environmental resources, as for example, partnerships to track, study, and restore salmon habitat have been widespread.

At the federal level, the 1994 Tribal Self-Governance Act permits federally recognized tribes to assume management responsibilities for trust assets and resources on their own behalf and on behalf of individual tribal members. This, coupled with the policy of comanagement, has led to tribes playing a larger role in planning projects in Washington State. The Duwamish, for example, have emerged as an important force in the cleanup of the industrialized Duwamish River in Seattle. Although they are not currently a federally recognized tribe, the Duwamish Tribe has claimed its interests by partnering with local non-native interest groups for remediation efforts and through the construction of their longhouse, which serves as an important cultural meeting and education space (Walker 2011).

Tribal Canoe Journeys

The Tribal Canoe Journeys, based on the canoeing cultures of the Coast Salish people, are particularly instructive as modern events that build on traditions of the past and hold long-lasting implications. The Tribal Canoe Journeys trace their beginnings to 1989, also the year of the Centennial Accord. As part of his role on the State Heritage Council and Centennial Commission, Quinault tribal elder Emmet Oliver successfully organized the first Paddle to Seattle, an event that has evolved into annual Tribal Canoe Journeys. Oliver and fellow Quinault member Philip Martin saw the journey as an opportunity to revitalize the oceangoing canoes that Martin had remembered as a boy while continuing the native presence in sites that had been claimed through settler colonialism (Bard 2011; Oliver 1991). The canoes that entered the Port of Seattle in July

Figure 13.2. Paddlers at the 2009 Paddle to Suquamish

1989 as part of the Paddle to Seattle thus marked a significant reclaiming of space by Coast Salish people.

Today the Tribal Canoe Journeys have grown to include more than100 canoes, with families representing locations throughout the Pacific Rim, including native Hawaiians, Maori, and Japanese, as well as other native nations in North America. Thousands of spectators attend the initial arrival of the canoes (Figure 13.2), and activities following the landing, including an extensive potlatch, or giveaways. The journeys are fairly brief, with the diplomatic and gift-giving protocol taking place over several days, with the paddlers (or "pullers") on journeys that last from several days to several weeks. But the effects can be long lasting.

In 2012, the landing of the canoes for the Paddle to Squaxin took place in downtown Olympia, Washington's state capital. The Squaxin Island nation is known as "People of the Water" as their aboriginal homeland encompasses seven inlets. The Squaxin Island tribe was dispossessed of most of this land through the 1854 Treaty of Medicine Creek, eventually forced to reside on one small island with no fresh water source. Today the tribe owns land in the Kamilche area, which has grown to a land base of almost 2,000 acres. There are no longer any full-time residents on Squaxin Island, although it serves as important site for fishing, hunting, shellfish gathering, and cultural activities (Henderson, VanderWal, and the Squaxin Island Heritage and Culture Committee 2002).

Figure 13.3. Mural by Joseph Seymour Jr. honoring the 2012 Squaxin Island Canoe Journeys, located next to Percival Landing in downtown Olympia

The Squaxin Island Tribe entered into a signed agreement with the city of Olympia for the canoes to land at the Port of Olympia at Swantown marina on Steh-Chass/Budd Inlet. While located in traditional Squaxin Island territory, today this site is a nontribal urban waterfront. The landing offered an accessible place to land in downtown Olympia that could accommodate huge expected crowds and that would raise the tribe's visibility; however, the waters of Budd Inlet and surrounding soils are contaminated by industrial waste. Between 2010 and 2012, the mile-long shoreline of the Port of Olympia and downtown Olympia was significantly improved. Creosote-contaminated wood pilings were removed from the long boardwalk, and several public art projects were commissioned. While the site continues to be the focus of remediation, the canoe landings in 2012 underscored the need to address the effects of pollution and that the Squaxin Island Tribe could be a valuable partner in those efforts.

As part of their responsibilities in hosting the 2012 Tribal Canoe Journeys, the tribe entered into a partnership with The Evergreen State College to create a number of art-making residences that were used to reflect the strong sense of place of the Squaxin Island people. These creative spaces extended outside reservation boundaries to downtown Olympia, and provided a lasting reminder of the Tribal Canoe Journeys. Squaxin Island artist Joseph Seymour Jr. created a mural funded by the Olympia Downtown Association that was inspired by the canoes and pullers that participated in the Tribal Canoe Journeys (Figure 13.3). The mural emphasizes how place is experienced by contemporary native people and ensures that the Squaxin Island Tribal Canoe Journey will continue to be visible well beyond the actual 2012 event.

Conclusion: Planning for Contemporary Partnerships

Today, both native and non-native policy makers can benefit from decades of hard-won progress in intergovernmental legal and political frameworks that have normalized interjurisdictional cooperation in the Northwest. Six guiding lessons can be drawn from these examples, based on a case study in the Skagit Valley area with the Swinomish Trib, (Zaferatos 2004, 93), summarized below:

- Employ a multiparty, government-to-government approach.
- Use continuous consultation and a forum for dispute resolution.
- Work to diminish historic barriers to institutional communication.
- Recognize that regional cooperation rquires time and commitments by elected officials and planning staff.
- Dedicate time and resources to education, orientation, and the development of skills among both policy makers and staff.
- Provide constant monitoring to protect the relationship.

These lessons did not come easily for this region, but planners today have an unprecedented opportunity to collaborate with tribal leaders in land use, infrastructure, economic development, and resource protection under a significantly improved intergovernmental context. With many legal and political barriers resolved, the interpersonal skills of planners and elected officials may rise to the forefront in creating true partnerships with tribal entities.

CHAPTER 14

Harmonizing the Natural and Built Environment on the Coast of the Salish Sea

Karen Dyson and Nicole Faghin

Our vulnerable coastal ecosystems in the Salish Sea—more than 4,000 miles of shoreline—are subject to impacts of development and require special attention. Consider these impacts: Shoreline armoring (built for coastal defense and erosion control) negatively affects nearshore fish distribution and behavior, alters aquatic communities, and eliminates upland vegetation (Toft et al. 2010). Coastal development also increases water pollution via urban stormwater runoff carrying sediments, nutrients, toxic chemicals, and bacteria (Waycott et al. 2009). While residents are drawn to, and value protecting, the region's beauty, preserving this beauty requires careful planning efforts that balance development with shoreline protection.

What tools can help planners incorporate coastal ecology into effective shoreline planning? How can we modify traditional planning systems designed for nonwaterfront projects to the waterfront?

Planning practitioners in the Salish Sea have created, adopted, and applied innovative planning tools that address the impacts of urban waterfront redevelopment on coastal ecosystems, in partnership with (and sometimes driven by) a strong scientific community and an environmentally aware citizenry. In this chapter, using examples from the Salish Sea region, we highlight environmental planning tools used in master planning, site planning, and site design that may be useful to planners in other coastal areas. These tools focus on addressing observed impacts of development, including restoring nearshore (shallow water) ecosystems, restoring connectivity between aquatic and terrestrial habitat, and reducing pollution from urban stormwater runoff.

The first case explores Bellingham's application of the Leadership in Energy & Environmental Design for Neighborhood Design (LEED-ND)—a rating system frequently used for urban infill projects—to develop a master plan for the redevelopment of former industrial waterfront property. The second and third cases explore two planning tools that specifically address waterfront development and lessons learned from their use: the development of the Green Shores Coastal Development Rating System (Green Shores) in British Columbia, which systematically integrates coastal ecology into site design and planning, and Seattle's experience using pilot projects coupled with scientific habitat monitoring to provide critical ecological information for site design (Table 14.1).

The first two cases are voluntary rating systems that highlight the difficulties of creating planning tools for waterfront brownfield redevelopment and the importance of participation during the formative stages of a project's development (Azhar et al. 2011; Desbois 2006). The third case explores using voluntary scientific monitoring to assess the ecological impact of potential site designs. In all examples, the programs were driven by community or stakeholder interests and went beyond regulatory compliance.

Taken together, these three cases demonstrate how coastal ecology can be integrated into planning tools to address the ecological issues of shoreline development, and that planning tools developed elsewhere may not be the most appropriate choice for shoreline development. These frameworks speak to the need other authors have voiced for planning tools based on scientific data that address ecological landscapes and their resiliency (Tramutola 2013).

TABLE 14.1. Three Cases of Coastline Development Project

Planning Application	Location	Planning tool
Master Plan	Waterfront District, Bellingham, Washington	Leadership in Energy & Environmental Design for Neighborhood Design
Site Planning	Olympic Village, Vancouver, British Columbia	Green Shores Coastal Development Rating System
Site Design	Seattle Seawall	Scientific habitat monitoring

Source: Karen Dyson and Nicole Faghin

The Setting

Waterfront development in the Salish Sea region is influenced by a community focus on the environment and a design aesthetic shaped by the natural environment and local history of the coast. Salmon in particular are powerful cultural icons.

Development in the region is also strongly influenced by the regulatory regimes of Washington State and British Columbia at the federal, state/province, and local levels. While the regulatory regimes of the United States and Canada differ, they are based on common principles including:

- Preventing impacts of piecemeal development
- Habitat protection
- Water quality protection
- Contaminated site mitigation and cleanup

These regulations (and particularly their permitting processes) can become the driving forces behind development decisions.[1] The planning tools described here may also be adopted at the outset of master planning and site-specific project design to facilitate permitting.

LEED-ND and the Bellingham Waterfront Redevelopment Master Plan

The LEED-ND rating system combines principles and objectives of green infrastructure and building, smart growth, and new urbanism. Since this framework prioritizes infill, waterfront redevelopment projects fit squarely within its purview. Here we examine how dissonance between terrestrial and waterfront land uses created problems when Bellingham applied LEED-ND development criteria to its Waterfront District Master Plan.

In December 2004, following two years of public meetings, the (port- and city-appointed) citizen-based Waterfront Futures Group (WFG) released a Vision and Framework Plan suggesting the port purchase a former industrial waterfront site owned by Georgia Pacific and recommending ecologically sensitive high-density, mixed use redevelopment (Port of Bellingham 2004).

In 2005, the Port of Bellingham acquired the 137-acre property and assumed responsibility for environmental cleanup. Following 100 years of industrial use, portions of the soil, groundwater, and sediments at the site are contaminated with mercury, petroleum products, metals, bioaccumlatives, pentachlorophenol, and other substances. Additionally, the historic mudflats and associated intertidal habitat have been destroyed (Port of Bellingham 2008). The city and port created a new advisory group, the Waterfront Advisory Group, to provide input on consistency with the WFG vision (Bellingham 2005).

After the Port of Bellingham acquired the Georgia-Pacific site, port planners realized many of the WFG recommendations paralleled the nascent LEED-ND program (Table 14.2).

The port and city of Bellingham joined the LEED-ND pilot program in 2007. Participation in the pilot program proved valuable to both Bellingham and the LEED-ND program.

TABLE 14.2. Comparison of Waterfront Futures Group Principles and LEED-ND Credits

Waterfront Futures Group Principles	LEED-ND Credits
Restore health of land and water (e.g. soften hardened shorelines)	Restoration of habitat or wetlands and water bodies
Manage stormwater to enhance estuarine habitats	Stormwater management; site design for habitat or wetland and water body conservation
Provide incentives and credits for "green" buildings	Certified green buildings
Make waterfront inviting for people on foot	Walkable streets; Tree-lined and shaded streets; visitability and universal design
Create mixed use areas	Mixed use neighborhood centers; Compact development; Housing and jobs proximity
Provide convenient connections between different modes of transportation	Transit facilities; transportation demand management
Create and connect large and small parks and open spaces	Access to civic and public spaces, public spaces, and recreation facilities

Source: Karen Dyson and Nicole Faghin

Applying LEED-ND to Waterfronts: Lessons Learned in Bellingham

Applying LEED-ND criteria during the design process helped Bellingham shape the Waterfront District master plan, encouraged adoption of specific policies that may not otherwise have been considered, and resulted in the Port successfully achieving LEED-ND SILVER Stage 1:Pre-certification—a valuable marketing tool to attract sustainability minded developers. However, incompatibilities between LEED-ND and waterfront brownfield redevelopment made it difficult for the Waterfront District Master Plan to qualify for some of the potential credits (Figure 14.1 and Figure 14.2).

For example, the port originally applied to certify the entire district, including the marine-industrial areas. Waterfront redevelopment under Washington State law gives preference to water-oriented uses (e.g., boat-building), which require large areas of open land (e.g., room for truck access and transporting boats). However, LEED-ND credits specify street trees, sidewalks, and minimum building density, and limit block size and surface parking, which are incompatible with marine-industrial uses. As a result, the port refocused their application on the mixed use nonindustrial portion of the site. Additionally, some LEED-ND credits require stormwater to be infiltrated into the soil on-site.

Figure 14.1. Aerial photo of the Waterfront District with Phase 1 development area highlighted

This practice is discouraged on brownfields with previous soil contamination as it is a pathway for waterway recontamination.

The difficulties faced in Bellingham illustrate the challenges inherent in adapting existing rating systems for use on large waterfront sites, and suggest that waterfront redevelopments will struggle to use the same planning tools and rating systems as upland developments. However, using LEED-ND has helped garner and retain public support for the redevelopment plans, and will help the port attract developers who share the WFG's vision. This and other feedback led to the revision of some LEED-ND credits (Garde 2009).

Green Shores: Developing Rating Systems for Waterfront Project Design

Like LEED-ND, Green Shores is a voluntary credit rating system that goes beyond regulatory compliance—although some municipalities are making

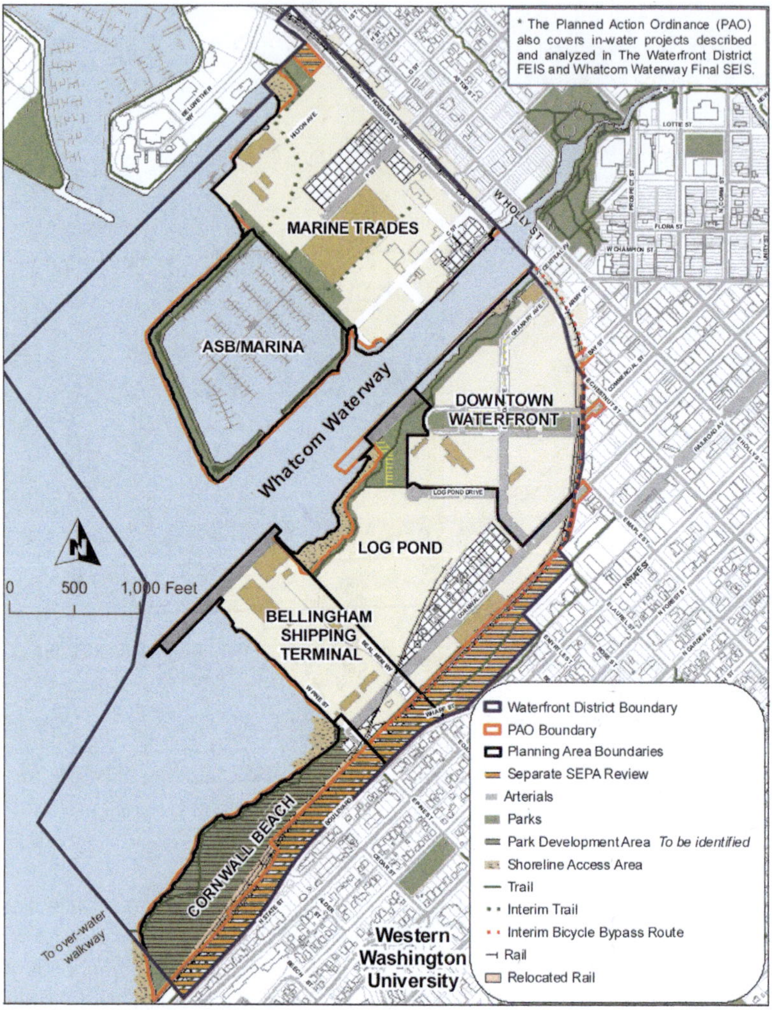

Figure 14.2. Bellingham Waterfront District redevelopment plans highlighting the proposed sub-areas

Green Shores mandatory. Project examples, an outreach program, and support for planning language were developed concurrently with the Coastal Development Rating System component of Green Shores. Unlike LEED-ND, Green Shores is a waterfront planning tool focused on coastal ecosystem health. This case uses Green Shores' pilot study of Vancouver's Olympic Village development to highlight the importance of integrating a rating system early in design development.

Spearheaded by the Stewardship Centre for British Columbia, a multidisciplinary technical team of planners, marine biologists, landscape architects, and coastal engineers adapted the LEED framework (Intent, Submittal Requirements, etc.) to create Green Shores. Green Shores' four guiding principles focus on preserving the integrity of coastal processes, enhancing habitat function, and reducing cumulative impacts (including pollution) to the coastal environment (Green Shores 2014).

In 2008, following peer review and public comment periods, the Green Shores technical team asked the city of Vancouver to participate in the pilot program, designed to evaluate the feasibility of applying the Green Shores Coastal Development Rating System and identify areas for improvement.

The technical team chose Olympic Village, located in the Southeast False Creek area of Vancouver, as the location to test Green Shores in a highly urbanized waterfront development. As in Bellingham, this former industrial area was proposed to be developed as a sustainable community (City of Vancouver 2006). Following a lengthy public process, construction on Olympic Village began in the winter of 2006–2007 and was completed in late 2009, prior to the 2010 Olympics (City of Vancouver Planning Department 1999).

The pilot project assessment was conducted in early 2009, before Olympic Village's completion. The team analyzed the Olympic Village (1,100 residential units including 252 affordable housing units), Hinge Park (a public

Figure 14.3. Hinge Park at Olympic Village

Figure 14.4. The completed Habitat Island at Olympic Village

park that also treats stormwater), and Habitat Island (designed and built as fish habitat remediation) (Figure 14.3 and Figure 14.4).

Applying Green Shores to Waterfronts: Lessons learned from Olympic Village

Results from this and other pilot projects led to revisions in the Green Shores rating system, both to the credits (e.g., adding credits focused on climate change and social sustainability) and to the credit review system (e.g., clearly defining required documentation for applicants). Although the tool demonstrated its ability to help planners incorporate coastal ecology into shoreline planning, the pilot experience also highlighted the need to integrate such a tool early in the planning process for it to be effective.

Olympic Village achieved some Green Shores credits (such as the riparian zone planting restoration credit) due to the Low-Impact Development and

LEED approach used to fulfill the city of Vancouver's sustainable community mandate. Unsurprisingly, other opportunities were missed. For example, one credit focused on shoreline conservation called for 75 percent of the shoreline to contribute to enhancing the local ecosystem. However, Olympic Village was designed as a fairly traditional hard-edged urban waterfront and only Habitat Island could contribute towards the credit. Had Olympic Village been able to utilize the Green Shores tool at the planning and design stage, planners could have designed the project to achieve this credit and made a potentially significant contribution to the coastal ecosystem.

Habitat Monitoring: The Science behind the Seattle Seawall Replacement

Scientific monitoring (data collection and assessment) is an important planning tool for waterfront redevelopment: It can be used prior to implementation to define project restoration goals; during the project design phase to increase the chance of a successful outcome; and after project construction to identify problems (Seattle 2012b). Scientific monitoring programs also provide site-specific information that complements rating systems' more general normative framework.

Seattle transportation planners engaged in an extensive scientific monitoring program to guide the Seattle seawall redesign process. During the planning stages, Seattle wanted the design to support migrating juvenile salmon (including Chinook, a threatened species under the Endangered Species Act); juvenile salmon hug the shoreline during their migration from river to open ocean, and so rely on the habitat provided by the Seattle seawall (Toft et al. 2010).

With this in mind, scientists developed two monitoring programs to facilitate design decisions benefiting salmon. The first monitoring study tested different designs for habitat enhancement of the seawall itself.[2] Seawalls typically lack the complexity associated with slope, crevices, and texture present on natural shorelines. Scientists tested six prototypes for seawall habitat enhancement designs using cast concrete panels bolted to the seawall. They found the textured (added microhabitat) and angled (horizontal and vertical surfaces) panels supported ecologically important species (specifically rockweed and mussels) (Goff 2010). Costs for including seawall texturing in the rebuilt seawall are expected to be minor, as the only added costs are those to make the molds and the extra concrete required.

The second monitoring study examined techniques to reduce the light/dark boundary caused by dock shading; juvenile salmon avoid these areas, and docks therefore interfere with their migration path. Monitoring results suggest that large glass panels installed in existing docks transmit enough light to encourage juvenile salmon to swim under (rather than around) the docks (Toft 2013). In both cases, the use of pilots and scientific monitoring provided important scientific data used to influence design decisions (Figure 14.5 and Figure 14.6).

Applying Habitat Monitoring to the Waterfront: Lessons Learned in Seattle

Results from both studies were incorporated in the final design of the Seattle seawall, and may help influence other seawall redevelopments in the Salish Sea region. These monitoring programs allowed Seattle to study the relationship between the built environment and the ecosystem and integrate coastal ecology into site design.

Without this tool, the city may not have determined until after construction whether their design provided the intended environmental benefits—or worse, without monitoring they could only assume the approach worked. Importantly, this was one of the first times such preconstruction monitoring and experimen-

Figure 14.5. (above) and Figure 14.6 (below). Seattle Seawall

tation had been used for a major public works project, and it was exemplary in its scientific rigor and the public availability of data and results.

Ecologically Sound Planning Tools for Our Coasts

Planning is the practice of turning knowledge into action—a role that is critical in (re)developing coastal landscapes (Sager 1995). We have the knowledge from ecological research concerning impacts from development—particularly shoreline armoring and stormwater pollution. Now urban planners need to combine planning tools for the built environment with this scientific knowledge to restore connectivity between aquatic and terrestrial habitat, restoring nearshore ecosystems, and reducing pollution from urban stormwater runoff (Toft et al. 2010).

For the extensive coastline of the Salish Sea, a strong scientific community and an environmentally aware citizenry have catalyzed planners' efforts to integrate this knowledge of coastal ecology into planning. The outcomes of applying these innovative planning tools provide planners elsewhere with important lessons learned.

The Port of Bellingham's experience with LEED-ND highlighted the unique challenges faced by coastal properties, and their experience suggests it may not be sufficient to apply the same planning systems designed for non-waterfront projects to the waterfront. LEED-ND may require adjustments to address critical shoreline issues such as rainwater as a vector for water recontamination and inadequate protection for coastal ecosystems.

Green Shore's pilot evaluation of Olympic Village demonstrates that robust protection of coastal ecosystems requires purpose-built planning tools. The Olympic Village, developed in an environmentally conscious manner using Low-Impact Development and LEED, did not provide the same level of protection for coastal ecology as dedicated coastal planning tools such as Green Shores. Applying Green Shores to Olympic Village post-planning also highlighted that to be effective, planning tools must be integrated early in the planning process.

The Seattle seawall project demonstrates the role scientific monitoring programs can play as planning tools for waterfront projects, both on their own and alongside rating systems like Green Shores. As this project highlights, testing design possibilities before they are widely implemented can help ensure that planning tools and project designs deliver the envisioned positive environmental impacts. This site- and environment-specific approach allows designers to tailor their design to their locale.

As in the Salish Sea, coastal ecosystems worldwide are impacted by development. New planning tools targeting coastal ecosystems, such as Green Shores and site-specific monitoring, can and should integrate coastal ecology into planning to orchestrate the balance between the built and natural environments.

Further, planners can go beyond "protection" to actively restore our environment. Rating systems (like Green Shores) can play a leading role in pushing design teams to consider not only how they can reduce the environmental impact of their project, but how they can actively enhance the habitat for the benefit of local species (Mapes and Wolch 2011). While urban areas may be irrevocably altered, it does not mean they should be abandoned. If anything, these areas are more important for conservation efforts because of the many people who come in contact with urban waterfronts on a daily basis. We have the tools; now we need to use them.

The information for this research is drawn from a larger study entitled "Planning and Management for Coastalscape Revitalization," conducted with funding from the Korea Maritime Institute (KMI) to the University of Washington School of Marine and Environmental Affairs. Authors on the original study include, from the University of Washington, Tom Leschine, Karen Dyson, and Nicole Faghin. Collaborators from KMI include Jay Nam and Jiyeon Choi. Additional collaborators include Sylvia Goodwin, the planning and development director of Port of Bellingham; Brian Emmett, senior partner with Archipelago Marine Research, Ltd.; and Jeffrey R. Cordell, principal research scientist with the University of Washington School of Aquatic and Fishery Sciences.

CHAPTER 15

Planning Without Borders in Cascadia

Angie Brewer, AICP, and Jeffrey B. Litwak

East of Portland, Oregon, and Vancouver, Washington, the Columbia River cuts a deep sea-level passage and forms the state line through the Cascade mountain range. Steep canyon walls and mountains—some nearly 5,000 feet in height—and dozens of waterfalls drop precipitously into the Columbia River. Along 85 river miles, temperate rainforest seamlessly transitions to fertile valley farmlands with apple, pear, and cherry orchards, to rare oak woodlands, and then to shrub steppe desert.

For more than 10,000 years, the Columbia River Gorge has been a route of passage and trade and home to tribal nations. Native American villages, camps, and hunting, gathering, and fishing sites still hug the shorelines.

Settlers from the East founded cities, company towns, and communities to take advantage of timber, agriculture, and fishing. Railroads on both shores of the Columbia River linked those towns west to Portland and Vancouver and east to the rest of the country, later followed by the historic Columbia River Highway along the Oregon shore, and the Evergreen Highway along the Washington shore. In the early 20th century, visitors came from all over the world to drive the scenic gorge highways and ride the trains (Figure 15.1). Burgeoning infrastructure, including the Bonneville Dam in 1937, The Dalles Dam in 1955, and Interstate 84 in the 1960s, changed the landscape at an unprecedented scale and transformed the gorge into an important economic artery.

In the 1950s, Oregon and Washington each established their own state Columbia River Gorge Commission. Sharing an executive director and meeting jointly, the two commissions advised state and local governments on plan-

Figure 15.1. Historic travel advertisement sharing an iconic view of Crown Point in the Columbia River Gorge from the Portland State Women's Forum overlook

ning issues and proposed development in the gorge. However, by the early 1980s, there were calls for additional planning and protections. In 1984, Oregon Senator Bob Packwood explained:

> The continuing pressures on the Gorge are clear to those who frequently visit the area. The Gorge sits at the end of a major metropolitan area of 1.15 million people. As the Portland-Vancouver area grows, so does the temptation to push suburban development deeper into the Gorge. . . . If we believe the Columbia Gorge is of national significance, it also deserves protection by the federal government. (Packwood 1984, 67–68)

More than just a river gorge, the Columbia River Gorge is the confluence of the geopolitics of four Native American tribes with treaty rights in the gorge, two national forests, two states, six counties, nearly 20 cities and unincorporated communities, and myriad ports and other special districts. In 1986, after several years of failed federal bills, Congress enacted the Columbia River Gorge National Scenic Area Act (Pub. L. 99-663, 100 Stat. 4274, codified at 16 U.S.C. §§ 544 to 544p). Although there is little legislative history for the Act, courts treat one law review article as the definitive summary of the various bills, debates, and hearings (Blair 1987).

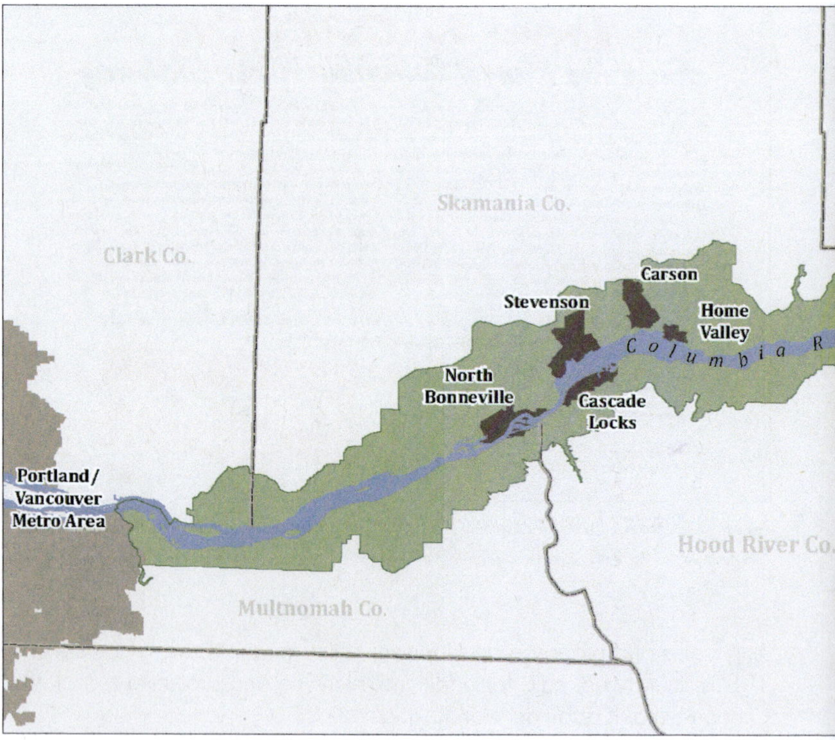

The National Scenic Area Act

The National Scenic Area Act states two purposes—(1) to establish a national scenic area to protect and provide for the enhancement of scenic, cultural, recreational, and natural resources of the gorge, and (2) and to support the economy of the gorge by allowing growth to occur in urban areas and by allowing future economic development in a manner consistent with the first purpose (16 U.S.C. § 544a). The Act also provided congressional consent for Oregon and Washington to enact an interstate compact to create a new regional Columbia River Gorge Commission—a bistate agency (16 U.S.C. § 544c). The Columbia River Gorge Compact is codified at Or. Rev. Stat. § 196.150 and Wash. Rev. Code § 43.97.015.

There are 13 urban areas (Figure 15.2) for which the existing local governments remain the primary planning entities and the National Scenic Area development regulations do not directly apply (16 U.S.C. § 544d(c)(5)(B)). Approximately 40 percent of the National Scenic Area is within one of four "Special Management Areas" (16 U.S.C. § 544b(b)). Remaining lands that are neither urban areas nor special management areas are "general manage-

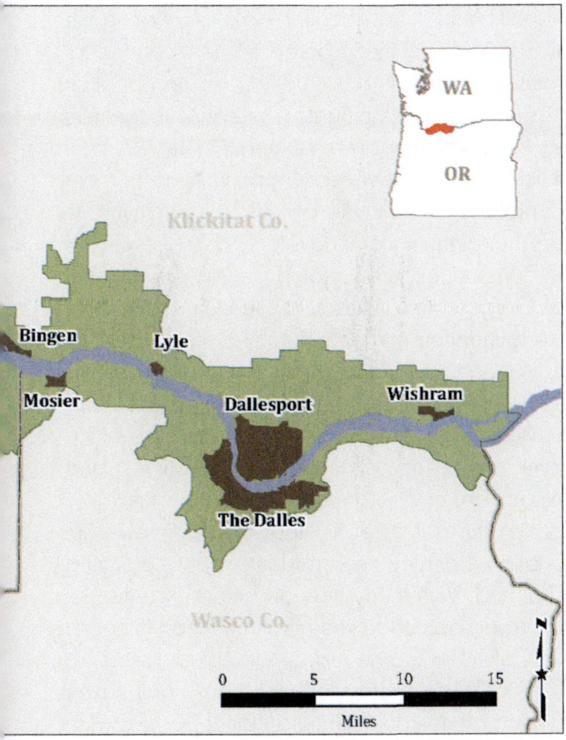

Figure 15.2. The Columbia River Gorge National Scenic Area is located immediately east of the Portland-Vancouver metropolitan area. It lies in two states and contains portions of six counties, 13 designated urban areas, and several rural communities.

ment areas," a term coined by early Scenic Area planners. The Act required the gorge commission and the U.S. Forest Service to develop a regional management plan for the National Scenic Area (16 U.S.C. § 544d) and provides standards for the plan, criteria for amending the plan, and criteria to change urban area boundaries. For all of this planning work, the Act also requires consultation with the four Native American tribes with treaty rights in the gorge (16 U.S.C. § 544d(e)), a responsibility the commission and U.S. Forest Service have elevated to formal government-to-government relations.

The Act allows the six counties with land area in the National Scenic Area to develop their own land-use ordinances, which the gorge commission and U.S. Secretary of Agriculture must determine are consistent with the Management Plan. The commission must adopt land-use ordinances for counties that do not administer their own.

The 1997 book, *Planning a New West: The Columbia River Gorge National Scenic Area*, recounts the numerous past planning efforts in the gorge dating back to the 1910s and the creation of the National Scenic Area in 1986, all of which had origins and champions in Portland. As the book suggests, "Seen in historical context, [the National Scenic Area] is one more entry on the long list of ways in which Portland has made the Columbia River Gorge its own" (Abbott, Adler, and Abbott 1997, 41). During the early years of the National Scenic Area, many gorge residents and local governments resented it because of this and chose protest over participation when the new gorge commission was developing its regional Management Plan. More recently, however, local governments are embracing the National Scenic Area and its legal structure as their own local opportunity to achieve regional solutions to regional problems that directly benefit their communities.

Some of this recent interest in planning is undoubtedly due to evolution in the economy of the gorge. When Congress created the National Scenic Area, many Columbia River Gorge communities still relied on commercial timber and agriculture for the foundation of their economies. Thus, the National Scenic Area Act and Management Plan contain strong requirements to support the ongoing use of timberlands for commercial timber use, and the use of high value agriculture lands for commercial agriculture. Since 1986, however, the economic model has changed. Timber harvest and grazing has declined. Farmlands are being converted to agritourism. New high-tech industries are choosing the gorge for its lifestyle, inexpensive energy, and access to transportation, bringing new residents with well-paying jobs. Recreation has also changed, with many new and more extreme activities, a trend that is happening at unprecedented and unplanned intensity. In the 1980s, there was one Columbia Gorge hiking guidebook listing 35 hikes (Lowe and Lowe 1980); in 2013, there are more than a half-dozen hiking guidebooks, one of which alone contains more than 100 hikes (Romano 2011). In addition to the millions of visitors who recreate in the gorge each year, the population of the gorge has nearly doubled from 40,000 to more than 70,000 since 1986.

However, the recent interest in locally sourced regional planning only gained momentum after a series of joint gorge commission and locally sponsored visioning projects, which developed fresh ideas for the gorge community that a few community leaders simply started to act on. In other words, local leaders are realizing that simply looking out for their individual communities is not economically sustainable when the public uses the gorge as a region.

Community-Based Visioning

With its 20th anniversary in 2006, the Columbia River Gorge Commission realized that it had spent most of its work focusing on resource protection and little on community building. A 2004 update of the Management Plan for the National Scenic Area was cut short due to budget constraints, leaving many local concerns and priorities unresolved. That update followed traditional rules of public participation—with commission and forest service staff doing much of the drafting and giving the public an opportunity for written and oral comment before the agencies adopted revisions. New rules and restrictions and unresolved policies frustrated landowners, local governments, and conservation interests. Observing this, the commission decided to shift gears and engage with local residents differently, encouraging the communities to think about what they wanted for themselves within the context of the regional landscape.

The first of these efforts was a 2007 visioning process called the Columbia Gorge Future Forum, initiated by the gorge commission, but controlled by the community. The purpose of forum was not to create another forecast for the commission, but to engage a cross section of the community—federal, state, local, and tribal elected officials and staff, special districts, business and NGO leaders, and interested citizens, in articulating their aspirations for the future (Columbia Gorge Future Forum 2008). Reflecting upon the 20 years since the passage of the Act, the forum introduced the first cohesive process to integrate ideas across geographical, tribal, social, and political borders to create a unified vision for the future of the gorge. The result was the first citizen-driven vision and strategies for the future of the region (Columbia Gorge Future Forum 2008).

Jessica Metta, then a planner for the Columbia River Gorge Commission, orchestrated this one-day event. A recent graduate from Portland State University's Master of Urban and Regional Planning program and a transplant from North Carolina, she brought fresh ideas without the personal "baggage" of past conflicts. With contagious excitement for the opportunities of this regionally significant event, she asked open-ended questions, listened thoughtfully, and reported everything that was shared.

The Columbia Gorge Future Forum produced a vision document that listed 75 specific strategies, four of which focus specifically on improved governance: regional planning and coordination, regional partnerships and coalitions, local government role, and financial tools and incentives (Columbia Gorge Future Forum 2008). Now a project manager for the Mid-Columbia Economic Development District, another agency focused on regional solutions in the gorge, Metta observes that the most significant result of the forum is that it "got people thinking regionally, and not just the decision makers, but the residents and general public, which has led to a significant shift in the way people think about their needs and goals" (Metta 2013).

In tandem with the Future Forum, the commission kicked off its Vital Signs Indicators Project, a regional resource monitoring effort that also responded to one of the forum-produced strategies. This time the commission asked citizens to identify resources that should be monitored as indicators of the condition of the gorge and about which the commission should have enhanced information for its policy work. A community advisory team and a technical advisory team met separately and jointly (and open to the public) more than 65 times to create a set of measures that could be backed by the best available science, and also embraced by the communities of the gorge (Columbia River Gorge Commission and U.S. Department of Agriculture 2009). Interestingly, from the heated conversations about conflicting values, many of the indicators mirrored the values, strategies, and concerns of the community expressed in the Future Forum. The teams also recognized that outside influences contribute to the condition of resources within the National Scenic Area, further illustrating the need for broad-based, systems—planning beyond any one jurisdiction or statutory authority.

In 2011, as the National Scenic Area approached its 25th anniversary, the commission took this milestone as another opportunity to engage with the communities and local leadership. This time the commission asked which parts of the National Scenic Area Act were worth celebrating. Focusing on the successes and unique solutions attributed to the Act channeled community, business, and NGO leaders to set aside past pessimisms and negative experiences. The committee set a goal of raising local, regional, and national awareness of the successes of the Scenic Area Act and the need for ongoing commitment for effective regional planning.

After several years of engaging the region, the commission was thus poised to take action. However, by the end of the global recession in 2012, the commission's planning staff had been cut by 70 percent and could not undertake all of the initiatives that the communities were now demanding. Again, the commission turned to the community to set priorities for the gorge. It contracted with Oregon Consensus and the William D. Ruckelshaus Center, two collaborative, problem-solving programs based at Portland State University and the University of Washington, to jointly conduct more than 80 stakeholder interviews to identify key issues that the commission and community could tackle through collaborative engagement (Columbia River Gorge Commission 2012). Using the centers' assessment, and through a collaborative decision-making process, the commission set three priorities that reflect the visions and strategies from Future Forum: (1) regional urban planning, (2) monitoring through the Vital Signs project, and (3) regional recreation planning.

Local Interest in Regional Planning

Following these efforts in regional planning, local community leaders are beginning to create their own regional planning opportunities. A common theme in planning literature is that individuals can make a difference (O'Connell 2009), and the gorge is no different. Take, for example, the cities of Cascade Locks in Oregon and North Bonneville and Stevenson in Washington. These three small communities are connected to each other by the Bridge of Gods and detached from the next closest towns by 20 miles.

In 2010, Cascade Locks, Oregon appointed Paul Koch, a former staffer for Oregon Governor Tom McCall, retired career city manager, and current strategic consultant, as its interim city manager. Koch, only half-jokingly, advertises himself as helping cities survive, "not that other 's' word" (referring to "sustainability"). Inspired by the commission's new approach to help gorge communities plan for themselves, Koch asked the commission if it would support an effort for Cascade Locks, North Bonneville, and Stevenson to cooperate across the state line. The three cities invited the commission to a first-ever joint meeting of their city councils in the late summer of 2012 to discuss how the National Scenic Area could help. Although still skeptical of working with the commission, they drafted a white paper outlining the issues, their goals, and their authority, and in early 2013, each city enacted resolutions pledging to cooperate in a "Three Cities Initiative." The white paper and each resolution referred to the unique legal structure of the National Scenic Area as authority for their interstate intergovernmental cooperation, notwithstanding state law that might otherwise not allow their actions.

One priority issue involves using the Cascade Locks, Oregon sewage treatment facility to treat sludge and waste from North Bonneville and Stevenson in Washington, both of which have treatment facilities at or near capacity. Oregon's Department of Environmental Quality initially informed the city that it could not import Washington's sewage for treatment, but now says there's no prohibition. Another priority involves figuring out how to share emergency services between the three cities where the two states have different certification standards.

To understand these communities' authority to cooperate over the objections of state officials and in the face of conflicting state statutes and regulations requires a short introduction to the law of interstate compacts. The National Scenic Area Act, as a congressionally enacted federal law, obviously preempts state law. But in *Cuyler v. Adams* (449 U.S., 433, 438–440 (1981)), the U.S. Supreme Court also concluded that an interstate compact enacted with congressional consent is itself federal law. Following this, courts have ruled that an interstate compact agency's regional plan and agency rules are the equivalent of federal law, superseding conflicting state law. Examples of such decisions include *Stephans v. Tahoe Regional Planning Agency* (697 F. Supp. 1149, 1152 (D. Nev. 1988)) and *Rhode Island Fishermen's Alliance v. Rhode Island Department of Environmental Management* (585 F.3d 42 (1st Cir. 2009)). It is this federal structure that gives the Columbia Gorge Commission the ability to devise the land-use planning program for the National Scenic Area to be responsive to the particular needs of the gorge, free from the restrictions and requirements of the states' own land-use planning programs.

This federal structure can also reach into city planning in the gorge. For example, by interpreting the second purpose of the Scenic Area Act (economic development) to include efficiency in providing government services, the National Scenic Area authorities may allow community cooperation across state lines in ways that state law might not otherwise allow—a form of "localism" (Davidson 2007). No court has had to consider whether the National Scenic Area Act preempts the relevant state law provisions that may be hindering the three cities from cooperating on their specific issues; still, the communities' work illustrates how local governments are leveraging the National Scenic Area authorities for their unique opportunities for problem solving.

Lessons Learned

For its first 20 years, the Columbia Gorge Commission struggled with mistrust from the gorge communities. Those communities began to realize they could work with the commission and the National Scenic Area authorities to achieve their own local goals only after the commission realized it had to work with the communities to achieve its regional goals. Following the commission's focused effort in convening community controlled visioning and planning, gorge communities are now suggesting ways that the commission can help them, which in turn helps achieve the purposes of the Scenic Area Act. The many possibilities for these interdependencies are still being explored, and are exciting to imagine.

The unique structure of the National Scenic Area Act is not the single solution for the communities of the Columbia River Gorge, nor is it even a necessary precedent for all solutions. Rather, it is one unique catalyst that gorge communities are discovering as a potentially powerful tool for their own creative problem solving.

CHAPTER 16

Building Balanced Communities: Equity and Inclusion

Kurt Creager and Paul Peninger

The Cascadia region is famous for an overriding environmental ethos, which is reflected as much in everyday attitudes and commonly held values as it is in comprehensive growth management laws and policies.[1] An integral part of these laws and policies is the inclusion of "adequate, affordable and appropriate housing" to ensure that Cascadia's urban areas are economically and socially diverse.[2] Despite this strong legislative framework, Seattle, Portland, and Vancouver, British Columbia, all face significant ongoing challenges in meeting affordable housing needs amidst growing local economies and rapidly changing land markets.[3]

This article describes specific developments and policy innovations for affordable and mixed income housing in the region's three largest cities. These approaches vary from jurisdiction to jurisdiction but share some common characteristics, especially a commitment to creativity and innovation. This chapter evaluates three broad trends across Cascadia: nonprofit and public-sector development, equitable TODs, and urban villages.

The Changing Role of the Public Sector and Nonprofit Development Culture

In the United States and Canada, the government's role in developing housing for low-income households has declined markedly over the past three decades as the private for-profit and nonprofit sectors have taken a larger role in developing new affordable housing. With public and private financing sources, private developers are able to assemble multilayered financing packages and target housing production to specific community needs with-

Figure 16.1. High Point community

out many of the obstacles that often constrain local public housing authorities (Bratt 2007).

In the United States, the role of private developers –whether nonprofit or for-profit—is strongly driven by the availability of equity capital for affordable housing generated through the Low-Income Housing Tax Credit (LIHTC) program, the most important resource for creating affordable housing in the United States.[4] Since 1987, the LIHTC program has provided the annual equivalent of approximately $8 billion in budget authority to issue tax credits for the acquisition, rehabilitation, or new construction of rental housing targeted to lower-income households.[5]

Nonprofit affordable housing developers in the Portland and Seattle metropolitan regions have developed a culture of entrepreneurship resulting in many affordable housing projects in urban infill locations that would not otherwise have been developed. They are often the first developers to enter urban locations, serving both households and communities that are underserved by the conventional private real estate market.

In Seattle, the Housing Authority (SHA) has also played a critical role in developing mixed income neighborhoods in partnership with nonprofit developers. In particular, SHA communities like New Holly, High Point, and Rainier Vista have become national models for the transformation of aging public housing projects into vibrant mixed income, mixed use neighborhoods (Figure 16.1). SHA is distinguished nationally because it serves as the master developer of its transformation projects rather than delegating responsibility to private companies. Its no-net-loss policy of affordable housing ensures that low-income SHA residents have the opportunity to return to their former neighborhoods, reducing disruption and gentrification.

Equitable Transit-Oriented Development

Cascadia's urban centers have also promoted equitable development in complete communities oriented around transit opportunities. This type of equitable transit-oriented development (TOD) "prioritizes social equity as a key component of TOD implementation . . . and aims to ensure that all people along a transit corridor, including those who are low income, have the opportunity to reap the benefits of easy access to employment opportunities offering living wages, health clinics, fresh food markets, human services, schools and child-care centers" (Pollack and Prater 2013).

One such development is Patton Park, the first major mixed use project to be developed along the Interstate Corridor in Portland's Northeast neighborhood. Sponsored by local nonprofit developer REACH Community Development, Inc., in partnership with the TriMet transit agency, Patton Park is a 100 percent affordable housing development with ground-floor commercial and community service uses (Figure 16.2). TriMet purchased the parcel directly adjacent to the North Killingsworth Max Station prior to the completion of the Yellow Line. In 2006, Tri-Met issued a request for proposals (RFP) seeking a developer to achieve the goals of activating the street through ground-floor commercial uses, providing affordable housing for families earning less than 50 percent of the area median income, and helping support transit ridership.

Figure 16.2. Patton Park Apartments

Project feasibility was aided by local planning regulations that allowed the developer to provide surface parking with a low parking ratio of 0.6 spaces per unit. The ground floor of the project has 4,500 square feet of commercial space occupied by the offices of a housing trust fund, a day care facility, and a therapist's office. These support local community and economic development goals.

Cascadia's Urban Villages

A central feature of planning in Cascadia has been a heavy reliance on neighborhood planning to gain consensus about appropriate ways to accommodate density and affordability. One outcome has been that higher densities are allowed in combination with additional urban amenities, open space, and community facilities. Community development corporations, public housing authorities, and some private developers are each—in different but symbiotic ways—providing a mix of housing options with a range of affordability within urban villages.

An industrial neighborhood for over 100 years, False Creek was first successfully redeveloped with a mix of housing from 1980 to 1986 and further transformed by the redevelopment of the Expo '86 site, adding still more density and urban amenities. The neighborhood accommodates a mix of uses, including some of the former manufacturing uses and the Granville Island Market, the venerable local source for fresh and local produce. Today, False Creek is a great success: walkable, vibrant, and well connected to downtown.

Other recent efforts by Vancouver to weave density and affordability (20 percent of the new housing units are expected to be affordable) into established neighborhoods have met with vociferous opposition that may not portend well for future success. The Vancouver EcoDensity Charter has effectively linked the reduction of greenhouse gas emissions to higher densities (Lee et al. 2008) and public criticism by planning and housing advocates has pressed for a systematic commitment to producing and preserving a mix of affordable housing choices. Vancouver's approval of Laneway Housing (accessory dwelling units for sale or rent) within single-family neighborhoods was partly in response to this criticism and adopted as policy in 2012.

Challenges and Opportunities

With robust public programs and policies that promote affordable housing in urban neighborhoods with access to transit, jobs and services, the region has been a leader in embracing issues of social equity. Still, building affordable housing faces a variety of challenges in Cascadia's large cities. Vancouver is Canada's most costly large city measured by median home prices, and Portland and Seattle are also comparatively costly with rental vacancy rates among the lowest in the United States. With strong economic growth and growing international profiles as magnets for talent, it is an ongoing struggle for these cities to marshal the financing and policy tools to address expanding needs for affordable housing. In each city, efforts are under way to address the policy and funding gaps to building equitable and inclusive communities, as follows:

- Vancouver Mayor's Task Force on Housing Affordability published a report in 2012 that could serve as a model for the rest of the region. The report combines recommendations for increasing the supply of nonprofit and social housing with broader recommendations on streamlining the approvals process. (Mayor's Task Force 2014) One key element is a robust but flexible inclusionary housing requirement for new development.
- Similarly, Seattle has recently undertaken a policy review of their Incentive Zoning Program to calibrate land-use incentives and ensure that zoning measures are working in concert with tax policy and funding programs for affordable housing.
- Although Oregon's State Legislature has prohibited inclusionary policies, Portland's use of Tax Increment Financing (whereby 30 percent of the funds are used for housing) has partly offset this barrier and has helped fund developers to provide a mix of housing in Urban Renewal Areas.

Conclusion

The approaches described in this article demonstrate that there are practical and effective solutions to building affordable housing in Cascadia's high-cost cities. However, the creativity and entrepreneurship of the region's nonprofit and public-sector developers have not been matched by concomitant state, provincial, or federal investments in housing and community development. Since safe, decent and affordable housing is the bedrock of healthy and equitable communities (Cohen 2011; Lubell 2007), these proven solutions merit additional financial and policy support at all levels of government to allow local actors to grow their activities to match the need. In Seattle and Portland, this support could come in the form of expanded use of inclusionary housing approaches and state legislative fixes to outdated laws limiting or prohibiting tools like Tax Increment Financing. In all three cities and throughout Cascadia, it is certainly time for state and provincial governments to identify permanent, ongoing financing sources to fully fund housing trust funds, and in so doing to make building equitable and inclusive communities a true priority.

CHAPTER 17

Blue-Green to the Extreme in Portland and Seattle

Nancy Rottle

The Blue Region

It rains in the Pacific Northwest. Predominant westerly winds regularly move cloud cover from the oceans across the landscape, dumping moisture on glacial-carved hills and valleys. Where the deluge and drizzle hit indigenous forest, most is caught by leaves and evapotranspired or infiltrated into the ground, with a fraction flowing to streams, rivers, and eventually the Pacific Ocean. However, where rain falls on urbanized impervious surfaces, flows across the landscape increase and accelerate, carrying with them eroded sediments and urban pollutants.

The region is also known for its abundant native salmon, a totemic and revered species by first peoples and valued by those who followed to populate the towns and cities along the rivers and inland seas. Early settlers wrote of being able to "walk across streams on the backs of salmon" and economies of both Seattle and Portland were built on the fishing, processing, and shipping of salmon. As land cover converted from forests to clearcuts and pavement, salmon populations declined, their spawning and rearing waters no longer hospitable to mature fish making their way upstream to dig gravel nests in calm, cool pools, their eggs suffocated by sediments and scoured by floods, and their young unable to find shaded clean water as they made their way back out to sea. By the 1990s, alarmingly reduced numbers of returning salmon resulted in the listing of salmonids as threatened species in both regions.

By the end of the 20th century, environmental degradation in metropolitan regions came to the forefront of the national environmental agenda.

In 1990, the U.S. Environmental Protection Agency (EPA) began requiring medium and large cities discharging stormwater into local receiving waters to obtain Municipal Separate Storm Sewer System (MS4) permits, which set conditions on the water quality discharged and required certain actions from cities. Another threat to the health of Washington's Puget Sound and Oregon's Willamette River recognized by the EPA was—and remains—the increasing frequency that urban sewers, swollen beyond capacity by rainwater, dump their contents through emergency overflow outlets into rivers, lakes, and bays. The EPA put Seattle and Portland on notice to reduce these combined sewer overflows. Additionally, research on local streams revealed a strong correlation between increasing imperviousness of urbanization with low biodiversity in streams and wetlands. In response to these scientific studies and regulatory drivers, Seattle and Portland have become leaders in the application of green stormwater infrastructure, pioneering practices that are being adopted nationally and internationally (U.S. Environmental Protection Agency 2010).

This chapter describes the evolution of these "blue-green infrastructure" programs in Portland and Seattle, focusing on their multifaceted, interwoven planning, programs, pilot projects, regulations, and funding mechanisms that have advanced over two decades. The stories of each city's progress are both parallel and distinct, and provide useful lessons for other municipalities addressing their stormwater issues.

Portland: Pioneering Blue-Green Urban Stormwater Management

> IN PORTLAND, LAND AND WATER ARE ELEMENTAL, THE VERY ICONS OF THE CITY. THE RAIN, OUR REGION'S RIVERS, AND OUR LAND—THE WATERSHEDS THAT GATHER, FEED AND PROTECT THEM—ARE OUR IDENTITY, THE ESSENCE OF WHO ARE AND WHERE WE'VE COME FROM
>
> —CHET ORLOFF (PORTLAND 2005)

Portland's leadership in advancing innovative green infrastructure emanates from this perspective, which is fortified by the city's focus on healthy watershed values and informing and engaging the public in advocacy and stewardship. Portland's story is one of recognizing water quality issues early on, looking ahead to regulatory requirements, and creatively crafting a multipronged program in response to permitting demands that includes combining green and gray techniques, monitoring, interdepartmental and multidisciplinary collaboration, and education. City government has focused its efforts on watershed processes and health, taking a methodical approach by planning and modeling how stormwater issues can be resolved basin by basin, innovating new prototypes distributed across the city, and valuing the multiple benefits that stormwater retrofit opportunities can provide for residents and the ecological health of the city and its water bodies.

Portland's urban areas primarily drain to the Willamette River, in a system comprised of both combined sewer and separated stormwater basins. In the early 1990s, Portland's Bureau of Environmental Services (BES) began to address their serious stormwater issues, responding to the EPA's 1990 MS4 requirements and its 1994 policy requiring large municipalities to develop and implement Long Term Control Plans in combined sewer basins. The BES began construction of a $1.4 billion "Big Pipe" to detain stormwater to limit combined sewer overflows (Slovic 2011), and also began experimenting with sustainable water management practices that mimic the way natural systems infiltrate, evapotranspire, and slow the release of rain runoff. To comply with the EPA's MS4 National Pollution Discharge Elimination System (NPDES) permit, the city committed to conduct research on their new approaches, as well as include education in their activities. Initial BES planning efforts strove to match stormwater requirements with best management practices, and in 1996 an Advisory Committee recommended new policies and codes. Funding for planning and pilot projects was provided by a stormwater fee that had been instituted in 1977.

Early Green Infrastructure Practices

Downspout disconnection

An early project was to encourage and assist residents living in combined sewer areas to disconnect their roof downspouts from the sewer line and instead direct the runoff to garden areas where the water could infiltrate into Portland's generally sandy soils. The 18-year program, which ended in 2011, prevented an estimated annual volume of a billion gallons of stormwater per year from entering the combined sewer system.

Bioswales, rain gardens, and green roofs

Another seminal project was the design, implementation, and monitoring of a series of swales in the Oregon Museum of Science and Industry parking lot to capture, infiltrate, hold, and clean polluted runoff (Liptan and Murase 2002). Tom Liptan, a landscape architect working for the BES, also began experimenting with green roofs, leading to the city's official recognition in 1999 of ecoroofs as stormwater management techniques (Portland 2008). Other innovative sustainable stormwater trials, such as planted infiltration basins, were also implemented and monitored for their ability to detain runoff and reduce pollutants.

1999 Stormwater Management Manual

Informed by research results that verified the effectiveness of green infrastructure practices, the city's 1999 *Stormwater Management Manual* required public

Figure 17.1. Rain garden at Portland Middle School

and private and new and redirected impervious areas greater than 500 square feet to retain as much runoff on-site and use as much green infrastructure as possible. The manual provided design guidelines, drawings, and sizing tools to assist stormwater designers.

Growing Sustainable Infrastructure: New Programs, Prototypes, and Funding

Sustainable infrastructure organizational support

Committing to continue its green infrastructure practices, in 2001 the city initiated its Sustainable Infrastructure program with establishment of a multidisciplinary Sustainable Infrastructure Committee, and, in 2002, a Sustainable Stormwater Management Division, both made up of representatives from multiple disciplines including planning, engineering, landscape architecture, and environmental science. Responding to policy requiring implementation of green stormwater approaches, the division's services included citizen assistance, partnerships with developers, advancement of funding approaches, monitoring, and education.

Pilot projects

BES followed its Sustainable Infrastructure mandate by designing and installing a series of urban features to test and demonstrate how stormwater can be detained and cleaned through green infrastructure. An initial green street design from 2003 featured the installation of simple curb extensions, which detain and treat runoff from the upstream portion of the street. To address combined sewer backups, the BES installed stormwater gardens at two schools, which performed as expected hydrologically and provided multiple benefits such as reducing classroom overheating (Figure 17.1) (Kurtz 2012).

Institutionalizing and financing watershed stewardship

A 2001 River Renaissance Initiative establishing a "Clean and Healthy River" theme set the stage for the city to focus on healthy watersheds, consequently expressed in the 2005 BES Portland Watershed Management Plan. Developed to comply with NPDES permit and other federal and state regulatory requirements in a holistic fashion rather than addressing each regulation separately, the watershed-based approach presented strategies and actions to produce multi-objective projects expressing a range of values.

External funding was an initial catalyst to accelerate Portland's blue-green infrastructure; between 2002 and 2009 the city implemented more than 30 projects funded by a $3.4 million EPA-funded "Innovative Wet Weather Program" to reduce the amount of stormwater entering the combined sewers. City-funded "Clean River Rewards" offer reductions in impervious surface fees for properties that manage their roof and paved areas through blue-green infrastructure, while the Community Watershed Stewardship Program (CWSP) provides small grants to community organizations for watershed restoration projects. Between 1999 and 2012, the CWSP had granted nearly $1 million to more than 200 projects (Portland 2013b).

Green building policy addressing stormwater

In the first part of the new millennium, Portland adopted a Green Building policy that required LEED Silver for city-funded projects, met through features such as ecoroofs, and awarded developers extra floor area and height in buildings with green roofs. In 2005, the city's standards for their own buildings were raised to LEED Gold and Silver. A Green Investment Fund, supported by the city of Portland and the nonprofit Energy Trust of Oregon, offered substantial grants of up to $425,000 for building projects that would significantly conserve water and energy, reduce stormwater, and recycle or reuse a substantial amount of materials, incentivizing 36 innovative projects from 2005 to 2009 (Portland 2013d).

Scaling up: Sustainable Stormwater Through Public and Private Partnerships

Green Streets Program

The momentum of these successful projects built political support for expanded implementation of blue-green infrastructure. In 2007, the city council established Portland's Green Streets Program, which required that "green streets" be incorporated into all city-funded right-of-way projects, and provided a Percent for Green Fund. These funds, generated by projects either unable or not required to comply with the city's *Stormwater Management Manual*, support construction of stormwater treatment facilities that are on public or private lands, and treat stormwater from the public right-of-way in projects that exceed the manual's requirements. Through the Green Streets program, the BES partnered with Portland's transportation department to implement stormwater treatment features that serve as aesthetic, traffic calming, and safety amenities, including roadside swales, planters, curb extensions, and pocket basins.

Grey to Green Program

The Grey to Green program was established in 2008. It allocated $55 million for green streets, street trees, ecoroofs, the purchase of land, maintenance, and culvert removal, funded by an increase of 0.1 percent in stormwater fees levied on new and retrofitted impervious surfaces. The five-year program brought BES staff together with other city agencies and community partners to implement sustainable stormwater practices and acquire and revegetate natural lands (Portland 2013e).

Private Property Partnerships

In 2009 Portland launched a Private Property Retrofit Program, which has funded up to $6 per square foot for stormwater retrofits projects that contribute to the "Tabor to the River" flow-control goals (see below). In the central city, developers were further encouraged to construct ecoroofs through the Grey to Green Ecoroof Incentive Program, which afforded $5 per square foot to eligible projects (Portland 2013e). Recognizing the value of tree canopies in intercepting and evapotranspiring rain, the city's 2010–14 "Treebate" program allowed citizens to recover up to 50 percent of the cost of planting trees on private property, with rebate values based on the height of the tree at maturity.

Tabor to the River

The largest and most comprehensive green infrastructure project BES has undertaken is in the 2.3-square-mile basin flowing from Mount Tabor to the Willamette River (Figure 17.2). With ever-expanding impervious surfaces and shrinking tree canopy coverage causing increased volumes of stormwater to overwhelm 100-year-old pipes, sewage was backing up in basements, flooding into streets, and overflowing to the Willamette River. In 2009, it was estimated that the municipality would save $63 million by implementing green infrastructure combined with pipes to address these issues. The Tabor to the River (T2R) program will incorporate tree planting, streetside stormwater gardens,

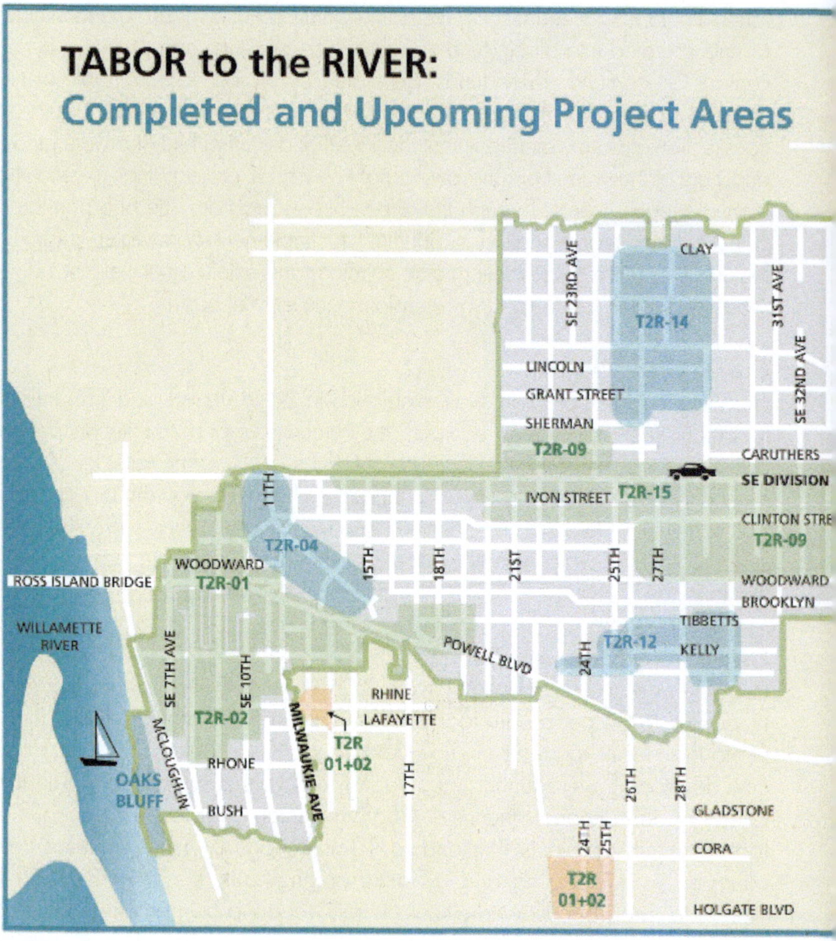

Figure 17.2. Tabor to the River program

sewer pipe repair, and wildlife habitat enhancement over its 15-year timespan (Portland 2013f). Extensive public outreach has been conducted, including two surveys in partnership with Portland State University to assess neighborhood concerns and preferences.

Multiple Benefits from Blue-Green Infrastructure

Ever cognizant of the need to fairly evaluate the full effects provided by the agency's green Infrastructure, the BES sponsored an evaluation of the corollary benefits of the Grey to Green program. The resulting 2010 report

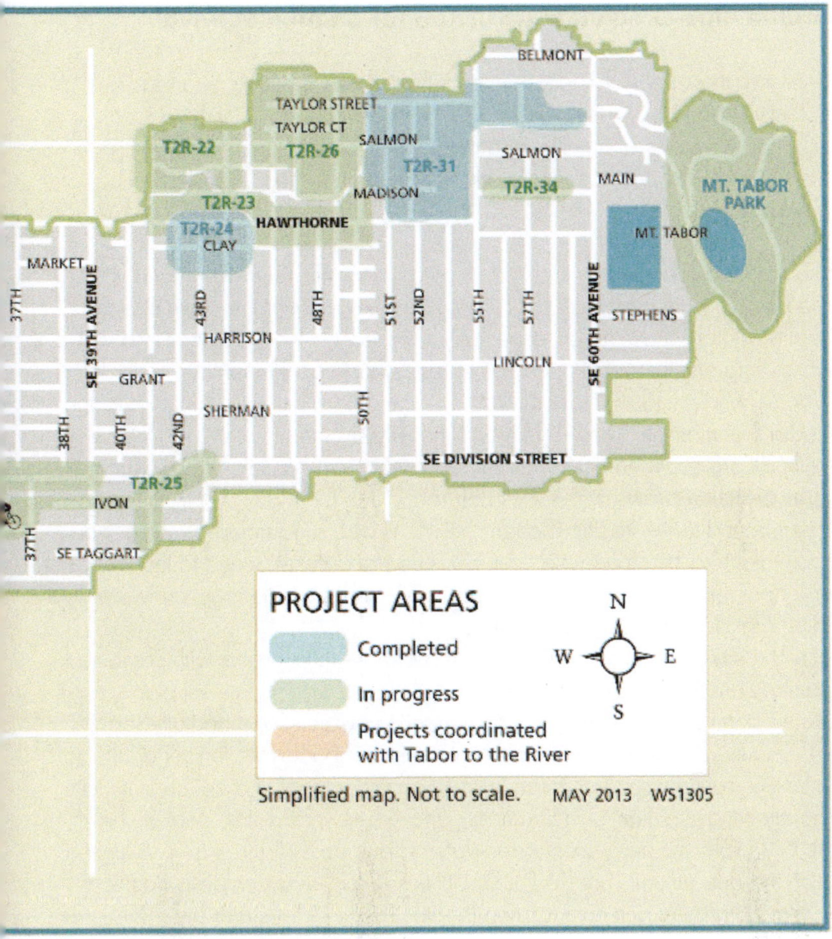

describes both qualitative and quantitative benefits related to health, community livability, and energy (Portland 2010b). Following the 2005 Watershed Management Plan, strategies to produce multi-objective projects were subsequently integrated by city bureaus such as in Urban Forest Plans, the Climate Action Plan, and the overarching 2012 Portland Plan. The municipality's Watershed Management Plan for 2012–17 underscores the relevancy of healthy watersheds to address multiple issues, proposing integrated strategies to address and monitor watershed health goals of water quality, flooding, air pollution, and urban heat island effects (Portland 2012).

Seattle Blue-Green Infrastructure for Salmon Survival

> From the shores of Puget Sound to the smallest tributary, Seattle is a city defined by water. . . . The City of Seattle is committed to restoring, protecting and enhancing these water bodies, and encouraging citizens and businesses to work with us in this effort. (Seattle Public Utilities 2008)

Like Portland, Seattle has focused its blue-green infrastructure around watershed health and mandates for cleaning up sewer outfall receiving waters. Seattle's efforts have been especially focused on the viability of salmon, which migrate through Puget Sound and the two primary river and lake systems whose mouths flow through the city, the Green-Duwamish and the Cedar-Sammamish. These rivers and the streams that flow through their watersheds are spawning grounds for the five species of salmon that lay their eggs and then grow as juveniles before making their way back out through Puget Sound to the Pacific Ocean. Seattle is also surrounded by water bodies—Lake Washington to the east, Elliot Bay and Puget Sound to the west—and contains several lakes, wetlands, and creeks conveying stormwater to Lake Washington and Puget Sound.

The city's stormwater system is a mosaic of piped basins with combined (sanitary and stormwater) systems flowing to wastewater treatment plants, separated storm sewers draining to local receiving waters, and partially separated systems with streets draining directly to water bodies while roof drainage enters the sanitary sewer system. In 1988 the city adopted a stormwater utility fee allowing creation of a drainage and wastewater utility, and in 1996, the city's solid waste, water, wastewater, drainage departments were united into one department, Seattle Public Utilities (SPU), embracing environmental stewardship as its common mission (Seattle Public Utilities and Lily 2004).

'Natural Drainage' for Creek Health

Initial trials—Seattle's SEA streets

With the listing of the Puget Sound Chinook salmon as a threatened species in 1999, and with several of the city's streams still flowing above ground, Seattle's initial innovative stormwater focus was on the health of Thornton, Piper's, Taylor, and Longfellow Creeks, basins where sanitary and storm sewer systems are primarily separated. A pivotal project to test the ability of streetside bioretention features to detain and treat stormwater were the experimental Street Edge Alternative (SEA) Streets, for which an interdisciplinary team redesigned two blocks of a ridgeline street and an adjacent steep street, both draining to Piper's Creek, which incorporated planted roadside swales to mimic the function of native vegetative cover and soils in holding and detaining stormwater. Monitoring found the trials to exceed performance expectations, and the published results heavily influenced Seattle's and other cities' policies for implementing urban low-impact development techniques (Seattle Public Utilities 2007; Horner, Lim, and Burges 2002). SPU applied these techniques in its expanded Natural Drainage System (NDS) program on several blocks in two creek basins, with institutionalization reducing the expense to below that of piped drainage systems.

New neighborhood housing applications
The success of the SEA streets also suggested use of NDS in an expansive Hope VI housing area retrofit at High Point in West Seattle, constructed from 2003 to 2010 on 120 acres draining to Longfellow Creek. Two years of monitoring confirmed that the system functions hydrologically as planned, with no overflows of the reduced-size detention pond into Longfellow Creek even during record-breaking rainstorms. In North Seattle, aspirations for daylighting a portion of Thornton Creek near its headwaters resulted in an artful water quality channel that acts as the central landscape feature between multifamily and senior housing on what was formerly a vast parking lot (Seattle Public Utilities 2009).

Institutionalizing blue-green infrastrucrure
In 2004, then Mayor Greg Nickels established the Restore Our Waters program, a cross-departmental strategy to integrate the city's growth targets with restoration of critical water resources. The aim of the program was to coordinate and integrate science into decision-making structures, and to provide education and incentives for public stewardship. By 2008 the program boasted a number of accomplishments, including strengthened regulations to protect creeks, shorelines, and wetlands; a comprehensive plan update and progress in overhauling the stormwater code to require use of green stormwater; and substantial progress on NDS projects (Seattle Public Utilities 2008).

Green Building to Address Blue-Green Infrastructure
Like Portland, Seattle has encouraged green building practices that contribute to stormwater control. In 2000 the city established the nation's first Sustainable Building Program, mandating that all city buildings over 5,000 square feet achieve at least Silver LEED rating, with living roofs subsequently installed on both the new Justice Center and City Hall. By 2009, Seattle had more than eight acres of living roofs, and another 33 acres of at-grade green roofs such as over city reservoirs (Seattle 2010a). The city's 2011 Sustainable Buildings and Sites policy requires that city buildings from all departments achieve LEED Gold and apply best management practices on all sites, such as through Sustainable Sites and Living Building ratings (Seattle 2011d). Additionally, in 2006 the city instituted the Seattle Green Factor code to increase ecological

function and visible vegetation in the city through private development projects, the first such program in the United States. The Green Factor requires new development projects in commercial, multifamily and other zones to achieve a minimum score through credits achieved by selecting and applying features from a menu of possible practices such as green roofs, permeable paving, rain gardens, deep soils, and tree retention and planting (Seattle 2013e).

Focus on Combined Sewer Overflows: A Learning Process

Lessons from Ballard's rain gardens

To comply with the EPA's requirements to limit combined sewer overflows and taking advantage of 2009 federal stimulus funding, SPU fast-tracked new design and construction of urban roadside rain gardens to temporarily detain stormwater in Ballard, a neighborhood with a high number of combined sewer overflows. However, during the design and construction phases the project met with several difficulties, resulting in nonfunctioning of a third of the rain gardens. Responding to neighborhood concerns, SPU removed a third and retrofitted another third of the bioretention cells with a shallower but more expensive design (Colwell and Tackett 2011). The retrofits have been successful, and SPU is applying lessons learned in continuing installation of the streetside rain gardens, this time in areas with verified permeable glacial outwash soils, and incorporating extensive study, design and community engagement, with emphasis on corollary benefits (Figures 17.3 and 17.4).

Seattle Rainwise

On a parallel track, SPU had conducted a pilot Rainwise program, supplying home owners with rain barrels that overflow to residential rain gardens, with positive stormwater performance results. Expanding the program in selected CSO basins, the agency's voluntary Rainwise program currently offers rebates of up to $3.50 per square foot of impervious surface that is mitigated by approved installation of cisterns and rain gardens. In its "slow it, spread it, filter it, soak it in" educational program, Rainwise encourages citizens to plant trees, reduce paved areas, improve soils with compost and mulch, and use permeable paving, and offers a suite of resources for citizens and contractors on its website (Seattle Public Utilities 2013c).

Coordinating for Blue-Green Multifunctionality

New green stormwater goals

Renaming its approach in ultraurbanized neighborhoods "green stormwater infrastructure" (GSI), in 2009 Seattle's new stormwater manual and a Director's Rule mandated that GSI be employed to the "maximum extent feasible" on all projects creating more than 2,000 square feet of impervious surface. A variety of GSI features may be used to achieve the target, utilizing infiltration

Figure 17.3 and Figure 17.4. Before (above) and after (below) green retrofitting in Seattle's Ballard neighborhood

Figure 17.5. Green stormwater infrastructure projects implemented in Portland and Seattle

IN PORTLAND AND SEATTLE

2005 2010 **PORTLAND**

SW 12th Ave Planters (2005): Stormwater planters on SW 12th Ave pioneered an urban raingarden typology.

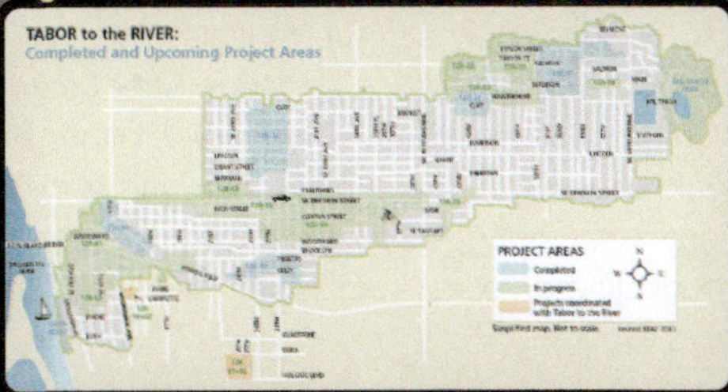

Tabor to the River (2009 - 2024): The Tabor to the River (T2R) program aims to plant 3,500 trees, install 500 stormwater facilities on the streets, assist with 100 private stormwater projects, repair or replace 81,000 feet of sewer pipe, remove invasive plants and improve wildlife habitat over its 15-year timespan. (Portland BES 2013c).

Tabor Middle School Rain Gardens (2006-07): Teachers report relief from reflected heat that previously emanated from the adjacent parking lot.

Rainwise Program (2010): By the end of 2013, over 300 residential raingardens had been installed as part of the Rainwise program.

Swale on Yale (2013): Four blocks of an urban, extra-wide planted biofiltration channel slow and treat a large volume of stormwater flowing from the dense Capitol Hill neighborhood before it is discharged into Lake Union.

Thornton Creek Water Quality Channel (2009): The meandering, deep constructed channel provides open space and wildlife habitat, and is designed to effectively filter 40-80% of the total suspended solids flowing from the 680-acre contributing basin (SPU 2009).

Ballard Roadside Raingardens (2010): Initial designs met with performance and acceptance obstacles, and have since been redesigned to address concerns.

2005 2010 **SEATTLE**

and reuse techniques such as bioretention cells, rainwater harvesting, permeable pavement with reservoirs, green roofs, and tree retention (Tackett 2012).

In the spring of 2013, then Mayor Michael McGinn issued an Executive Order establishing a citywide goal of annually managing 700 million gallons of stormwater with GSI by 2025, directing city departments to collaborate and coordinate to achieve multiple objectives. Such integration incorporates streetscapes, aesthetics, signage, tree canopies, neighborhood engagement, and stewardship, with considerations for creating walkable, bikeable, climate-responsive neighborhoods and a six-fold increase in the amount of stormwater managed by green infrastructure (Seattle 2013c). SPU is currently conducting an ecosystem service study to evaluate the multiple benefits of the city's GSI.

New partnerships

This new regulatory development was crowned with completion of a stormwater treatment project several years in the making, the Swale on Yale, developed in partnership with a LEED Platinum housing project that collects and reuses water for its irrigation (Seattle Public Utilities 2013a). The agency is also partnering with King County in expanding its Rainwise home owner rebate program; more than 40,000 homes are now eligible to participate in basins managed by either Seattle or King County-Metro.

Innovating with the EPA

In 2013 Seattle Public Utilities signed a Consent Decree with the EPA, the first in the nation to allow NPDES permittees to integrate both combined sewer outflows and stormwater into one permit. Responding to criticism that the EPA's focus on CSOs ignored the more voluminous and probably more damaging stormwater discharges, and with CSO prevention costs crippling municipal agencies' abilities to respond to this need, the EPA agreed to an Integrated Plan alternative that would allow the city to address its stormwater outflows prior to its combined overflows (Seattle Public Utilities 2013b).

Lessons for Achieving Blue-Green to the Extreme

As Portland and Seattle both show, achieving blue-green to the extreme is a process that takes time and civic commitment, aided by external requirements and funding. Both municipalities have begun with pilot projects demonstrating diverse design approaches to fit specific contexts, starting small and then scaling up into city policy, funded programs, and whole-basin approaches. Monitoring the effectiveness of these pilots in their local hydrological contexts has been instrumental, with iteration and refinement of design approaches for increased success in subsequent applications. Figure 17.5 shows the sequence of key pilot projects described above.

TABLE 17.1. Blue-Green Infrastructure Evolution in Portland and Seattle

	Initiation Stage	Growth Stage	Integration Stage
Institutional Organization	Green Stormwater Team	Expanded Green Stormwater Team; private, NGO, and public partnerships	Executive and city council directives; integrating agency
Planning	Goals, aspirations, response to regulatory and watershed health drivers	Watershed-based planning and action plans	Integrated planning across departments and CIP coordination
Projects	Demonstration projects	Expanded application and prototype design and construction	Design,construct, and support integrated projects
Performance	Monitor project performance	Monitor expanded application and prototypes; response to science and requirements	Assess multiple benefits, ecosystem services
Programs		Citywide implentation programs, incentives for private landowners, government practices, partner programs	Integrated implementation programs (e.g. Urban Forest, Transportation, Development, Park, Climate)
Standards and Codes		Revised *Stormwater Manual*, requirements and codes	Green stormwater integrated into development, street, etc. codes
Education, Public Engagement	Watershed education plus project-specific issues and solutions	Basin and citywide educational materials, outreach, training,tours	Messaging includes multiple benefits and opportunities

Source: Nancy Rottle

Both municipalities rely upon regulation as well as incentives and partnerships, initiating work in the city-owned rights-of-ways while encouraging water-sensitive new construction and retrofits on private lands. Both cities also recognize the value of a hybrid system, mixing green and gray methods to solve stormwater problems, and have evolved to value the integrated multiple benefits green practices offer. Table 17.1 shows a simplified summary of the phases Portland and Seattle manifested in the development of their blue-green infrastructure systems.

Yet the conditions and success factors are different in each city. Where Portland's generally sandy soils facilitate effective functioning of its blue-green infrastructure, Seattle's glacial tills and extensive fills pose infiltration challenges that require careful engineering for optimum success. Portland attributes its gains to integration of diverse professionals, including engineers, environmental specialists, and landscape architects, and coordination between multiple agencies and programs for maximum integrated benefit. Seattle has relied upon monitoring and proven science to guide the way, taking a focused view of how to best and most cost effectively solve its stormwater issues. Seattle is now following Portland's lead in working to transcend departmental barriers, and is increasingly addressing public aesthetic and functional concerns and highlighting the co-benefits of green infrastructure.

Portland and Seattle rely equally on advocacy from their citizens, and prioritize education and enabling of best practices and stewardship. A focus on overall watershed health, at all scales, has been a guiding framework to promote holistic, goal-based actions. A critical position for both cities has been the importance of evaluating, valuing, and cultivating appreciation for the multiple environmental, social, and economic benefits that blue-green infrastructure can deliver, enlarging the scope of education and sphere of influence to affect triple-bottom-line decision making and associated funding appropriations. With successful on-the-ground projects, and awareness of their broad and compounding value, a culture of care is fueled. Such a culture may then build upon itself in a "virtuous cycle," fostering actions that shape the urban environment so that it may continue to cultivate awareness, environmental appreciation, and stewardship.

CHAPTER 18

The Columbia River: Community Participation and Science-Based Planning

Nicole Lewis, AICP

As the largest North American river to flow into the Pacific Ocean, the Columbia River is an inextricable part of both natural and built systems in the Pacific Northwest. The Columbia and its tributaries have been a symbol and source of bounty and a means of livelihood and mobility for the people of the Pacific Northwest for thousands of years. While the damming of the Columbia River brought inexpensive electrical power to fuel growth and development in the region, it also destroyed natural habitat for salmon and other species and affected many native communities and traditions. Preservation and restoration of the many roles that the Columbia River plays for the people of the Pacific Northwest is of paramount importance. For some, this restoration is as much about respectful enjoyment of wild and remote rivers as it is about the return of salmon to local streams.

Using salmon habitat restoration and river recreation as examples, this chapter explores the challenges to plan for the use of our shared resources in ways that pursue multiple objectives and are both science-based and responsive to community needs and expertise.

Salmon Recovery in the Columbia River Basin

Until recently, our history of planning and river management focused on achieving single objectives and, consequently, risked the health of entire natural systems. This reality shaped today's litigious, high-stakes natural resources planning and policy environment. When it comes to contemporary resource planning in the Pacific Northwest, perhaps no issue is as politically charged as salmon.

Since 1991, 12 specific populations of Columbia River Basin salmon and steelhead and two resident fish species have been listed for protection under the Endangered Species Act, beginning with the Snake River sockeye, which was listed following petition of the Shoshone-Bannock Tribe in southeastern Idaho (Harrison 2011). The new federal status of these populations fostered the emergence of a political, organizational, and financial complex built to recover these and other threatened and endangered fish species.

Columbia River salmon recovery strategies address the need for action in four sectors, or the "four Hs" as they are commonly called: habitat restoration, hydroelectric dams on migratory rivers, fish harvest, and hatcheries. Investment in habitat restoration—one piece of the puzzle—is tremendous. According to the Upper Columbia Spring Chinook Salmon and Steelhead Recovery Plan,[1] the initial estimated cost of restoring habitat for Spring Chinook, steelhead, and bull trout in the Upper Columbia Basin alone was at least $296 million over the first 10-year period. Implementation actions beyond this first 10 years were anticipated to cost from $150 million to $200 million (Upper Columbia Salmon Recovery Board 2007).

The Practices and Politics of Large Wood

To enhance the function of natural systems and create habitat for imperiled fish species, habitat restoration biologists today are adding wood to rivers and streams. This growing practice seeks to mitigate forestry and river management practices of the past. Large wood enhancement projects are commonplace in

Figure 18.1. Yakama Nation Habitat Fisheries biologist Chris Butler looks at a recently completed large wood enhancement project on the Twisp River, located upstream of Twisp, Washington.

the Pacific Northwest, and can be found on private lands, in local and regional parks, and on state and national forestlands (Figure 18.1).

Foresters and biologists are not the only ones lending a hand in large wood management, although objectives for doing so vary. Some whitewater boaters take it upon themselves to remove large wood from favored boating reaches where it spans rivers, constitutes a hazard or obstacle, or otherwise creates risk or inconvenience for boaters. As written by American Whitewater National Stewardship Director Kevin Colburn in an article encouraging ecological and ethical considerations in wood management, "Logs are the predators of paddlers and we treat them how our ancestors in this country treated wolves and mountain lions. They are generally disliked, their importance to the ecosystem is completely misunderstood, they are removed whenever possible, and if one is ever implicated in the injury or death of a human it is ceremoniously destroyed." (Colburn 2001, 57)

While an antagonistic attitude toward large wood persists among a minority of whitewater boaters today, many understand and respect its ecological value. However, even the most environmentally conscious paddlers, according to one, may also believe that "large woody debris should not be regarded as sacrosanct" and that "in certain cases . . . should be fair game for removal" (Yakama Nation 2013).

Large Wood and Community Safety

While driven by an urgent environmental, cultural, and legal mandate, large wood placement for salmon may have unintended consequences. The safety of boaters and the liability of landowners and agencies implementing large wood enhancement projects are among the concerns that have garnered the most interest and action politically.

King County, Washington, led the way to address these issues in the Pacific Northwest by establishing a Large Wood Stakeholder Committee in June 2009. The purpose of the committee was to advise the county's Natural Resources Department regarding large wood management practices and protocols (King County 2009). At a statewide level, the governor of Washington signed House Bill (HB) 1194 into law in 2013, requiring that a designated lead entity in habitat project planning establish a committee "to provide a citizen-based evaluation of the projects proposed to promote salmon habitat" (Washington 2013, 2). Focused, in part, on the design and placement of large wood and other structural habitat enhancements, HB 1194 seeks to protect landowners from civil liability for property damages resulting from a project located on their lands.

Paddling Perspectives

While salmon habitat restoration is a critical and evolving part of the culture and economy of the Columbia Basin, so is recreation. The same streams and river valleys that exhibit potential in salmon recovery are veritable playgrounds for river recreation and whitewater enthusiasts. More than 40 percent of participants in a 2005 study identified proximity to recreational opportunities as their top reason for moving to or visiting the Methow Valley. (Methow Conservancy 2005)

In a recent series of studies, the Yakama Nation[2]—a key player in salmon recovery in North Central Washington—reached out to hundreds of local and visiting boaters across five Upper Columbia subbasins to learn from their experiences and expertise. Primary methods included personal interviews and a detailed questionnaire. The intent was to better understand the nature, extent, and locations of boating use to inform river restoration and management activities.

Study participants were asked to express their level of support for management activities intended to mitigate unintended consequences of large wood placement and to improve boater safety. The clear majority of participants who shared an opinion about river restoration voiced support for local river restoration activities. One individual stated, "As a competent river user, I fully support river restoration efforts. [Inexperienced] tubers have no business standing the way of restoration." Another expressed that "Recreational boating should only be a secondary use when compatible with other natural river functions" (Yakama Nation 2013).

The majority of respondents (in this case, skilled whitewater boaters) shared the following perspectives related to personal risk and responsibility:

- "The river should not be made 'safe' for boaters through government regulation."
- "People need to take more personal responsibility for their own safety and not rely on others to warn them of every possible hazard."
- "It's normal for boaters to be aware [of] and manage their own risk, even when it comes to man-made structures and enhancements."[3] (Yakama Nation 2013)

Very few participants expressed opposition to large wood placement. However, one participant called recent restoration work "an eyesore." Another suggested that other methods might be more effective: "As long as the Columbia Dams exist the salmon will be endangered. . . . I believe that river restoration should be more about removing man-made structures like riprap and diversions than modifying or adding features."

Two paddlers declined to participate, stating they were "not interested in helping anyone who will deliberately put wood in the river." In related communications, they expressed concerns regarding the "dangerous combination" of wood projects and paddlers, and the lack of research proving the effectiveness of wood placement for salmon recovery.

Many restoration strategies are considered works in progress involving long-term monitoring. Large wood projects are recognized as immediate, short-term actions to improve habitat diversity as other actions are also used to restore natural watershed processes (UCSRB 2007) As noted in the Upper Columbia Spring Chinook Salmon and Steelhead Recovery Plan, " . . . at some point in the future, habitat improvements through protection and restoration will have a limited effect on fish habitat." (Upper Columbia Salmon Recovery Board 2007, p. x1)

The Yakama Nation study captures a snapshot of today's fluid context of natural resource planning including social, cultural, and natural science factors. Strong individualistic values are meeting the realities of ecological restoration. Values that drive resistance also support the insistence to be involved and be heard. Scientific knowledge is also on the move as new research and experimentation shape new interpretations and actions. Adaptive management approaches involving ongoing learning and knowledge creation—substantive and procedural—replace the quest for defined, once-and-for-all-solutions. Planning for rivers is about cultural shifts and changes in planning that are accelerating as the limits of these natural resources are pushed to the edge.

The Future of the Columbia River

The roles and values we assign our rivers in the Pacific Northwest have changed dramatically over time. In parallel, the nature of planning has evolved as well.

Today, even the most pristine and remote rivers are part of a managed system, and are regulated and manipulated in a variety of ways. Countless cities and towns rely on the flood protection the Columbia River provides and the hydropower it generates. These benefits are governed by the 1964 Columbia River Treaty, a binding accord between the governments of the United States and Canada focused on operation of the Columbia dams. The treaty has no end date, but it includes an option for either country to terminate most treaty provisions anytime after 60 years (i.e., September 2024), given at least 10 years' advance notice. In 2014, the two governments are reviewing the future of the treaty. The stakes are high for everyone, and final outcomes will largely dictate future management of the Columbia River system and play a central role in shaping the future of the Pacific Northwest.

The treaty originated in a time when our approach to planning and managing freshwater and riparian resources was focused on a few objectives. The accompanying planning processes were centralized and both participation and outcomes were limited. Today, natural resource planning has a more resilient and indeterminate quality based on engaging a multitude of issues and a process inclusive of community members, non-agency interest groups, and tribal governments.

Federal mandates for recovering the endangered salmon, requirements by the state for community participation in river restoration projects, and discussions as far reaching as the Columbia River Treaty are challenging opportunities for creativity, innovation, and idea-sharing in planning, including:

- Adapting management practice to advance scientifically sound environmental management practices, and apply, evaluate, and recalibrate them in a dynamic process.
- Determining the most relevant planning methods for stakeholder analysis and for engaging and addressing many, often divergent community needs spread over a geographically extensive region.
- Figuring out how to learn together to effectively connect science-based knowledge with community-based knowledge.
- Determing how to protect diverse local cultures and economies dependent on a resource that spans an international boundary, flows through seven states, crosses multiple agency jurisdictions, and touches so close to home.

Natural resource planning for the river will continue to evolve, drawing on collaboration among disciplines and across the full spectrum of community interests. Increasingly, participants in this work will listen and learn together, finding ways to view an issue with a variety of tools and perspectives. Planners will have a role in designing and facilitating these processes but also, as participants, will learn as well. Recognizing the limitations of any single approach, planning can assist participants in working toward more holistic, integrated solutions. Planning can also frame the work to overcome jurisdictional boundaries, keep the focus on looking ahead—envisioning a future—rather than trying to recapture the past, and maintain the spirit of the Columbia not as prescriptive condition, but as one full of possibilities.

CHAPTER 19

The Cloud Beneath the Clouds

Kristen A. Vitro and Jan Whittington

The Pacific Northwest is known for its persistently gloomy winter weather. Despite the misty drizzle that would drive many sun-loving people far, far away, major cities such as Seattle, Portland, and Vancouver, British Columbia, are thriving. But the overcast sky is not the only type of cloud this area of the country is known for. Cloud computing and data centers have been springing up across the Columbia River basin. Is the presence of the digital cloud beneath our overcast skies merely a coincidence, or are other factors influencing the placement of this critical 21st century infrastructure?

Seattle's metropolitan area is home to a number of large technology companies, including internationally known firms such as Boeing, Microsoft, and Amazon, which employ thousands of local residents. Seattle has also become a top U.S. city for technology-related startups, attracting young people with degrees in engineering and computer science (Cook 2012). The explosion of application development for smartphones and other Wi-Fi-enabled devices has increased the demand for cloud computing capacity, and the region's proximity to several major transpacific submarine cables provides excellent connections to the global Internet backbone.

The explanation as to why so many cloud computing data centers are located in this area may seem simple at first glance. The prevalence of technology firms and their computing demands created a need for increased data capacity, thus facilitating the siting of data centers nearby. However, this isn't the whole story. Computer infrastructure investment in the Pacific Northwest is not limited to companies headquartered in the region. Google and Facebook, two firms with huge data requirements, have also begun to move some of their operations to the Columbia River Basin, locating data centers in The Dalles and Prineville, Oregon, respectively (Facebook 2011; Google 2014). What attracts technology firms to the Pacific Northwest? Why are global firms planning to locate their cloud computing assets under the clouds?

One of the many explanations for this attraction is the availability of abundant, inexpensive electricity. During the fall and winter, heavy precipitation along the western side of the Cascade and Rocky Mountain ranges ensures ample electricity generation as surface waters drain through the hydroelectric turbines that dot the Columbia River basin. The spring and summer months see a melting of snow at higher elevations, allowing for consistently reliable year-round power generation.

The management practices and physical features of the federal Columbia Power System's dam network result in electricity rates that are persistently low in comparison to other parts of the country. This is a point of critical importance for computer-based technology operations: Data centers require massive amounts of electricity, and that electricity consumption must be paid for. Facebook's new server campus in Prineville, Oregon, is estimated to draw a total 78 megawatts when its three-phase construction is complete (Miller 2012). In the Northeast, where hydropower is less abundant, coal, natural gas, and nuclear power make up a greater percentage of the energy mix. In general, these sources and facilities are more expensive to operate, and that increased cost is ultimately passed down to the consumer. Officials of the Port of Quincy (Washington), home to data centers for Microsoft, have specifically noted that low electrical costs make the area an attractive option for technology companies investing in data centers (Hernandez 2013).

While lower hydroelectric power prices are a factor, there is another benefit of locating these facilities close to dams along the Columbia River. Because of their importance, dams are often classified as critical infrastructure and are safeguarded by additional security measures. Consider the impacts of a dam failure: A breach in the structure could result in highly destructive flooding that poses a threat to health and safety and insufficient electrical supply for the area. In a world where terrorism has become a real threat, security around critical infrastructure, dams and bridges alike, has increased. Now consider the importance of data centers. As our society becomes increasingly reliant on technology for personal communication, banking, and business, the protection of data is also of paramount importance. Our electronic cloud is, like the dams on the Columbia, critical physical infrastructure. The colocation of hydroelectric dams and data centers not only provides access to low-cost electricity, but can also generate security co-benefits.

Climate may be yet another factor influencing the location of data centers in the Pacific Northwest. Washington and Oregon enjoy a temperate climate, cooler on average than temperatures in California's Silicon Valley. During their operation, server farms generate a significant amount of heat and need to be cooled to avoid hardware damage. Excess heat can destroy computer components and impact data availability. Locating data centers in cooler climates avoids issues with extreme outdoor ambient heat, which can help reduce cooling demands and thus lower the operating costs for each facility.

One final factor that may explain the prevalence of data centers in the Pacific Northwest has nothing to do with electricity generation and its pricing, or the area's climate, but rather planning and economic development. The construction and operation of data centers provides jobs for the communities that they are located in. An economic impact study of Facebook's Prineville data center investment found that capital spending for the phased project may result in more than $140 million in economic activity from both wages and related costs of construction, including food and lodging for workers (Cascade Business News 2012). Operation of the first phase was estimated to have generated approximately $21 million in economic activity for the area in 2011 (*Cascade Business News* 2012). In addition to the temporary construction jobs created during the capital phases of this project, the project has led to permanent technology jobs dealing with the operation and maintenance of the facility. Local construction-related spending, property taxes, and the generation of long-term employment prospects are attractive to smaller municipalities, and some have gone to great lengths to ensure this kind of economic investment in the community. To Facebook's benefit, the company was charged only $3 million for its purchase of 124 acres of land, a deal that also included a 15-year agreement that their property taxes would only be assessed for the unimproved value of the land (Williams 2010).

Other companies, including Amazon, have also made recent land purchases around the state for the expansion of data center facilities. Amazon's data arm, Vadata, has begun operations at their Port of Umatilla center, which was recently annexed by Umatilla, Oregon, to allow the facility access to municipal water and sewer systems in the event of a future expansion (Miller 2011). Amazon expressed several reasons for its decision to locate its new center in this area, noting the availability of cheap and abundant hydropower and a cooler climate. Microsoft has also branched out from the greater Seattle area, establishing a new data center in Quincy, just upstream of Umatilla (Data Center Knowledge 2014). Both sites are along the main stem of the Columbia River.

Cloud computing is on the rise, and the need for data centers will continue to grow. Although these facilities will pop up around the world, their siting is not random. The Pacific Northwest will continue to be an attractive location for future facilities, ensuring continued investment in the cloud beneath the clouds.

CHAPTER 20

A Bicycling Haven

Paula Reeves, AICP CTP

The Pacific Northwest is well known for its bicycle culture, bicycle economy, and safe and scenic bicycling; as a result, the region is experiencing a substantial increase in bicycle commuting and tourism dollars. For the seventh year in a row, Washington State has been named the nation's most bicycle-friendly state and Portland has claimed recognition as the most bicycle-friendly city. Seattle is also recognized as a world-class cycling city (League of American Bicyclists 2013b).

Our Natural Environment and Expanding Bicycle Culture

It is nearly impossible to be in the Pacific Northwest and not be conscious of the natural environment, the beautiful coastlines, spectacular mountains, temperate rain forests, and high desert and alpine landscapes. It is also nearly impossible not to be drawn out into these amazing natural settings and want to work to help steward them. This is evidenced by the flourishing outdoor recreation economy, which generates more than $35 billion annually in Washington and Oregon and the legacy, strength, and number of environmental organizations in the region (Outdoor Industry Association 2012; Chapman 2010).

The Pacific Northwest states of Washington and Oregon are also famous for their bicycle culture, comprised of a growing number of bike-friendly businesses, increasing population of everyday-everywhere bicyclists, strong environmental consciousness, rapidly developing cycling infrastructure, relatively courteous and mindful automobile drivers, and of course, great bicycle plans from the neighborhood to state level. Maybe this is why Washington and Oregon top the list of the bicycle-friendliest states in the United States (League of American Bicyclists 2014).

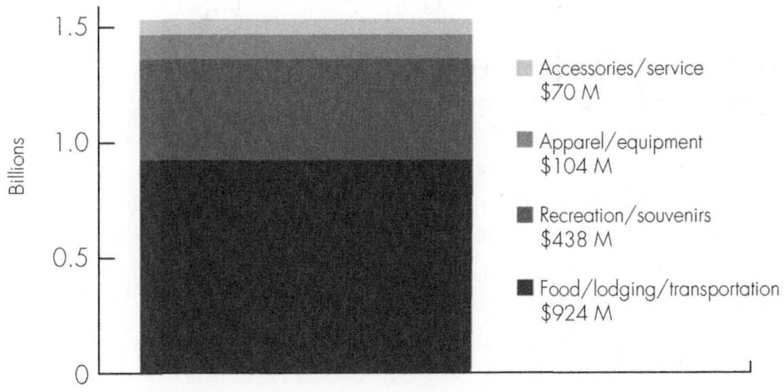

Figure 20.1. Annual spending on bicycling in Washington (Source: Data from Outdoor Industry Foundation 2006; analysis by Paula Reeves)

Bicycling is big business in the Pacific Northwest

Washington is a leader in outdoor equipment development, and the bicycle industry is a large part of this, with companies including Raleigh, REI, Seattle Bike Supply, Transition Bicycle Company, Kona, K2, and Torker headquartered in the state. The League of American Bicyclists (2013b) reports the annual gross income from bicycle retail stores in Washington at more than $160 million. For every dollar spent on gear and bicycle equipment, the Outdoor Industry Association estimates an additional $4 is spent on trips and travel, which means that as much as $650 million is spent by Washingtonians annually on bike travel (Figure 20.1) (Outdoor Industry Association 2012).

Boasting the only State Scenic Bikeway system in the nation, Oregon is famous for its world-class bicycle touring routes, as well as its bicycle economy. These diverse Scenic Bikeway routes have been officially reviewed and adopted by Oregon State Parks and Recreation Department, and they accommodate everyone from beginning to advanced riders (Travel Oregon 2014). Travel Oregon estimates that recreational bicycle travel accounts for $400 million, or 4.4 percent of Oregon's annual $9 billion tourism industry (Travel Oregon 2013).

From Seattle to Portland and many communities in between, bicycle-friendly businesses—ranging from bicycling coffee roasters to bike-friendly grocers and bicycling chiropractors that offer customers and employees bicycle facilities, services, and incentives—are increasing rapidly. The League of American Bicyclists has seen bicycle-friendly businesses in the Pacific Northwest more than double in the past five years, benefiting 97,000 employees in Washington and Oregon in 2013 along with many more customers (League of American Bicyclists 2013a).

Bicycling by the Numbers in the Pacific Northwest's Major Cities

The two largest cities of the Pacific Northwest, Portland and Seattle, have been identified as world-class cycling cities by a number of industry experts and organizations including the League of American Bicyclists, *Bicycling* magazine, and CNN Travel. Bicycle commuting in these cities is growing rapidly. From 2000 to 2012, the percent of bicycle commuters in Portland grew 250 percent to more than six percent, the largest in the United States, and Seattle's bicycle commuting grew 120 percent (League of American Bicyclists 2013b). These cities offer extensive bicycle transportation systems that include trails, bicycle lanes, cycle tracks, bicycle boulevards, directional signage for bicyclists, shared lanes, bike boxes at intersections, and other features like bike share and bicycle stations for convenience and safety. Seattle's bicycle network is an extensive 236 miles, and Portland has created a network of 319 miles traversing the city (Portland 2010a; Seattle 2013f).

These impressive bicycling statistics and networks of bicycle-friendly streets, trails, and connections did not come about by chance. Oregon and Washington have plans and legal frameworks that support bicycling as part of their transportation systems and strong leadership support at federal, state, regional, and local levels of government. The largest cities, Portland and Seattle, also have a history of planning for bicycle transportation, integrating bicycling into land-use planning, setting specific goals, and identifying specific projects across their cities that are necessary to meet those goals. Additionally, increasing bicycling is identified as a key strategy for reducing greenhouse gas emissions at the state and local levels. Seattle's 2013 Climate Action Plan establishes the aggressive goal of tripling bicycling from 2007 levels by 2017 to achieve reductions, and Portland's goal is to have 25 percent of trips in the city being made by bicycle in 2030.

Portland's Bicycle Planning Legacy

Portland may have the longest history of planning for bicycling, starting with its first Bicycle Master Plan in 1973. This first-of-its-kind plan called for 190 miles of new bicycle infrastructure and created a bicycle program within the city's Transportation Bureau (Initiative for Bicycle & Pedestrian Innovation 2010). After reaching the goal set in the 1973 plan, Portland adopted its second Bicycle Master Plan in 1996. This plan also set a very specific and aggressive goal of developing an additional 445 miles of bicycle infrastructure by 2016, the 20-year planning horizon, to implement the city's broader Comprehensive Plan Goal:

> Make the bicycle an integral part of daily life in Portland, particularly for trips of less than five miles, by implementing a bikeway network, providing end-of-trip facilities, improving bicycle/transit integration, encouraging bicycle use, and making bicycling safer. (Portland 1996)

In 2010, Portland revised its Bicycle Master Plan again, taking additional steps and setting even more aggressive goals. The Portland Bicycle Plan for 2030 identified more than $600 million in bicycle infrastructure needs and expanded the goal of constructing 630 miles of new bicycle infrastructure by 2016 to over 900 miles by 2030, the planning horizon, which they appear well on track to accomplish (Portland 2010a). Important recent state legislation provides Oregon cities the authority to establish speed limits on neighborhood streets and will support the neighborhood greenways outlined in Portland's plan (HB 3150; Portland 2011).

Grassroots Planning for Bicycling in Seattle

Although Seattle was later than Portland in adopting its Bicycle Master Plan, the city has a long history of making bicycling improvements in response to needs identified by neighborhoods and community groups. Seattle's 2007 Bicycle Master Plan set two goals for the planning horizon year of 2017: to triple bicycle trips and reduce bicycle crashes by one third. To accomplish these goals, the plan identified 450 specific improvements to infrastructure, in addition to education and enforcement efforts (Seattle 2007).

In 2012, Seattle started an update process to develop a 2014 Bicycle Master Plan, which is focused around neighborhoods and sectors of the city. City leaders specified that this plan include neighborhood greenways, an idea gaining popularity among Seattleites—even residents who do not bicycle (Seattle 2013).

Neighborhood Greenways

These major cities of the Pacific Northwest have embraced the concept of neighborhood greenways. Neighborhood greenways, as defined by the city of Portland, are residential streets with low volumes of auto traffic and low speeds, where bicycle and pedestrians are given priority. Goals include:

- **Reducing auto cut-through**. Speed bumps and traffic diverters discourage drivers who try to avoid busy main streets by cutting through on neighborhood streets.
- **Providing safer bicycling and pedestrian connections.** Pavement markings alert drivers to expect bicyclists; improved crossings and curb ramps make pedestrian mobility easier and safer.

- **Reducing auto speeds**. Speed bumps help slow automobile traffic on greenways.
- **Helping people across our busier streets**. Improved crossings at main streets help people walking and bicycling cross more easily.
- **Guiding people on the route and help get them where they are going**. Markings on the pavement and signage let users know where the greenway goes and informs them of nearby attractions, such as parks and business districts.
- **Providing more "eyes on the street."** More people out on the street bicycling and walking leads to safer streets (Portland 2013c).

Portland has developed 82 miles of neighborhood greenways. Seattle has completed about six miles, but has outlined a plan to develop a network of 244 miles of neighborhood greenways in the 2014 Bicycle Master Plan.

Bicycle Planning in Communities Across the Pacific Northwest—A Smorgasbord of Awesomeness

More than 20 cities in Washington and Oregon have received the Bicycle Friendly designation from the League of American Bicyclists for their accomplishments in improving conditions for biking and walking. A few examples include Ashland, Oregon, recognized for its grassroots bicycle safety education program and Bellingham, Washington, which was recognized for its innovative approaches to bicycle planning and funding. Additionally, Washington County, Oregon, recently completed a Bicycle Facility Design Toolkit that provides a model for county-level bicycle planning in suburban communities.

So Why is the Pacific Northwest a Bicycling Haven?

Part of it appears to be luck—the good fortune to have a beautiful natural environment that draws people outdoors and fosters environmental stewardship. Communities across the Pacific Northwest have also employed smart planning and have citizens and leaders who recognize the connection between transportation, sustainability, and economic vitality. A final important factor is the entrepreneurial nature of Pacific Northwesterners, who are defining and developing a bicycle culture and a bicycle economy all their own.

CHAPTER 21

Energy Efficiency the Cascadia Way

Andrea Petzel, AICP, and Valerie Pacino

Federal funding through the 2009 American Recovery and Reinvestment Act supported pilot programs in Washington and Oregon that explored new models for achieving increased energy efficiency in existing homes. As community energy-efficiency programs, these programs provide approaches that can serve as a model for other cities and energy providers by integrating social equity and workforce development into program design and delivery.

Testing the proposition that a robust and thriving clean economy reaps significant environmental, economic, and social benefits, Seattle's Community Power Works and Oregon's Clean Energy Works have changed the way building owners, their tenants, contractors, utilities, lenders, labor, environmental groups, and the broader community engage in energy efficiency across Cascadia (Figure 21.1 and Figure 21.2).

In April 2010, the U.S. Department of Energy's (DOE) Better Buildings Neighborhood Program awarded Seattle $20 million to pursue a pilot project designed to encourage efficiency upgrades for single-family and multifamily residences, small businesses, hospitals, and large commercial and municipal buildings. The majority of grant funding was directed toward the single-family sector with the goal of encouraging deep energy savings to traditionally underserved communities. The grant was administered by the city's Office of Sustainability and Environment (OSE) under a program called Community Power Works for Home.

Concurrently, the DOE awarded $20 million to Clean Energy Works to fund a statewide initiative in Oregon. Already successful with a pilot project in Portland, the Clean Energy Works program had demonstrated that par-

Figure 21.1. Community Power Works

Figure 21.2. Clean Energy Works

ticipants were willing to undertake deeper upgrades than their counterparts in utility and local energy efficiency programs, and the program moved to scale-up statewide operations.

Together, the two programs shared some significant costs for program design and development. However, each program piloted a number of innovations over their separate grant periods, including suites of incentives and rebates, robust customer service, accessible IT platforms, low-interest financing and repayment options, third-party quality assurance, auditing tools, and approved pools of contractors governed by national model community workforce agreements.

Setting the Bar

The hallmarks of both programs include whole-house retrofits for deep energy savings, active stakeholder involvement, adaptive management, and an emphasis on the community benefits of workforce development.

Deep Energy Savings

Both programs built service-delivery models based on achieving deep energy savings through a whole-house performance-based approach, rather than single-measure efforts. Rebates to home owners were reflected in the overall amount of energy saved, rather than a flat amount for a specific installed measure (such as a ductless heat pump or high-efficiency furnace). DOE standards mandated that all grant recipients achieve 15 percent energy savings across their respective portfolios. Both programs surpassed all expectations by achieving 30 percent average energy savings, with hundreds of homes achieving more than 50 percent energy savings, and some homes achieving as much as 80 percent energy savings.

Active Stakeholder Involvement

Both programs have actively engaged stakeholders, including representatives from local government, labor unions, community organizations, utilities, and contractors, at all levels of program design, operation, and sustainability planning. This engagement process helped program administrators identify and remove barriers to program access for customers, contractors, and other stakeholders who interact with the program.

Adaptive Management

Community Power Works and Clean Energy Works are committed to adaptive management—perhaps their most valuable innovation. Building many systems from the ground up and deploying untested strategies, both programs recognized the value of real-time evaluation and adaptive strategies to ensure resources were allocated best. As systems, tools, and delivery models are deployed, assessed, and refined, the programs demonstrate success by breaking down barriers between evaluators and programs through rapid learning and iterative program monitoring.In addition to energy savings, these community-based energy efficiency programs have supported job creation and economic development by negotiating and piloting robust community workforce agreements called Community High Road Agreements (HRA).

HRAs provide a framework of workforce and community standards, targets, and benefits as summarized below:

- Requirements for contractor participation (e.g., local hire, paying family-supporting wages, and hiring from designated training providers)
- Incentives for meeting specific objectives (e.g., providing health care insurance, employing a diverse workforce, being or contracting with a historically underrepresented businesses, mentoring other contractors)
- Support for approved and emerging contractors (e.g., training and continuing education resources, business classes, business coaching, peer mentoring, access to working capital, and engagement and outreach efforts targeting underrepresented and economically disadvantaged contractors)
- Resources for continuing education and certification to those coming into the home performance industry and to those ready for opportunities for promotion and upward mobility through career pathways and entrepreneurship training

By applying HRA standards, Community Power Works and Clean Energy Works demonstrated that energy efficiency programs can include community benefits through workforce and economic development. Both programs found that HRA standards work well as a flexible, efficient system for assuring quality installations and living-wage jobs. Reporting has been comprehensive, efficient, and accurate. The model and associated reporting and enforcement mechanisms have solid buy-in from contractors. Consequently, verified compliance rates are close to 100 percent.

Results and Long-Term Viability

With nearly 5,700 homes upgraded, Community Power Works and Clean Energy Works have demonstrated that the program model can create dramatic energy savings, provide economic and social benefits, and be replicated.

As Community Power Works transitioned from its pilot phase into a public-private partnership with a long-term business model, Clean Energy Works and its team of local partners was selected to take over the planning process. Clean Energy Works worked closely with OSE and Seattle City Light, the city's municipally owned utility, to develop a funding, management, and streamlined operations model to take Community Power Works into the future. The program will expand beyond the city's borders throughout Seattle City Light's utility territory to offer service and financing to many additional single-family homes.

Conclusion

Both pilot programs demonstrate the success of a community-based approach to increase community engagement, reduce energy use, and build the economic and workforce base of the community. While it remains to be seen what the programs can do without grant funding support, the programs see potential for regional partnerships with other community energy programs. Such regional partnerships can create economies of scale, leverage the experience and resources of a greater number of partners, and help create consistency and predictability for large regional partners.

CHAPTER 22

From Table to Tank: Biodiesel in Washington

Eric J. Howard

Standing on a corner in the new urbanist community of Snoqualmie, you may catch an unexpected whiff of french fries. Taking pride in its efforts to be sustainable and resilient, this city has formed a unique partnership with the Snoqualmie Tribe, King County Metro, and Snoqualmie Valley Transit to use waste cooking oil to power local transit services.

Incorporated in 1903, the city of Snoqualmie is located 25 miles east of Seattle in the foothills of the Cascade Mountains. Extensive development in the early 2000s reshaped this small town of 1,500 people to a growing city of over 12,000 people, a large share of that new population from Microsoft and other eastside tech firms (Snoqualmie 2014). By 2008 the Snoqualmie Tribe embraced the opportunity to serve that new population and a steady stream of visitors with a full service casino, including six restaurants and cafes.

In Washington, tribes developing casinos on reservation lands are required to work with the State Gambling Commission, adjacent cities, and the county to develop a State Compact that commits two percent of their net revenue to mitigate impacts to the local area and region. For the Snoqualmie casino, discussions led to a partnership in which waste cooking oil (from french fries and other cooking) at the tribe's facilities is used to power biodiesel passenger vans. Originally serving simply as a local dial-a-ride, with King County Metro's expertise the system now provides shuttle services to a large region of the Snoqualmie Valley communities (Larson 2014).

Snoqualmie Mayor Matt Larson explains: "The city's role in this process was to bring the parties together and to help facilitate the discussions. We provide parking facilities for the buses when they are not in use and regularly use the buses for touring visiting dignitaries. Most importantly, the waste oil is used productively and the buses provide great public transportation in an area that is underserved by other transit services" (Larson 2014).

What Is Biodiesel?

The Snoqualmie case exemplifies what has been, in the state of Washington, a fervent movement in policy and practice toward the adoption of biodiesel.

Biodiesel is a type of diesel fuel that is made by processing triacylglycerols, or fatty acids, which are found in vegetable oils and animal fats (Encinar, González, and Rodriguez-Reinares 2005; Knothe, Van Gerpen, and Krahl 2005). Waste fryer grease and clean vegetable oils, like canola oil, are typically used in this process (Figure 22.1). These fatty acids are broken down through a chemical reaction called transesterification. This involves mixing lye (or some other type of base catalyst) with methanol to form methoxide, which is mixed with the triacylglycerol (Knothe, Van Gerpen, and Krahl 2005). The

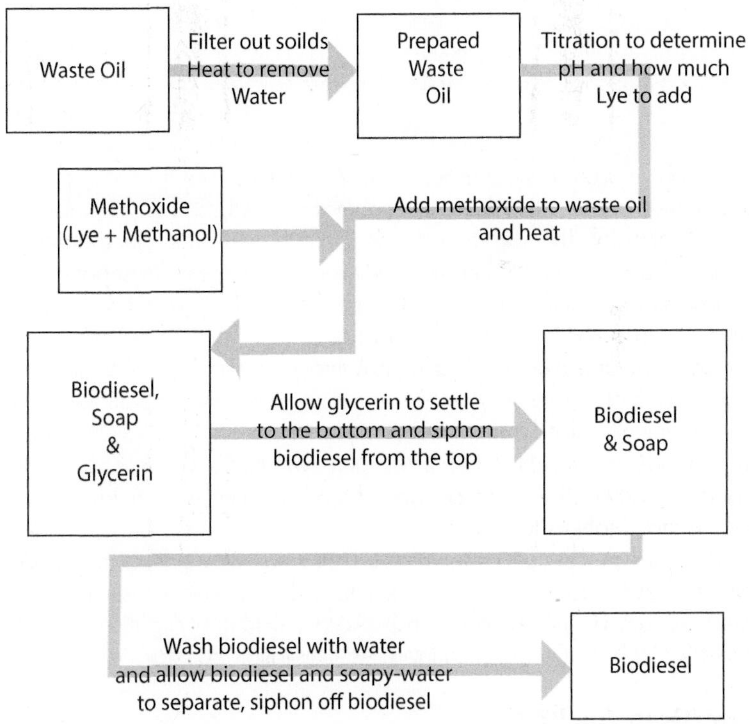

Figure 22.1. Biodiesel production process (Source: Information from Encinar, González, and Rodriguez-Reinares 2005 and Knothe, Van Gerpen, and Krahl 2005; figure created by Eric Howard)

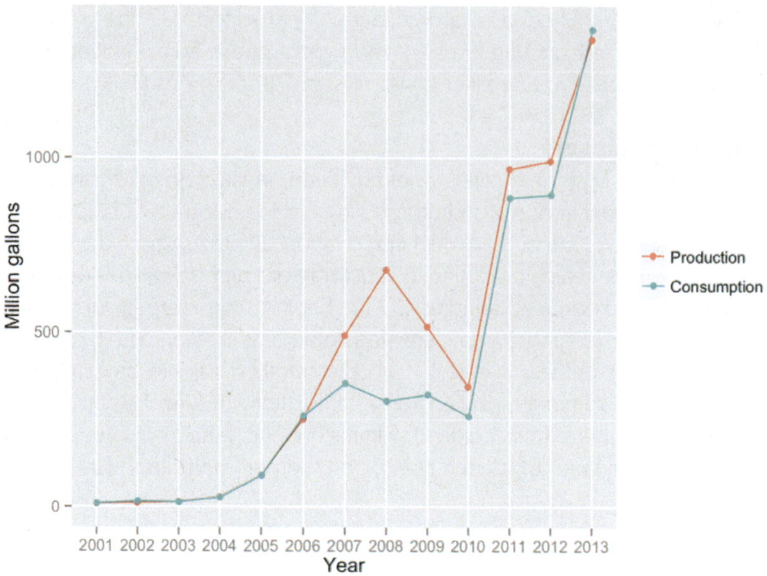

Figure 22.2. U.S. biodiesel production and consumption (Source: U.S. Energy Information Administration 2014a)

amount of lye used in the reaction is based on the pH of the triacylglycerol used in the process, while the amount of methanol is based on the volume of the triacylglycerol. The result is a mixture that can be used in place of normal diesel fuel and glycerin. After the biodiesel and the glycerin separate, the biodiesel is washed to remove any excess soap and is then ready to use as fuel in a diesel vehicle or for home heating.

Commercially, biodiesel is available through a select set of suppliers for home heating and other uses, and at a few pumps for use in automobiles. Biodiesel is typically mixed with normal diesel for commercial use in automobiles. These blends are typically labeled with acronyms that have the letter B at the beginning followed by the percentage of biodiesel they contain (Knothe, Van Gerpen, and Krahl 2005).

Biodiesel production in the United States has grown from nine million gallons in 2001 to 1,359 million gallons in 2013, and consumption has increased from 10 million gallons in 2001 to 1,404 million gallons in 2013 (Figure 22.2) (U.S. Energy Information Administration 2014a).

How 'Green' Is It?

The sustainability of biodiesel is directly related to the feedstock, or source of triacyclglycerol, used in the chemical reaction. If waste fryer grease is used then a waste product is being recycled into something useful. If virgin materials are used, the long-term sustainability of the fuel is not as promising, as would be the case if the feedstock were a common food crop such as soybeans.

Regardless of the feedstock, biodiesel burns more cleanly than regular diesel fuel. A study conducted by the National Renewable Energy Laboratory found that a B20 blend of biodiesel had 16 percent lower particulate emissions and 17 percent lower carbon monoxide emissions when compared to standard diesel fuel (McCormick et al. 2006). Additionally this study found that B20 had 12 percent lower hydrocarbon emissions, and no significant changes in nitrous oxide emissions.

Biodiesel is not perfect. Some studies suggest that it may increase nitrous oxide emissions (Hajbabaei et al. 2012), and it is dependent on readily available renewable feedstocks. Also, the clog point of biodiesel produced from waste grease is approximately 48 degrees Fahrenheit. Below this temperature the biodiesel needs to be blended with other fuels to prevent the fuel filters from getting clogged (Knothe, Van Gerpen, and Krahl 2005). Additionally, biodiesel production needs to be done in a safe manner in a well-ventilated place. In the production process the combination of lye and methanol produces methoxide, a neurotoxin, and can be harmful if inhaled. However, biodiesel does provide significant air quality gains over standard diesel fuel.

Washington's Supportive Biodiesel Policies

Washington currently ranks as the number two state in the nation in terms of the number different of laws, regulations, and incentives that address and support biodiesel production and consumption with 17 polices or programs, just one short of Virginia's 18. (U.S. Department of Energy 2014d). These policies include four prominent tax incentives (U.S. Department of Energy 2014b):

- A distribution tax exemption on retail fuels sales and use taxes on biodiesel blends of 20 percent or more
- A tax deduction for businesses involved in the sale or distribution of biodiesel
- A production tax exemption on the land, buildings, and equipment used in the manufacturing of biodiesel, including feedstocks
- A feedstock tax exemption, which is a state sales and use tax exemption available for the collection and processing of waste vegetable oil for use in biodiesel production for personal use

Beyond tax incentives, Washington has a set of policies that promote biodiesel production and use. Renewable Fuels Standards require that at least two percent of all diesel sold in the state be renewable. This standard will increase to five percent if the Washington State Department of Agriculture finds that enough in-state feedstock production capacity exists to meet anticipated demand. The state also requires that at least 20 percent of the diesel used by state agency vehicles be biodiesel. Finally, Washington has an alternative fuel use requirement that state agencies must use 100 percent biofuels or electricity to operate publicly owned vehicles by June 2015 (U.S. Department of Energy 2014a). Because of these policies the production and use of biodiesel will likely continue to grow for years to come.

Uses of Biodiesel in Washington State

Biodiesel is driving the green future forward in Washington, and Snoqualmie is not the only example worth mentioning. Biodiesel is used as a replacement for traditional diesel fuel in a variety of applications throughout Washington State, including home heating and transportation. Washington currently has 38 different retailers that sell biodiesel (National Biodiesel Board 2014). A number of commercial fleets are also using biodiesel in the their daily operations. Essential Baking Company—a local bakery that supplies a variety of baked goods to restaurants, grocers, and cafes in Seattle—has been using biodiesel to fuel its delivery vans for the past eight years. According to a tracking system provided by Propel, Essential Baking Company's biodiesel supplier, the company reduced its carbon dioxide emissions by 320,000 pounds and saved approximately 400 barrels of oil between 2006 and 2012 by using biodiesel (Sutor 2012).

Who knew those tasty fried foods would be giving us alternative transport?

CHAPTER 23

Process Makes Perfect? Replacing the Great Alaskan Way Viaduct

Ian Nunley

Scheduled for completion in 2017, the new State Route 99 tunnel under the heart of downtown Seattle will bring to an end a 20-year debate about what to do with one of the Pacific Northwest's most important infrastructure systems. The 1.7-mile-long underground tunnel will replace a double-decker arterial that has lined Seattle's waterfront since 1953. How did Seattle arrive at this alternative and why has it taken nearly two decades for a viable substitute to take shape? The answer to this question is one intrinsic to this city and its political culture. Known colloquially as the "Seattle Process," the term exemplifies the historically methodical and incremental nature of political deliberation, public involvement, and dialogue surrounding major municipal projects in this region (Follansbee 2012).

Origins of the Viaduct

In the early 1900s, Seattle was a small but steadily growing city of 80,000 with an economy focusing on timber, shipbuilding, and trade in and out of the local port (Washington State Department of Transportation 2011a). The Great Northern Railway extended to Seattle in 1884, cementing the city's role as a major player in the movement of goods (Ott 2011a). World War II brought a new economic boom to the city. By 1939, workers began streaming into Seattle for the shipbuilding, manufacturing, and other jobs supporting the American war effort. Boeing became a leading manufacturer of airplanes and a staple of employment in the region. Along with the population growth and economic boom came problems of traffic congestion that hampered local connectivity. Initial planning for the viaduct began in the 1930s, but the Great Depression, national focus on the war effort, and a lack of funding delayed development of the project (Washington State Department of Transportation 2011b).

Following World War II, the rise of suburbanization and a burgeoning autocentric consumer culture sent many cities scrambling to improve local infrastructure in order to meet increasing demand, and Seattle was not immune to the movement. The city and many of its neighbors in the Puget Sound region began recognizing a need for freeways to appropriately accommodate growth and establish a more robust regional economy (Ott 2011b). Freeway extensions reached out to suburbs located to the north, south, and east of the city, representing the first calculated attempts at truly cooperative regional planning in the Pacific Northwest.

Creating a north-south thoroughfare expediting the delivery of goods out of the Port of Seattle was paramount, linking the city with the industrial hub of Tacoma to the south, rapidly expanding suburban landscapes to the north, and relieving severe traffic congestion. A comprehensive traffic study completed in 1947 proposed two major north-south freeways, with an elevated double-deck, six-lane highway running along the Elliot Bay waterfront (Washington State Department of Transportation 2011b). The viaduct project was given developmental priority because a large portion of the proposed

Figure 23.1. Alaskan Way Viaduct, 1951: A view northward, with old train tracks in the foreground and pillars of the new viaduct in the background

route had already been built along Aurora Avenue and remaining segments were located on the right-of-way of the already existing Alaskan Way and old railway lines. The 1947 study also proposed a second major north-south arterial, which would not take shape for more than a decade with the development of Interstate 5 along the eastern section of the city (Kueter 2001).

Once plans were finalized in 1947, the city passed a resolution promising nearly $1.5 million in funding in addition to the nearly $2 million pledged from the state development fund and $1.5 million in allocations from the Federal Aid Highway Bill of 1944 (Ott 2011c). Despite the passage of adequate funding, many local businesses and architects continued to have reservations, including compensation for the loss of surface parking, impacts on future development, and the perceived damaging aesthetic caused by the creation of a concrete leviathan fencing in valuable real estate along the shoreline. Ongoing debate and concerns delayed the start of construction until the spring of 1950. The first section opened to automobile traffic in April 1953 (Figure 23.1) (Ott 2011c). With the completion of the last on-ramp along Columbia Street in 1966, nearly 30 years of planning and 16 years of construction finally drew to a close.

Nisqually Necessitates Change

Over the next 30 years, the Alaskan Way Viaduct became an essential system for port and industrial traffic through the greater Duwamish, Ballard Locks, and the Aurora Avenue corridor, as well as a major route for commuters to downtown and surrounding neighborhoods (Figure 23.2) (Holden 2011). Questions about the long-term viability of the Alaskan Way Viaduct arose when the similarly designed Cyprus Street Viaduct in Oakland, California, took on heavy damage during with the 1989 Loma Prieta earthquake (James et al. 2006). A follow-up study in 1995 from Washington State Department of Transportation (WSDOT) engineers raised concerns about the foundational integrity and overall resiliency of the Viaduct (Kramer and Eberhard 1995).

These fears were realized on February 8, 2001, when the 6.8 magnitude Nisqually earthquake, with an epicenter situated just south of downtown Seattle, shook the entire Puget Sound along the Cascadia subduction zone. More than 400 injuries were reported throughout the city and a number of unreinforced concrete and masonry structures showed heavy damage, including many of the support columns running along the viaduct's double-decker structure. WSDOT took immediate action by investing $14.5 million in emergency funds to rehabilitate the viaduct and its supporting seawall (U.S. Department of Transportation et al. 2009). These funds were not meant to solve the structural instability problem, but rather act as a temporary remedy until a more permanent solution could be analyzed, agreed upon, and implemented. Our fair city spent the next decade in public and political debate over the issue, a slog wholly demonstrative of the "Seattle Process."

Figure 23.2: Alaskan Way Viaduct, 2008: The view southward

A comprehensive resolution for replacing the crippled viaduct required coordination and collaboration between transportation agencies at the local, state, and federal levels. Seattle assumed financial responsibility for replacing the viaduct and the damaged supporting seawall, and WSDOT took charge of assessing policy alternatives and associated environmental impacts (Washington State Department of Transportation 2009). An environmental impact statement (EIS) conducted in 2004 identified the "cut-and-cover" tunnel option as the preferred alternative. This option would allow for north-south movement of freight and cargo, provide access points to downtown, and open up over two miles of newly accessible land that had been long hidden under the shadow of the viaduct. However, a second round of environmental impact assessments carried out in 2006 raised concerns about budgetary implications and the ability to address potential cost overruns associated with the project (Washington State Department of Transportation 2006). Unsure of how best to move forward, local and state leaders, including Gov. Christine Gregoire, put decision-making power in the hands of Seattle voters by calling for a public advisory vote for both alternatives. The general public showed little support for either option, voting down both by an overwhelming majority (U.S. Department of Transportation, Washington State Department of Transportation, and City of Seattle 2011). Just like that, Seattle and its rapidly deteriorating infrastructure system were back at square one.

Collaboration, Partnership, and Alternatives

Seattle residents took their elected officials to task, resoundingly showing their disapproval for the first set of proposed alternatives. Gov. Gregoire and other elected officials were forced to regroup and began developing new processes for collaboration, communication, and public participation (Washington State Department of Transportation, King County, and City of Seattle 2009). The governor called for the formation of a Stakeholder Advisory Committee, comprised of individuals representing various economic, social, and community interests associated with the project. Gov. Gregoire, King County official Ron Sims, and Seattle Mayor Greg Nickels took on the task of formulating a set of guiding principles for the collaborative planning process. The six guidelines included maintaining fiscal responsibility, improving public safety, enhancing public accessibility to the downtown waterfront, improving efficiency in the movement of goods and people, ensuring environmental sustainability, and supporting local, regional, and state economies.

With principles in hand, the 29-member committee started by creating a set of criteria for evaluating the relative effectiveness of each proposed alternative in meeting the guiding principles (Litman 2014). They also considered the relative impact of each alternative in terms of the environment, mobility, connectivity, and equity. With more comprehensive metrics, coupled with increased public involvement, the committee moved forward with three possible scenarios for replacing the Alaskan Way Viaduct: a new elevated structure similar to the original viaduct, a comprehensive plan incorporating surface street improvements with increased capacity for public transit and Interstate 5, and a bored tunnel option.

Alternative 1: A New Elevated Structure

In this scenario, the original viaduct would be demolished and replaced with a more seismically sound elevated structure. While generally unpopular with committee members, this alternative remained in consideration because it maintained and improved established levels of traffic mobility with a palatable price tag. However, the elevated structure would continue acting as a barrier to the waterfront while generating numerous negative externalities, such as noise pollution and diminished property values. Seen as the least desirable of the three remaining alternatives, the elevated structure option was kept largely as an element for comparison with the other two scenarios.

Alternative 2: Comprehensive Surface Street Improvements and Increased Transit Capacity

Under this proposal, the viaduct would be razed, with the resulting capacity loss counterbalanced by a comprehensive set of smaller scale infrastructure improvements (Ott 2011d). State Route 99 would be converted into a couplet with three automobile lanes and one bicycle lane running north along Western

Avenue and southbound traffic moving along the old Alaskan Way. The proposal also recommended a number of transit infrastructure improvements aimed at improving existing routes to Seattle's central neighborhoods and regional connections to nearby suburbs (Ott 2011d). The proposal also called for the expansion of Interstate 5 to include a new northbound travel lane and numerous additional surface street improvements.

This proposal drew wide acclaim from the committee for a variety of reasons. By focusing on multimodal improvements, the proposal supported horizontal equity, spreading the cost and benefits over a wide variety of users. Pedestrian, bicycle, and automobile systems would each receive significant improvements to their carrying capacity, accessibility, and connectivity within the downtown landscape. Furthermore, this option carried the cheapest total construction cost with an estimated $2.8 billion price tag (Seattle City Council 2006). While the diminished capacity of State Route 99 would increase travel time for traffic continuing through the city and the couplet design made waterfront accessibility a major challenge, this option gained resounding support from the committee due to the other benefits.

Alternative 3: The Bored Tunnel

The final alternative considered by the committee featured a new twin-bored tunnel. The twin formation would provide a set of northbound lanes running on top of southbound lanes, all encapsulated within a single tunnel. (Washington State Department of Transportation, King County, and City of Seattle 2009). The subterranean bored tunnel alternative would maximize expansion of the public realm along the waterfront while maintaining capacity and mobility for humans and freight. The tunnel option would also allow the viaduct to remain open during construction, thus allowing traffic to continue unimpeded throughout the lengthy process. So what prohibited the committee from throwing its full support behind the tunnel? There remained the matter of the approximately $4.50 billion price tag associated with such a development (Seattle City Council 2006). By far the most expensive of allthe options considered, the truly massive endeavor shattered previous funding allocation options and the guiding principle of generating a fiscally responsible alternative.

The Decision

At the end of their yearlong deliberation, the committee brought forth its final recommendation. It called for funding for the planning and design of the comprehensive surface street/transit option while also providing for further economic and environmental review of the bored-tunnel alternative. In spite of these recommendations, in 2009, elected officials unilaterally advanced the bored-tunnel option without future study. The tunnel was to be combined with some surface street and transit improvements outlined in the second alternative, but the multimodal investments would fall short of the full recommendations from the second option. The state legislature quickly approved $2.8 billion in funding for the project (McGann 2008). The Port of Seattle, King County, and the city government pledged a further $1 billion in funds, but the project still remained roughly $400 million short of the estimated total cost of $4.50 billion. To meet this budgetary shortfall, a decision was made to institute tolling provisions for accessing the tunnel with rates set by the Washington State Transportation Commission (Washington State Department of Transportation 2012).

While demolition of sections of the viaduct began in 2008, physical boring of the tunnel did not begin until five years later. Many in Seattle were infuriated that the matter was not put up for public referendum, and that responsibility for cost overruns associated with the project would lie explicitly with Seattle and its inhabitants. This, coupled with a plethora of lawsuits, delayed implementation of the project. It was not until the summer of 2013 that the tunnel-boring machine took its first bite out of Seattle ground.

Designed by the Japan-based Hitachi Zosen Corporation, the $80 million machine—nicknamed "Bertha"after Seattle's first female mayor, Bertha Landes—is the largest machine of its kind in the world (Paanenen 2010). Weighing in at roughly 7,000 tons, the 326-foot-long machine includes a cutter head stretching 54 feet in diameter, and requires a crew of 25 to operate. Starting at the south tunnel portal near Seattle's SoDo neighborhood, the machine was slated to drill at a rate of 30 to 70 feet per day until it reached the north portal exit at the intersection of Sixth Avenue and Harrison Street. In total, engineers estimated that Bertha would dig through nearly two miles of underground dirt and debris in creating the new tunnel. At the time of this writing, however, Bertha had been shut down for more than a year due to a blockage identified as a steel pipe fragment left from a 2002 groundwater survey. Seattle Tunnel Partners have completed excavation of a 120-foot-deep shaft that will allow engineers to bring the cutter head to the surface and make the necessary repairs to get Bertha up and running again. The final completion date for the project has been revised several times and is currently projected to be August 2017.

When finally completed, the tunnel will finally spell the end for the Alaskan Way Viaduct and Seattleites may, at long last, reclaim accessibility to the downtown waterfront and Elliott Bay. While final designs for the new waterfront have yet to be completed, conceptual planning and design includes bountiful new public spaces, high-density residential development, and the expansion of commercial enterprise (Waterfront Design Honored 2013). Current estimates indicate waterfront redevelopment will likely continue through 2021 (or more), a full 20 years after the Nisqually earthquake shook the Pacific Northwest.

CHAPTER 24

Preserving Seattle Grunge in the Pike/Pine Neighborhood

Manish Chalana

In November 2007, the 500 block of East Pine Street in the Pike/Pine section of Seattle's Capitol Hill was demolished to make way for a new luxury residential development. This block had housed an eclectic set of small local businesses, including bars, restaurants, and shops, in a series of brightly painted one-story spaces, with a three-story affordable-housing apartment building at one end. Of the seven businesses displaced, only four relocated in the neighborhood, one of which has since shut; the others simply closed shop for good. As the owner of the bar Man Ray summarized: "You just can't take the spirit of the place and try to transplant it" (Barnett 2006a).

After demolition and before new construction, the Great Recession hit, and the property languished for three years as a parking lot. Finally, the Terravita Luxury Apartments began construction, opening in 2012 (Figure 24.1). Offering 108 units at rents nearly twice the city's average, the six-story building maximizes the site's development potential with monolithic massing. The ground floor contains two larger businesses (a fitness center and upscale bar) in place of the previous seven. In all of these details, the redevelopment of the 500 block is representative of the types of new construction and spatial and social changes occurring in the neighborhood.

Many residents were outraged, seeing it as the final straw in a long process of gentrification that had been erasing Pike/Pine's campy and grungy local flavor. Many felt that the neighborhood's entire character, unique in Seattle and rare nationwide, was rapidly being replaced with simply a denser version of "everywhere else." This concern played out in countless blog postings, newspapers, and magazine articles. A neighborhood resident created a "Requiem

Figure 24.1. The Terravita Luxury Apartments in 2014, showing its monolithic six-story massing

for a Block" website, documenting personal histories from displaced businesses (Barnett 2006b). In summer 2009, neighborhood artists held a remembrance for the lost block—described as the "little section of heaven that was so violently ripped out of our hands"—with large screens flashing scenes from the lost social spaces (Carder 2009). Another group, People's Parking Lot, created a temporary art installation and community garage sale on the site as part of a larger effort to reclaim open spaces for public uses (Figure 24.2) (Harris 2013).

Of course, there are varying perspectives on the type of urban transformations occurring in Pike/Pine. The city and developers argue that they are promoting a form of sustainable development that concentrates growth into urban neighborhoods and prevents sprawl. Developers describe themselves as partners in perpetuating neighborhood character by introducing new residents who value its unique amenities. For example, Terravita touts proximity to coffeehouses as a major draw, listing local businesses on their website and on a six-foot-tall map in their leasing office (Terravita 2014). Ironically, the Press Condos across the street used similar promotional maps that listed the now-lost businesses of the 500 block that Terravita replaced; indeed, by one account half of the businesses on these maps were soon demolished (Barnett 2006a).

The frustration with Pike/Pine's rapid transformation, and particularly of the 500 block, caught the city's attention. In 2009, under the leadership of city council member Tom Rasmussen, the existing Pike/Pine Overlay District

Figure 24.2. Using the 500 block of East Pine for a community garage sale in 2010

was expanded and renamed the Pike/Pine Conservation Overlay District (PPCOD), with the goals of protecting the historic built environment and maintaining and encouraging local and small businesses (Figure 24.3) (Seattle 2009). In exchange for protecting historic fabric, developers could avail themselves of zoning incentives such as increased floor area ratio. A second ordinance was adopted in 2010, revising the neighborhood design guidelines for height, bulk, and scale to better achieve preservation goals (Seattle 2010b). The third phase in 2011 created a smaller conservation core zone within the PPCOD and established a Transfer of Development Potential program to divert air rights outside the conservation core, but within the PPCOD (Seattle 2011b).

This set of ordinances is unique in Seattle in the degree to which it explicitly identifies protection of neighborhood character beyond architectural history as the primary outcome. Seattle has eight other designated historic districts, in which maintaining historic significance and integrity of contributing buildings are the primary goals. But for Pike/Pine, Seattle opted to create its first conservation overlay district, following the lead of cities like nearby Portland (Miller 2004). In this approach, historic preservation is seen not only as an end in itself but also as a "way to maintain space that is affordable

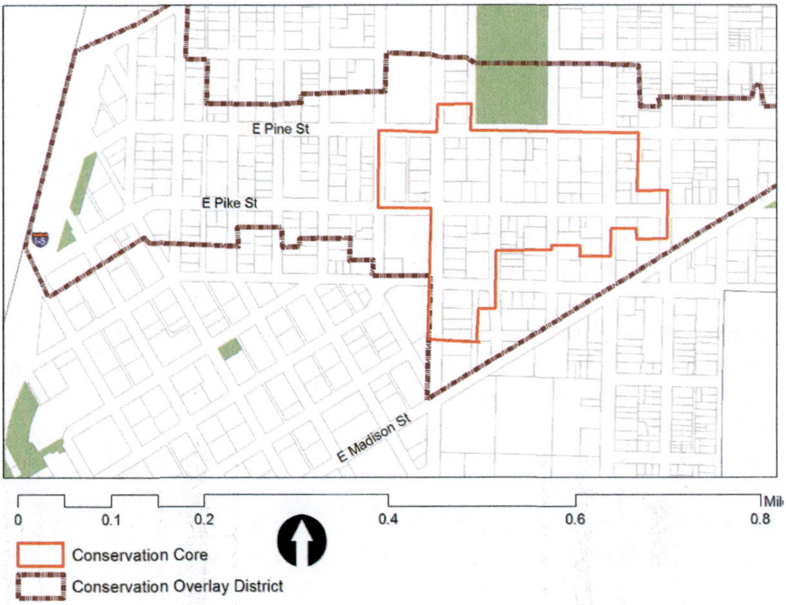

Figure 24.3. Pike/Pine Conservation Overlay District showing the newly designated Conservation Core

and conducive to small business uses." (Lund Consulting 2008). In addition to the built form itself, the PPCOD ordinance explicitly attempts to maintain the area's "gritty and authentic" uses, "bohemian and alternative" nightlife and culture, and socioeconomic and sexual diversity.

However, despite explicit recognition of Pike/Pine's unique neighborhood character, the conservation overlay ordinance is operationalized largely in terms of spatial characteristics of the built form. These are based upon the neighborhood's specific history, dating to its development in the 1920s as an auto-row district of car showrooms, garages, and auto-parts stores. The most common built form included high-ceilinged showrooms with large display windows and wide-span garage doors. Street-facing facades were carefully crafted with bricks and terra cotta to convey strength and reliability. Despite auto-oriented services, the area evolved into a varied, dense urban form in a walkable environment by the 1940s. With mid-century suburbanization, Pike/Pine's auto businesses started relocating. By the 1970s, Capitol Hill began emerging as a gay neighborhood, with Pike/Pine developing associated bars, bathhouses, and social services. This repurposing was aided by the auto-row structures' unique open floor plans, which were easily divisible into separate businesses along the bays. The result was an area in which small, eclectic local businesses could locate at reasonable rents, find clientele, and gain acceptance. The area retained its broad "countercultural" flavor throughout the '80s, and became one of the incubators for the music scene that went global in the 1990s under the apt name "grunge." However, by the 21st century the neighborhood began shifting directions. Inspired by cities like Vancouver, British Columbia, Mayor Greg Nickels' administration introduced a new Center City Strategy that encouraged inner-city densification through various zoning changes. This is the context for the demise of the 500 block, fueling the backlash that inspired the PPCOD's creation.

The ordinances of the PPCOD have led to some successful cases of adaptive reuse of auto-row buildings that maintain the fine-grained urbanism and bring new uses to the neighborhood. In this category is Elliott Bay Books, formerly an anchor business within Seattle's first historic district (Pioneer Square). Relocated to a Pike/Pine warehouse in 2010, the bookstore and the quality of the restoration have contributed to creating a broadly popular destination retail space. Another example is the Melrose Market, which relocated into a formerly empty 22,000-square-foot warehouse. This was fully renovated and divided into several smaller tenant spaces, almost all of them specialty food and drink vendors. Care was taken to integrate the building with the street through design elements and a sidewalk cafe. The project demonstrates how an auto-row building can be updated to current building and seismic codes while maintaining its original features.

Other more complex cases involve a core preservation project with some demolition and integration of new construction, An examples is the Trace Lofts, which converted a former commercial building into residential space with two additional setback penthouse floors built above and new mixed use buildings adjacent. Just as common, however, have been various "facadism" cases retaining a minimum of street-facing facades, employing the same incentives through the PPCOD as preserving the entire structure. The Packard Building project is one example, highlighting its preservation story in promotional materials while simultaneously being selected as one of six "horrible facadism renovations" worldwide in the *International Business Times* for the trivial amount of preservation involved (Smith 2012).

Other neighborhood sites have seen complete demolition and new construction. The most famous case is the Bullitt Center, purported to be the "greenest building in the world." Seattle has been promoting "super-green building" through its 2030 Challenge, prioritizing and streamlining the green permitting program. A six-story structure with 50,000 square feet of space, the Bullitt Center is set to meet the Living Building Challenge—the world's highest sustainability measure. While the Bullitt Center is undoubtedly a major advancement in sustainable development practice and an important neighborhood addition, it did displace a popular, affordable watering hole, CC

Attle's, which served as an informal community center for the city's large "bear" community of gay men outside the generally youth-oriented and body-conscious world of gay nightlife.

Pike/Pine has thus continued to see a host of changes to its physical and social form since the introduction of the PPCOD ordinances. While some adaptive reuses have successfully maintained historic structures, many price out the existing community. In turn, this is fueling further loss of other businesses on the "grungier" side, including a bathhouse, used record stores, and other bars. In 2012, Travelers—which sold an eclectic assemblage of goods from India and contained a chai house and popular gathering space for a wide cross section of area residents—moved out, no longer able to afford the rising rents. As one blog poster summarized:

> Oh no. I am so sad to see this go, although the writing has very clearly been on the wall for ages. Lovely, delicious, individual, unfashionable and slightly shambolic Travellers has no place in the bright new yuppie future of Capitol Hill. (Carder 2012)

In other words, for many it feels like the story of the 500 block is repeating itself regularly, regardless of the PPCOD.

The Seattle City Council remains aware of the ongoing issues, and is making further efforts to address them. For example, they recently instituted plans to increase demands on developers who want to utilize the full zoning incentives, requiring projects to partially retain all character-defining structures on the project site (Seattle 2013). However, developers are lobbying to block the new rules, arguing that they would discourage redevelopment, creating "adverse physical and aesthetic impacts" resulting from "vacant lots and deteriorated buildings" (Cohen 2013).

Ultimately, however, it is not clear to what degree this—or any other conservation ordinance—can preserve something as elusive and subjective as neighborhood flavor. To borrow the words of Berlin mayor Klaus Wowereit, Pike/Pine has long been "poor but sexy." Its poor-but-sexy businesses are now mostly being replaced by others that are still small scale and independent (as encouraged by the ordinances), but rich and trendy. On paper, then, they fulfill the classic criteria for maintaining neighborhood character. And this is indeed a big step forward relative to past gentrification in other neighborhoods that led to an influx of large-scale national chains. Nevertheless, the changes are still, in many residents' eyes, taking away all that makes the neighborhood classically Seattle.

The city has shown its willingness to listen to the community vision and to revise its ordinances to better achieve this vision. It remains unclear whether these changes will be able to keep up with the rapid pace of development and retain the mix of ages and scales necessary for building "that illusive synthesis known as urban character," as described by Ada Louise Huxtable (2008). What is certain, though, is that Seattle's Pike/Pine corridor will be a crucial place for urban preservation planners to watch for the next decade and beyond.

CHAPTER 25

A Tale of Three Cities on the Road to Smart Green Growth

Julie Kriegh, Nancy Rottle, Hillary Pritchett, and Cayce James

Three cities in the Pacific Northwest independently recognized the need for growth and rejuvenation in each of their downtown and commercial centers. Their similar desires were to promote economic viability, ecological sustainability, and housing affordability, as well as to highlight the unique character inherent in each individual town center. In response, city planners sought planning tools designed to achieve desired urban form incorporating green features, accountability to community goals, and predictability for developers to spur development. For all three cities—Bainbridge, Edmonds, and Burlington, Washington—integrating sustainable urban form with the Northwest's natural environment was foundational.

The authors of this chapter have been involved in planning activities with these communities sequentially over five years. Consequently, each plan has benefited iteratively from its precursor. Therefore, we are uniquely positioned to describe the planning processes, public engagement opportunities, recommendations, and comparative outcomes related to the processes. We are also able to distill lessons learned on the road to implementing smart green growth.

Each town has included public open space, housing affordability, and green building and infrastructure strategies in its overarching definition of "sustainable" community goals. Because each town has prioritized distinct goals and utilized different planning approaches, their stories are unique while parallel. Table 25.1 shows the distinctions between the three cities by summarizing the community processes of Bainbridge, Edmonds, and Burlington as well as various features of the cities' smart growth planning approaches and their particular requirements.

TABLE 25.1. Cities of Bainbridge, Edmonds, and Burlington: Smart Growth Planning Comparison

Planning Code Comparison	Bainbridge 2009–2013	Edmonds 2011–2013	Burlington 2013
Intent	To promote: innovative housing design and diversity and housing affordability with increased environmentally sustainable development	To promote: local and regional gateway; vibrant compact mixed use development; economic strength; increased ecological function; environmentally sustainable development; and housing affordability	To promote: local and regional connectivity; vibrant compact mixed use development; economic strength; increased ecological function; environmentally sustainable development; and housing affordability
Code	Housing Design Demonstration Program–Housing Diversity Program	Special District Form Based Code: Westgate and Five Corners	Comprehensive Plan update
District	Winslow Downtown District	Special Districts: Westgate and Five Corners neighborhoods	Downtown District, Commercial Core, Gages Slough Corridor and Drainage Basin, and Skagit River Park
Population	23,000	40,000	8,500
Area	65 square miles	18.4 square miles	4.4 square miles
Increased Connectivity and Transportation Options (Multimodal)	Pedestrian and bike trails encouraged	Enhanced mult-modal transportation connectivity is encouraged	Enhanced multimodal transportation connectivity is encouraged locally within city limits and regionally in Skagit County, the business community and the city are considering partnering to develop a trolley loop
Sustainable High Performance Buildings	Requirements vary with developmental tier	Required levels and incentivized levels for LEED, Passive House, Built Green, and Evergreen Sustainable Development	Encouraged
Green Stormwater Infrastructure Requirement	Requirements vary with developmental tier	Required levels and incentivized levels	Demonstration strategies are being developed and installed throughout the city as GSI and green wayfinding techniques

TABLE 25.1. **Cities of Bainbridge, Edmonds, and Burlington: Smart Growth Planning Comparison**

Planning Code Comparison	Bainbridge 2009–2013	Edmonds 2011–2013	Burlington 2013
Public Open Space, Trails, and Plazas	Requirements vary with developmental tier	Required levels and incentivized levels	Public park and plaza to be developed by the city as a demonstration project
Life Space Building Methodology	No	Yes	Yes
Housing Affordability Component	Requirements vary with developmental tier for % of affordable units, range of unit sizes, and number of different unit types	Requirements regulated by a range of unit sizes, and number of different unit types	City is actively working with area nonprofits and Skagit Valley Housing Autority to provide affordable housing units
Public Participation Process	Public hearings at planning commission and city council as well as a task force with local citizens	Extensive public process including multiple public forums led by the UW Green Futures Lab, public online survey, public polling, day-long workshop with PNW area design professionals, and public hearings at planning commission and city council	Extensive public process including multiple public listening sessions, presentations and forums led by the UW Green Futures Lab, presentations by the Urban Land Institute, and public hearings at planning commission and city council
Plan Adoption	The pilot program has been adopted as a permanent code optional track for dovolopment	Pending adoption, the FBC will become code within the special districts	The plan is slated to be a strategic element of the Comprehensive Plan update
Development Predictability	Low	High	Medium
District SEPA Review Plan	No	No	Yes
Indentify community goals and available utilities for available parcels	No	Yes, through form-based code process	Yes, city is taking the lead on creating a developer's manual for this purpose
Market Study	No	Yes	Yes
Form Based-Codes	No	Yes	No

Source: Kriegh Architecture Studios and Green Futures Lab, University of Washington, Seattle

City of Bainbridge

> IN ADDITION TO INCENTIVIZING PARTICIPATION IN A GREEN BUILDING CERTIFICATION PROGRAM, THE HOUSING DESIGN DEMONSTRATION PROJECT PROGRAM PROMOTED SMALLER DWELLINGS OF ALL KINDS, BROADENING THE SPECTRUM OF PEOPLE THAT CAN AFFORD TO LIVE IN OUR DOWNTOWN NEIGHBORHOODS.
>
> —JENNIFER SUTTON, AICP, SPECIAL PROJECT PLANNER, CITY OF BAINBRIDGE

Bainbridge, an island west of Seattle with finite land, water, and energy resources, sought an inclusionary code targeting new sustainable residential development proposals in the downtown core from 2009 to 2013. City planners used conventional public processes (focus groups, public hearings, and city council deliberations) for adoption of a pilot program. The program, based on specific qualifying metrics and development incentives, is called the Housing Design and Development Program (HDDP) (Bainbridge 2009, 2013).

The HDDP was initiated to incentivize housing affordability, sustainable buildings and sites, and open space for public benefit. Featuring a menu of development tracks with specific metrics, development is incentivized through increased density allowances. The highest level sustainability track endorses state-of-the-art building practices such as Living Building Challenge, LEED for Homes, and Passive House; innovative site strategies for low-impact site design; public open space, including expanded trail networks; multimodal transportation options; biodiversity offsets; and the promotion of housing diversity. The mid- and lower-level tracks have successive reductions in the above requirements. An applicant's project is scored on a point system to determine the qualifying level and corresponding density bonus.

Ferncliff Village and Grow Community are the first two projects permitted under this code. Ferncliff Village has 24 single-family and 24 multifamily homes (Figure 25.1).

This project garners the highest-level rating and corresponding density bonus due, in large part, because the units are designated affordable for 50 years. This development was scored and permitted with compliance metrics for low-impact site design and LEED for Homes criteria, a network of trails, active and passive public open space, forestland, and community gardens. However, during the Great Recession, the developers chose to comply with minimal sustainable building, site, and open space standards, focusing instead on 100 percent housing affordability.

Although the outcome is laudable for its affordability, it demonstrates the inherent difficulties in follow-through when market forces impact development costs and, as a result, project compliance with permit stipulations. Many of

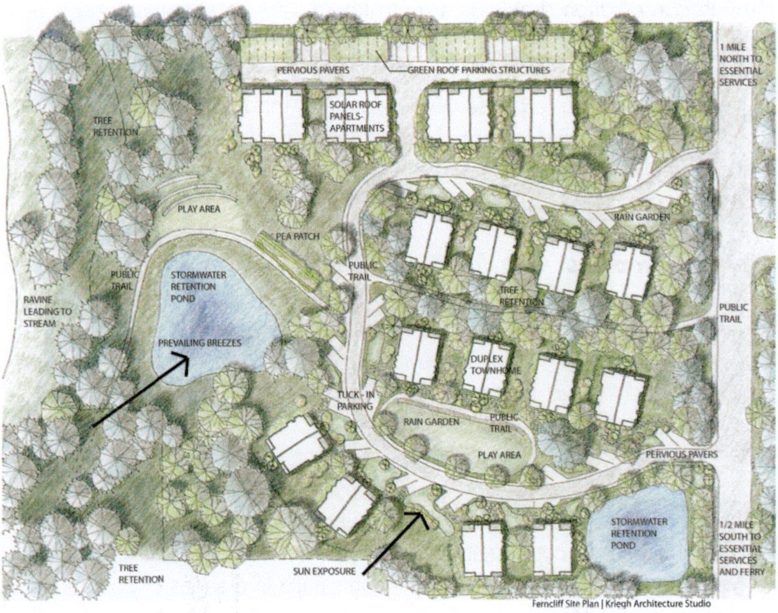

Figure 25.1. Ferncliff Village Master Plan, Bainbridge Island, Washington

the sustainable features and open space standards were compromised in the final build-out.

The Grow Community is comprised of 131 single and multifamily residences, and is being built in two phases. This project has a mid-level ranking featuring: 5-Star BuiltGreen and One-Planet-Living certification, which requires a higher performance standard for energy, water, waste, and pro-environmental behaviors; open space community gardens and connecting trails; on-site renewable energy systems; and a community bike- and car-share program. Although homes are small (1,000 to 1,800 square feet) at $300 per square foot, housing affordability is not a priority. Phase two will consist of town homes and apartments surrounding two semiprivate courtyards instead of one larger public open space as first permitted. It is uncertain if One-Planet-Living certification and the other pro-environmental aspects of phase one will continue. In this case, the project was accepted into the HDDP program and granted incentive bonuses based on the ranking of the entire project, yet as developers change course, community expectations are challenged.

By incentivizing developer participation, the HDDP program successfully broadened the spectrum of options for housing in Bainbridge's downtown. A second realized goal was encouraging innovation in resource protection through conservation strategies. Due to liberal scoring options, public open-space objectives have become less fully realized. These two projects demonstrate that divergent outcomes are possible under the same code from project to project and phase to phase. While laudible for meeting housing diversity goals on the one hand and pro-environmental goals on the other, a project that accomplishes the combined goals of sustainability, affordability, and public open space in the same development has yet to be achieved.

City of Edmonds

> FORM-BASED ZONING FEATURES PROVIDE A GREAT WAY OF ENHANCING OUR PLANNING AND ZONING APPROACH TO KEY INFILL REDEVELOPMENT OPPORTUNITIES, ESPECIALLY IN WORKING TOWARD DEVELOPING WALKABLE NEIGHBORHOOD CENTERS.
>
> —ROB CHAVE, AICP, PLANNING MANAGER, CITY OF EDMONDS

Edmonds, located on Puget Sound just north of Seattle, sought rejuvenation of an aging suburban commercial shopping center by emphasizing economic growth and urban form. Engaging the community in a series of public design workshops and feedback forums, city planners and the University of Washington Green Futures Lab (Green Futures Lab 2010) developed a form-based code called The Westgate Special District Form-Based Code (FBC).

Building upon lessons learned from the HDDP, the Edmonds FBC not only offers a menu of options for compliance, but also ensures greater predictability in building form, green building features, housing options, and site design strategies that encourage walkable, sustainable mixed use development in the suburban commercial center. In addition to addressing physical form, this FBC framework incorporates aspects of the Bainbridge HDDP and the guiding principles of a "life-space-building" methodology, promoted by Gehl Architects, so that life (activity), determines the arrangement of spaces, and only then placement of buildings. Finally, the proposed code incorporates a "green factor" overlay emulating Seattle's successful program to integrate ecological and green site features into new developments.

The proposed code supports mixed use, three-story developments including a variety of smaller, more affordable residential units attractive to young singles and senior citizens. Suggested improvements in pedestrian and bicycling facilities will provide linkages within the neighborhood and to larger routes through the city. The FBC requires amenity spaces for outdoor gatherings and events as well as green infrastructure features to filter stormwater. The "green factor" overlay offers a menu of sustainable site ecological features that project developers can use to achieve a minimum required score. A bonus system allows for developers to build projects with as many as five floors

	Housing Unit Size (see Section 3.4)	Cumulative **4 Points**
Prereq.	**Number of units < 900 sq. ft.,** 10%	Required
Prereq.	**No units ≥ 1,600 sq. ft.**	Required
Credit 1	**Number of units < 900 sq. ft. 20%**	1
Credit 2	**Number of units 900-1000 sq. ft.** 10%	1
Credit 3	**Number of units 1001-1200 sq. ft.** 10%	1
Credit 4	**Number of units 1201-1400 sq. ft.** 10%	1
	Green Building Program (see Section 3.4)	**4 Points**
Prereq.	**Built Green® / LEED®** Certified Rating or equivalent	Required
Credit 1	**LEED®** Silver Rating / **Built Green®** 4-5 / **Evergreen Sustainable Development Standards**	1
Credit 2	**LEED®** Gold Rating	2
Credit 3	**Passive House Standard / LEED®** Platinum Rating	3
Credit 4	**Living Building®**	4
	Green Factor (see Section 2.3 and 5.2)	**5 Points**
Prereq.	**Green Factor Score** 0.3	Required
Credit 1	**Green Factor Score** 0.4	2
Credit 2	**Green Factor Score** 0.5	3
Credit 3	**Green Factor Score** 0.6	4
Credit 4	**Green Factor Score** ≥ 0.7 Sustainable Sites Initiative™, or equivalent	5
	Amenity Space (see Section 5.3)	**4 Points**
Prereq.	**Percentage of amenity space of lot size** 15%	Required
Credit 1	**Percentage of amenity space of lot size** 20%	2
Credit 2	**Percentage of amenity space of lot size** 25%	3
Credit 3	**Percentage of amenity space of lot size** ≥ 30%	4
	Alternative Transportation (see Section 5.6)	Cumulative **5 Points**
Prereq.	**Meet street standards, including; bikeway and pedestrian networks, and vehicle parking**	Required
Credit 1	**Car share parking,** minimum 2 parking spots	1
Credit 2	**Charging facility for electric cars**	2
Credit 3	**Indoor bicycle storage and changing facilities**	1
Credit 4	**Priority parking for sub-compact (Smart Cars™ and motorcycles)**	1
	One-story Bonus requires 8 Points **Two-story Bonus** requires 12 Points	
	Points in at least 4 categories	Required

Figure 25.2. Westgate Height Bonus Score Sheet from Edmonds, Washington

in specified locations, provided that the development incorporates community benefits such as additional open space, green features, affordable and workforce housing, and alternative transportation incentives (Figure 25.2).

With the reviving economy, developers are moving ahead with conventional projects while the proposed code moves slowly through the city's review process. Despite the project's exceptional participatory public process, adherence to community values, and a clearly defined menu of development options and incentives, delays in code adoption, coupled with market forces, have made it difficult to achieve some of the unique aspects of this district-wide plan.

City of Burlington

> THE DOWNTOWN FUTURES AND THE BURLINGTON COMMUNITY TASK FORCES ARE ALREADY TAKING ACTION LOOKING AT COMPLETE STREETS, A DOWNTOWN HISTORIC DISTRICT, AND A RANGE OF IMPROVEMENTS TO AND CONNECTIONS WITH THE RETAIL CORE IN THE I-5 CORRIDOR.
>
> —MARGARET FLEEK, PLANNING DIRECTOR, CITY OF BURLINGTON

Burlington, an agricultural town located in the Skagit Valley north of Seattle, focused on ecological sustainability by integrating water quality improvements to the Gages Slough with the redevelopment of its historic downtown and commercial shopping centers. Hosting regional experts including the Urban Land Institute (ULI), Downtown Business Association, Skagit Housing Authority, local government leaders, and developers, city planners and the GFL convened numerous public workshops, forums, and presentations to identify a cohesive set of values, goals, and strategies in the plan Burlington at the Crossroads (BATC) (Green Futures Lab 2014). Following ULI recommendations, the BATC plan proposes the use of commercial shopping center tax revenues to support investments in civic buildings, public housing, and green stormwater infrastructure demonstration projects to lead the way for future development.

As in Edmonds, a public engagement process employing the Life-Space-Building methodology was central to the recommendations produced. Strategies for improving ecological sustainability and housing affordability were seen as mutually interrelated and highly valued by stakeholders as a means to achieve greater revitalization. Promoting Burlington as a regional service center, the BATC plan encourages residential mixed uses, sustainable building practices, municipal green stormwater infrastructure systems, regional and local bike and pedestrian connections, and the enhancement of Gages Slough—a central city feature plagued by poor water quality—as opportunities for smart green growth.

A denser mixed use infill development is proposed at the main entry to the downtown district to inspire a lively pedestrian-oriented main street culminating in a renovated public park. The park is designed as a major public gathering space for activities and civic events such as farmers markets and festivals, and features multiple green stormwater demonstration projects (Figure 25.3).

The effects of the BATC recommendations have already had a broad impact: the plan will serve as the guiding vision for the city's 2016 Comprehensive Plan update; a grant will fund events for the historic town center such as wine and microbrew tasting, outdoor movies, and live music; and local businesses are proposing to showcase Skagit Valley produce.

Figure 25.3. Proposed Crossroads Park, Burlington, Washington

Perhaps the greatest lesson to be gleaned from the Burlington case study is the small city's commitment to put words into action through demonstration projects and code adoption in order to build an economically vibrant, ecologically sustainable, and socially just future.

Lessons Learned

These three Pacific Northwest cities recognized the need for growth and rejuvenation in their downtown and commercial centers. They each prioritized overarching goals for housing affordability, economic viability, and ecological sustainability according to the unique attributes of the community at large and an innate sense of place in their town centers. What are the lessons inherent in bringing each plan to fruition?

First, incentivizing developer participation can promote sustainable development. Bainbridge achieved housing affordability goals on the one hand and pro-environmental goals on the other, but a project that accomplishes the combined goals of sustainability, affordability, and public open space in the same development has yet to be achieved. The HDDP menu might benefit from rebalancing.

Second, extensive public process can galvanize community priorities to spur predicable building form and economic development. However, in Edmonds, delays in code adoption, coupled with market forces, have made it difficult to achieve the intentions of the FBC. Edmonds might benefit from a city-led incremental implementation approach to validate the FBC through demonstration projects in the public realm.

Third, comprehensive research coupled with a transparent public process can stimulate a commitment to ecological sustainability and housing affordability to achieve revitalization. Holding these values to be equal and interdependent, Burlington's civic and citizen leaders have begun implementing the recommendations through demonstration projects and community activities even before they are adopted as code.

By integrating growth into preservation and enhancement of their natural environments to create economically vibrant, ecologically sustainable, and livable downtowns, Bainbridge, Edmonds, and Burlington have charted unique paths toward their community-envisioned destinations, setting out instructive courses on their roads to smart green growth.

CHAPTER 26

Ecological Repair and Neighborhood Revitalization: The Foster Floodplain Natural Area

Marie Walkiewicz

> The physical problems of Johnson Creek, resulting from urbanization, channel restrictions, water quality and flooding are so inter-related in terms of cause and effect that no single-purpose proposal will ever achieve the necessary results. (Emery 1977)

High Water

January 19, 2012. After a day's reprieve, the rain started up again around midnight. The ground was already saturated. By 9 a.m. the Johnson Creek team was mustered to go out in the field. The creek was expected to crest at 13 feet—two feet above flood stage—at 4 p.m., just before dark. Conditions were perfect for seeing what would happen, how the creek and floodplain would handle the high water.

Crews worked up and down Johnson Creek checking river gauges, measuring flood extents, and monitoring other restoration sites. But Maggie Skenderian, manager of the Johnson Creek Watershed Team at Portland's Bureau of Environmental Services (BES), was staying put at the Foster Floodplain Natural Area, previously known as the East Lents Floodplain Restoration Project. More than halfway through the site's restoration effort, the former steep and armored creek banks were now laid back in a much more natural contour. Where a neighborhood of 62 houses once stood on almost 50 acres, about 50,000 cubic yards of soil had been removed and a new overflow channel was under construction. Only a year before, wet lawns and visiting ducks hinted at the area's remnant wetlands. Now, midway through the restoration effort, the site's natural features were overt, though still a bit raw, waiting to be planted.

By 10 a.m. the creek was at 10 feet. Rain added definition to the creek channel and floodplain. High water wended around brush piles, which provided wildlife habitat. The day before, Foster Floodplain looked muddy with faint green sprouts. But today the changes to the land were distinguished as water filled the low points (Figure 26.1).

Figure 26.1. Shown during normal winter conditions, Johnson Creek is at six feet of elevation (above). The creek reached bank full conditions, 10 feet, at noon, January 19, 2012 (below).

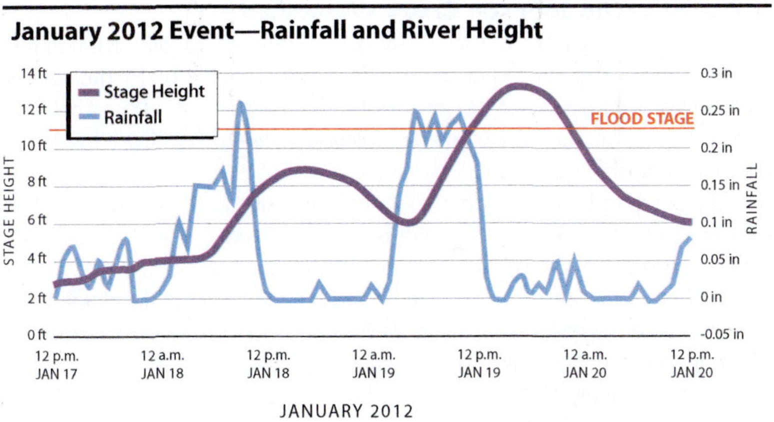

Figure 26.2. Rainfall and river height, January 18 to 20, 2012

By midday, the creek was nearly full and water was starting to spill into the overflow channel, which was not yet completed. Then the gravel road breached: Water cut across and began to erode the road bed exactly where excavation of the channel would be completed next summer. Residents considered trying to forge into the rising water, then thought better of it.

As the creek rose, neighbors gathered. At 3:30 p.m., the owner and staff from a nearby motorsports business came to watch Johnson Creek. A woman from the neighborhood brought her daughter and son to see what would happen.

Everyone was excited and anxious. Skenderian beamed. The damage to the road would be a problem for a few months, but Johnson Creek and the restoration site were holding the flood waters.

At 4 p.m., the river gauge at Brookside Wetlands, just 100 feet from the site, measured 13.21 feet, well over the 11-foot flood stage. Before Foster Floodplain was built, a similar storm would have flooded the motorsports store, acres of auto salvage yards, many homes, and an electrical substation. Foster Road would have been closed, blocking access to the industrial area, nearby residents, and commuters from rural communities to the east.

Where were the news crews? It was a tradition—every other year television reporters would stake out this spot and wait for the road to flood and shoot footage of people four-wheeling around the barricades. But the news crews didn't come. Foster Road didn't flood, so there was no story to cover.

After almost 20 years of planning, land acquisition, project design and perseverance, the Foster Floodplain Natural Area was nearly done and had already it proved a success (Figure 26.2).

A Profile of the Johnson Creek Watershed

Johnson Creek originates in Boring, Oregon, and flows 26 miles through two counties, three cities, farmland, residential neighborhoods, and industrial districts before reaching its confluence with the Willamette River. About 180,000 people live within the 52-square-mile watershed; over 120,000 of them are within the city of Portland.

The 63-acre Foster Floodplain Natural Area sits at about river-mile eight on Johnson Creek. Built by BES, the natural area reduces local flood risks, improves fish and wildlife habitat, and improves the water quality of Johnson Creek by allowing sediment in high water to settle onto the floodplain. The project restored a half mile of the creek for native salmon, trout, and lamprey (Portland 2014d). Pond and wetland enhancements benefit sensitive amphibians. A wide variety of birds, including hawks and bald eagles, use the site, as do small mammals, deer, and coyote.

Lents

The Foster Floodplain Natural Area is in Portland's Lents neighborhood, at the intersection of the Springwater Corridor and Foster Road, a major arterial. In 1983, Lents was divided by the I-205 freeway. The west side of the neighborhood includes small businesses while an industrial district straddles Foster Road east of I-205. Businesses, primarily materials suppliers and auto recycling services, provide about 450 jobs (Cronin 2014).

Johnson Creek floodplain in Lents covers about 330 acres. Public open space is the predominant land use, followed by residential land uses and industrial (Table 26.1).

About 650 residential properties and 40 business properties in the Lents area are currently at risk from a 100-year flood. As of 2013, estimated an-nual flood insurance premiums in the area are about $770,000 and the average cost of flood insurance is about $1,100 annually per single-family home.

TABLE 26.1. Johnson Creek Floodplain Land Uses

Land Use	Approximate acreage in floodplain
Industrial	70
Commercial	8
Single-family residential	94
Multifamily residential	31
Open space	128

Source: City of Portland, Bureau of Environmental Services

Within the area, the smaller nuisance floodplain (the area with a 10 percent likelihood of flooding in any given year) covers about 140 acres. About 65 percent is publicly owned open space, 30 percent is industrial or commercial uses, and five percent is residential property.

Compared to Portland overall, Lents is a relatively diverse neighborhood. Twenty four percent of residents are nonwhite and 16 percent are Hispanic. Resident incomes are lower than the city's median. Languages spoken in the neighborhood include Vietnamese, Chinese, Spanish, Russian, Somali, and Nepali.

History

Flooding is not a new problem along Johnson Creek in Lents. In fact, the extent of the floodplain is attributed to the Missoula Floods, which helped shape the Columbia River basin 13,000 to 15,000 years ago and created the large, flat floodplain in Lents (Allen, Burns, and Burns 2009).

Before white settlers arrived, the Johnson Creek watershed was a diverse mix of upland and wetland forests, marshes and scrub-shrub habitats. Elk, deer, and fish thrived in the watershed. Native Americans set up summer camps in the area to fish, hunt, and forage along the creek. Until a few decades ago, salmon and trout were plentiful in the creek.

White settlement began in the mid-1800s. Over time, farms were established in the floodplain to take advantage of the fertile soil. Within Portland's city limits, farms were replaced by industry and homes. But small farms, nurseries, and ranches continue to operate upstream. Legacy pollutants from past farming, including DDT and dieldrin, are still found in the creek.

As homes and businesses replaced farmland, flooding was seen as a problem, and pressure mounted to do something. Nearly every decade, from the 1930s to present day, saw at least one major initiative to stop or reduce flooding along Johnson Creek.

Early Flood Control Efforts

During the Great Depression, the Works Progress Administration (WPA) straightened and rock-lined much of the creek, creating a smooth trapezoidal channel. While the craftsmanship was remarkable, the approach exacerbated flooding (Figure 26.3).

In later decades, the U.S. Army Corps of Engineers, a special local water control district, and an early regional planning agency all proposed flood control projects. Most called on property owners to contribute toward project costs or hold the sponsoring agency harmless should flood control projects impact their homes or businesses. Ultimately the technical, financial, and political challenges of flood mitigation proved overwhelming and no actions were taken.

Figure 26.3. In the 1930s, the Works Progress Administration straightened and rock-lined 15 miles of Johnson Creek in an unsuccessful attempt to reduce flooding. Johnson Creek experienced one of its largest floods in 1962.

Proposals were often controversial and Johnson Creek residents were cynical about government efforts to reduce flooding. Yet community members didn't agree on the nature of the problem, how to address it, or who should pay for changes. Most creekside residents valued where they lived, despite the risk of flooding, and resisted proposals to change the creek's relatively natural character. Uplanders didn't believe that their actions affected the creek and didn't want to pay for projects that would increase creekside property values. Without a common understanding about the nature of the flooding problems and how to solve them, successful implementation was unlikely.

Restoration Planning Versus Flood Control

The nearly two-decade journey to the completion of the Foster Floodplain Natural Area started with a different premise than previous efforts. The new thinking considered how to use nature as a partner—to recreate and mimic more natural floodplain functions to reduce flooding while also improving water quality and helping restore native salmon and trout populations.

Johnson Creek Resources Management Plan

This new approach was prompted in part by the city's annexation of much of east Portland in the 1980s when BES was given responsibility for preparing a drainage master plan to manage stormwater in the area (Johnson Creek Corridor Committee 1995).

A watershed-wide consortium of neighbors, environmental groups, business people, and public agency staff calling themselves the Johnson Creek Corridor Committee sought solutions to Johnson Creek's problems. Supported by BES, the planning process sought to involve all stakeholder groups with a potential interest in the plan and its implementation to develop a plan to address all of the watershed's problems, rather than flooding alone.

Building from this foundation, the Johnson Creek Resources Management Plan (RMP) documented the connections between stormwater management, water quality, flooding, habitat, and local quality of life. It also provided the rationale for investing in a watershed-wide approach to flood mitigation and stormwater management. For community members, the plan supported their interests in preserving and enhancing the natural qualities of the creek and its watershed.

The plan called for managing stormwater in strategic locations on public land acquired from willing sellers (rather than from condemnation). While previous proposals forwarded technically based flood-control projects funded through property assessments, the RMP offered residents a healthier creek that everyone could enjoy. Most project funding would come from local jurisdictions, which expected to recoup their investment through increased property values.

Although the promising plan was not implemented, it provided the technical, philosophical and political basis for the planning and restoration work that was to follow. Also emerging from this effort, the Johnson Creek Corridor Committee evolved into the nonprofit Johnson Creek Watershed Council, which coordinates projects and research across jurisdictional boundaries, and supports community-based stewardship.

The Johnson Creek Restoration Plan

> Experience has shown that fighting a creek's natural tendencies is often more costly and ineffective for a long-term solution. . . . It is now recognized that it may be more cost-effective and environmentally sound to work within the creek's natural dynamics. (Johnson Creek Corridor Committee 1992 quoted in Portland 2001a, 3-4)

Soon after the RMP was completed, Johnson Creek runs of steelhead trout and Chinook salmon were listed as threatened under the federal Endangered Species Act. In response, the Portland City Council set an ambitious goal to reestablish self-sustaining populations of threatened fish in Portland rivers and streams. While the principles of the RMP remained valid, many of the projects it recommended proved infeasible given new permitting and policy direction.

Building on the organizational structure, policy basis and technical underpinnings of the RMP, the Johnson Creek Restoration Plan (2001) began with three simultaneous goals: to improve water quality, enhance fish and wildlife habitat, and mitigate flooding.

These goals recognized that flood mitigation and other creek improvements would yield complementary benefits. Given the extent and frequency of flooding, the plan didn't aim to stop flooding entirely. Rather, BES proposed to manage nuisance floods by restoring the creek channel and floodplains on about 260 acres in four target areas along Portland's stretch of Johnson Creek. For neighborhoods like Lents, this would represent a significant improvement over the flooding they were enduring about every other year.

Johnson Creek Willing Seller Program

The primary tool for achieving the Restoration Plan's goals is the Willing Seller Program (Portland 2014e), which identifies potential properties for floodplain restoration in four target areas. The program recognizes that successful floodplain restoration depends on public support so all transactions are voluntary. While many property owners were initially skeptical or hostile about the idea of selling, BES negotiated the purchase of 222 acres by 2010.

Early acquisitions were funded in part by the Federal Emergency Management Agency (FEMA), after two major floods in 1996, and federal Community Development Block Grants. Other funding came from the Metro Regional Government and Portland Parks & Recreation. Of the public properties within the Johnson Creek target areas, BES owns about 68 percent of the land; Portland Parks & Recreation or Metro have sole or partnership interests in the remaining properties.

Creating the Foster Floodplain Natural Area

After most of the properties at the Foster Floodplain site were acquired, BES received a $2.7-million FEMA Pre-Disaster Mitigation Grant for project construction. The program funds projects that reduce the risks and costs associated with hazards. The Foster Floodplain's multi-objective approach made it a good fit for FEMA's grant program, which gives priority to projects that protect or enhance natural functions while also reducing risks.

Design

Project design, which began in 2007, was initially complicated because a few properties remained in private ownership. Analysis of several design alternatives determined that restoration could potentially impact them, so BES intensified acquisition efforts for the remaining properties.

When all properties were secured, the design was finalized. It called for removing three bridges and roads, widening the creek at previous pinch points, and expanding the scale of floodplain enhancements. The needs of

Figure 26.4. Before restoration, the creek banks were narrow, rock lined, and covered by invasive plants. During restoration, crews installed hay bales wrapped in coir fabric to stabilize the banks while vegetation becomes established. After restoration, lupine was one of the first native plants to establish on the site.

long-term maintenance and environmental education influenced the design, which added a paved path and provided a parking lot large enough to accommodate school buses for environmental education programs.

Concurrently, BES's Brownfield Program cleaned up contamination on an adjacent site and integrated that work into the Foster Floodplain design. Funded by a U.S. Environmental Protection Agency bioremediation grant, the Brownfield Program used bacteria to clean up petroleum contamination at a former gas station site (Portland 2014b). The site includes an informational kiosk covered by a green roof. Interpretive signage describes the brownfield reclamation, the history of local flooding, and the restoration of the Foster Floodplain Natural Area (Figure 26.4).

Construction

Restoration work at the Foster Floodplain Natural Area took two years to complete. In 2011, the WPA's rock armoring was removed from the creek, the bank was laid back, and large wood and boulders were installed for in-water habitat. Workers excavated the floodplain and created an overflow channel and a floodgate at the downstream end of the site. In 2012, the bridges were removed, as was a 72-foot culvert that previously bypassed a portion of the creek during high flows. The overflow channel was finished, followed by a pedestrian bridge, an Americans with Disabilities Act-compliant trail, and interpretive kiosk and a parking lot. The BES Revegetation Program began removing invasive plants from 63 acres, replacing them with 20,500 native trees, 70,500 native shrubs, 4,750 wetland plants, 200 pieces of large wood habitat and 1,000 pounds of native grasses, sedges, and forbs. This effort will continue for five years (Portland 2014c).

The completed project features 140 acre-feet of flood storage (enough to cover the site with about two feet of water), which will reduce local flood risk from every other year to an anticipated average of about every six to eight years.In addition, 18,000 square feet of landscaped stormwater facilities treat Foster Road runoff, which previously flowed untreated into Johnson Creek.

Celebration

In April 2013 just after Earth Day, nearly 150 neighbors, project staff, and local elected officials gathered in the sunshine to celebrate the project's completion. Native American elders drummed and blessed the land. Students from Kelly Elementary School paraded onto the grounds carrying flags from their many homelands (Figure 26.5). BES director Dean Marriott welcomed everyone. Amy Fraenkel from the United Nations' World Environment Programme congratulated Portland as the 2013 North American host for World Environment Day.[1]

In a neighborhood that has experienced many challenges, the Foster Floodplain represents a renewed connection to Johnson Creek and a growing sense of hope for the creek, the watershed, and the community.

Foster Floodplain Today

The Foster Floodplain Natural Area is now the most accessible place to view Johnson Creek. When the project was designed, public access was a secondary consideration, so its popularity came as a surprise. Larger than several of Portland's well-loved Olmsted brothers parks, Foster Floodplain is a unique urban open space where nature and natural processes are on ready view (Portland 2007).

The Foster Floodplain's popularity represents an opportunity for Portlanders to learn about Johnson Creek, to see that even in the city, creeks are alive

Figure 26.5. Kelly Elementary students and fancy dancers helped celebrated World Environment Day at Foster Floodplain Natural Area.

with fish and wildlife and that restoring natural functions benefits people too. The hope and potential embodied in the site seems to resonate with locals and visitors alike. Schoolchildren visit the site to test the creek's water quality or work on an adjacent property, removing invasive weeds and planting native plants. Delegations from Great Britain and China come to the site to learn about the project and Johnson Creek restoration efforts.

Foster Floodplain is part of a natural "string of pearls" in east Portland along the Springwater Corridor Trail. Wetlands, buttes, a botanical garden, and a nonprofit farm form a network of natural areas that would be enviable in most communities. As part of that network, the Foster Floodplain Natural Area represents a fundamental shift in Lents and nearby neighborhoods.

Renewed pride in Lents and Johnson Creek is evident in the actions of the residents. Longtime community champions Ernie and David Francisco donated part of their creekside land to the city for preservation. Ed Kerns continues to lead students in cleaning up and replanting parts of the Springwater Corridor Trail. Younger residents are moving to Lents, attracted by affordable homes and the ready access to nature. The Foster Green EcoDistrict (2014) promotes sustainable community development across several southeast Portland neighborhoods and Green Lents (2014) sponsors creek cleanups and watershed stewardship projects.

In fact, Foster Floodplain's popularity is one of its challenges. For many visitors, the floodplain looks like an open area awaiting their exploration. They traverse the site for discoveries without realizing that they (or their dog) might inadvertently harm nesting killdeer, eggs of red-legged frogs, or habitat for other sensitive species. Park rules are posted, but the site's long-term management may require special outreach programs to educate visitors about Foster Floodplain's natural features.

What Does the Future Hold?

While the Foster Floodplain Restoration Project is complete, about 40 acres are still identified for acquisition in the Johnson Creek watershed. BES now acquires upland wetlands and forests to reduce impacts on Johnson creek. The Johnson Creek Team is initiating a subwatershed plan to guide future improvements to Johnson Creek tributaries, pipesheds, and uplands. Citywide, BES invests in natural resource preservation and enhancement projects and green infrastructure projects, such as eco-roofs, green streets, and stormwater swales, to manage stormwater close to its source.

The impact of the Foster Floodplain on the Lents neighborhood isn't fully understood at this time. Some business owners report that they are investing in their properties as a result of this project. However, the complexity of funding and permitting development in the floodplain is likely to hinder job growth in the area. And increasingly the cost of flood insurance is burdening vulnerable households.

A recent study commissioned by BES indicates that additional floodplain restoration could manage the 100-year flood in Lents, although such an effort would require a complex master-planning process. Currently there is no clear champion for such an effort.

It is clear that the Foster Floodplain Natural Area is making a difference. Its flood mitigation benefits are already demonstrated, and its water quality and wildlife habitat impacts are being tracked. Already, wildlife surveys found that red-legged frogs are breeding in the site's wetlands.

The Foster Floodplain project demonstrates that it is possible to solve problems for people and the environment simultaneously. Where local planning philosophy once held that managing growth meant sacrificing urban natural areas, today watershed health goals are informing the update to Portland's Comprehensive Plan. Planners, designers, engineers, and community members understand that improving watershed functions through infrastructure investments is a commonsense, cost-effective way to provide essential public services while also creating more distinctive, beautiful, and highly livable neighborhoods.[2]

SECTION 3
PLANNING PROSPECTIVE: WHAT'S NEXT?

Introduction

Jill Sterrett, FAICP, and Dennis Ryan

Perhaps by now you are catching a glimpse of the Northwest planner. As written in the opening Introduction, it's "like birding: you have to relax and look for the movement out of the corner of your eye to actually find what you're looking for." But to portray planning in a region where "we expect planning to make change," our picture of the Northwest planner cannot be complete without exploring what's next. What are the changes that planners in the Northwest are seeking to make? How are we engaging in the emerging issues that will define our region for the 21st century?

Section 3 opens with Tillett's call for "Redefining Planning in Cascadia," which asks planners to take a broader view of their role. He calls on planners to be more interdisciplinary, more integrative, and to become "capable conductors of an orchestra" of the many disciplines needed to address the complex challenges we face.

The challenges we face are not unique to the Northwest. The Sterrett/Campbell chapter, which concludes Part 3, identifies four of the many:

- Climate change—global climate change that will further stress natural systems and have severe effects on our communities
- Ecosystem damage—accelerating degradation of natural resources due to population growth and unsustainable rates of consumption

Late Summer 2013 #3. *James Lavadour, born in Pendleton, Oregon, is a contemporary artist whose work is exhibited at the PDX Contemporary Art Gallery in Portland, Oregon.*

- Changing economy—the economic recession, with a "new normal" that is likely to be slow growth for years to come
- Polarized public interest—increasing economic inequities, income disparity, and demographic changes that undermine a middle class with shared values

These challenges are complex, interrelated, and systemic. They are truly "wicked problems"—a term coined in the 1960s and immortalized in an article by Rittel and Webber (1973). They argued that planning has successfully applied a rational approach to solving physical problems—roads are paved, buildings are safe, clean water is provided, and waste is removed. Those are "tame" or "benign" problems in their view. By their era of the 1970s, the planning profession had turned to social and policy distributional issues that are much more systemic. That era of change in the 1970s is where we begin the story of Planning in the Pacific Northwest, as we saw in Part 1.

What is a "wicked problem"? Rittel and Webber list and describe 10 characteristics. One of them is that there is no definitive formulation of the problem itself and every wicked problem can be considered a symptom of another problem. Thus, defining a wicked problem *is* the problem. Furthermore, there is no method to test a solution to a wicked problem since solutions generate waves of consequences over an extended period of time.

Although Rittel and Webber were writing in the 1970s, the social and distributional problems they identified are still with us. We also have new problems in our "supersized" world. A 2012 *Policy Science* article expanded wicked problems to "super wicked problems" in reference to contemporary social problems (Levin et al. 2012). For these, they identify four additional key features:

- Time is running out.
- Those who cause the problem also seek to provide a solution.
- The central authority needed to address it is weak or nonexistent.
- Policy responses discount the future irrationally.

In keeping with our increasingly globalized world, the wicked problems identified for the Pacific Northwest are not limited to our region, but are common threats throughout the country. Can the experience of the Northwest provide useful examples for other states or regions?

This section takes a look at how planners in the Pacific Northwest are dealing with the challenges and emerging issues of the 21st century. Among the litany of these challenges, first and foremost, is climate change. Whether dealing with mitigation (reducing carbon emissions) or adaptation (responding to the effects of climate change), planners in the Northwest are exploring these issues. Authors addressing climate change, in terms of alternative energy in Part 3 include: Whittington and Young, addressing the effects of climate change on the region's pervasive hydropower; Hill, who looks at solar power in a not-so-sunny environment; Russett, addressing planning for greenhouse gas reduction; and Cutler, who examines tactical sustainability efforts that bring together practice and action.

In addition to climate change, we also see that strong environmental theme, which carries throughout the book, continuing into this part with chapters that reflect changing attitudes on "taming" our rivers in Yocom's article on the evolution of environmental ethics as well as new attitudes on integrated planning approaches in Roderick's "Green Infrastructure Mashup."

Emerging issues are addressed in chapters covering food systems planning (Born and Horst) and the new economy, such as Portland's artisan economy (Heying) and the food truck scene in the Pacific Northwest (Mooney). Also, we are rethinking our cities to be increasingly dense and more socially equitable, while providing public spaces that are more people-friendly in the chapter "Growing Transit Communities" and reusing urban spaces in Nelson's chapter on "Car Spaces into People Places." And we are looking at new metrics to determine if we are successful, described in "The Happiness Factor."

Beyond the practice of planning here in the Northwest, the chapters can be read for the future of issues facing this field as well as for indicators of changes in planning practice—what we do and how we do it.

Heying's story of the emerging economy as "disruptive innovation"—an upending of the old industrial model of development where economies had boundaries and where wealth only came from production—may be an equally appropriate metaphor for thinking about the emerging future of planning. At least, it raises questions. As the contexts of economic activity shift, how does this affect our definition of practice? How closely intertwined is our understanding of planning with the conventional models of development? Sifting through the language of these articles is instructive. While the strong narrative thread in all is about the planning case or project, the reader will also catch a glimpse of practices attuned to an unfolding future.

Saul Bellow once wrote, "I know how to transform common matter." Isn't good planning often about doing the same?

The authors, in Part 3 and throughout the collection, write with enthusiasm about the everyday work of planning—the power of collaborative and interdisciplinary efforts, the special expertise for facilitation among technical fields as well as within communities, and the attention to designing a process that can sustain, excite, and get the job done. Stay curious, notes one author. Ask "Why Not?"

Other tools addressed here include the high value for planning of close partnerships with universities, using real-time experimentation and demonstrations along with close evaluation, and taking advantage of new technologies for visualization. Increasingly we are using software advances for mining data large and small, for facilitating and sharing collaborative knowledge building, and for supporting interdisciplinary learning.

Jaron Lanier's book, *Who Owns the Future?* (2013), looks at how changes affect fields. Software substitution, algorithms, and wikis are replacing former activities in planning and propelling us into the kind of higher-value work exemplified in these articles.

Planning's ways of thinking and acting—the epistemology of this field—shapes everything including knowledge and understanding, values, identities, skills, and social practices. These articles are snapshots of planning in the Pacific Northwest; a cultural text that can be read as a compelling demonstration of what engages us and of what we see coming around the corner.

When you read these—with your Starbucks coffee or your Northwest wine or local brew in hand—consider this: Are we living up to Tillett's view of the larger role of planners? Are we initiating a movement, as Sterrett and Campbell call for? And is that happening in your corner of the country as well?

CHAPTER 27

Redefining Planning in Cascadia

Paddy Tillett, FAICP

Ask any businessperson or politician and they will tell you that planners can be a pain in the neck when they get in the way of a deal. There are many instances when we should "get in the way" because we have the breadth of knowledge to recognize disastrous long-term consequences of a course of action designed to make short-term gains. Too often we have allowed ourselves to be sidelined as "specialists" in silos unable to influence the big picture. It is incumbent upon planners to take initiative; the alternative is passive planning—an oxymoron.

Though plans of human habitation are as old as civilization, the planning profession is relatively new, lacking the centuries of status and respect accorded to medicine, law, and architecture. In our society, being a "specialist" confers credibility, and perhaps this is why we have allowed the scope of our activities to be narrowed. Educators have had to prove the validity of planning as a profession through accreditation—which has had the effect of dividing planning into a legion of special topics—inviting students to select a pigeonhole. Yet taken as a whole, our education spans a range from global trends to ethics to details of street design. It is time to find our way back to a place where we use our breadth of knowledge and perspective to address the big issues that shape our future. To do so, it is necessary to understand the complexity of the challenges that confront us, then identify practical initiatives that can help us to succeed, knowing at the outset that there will be no simple answers.

The big challenges are issues that our conventional decision-making machinery is ill-equipped to address. The problems posed are global, but are felt locally. A good place to begin would be to develop regional initiatives to address them. The broadest perspective of planners will be needed to span such obstructions as jurisdictional boundaries, self-interest by commercial and political interests, and a sclerotic mesh of regulations and conventions. These issues include:

- Climate change that is causing more extreme weather events and may prompt mass migrations to water-rich regions including Cascadia
- Depletion of natural resources due to population growth and unsustainable rates of consumption
- An aging population that places the burden of supporting them onto a diminishing workforce.
- Changing employment norms and increasingly polarized wealth distribution in most developed countries including the United States and Canada

There are international efforts to address some of these same challenges at the worldwide scale. In 2013 the Oxford Martin Commission for Future Generations published *Now for the Long Term*. The Oxford Martin School was founded in June 2005 as the James Martin 21st Century School at the University of Oxford in England. The school supports more than 300 researchers, drawn from across Oxford and beyond, working to address the most pressing global challenges and opportunities of the 21st century.

A prestigious international panel identified seven megatrends:

- Demographics—large aging populations
- Mobility—urbanization and a growing middle class
- Society—inequality and unemployment
- Geopolitics—power transitions
- Sustainability—resource insecurity
- Health—shifting burdens of disease
- Technology—information and communications revolution

The commission went on to identify five shaping factors that frustrate positive responses to the challenges embedded in these topics:

- Institutions—Too many have failed to adapt to today's global information system.
- Time—Short-term interests direct political and business cycles.
- Political engagement and public trust—Both eroded by questionable practices.
- Growing complexity—Problems can defy simple definition.

- Cultural biases—Globalization can amplify cultural differences and exclude key voices.

The relevance of these points is clear: Short-term expediency, wavering public trust, complexity, and social injustice are all familiar enemies of sound planning. Too often they result in expedient short-term solutions that fail to address long-term problems. The Oxford Martin School provides its researchers with the opportunity to interact directly with policy makers and industry leaders around the world: a top-down approach. Our need in Cascadia is for a bottom-up approach implemented through specific initiatives, practical measures that can be put to work immediately.

In Cascadia we have some additional challenges to address. One is the threat of an imminent seismic event similar in scale to the one that struck our shores at 9 p.m. on January 26, 1700. [Thanks to the diligent record keeping of Japanese harbormasters, we can pinpoint the time and location of the event]. Although it happened more than 300 years ago, our knowledge of it is remarkably precise. The event was centered just off our coast, dumping a hefty stratum of sand on the peat beds of coastal lakes and wetlands. It is all there to see in the geological maps of the coasts of Oregon, Washington, and Vancouver Island; they show the extent of tsunami and landslide damage to estuaries and hillsides from that magnitude 9.0 earthquake. We also know that a repetition is due any time now.

We should expect as much damage and more when the predicted earthquake, the "Big One," strikes this time—yet we continue to allow development on steep slopes and in coastal plains known to be vulnerable. There have been enough seismic disasters elsewhere around the Pacific Rim in recent years to drive the message home. Planners understand the full spectrum of consequences when we build in dangerous places, yet we seem unable to act on that knowledge to keep people and facilities out of harm's way. Our tools are limited to applicable regulations and reach is limited by jurisdictional boundaries—and therein lies the problem. An accretion of rules and limitations laid over old lore makes fundamental change very difficult to achieve. The sanctity of property ownership, for example, all but denies the possibility of a development ban on vulnerable sites. Yet it is clearly irresponsible to allow homes to be built in the near-certain path of a tsunami or a landslide.

Other than planners, who is there to address such major issues without political or economic taint? Planners by definition have a long-term perspective, and are perhaps uniquely positioned to advocate for responsible long-term use of natural resources, by focusing on resilience, inclusiveness, and sustainability. These are terms that have traction with the electorate, and may be the means by which we can combat the seismic risks.

Figure 27.1. TriMet, the transit agency, selected a design team led by architects and landscape architects knowing that they could communicate effectively with all the engineering disciplines involved and with businesses along the street. From the outset, a holistic view of street functions and an enfolding design concept that included building frontages and everything in the 80-foot right-of-way drove the design toward a solution that is equitable, safe, and enjoyable for all users of the streets—and it fulfills its many functions completely.

There are instances where the profession—collaborating with fellow design professionals—has overcome the rigidity of rule book and convention. Every city has encoded street standards that favored motorized vehicles above other modes and considerations. The Complete Streets initiative is steadily reversing those diktats.

Too many streets have been designed purely as vehicular conveyances, resulting in the sterile antithesis of a walkable environment. Focusing on equity for all street users leads to a very different perception of street function. First of all, the street includes land uses on either side of it, and the access they need. Besides serving motorists, bicyclists, and pedestrians equally, should the street contribute to the urban forest, controlling the heat island effect and providing habitat continuity and biophilic relief? What about lighting and signage? Are there things that can make the environment of the street more accommodating to those who use it, such as seating, artwork, quality paving, and other sustainable materials? Can it enrich the lives of those whom it serves?

Design for a complete street should at a minimum be a portrait of a place that is safe, efficient, enjoyable and sustainable, and it should express the character of its location. This can happen when planners, engineers, architects, and landscape architects collaborate as participants in a single conversation about how to optimize every aspect of the street—the way it is built and maintained, the different functions that it should fulfill, the way it looks and the behaviors it evokes. Effective collaboration with another design professional demands some understanding of what they care about and why. Each must become less of a specialist and more of a generalist in the broad fields of design. When they work as a collaborative team, each aware of the other's objectives and of the greater common purpose at hand, then masterful work can be done (Figure 27.1).

Scaling "complete streets" up to complete planning of natural and man-made environments is a mighty challenge, demanding an understanding of hydrology, geology, flora and fauna, and a great deal more. The generalist planner (for "generalist" read: accomplished polymath) should know enough about these and other collateral topics to be able to read the entire landscape, to recognize the contribution that each feature and quality can make. A planner should be able to read the environment like an orchestra score, with every component adding its particular voice to a harmonic whole. Only then can the full potential of a place be revealed and capitalized upon.

Few work environments provide an opportunity for interdisciplinary collaboration, but there are trends that are beginning to force such intermingling of professions. Design of sustainable environments, whether buildings or landscapes, engage multiple engineering and design disciplines. Ecodistricts enmesh planners more directly with these other designers. As each becomes more comfortable in the realm of the other, so the opportunities for creative, interdisciplinary solutions multiply.

The British often refer to "town and country planning"—rather a quaint term, but it captures the scope of the planning profession's work quite well: responsibility for the wise conservation and development of both man-made and natural environments. That is an undertaking worthy of intellectual giants, yet for most planners in practice the scope has been narrowed to a mere pinhole: not much more than the upkeep and administration of rules within a rigid yet inadequate framework. There are means by which a nobler scope of planning can be regained: by refocusing on the greatest issues that confront us, and by broadening our professional capabilities.

Something similar happened to architects, who descended from being scholarly master builders to a recent dark age of postmodernism in which many transformed themselves to architectural cosmeticians: providing a pretty skin to cover the engineers' work (Figure 27.2).

Architects are reemerging as capable conductors of an orchestra of numerous consultants to design buildings that perform many complex functions in near perfect harmony. Planners are poised to undergo a similar renaissance and nowhere more so than in the Pacific Northwest where the man-made and natural environments are under threat in some extraordinary ways.

Figure 27.2. Modernism and brutalism had left many people with the sense that architects were out of touch with current values. Postmodernism confirmed this suspicion. Architects have since redefined themselves as polymath creators of high-performance built environments. The planning profession needs a similar redefinition of its role.

If we are to rise to the challenges presented by climate change, demographic shifts, cultural injustice, political polarization, and natural disasters such as earthquakes, we need a better set of tools than we have today. We need tools that can get past obsolete jurisdictional boundaries such as county lines. We need the boldness to find equitable ways to shift people and buildings out of harm's way. We need to expand the reach of planning beyond the short-term ambitions of a political term or a business agenda. Planners can achieve the greater stature needed for such challenges by broadening their knowledge-based authority and their professional affiliations to be the capable generalists on whom leaders can rely. It is time to leave the silo and take giant steps to empower ourselves to guide the future.

CHAPTER 28

Car Spaces into People Places

Alyse Nelson, AICP

Transforming streets from automobile-dominant spaces to people places is a powerful process. It opens up peoples' minds to the opportunities that exist in our street rights-of-way. Cascadia's cities are faced with a tall order: add density to developed areas without sacrificing quality of life. As land costs rise and availability decreases, cities must resourcefully use their existing public land to create quality open spaces.

Streets make up to one-third of all public land in cities, making them an important asset already available and awaiting transformation (Bain, Gray, and Rodgers 2012). By taking space away from cars and giving it to people, cities have a valuable tool for creating a quality public space system. Cascadia's three largest cities—Vancouver (British Columbia), Seattle, and Portland—are each experimenting with repurposing the right-of-way. This chapter will explore some of the ways these cities are taking car spaces and creating people places.

VIVA Vancouver

Since 2011, Vancouver has used the VIVA Vancouver program to implement temporary events and installations throughout the city. "Streets and sidewalks are a significant part of the public realm," reads the city's Transportation 2040 Plan. "They are not just spaces to move through, but places to be" (Vancouver 2012, 24). The VIVA program is seen as critical to the development of a lively public realm and as a way to test creative ideas (Figure 28.1 and Figure 28.2).

The Transportation 2040 Plan identifies proposed downtown pedestrian-priority streets and spaces—places the city hopes to transform into vibrant

Figure 28.1 and Figure 28.2. The 800 block of Robson Street is just a regular downtown street (above) that is transformed from Canada Day (July 1) to Labour Day into a summertime plaza (below) through the VIVA Vancouver program.

people places while balancing transportation needs. Like the summertime closure of Robson Street, VIVA has brought temporary activities that bring people out to these planned pedestrian-priority streets. Through the VIVA program, Vancouver has introduced parklets, downtown weekend festivals all summer long, painted murals and crosswalks that bring color to neighborhoods, and a farmers market. These transient activities bring people to the space, which help them imagine what it could be if the short-term changes VIVA brings were to become permanent.

Portland's Intersection Repair

In Portland's Intersection Repair program, city residents join together to paint a neighborhood intersection as a public square. The city's first Intersection Repair was implemented in the Sellwood neighborhood in the mid-1990s. Its goal was to create a community space in a place previously focused on moving traffic. Subsequent resident surveys showed that Sellwood neighbors felt safer and more connected to their community—invaluable benefits that came at no cost to the city budget (Figure 28.3).

Since the first Intersection Repair, Portland's city council has passed a citywide ordinance to allow similar projects throughout the city. The nonprofit group City Repair formed to facilitate hundreds more community projects throughout Portland and beyond.

To retain their permit for an Intersection Repair, neighbors need to keep their painted mural vibrant. Sellwood neighbors have been painting their

Figure 28.3. Neighbors repainting Share-It-Square in Portland's Sellwood neighborhood in 2013

Figure 28.4. Seattle's Bell Street Park features a curbless street, landscaping, and a variety of street amenities to encourage its use for recreation as well as for transportation.

intersection every few years since the mid-1990s. This helps introduce new residents into the community and helps maintain the relationships established over paintbrushes. This collaboration between neighbors makes an effective Intersection Repair because, as City Repair coordinator Mia Van Meter explains, the project site is "just a space until they create meaning together that makes it their place" (Van Meter 2013).

Seattle's Bell Street Park

About 9,000 people live in Seattle's Belltown neighborhood, which sits just northwest of downtown (Downtown Seattle Association 2012). Seattle planners estimate the neighborhood needs about nine acres of open space (Seattle 2014b). Yet the neighborhood has only one half-acre park—the Regrade Dog Park along Bell Street and 3rd. Like many dense urban neighborhoods, land availability is low and prices are high, making it challenging to plan for more urban open space within the neighborhood.

The Belltown community came up with a creative solution in the Belltown Neighborhood Plan adopted in 1999. One key strategy of the plan was to develop green streets and open space connections to "provide parks and open space opportunities for residents . . . without a significant expenditure

Figure 28.5. Seattle residents take to the street to enjoy the newly completed Bell Street Park at a grand opening celebration in April 2014.

of public funds for land acquisition" (Seattle 1998, 16). Bell Street was identified as an important green street because it traverses Belltown and links the neighborhood to Elliott Bay (Figure 28.4) (Seattle 1998).

Ten years later, the project came to fruition after the 2008 Parks and Green Space Levy passed. Led by the Seattle Parks Department, the Bell Street Park project design encompasses four full blocks of Bell Street, where the street will become a shared space between cars, bicyclists, and people (Figure 28.5).

Removing a vehicle lane and reducing on-street parking created more space for pedestrians. The street sits at one level—no curbs separate pedestrians from vehicles. This encourages people to cross the street whenever it's convenient and it makes it easier to hold community events. Landscaping and street furniture provide respite for residents and visitors. Outdoor dining nodes provide opportunities for neighborhood restaurants to establish outdoor cafes.

Bell Street may not be a traditional park, but it has added about an acre of open space to an urban neighborhood. This may be a more likely future for cities, as Patrick Donohue of the Parks Department explains: "As density becomes inevitable, we'll have to carve out more open space out of right-of-way." (Donohue 2013) Seattle is exploring similar projects in two other neighborhoods.

Conclusions

People have choices about where they will live, so creating a quality public realm is essential if cities want to flourish. Today's city planners are faced with tight budgets with which to transform cities into livable places with open space, dense urban areas, and a multimodal transportation system. Through temporary events during the summertime, neighborhood painting projects, and implementing shared streets to meet open space goals, Cascadia's cities demonstrate the power of experimenting with city streets. Turning car spaces into people places is a powerful tool for cities.

CHAPTER 29

Lights On or Off? Hydropower in a Changing Climate

Jan Whittington and Stefanie Young

Hydroelectric dams along the Columbia River and its tributaries allow the Pacific Northwest to generate the cleanest power in the nation. One megawatt (MW), a standard measure for bulk electricity, can power about 600 homes in the Pacific Northwest (Harrison 2008d). Total generating capacity in the United States from hydropower is 80,000 MW. Washington State alone provides 11,000 MW of this capacity, more than double the amount of any other state (U.S. Department of Energy 2004). Unlike coal, petroleum, or natural gas-fired plants, hydroelectric facilities produce no carbon emissions, helping to limit greenhouse gas emissions and curtail climate change.

Since both the supply and demand for hydroelectric power are strongly influenced by precipitation and temperature, changes in climate already forecasted for the region will bring a host of challenges to the planners and operators of the Columbia basin's electrical system. This chapter explores the interplay between climate mitigation, climate adaptation, and the supply and demand for hydroelectric power in the Pacific Northwest.

Hydroelectric Assets

The Columbia River is the single largest source of energy for the Pacific Northwest. (Northwest Power and Conservation Council 2013c). As the fourth-largest river system by volume in North America, the Columbia drains an area the size of France, covering territory in seven states and the Canadian province of British Columbia on its 1,200-mile course (Center for Columbia River History 2014; Harrison 2008b).

The Columbia is the most hydroelectrically developed river system in the world (Center for Columbia River History 2014). The first known dam was completed in 1932. By the 1970s, the river and its tributaries were blocked and tapped by more than 400 dams. Three dams in the Canadian portion of the basin were constructed, in accordance with the 1964 Columbia River Treaty, to serve the joint needs of Canada and the United States for electricity and flood control (U.S. Army Corps of Engineers and Bonneville Power Administration 2014). In an average water year, the dams in the American portion of the basin provide more than 16,000 average MW of renewable electricity to an estimated 13.5 million people (Northwest Power and Conservation Council 2013c). The region also uses energy from coal, natural gas, nuclear, wind, and biomass. However, while 70 percent of the electricity consumed across the nation comes from fossil fuels, in the Pacific Northwest, about 70 percent of capacity is carbon-neutral (Table 29.1) (Northwest Power and Conservation Council 2013c; U.S. Energy Information Administration 2012a).

TABLE 29.1. **Pacific Northwest Energy Capacity and Supply by Source, 2013 estimates**

	Capacity *Megawatts*	Supply *Average Annual Megawatts*
Biomass	1,091	750
Coal	7,318	5,662
Hydro	34,247	16,279
Natural Gas Baseload	7,677	7,627
Natural Gas Peaking	1,706	N/A
Nuclear	1,200	978
Wind	8,551	2,607
Other*	512	131
Total	62,301	34,034

* *Geothermal, Petroleum, Pump Storage, Solar*

Source: The Northwest Power and Conservation Council

Benefits of the Region's Hydroelectric Dams

The dams in the U.S. portion of the Columbia basin are owned and operated by many entities and coordinated by the Bonneville Power Administration, an agency within the U.S. Department of Energy formed in 1937 with a mandate to provide energy at cost and prioritize service for the benefit of public utilities (Harrison 2008b).

About 40 percent of the electricity used in the region comes from federally owned hydroelectric dams, and is sold through Bonneville. As of 2013, there were 33 federally owned dams in the Columbia River basin, providing nearly 21,000 MW of power generation. Over time, this inexpensive and reliable supply has attracted substantial economic investment in aluminum production, shipbuilding, aerospace, biotechnology, computer systems, information technology, and e-commerce (Center for Columbia River History 2014).

Many dams in the Columbia Basin were designed for flood control or to extend navigable waterways inland (Bonneville Power Administration, U.S. Bureau of Reclamation, and U.S. Army Corps of Engineers 2001; Northwest Power and Conservation Council 2013c). The average annual runoff estimated to flow from the mouth of the Columbia is nearly 200 million acre-feet, yet the total amount of storage available is only 60 million acre-feet, and the system is operated to supply only about 40 million acre-feet on average to industrial, municipal, or irrigation uses (Harrison 2008b). Thus, quite unlike other major river systems in the United States, the bulk of annual flows in the Columbia pass through the system. Flows are stored and released seasonally through energy-generating turbines or over spillways. Bonneville and the U.S. Army Corps of Engineers draw down reservoir levels in the fall to provide the capacity needed for flood management as winter approaches, rely on monthly forecasts of runoff volume from January through April to provide space for precipitation and snowmelt, and aim to begin July with full reservoirs to meet late spring and summer demands for energy and water (U.S. Army Corps of Engineers and Bonneville Power Administration 2014). Dams are the only significant method currently available for storing electricity.

The Impacts of Concentrated Investment in Dams

The dams of the Columbia have inevitably altered fish habitat, reducing populations and prompting many decades of investment in over 150 fish hatchery and farming operations (Harrison 2008a). The reaches of the Columbia and its tributaries are home to a diverse array of fish species, including numerous salmon, sculpin, sucker, and minnow species (U.S. Department of Energy 2014c). Researchers estimate that between 10 and 16 million salmon and steelhead once populated the Columbia (Harrison 2008a). By the late 1970s, annual returns were down to 2.5 million fish (Northwest Power and Conservation Council 2012). In 2013, the biological opinion issued by the fisheries division of the National Oceanic and Atmospheric Administration identified 13 isolated runs of fish protected under the Endangered Species Act because of the effects of the operation of federally owned dams in the Columbia basin (National Oceanic and Atmospheric Administration 2014).

Figure 29.1. Native American fishing at Celilo Falls, 1950

Perhaps no other group has felt the impact of dam construction and fish decline quite like the Native American tribes of the region. By the time of contact with Europeans, Native American tribes lived in well-established settlements along the rivers of the basin or gathered seasonally at fishing sites (Harrison 2008c). The dams of the Columbia basin destroyed the historic fishing grounds and many sacred sites of the tribes, and blocked the passage of fish through hundreds of miles of river. For decades, tribes have invested in hatcheries to revive stocks depleted by commercial operations and habitat destruction, joined by state and federal agencies (Figure 29.1) (Bonneville Power Administration 2011). Today, tagging studies indicate that more than 90 percent of the salmon caught in the Columbia River are the product of fish hatcheries (Washington Department of Fish and Wildlife 2014).

Climate Change in the Columbia River Basin

The Intergovernmental Panel on Climate Change, the world's leading scientific body for the assessment of climate change, projects global temperatures to increase by at least two degrees Celsius by 2045 due to greenhouse gas emissions in our atmosphere (IPCC 2014; World Resources Institute 2013). This change in temperature will cause stress on every facet of our society (U.S. Environmental Protection Agency 2014).

The Climate Impacts Group, an internationally recognized research group within the University of Washington, downscales global models from the IPCC for the Pacific Northwest (Climate Impacts Group 2014a). The Climate Impacts Group (Climate Impacts Group 2014b) projects an increase in annual average temperature of 1.8 degrees Celsius (3.2 degrees Fahrenheit), with greater variation in precipitation (decreases in summer, increases in winter) within the next 30 years, with several resulting effects, including:

- Increase in summer droughts due to warmer temperatures
- Increase in winter flooding
- Reduced snowpack for late summer stream flows
- Greater uncertainty regarding intensity of precipitation

The degree to which snowpack is forecasted to change is striking, and of profound significance for the management of the Columbia River basin. Snowpack is, after all, a "free" form of water storage that helps maintain stream flows during otherwise dry times of year. Forecasts of change in snowpack, measured as snow water equivalent, have prompted organizations in the Pacific Northwest to take action to mitigate greenhouse gas emissions and to prepare to adapt to changes in the hydrologic cycle.

Planning for Hydropower in an Era of Climate Change

Since 1980, when Congress passed the Northwest Power Act, planning for the hydroelectric assets of the Columbia River basin has been the responsibility of the Northwest Power and Conservation Council, comprised of two appointees each from the governors of Washington, Oregon, Idaho, and Montana. The plan adopted and periodically amended by the council sets goals for the Bonneville Power Administration (Northwest Power and Conservation Council 2012).

Besides planning for electrical power, the efforts of the council include plans and programs to protect, mitigate, and enhance fish and wildlife affected by the construction and operation of dams in the Columbia basin. These plans and programs are paid for with Bonneville funds, and must be consistent with state and local property rights, water rights, and the rights of the region's tribes.

The Northwest Power Act directs the council and Bonneville to give priority to cost-effective energy efficiency and renewable energy sources in meeting the region's needs. This mandate places Bonneville and the Pacific Northwest on a path of demand management, congruent with climate mitigation, for the foreseeable future. Forecasts suggest, however, that adaptive management challenges lie ahead.

Greenhouse Gas Mitigation Under Way

The council issued its Sixth Power Plan in 2010 (a five-year plan), at a time when Congress was debating federal legislation to reduce greenhouse gas emissions (Northwest Power and Conservation Council 2013b). Although efforts in Congress waned, multiple forces in the region have had the effect of reducing emissions to a substantial degree. These effects, supported by the council and Bonneville, can be summarized as follows:

- **Eliminating Coal-Fired Plants**. Rising coal prices, the aging of plants, more stringent federal mercury and air toxics standards, and the prospect of state-level standards for greenhouse gas emissions have contributed to plans to eliminate coal-fired power (Northwest Power and Conservation Council 2013b). The last two plants in the Pacific Northwest, a 550-MW plant in Boardman, Oregon, and a 1,340-MW plant in Centralia, Washington, are scheduled to close in 2020 and 2025, respectively (Kuipers 2011; Northwest Power and Conservation Council 2013b).
- **Promoting Efficiency**. By 2010, investments in energy efficiency in the Pacific Northwest amounted to 4,700 average annual MW, reducing the net amount paid for electricity by $2.5 billion. Expressed as generated electricity, this is enough to power Idaho and western Montana for a year, with enough left over to serve a city the size of Eugene, Oregon (Northwest Power and Conservation Council 2013b). In the 2010 plan, the council proposed acquisition of 1,200 MW in efficiency over the next five years. Bonneville, the Energy Trust of Oregon, and the Northwest Energy Efficiency Alliance act on these goals through transforming markets for durable goods, promoting new building codes and standards, and promoting programs by local utilities. One interesting effect was the agreement of retailers to limit stock of televisions to low-energy-using models when cable and broadcast services were transitioning to high-definition service, thereby resulting in lower household energy demand (Northwest Power and Conservation Council 2013c).
- **Pricing to Reduce Demand**. In October 2011, Bonneville began charging tiered rates for wholesale power. Tier 1 rates are based on the embedded cost of the federal power system. At about $30 per megawatt hour (March 2013), Bonneville's tier 1 price is reliably low compared to wholesale spot markets, which tend to fluctuate with the price of natural gas. Tier 2 rates reflect Bonneville's cost to develop new generation. Over the long term

these price signals should inspire local utilities to reduce demand (Northwest Power and Conservation Council 2013b).

- **Investing in Renewables**. Apparently driven by state renewable portfolio standards, investments in wind capacity have amounted to 7,300 MW and the costs of photovoltaic systems have plummeted, making solar power as marketable as wind power. As the council noted in its 2013 scan of the market for renewables, "the economic and commercial viability of solar power is improving and merits further investigation" (Northwest Power and Conservation Council 2013b, 16).

Investments in efficiency cost much less than new generation (two cents per kilowatt-hour), and wind and solar—like hydroelectric power—have very low incremental operating costs in comparison to fossil-fuel power plants (Northwest Power and Conservation Council 2013b). The council and Bonneville are investing aggressively in efficiency because it is cost-effective, but also because they prefer to delay the need to invest in new plants until alternative low-carbon energy sources have matured in technology and cost, and future environmental legislation or implementing regulations have become clear (Elsner 2009).

Up to this point, the bulk of new renewable investment has been in wind, which can exhibit extreme fluctuations over very short time frames. Therefore, utilities seek out additional energy resources to hold in reserve and balance loads. Despite the success of programs for efficiency and renewables, over 4,700 MW of natural gas-fired generation have been added in the region since 2000. If hydroelectric assets are already operating at the capacity allowed by multiple objectives, managers of the utilities in the region may demand more new generating facilities from nonrenewable sources.

Adaptation Challenges Ahead

Forecasted changes in climate are predicted to impact both the supply and demand for hydroelectric power in the Pacific Northwest. The ability to supply hydropower is strongly affected by climate-related changes in the amount and seasonal timing of stream flow. Demand for power is expected to increase with population growth, but also because warmer temperatures can affect the demand for energy for cooling (Elsner 2009). Unfortunately, the greatest impacts appear forecasted to occur in seasons and locations that may already be experiencing the greatest stress.

Seasonal changes in annual stream flow are expected to be substantial. Significant reductions in snowpack and modest increases in precipitation portend increased flows in the winter and spring months, when releases from dams are needed for flood control, and the hydroelectric system already produces more supply than the region can consume (Elsner 2009; Northwest Power and Conservation Council 2013b). In the summer and fall months, forecasted reductions to snowpack and stream flow are anticipated to decrease hydroelectric production by 10 percent in the 2020s and more over time. These reductions are expected to impact the peak period of demand for air conditioning, which occurs at a time of multiple competing demands for water supply, including flows over spillways for migrating threatened and endangered species.

Forecasted changes in snowpack and stream flow are not evenly distributed across the basin (Casola et al. 2005). On the basis of the IPCC medium emissions scenario, with a best estimate temperature rise of 2.8 degrees Celsius (likely range of 1.7 to 4.4 degrees Celsius), the Climate Impacts Group forecasts a near complete conversion of the Yakima River basin (part of the Columbia system), from snow-fed to rain-fed seasonal flows (Elsner 2009). It is difficult to visualize the effect this transformation will have on water and its uses in the Yakima River. The basin is agriculturally rich and has experienced development pressure in recent years. For more than a decade, the Washington State Department of Ecology has identified Yakima and its tributaries among the basins suffering from a critical shortage of water for endangered fish species (Washington 2002).

Keeping the Lights On

As a carbon-neutral source of power, hydroelectricity has played—and will play, in the face of climate change—a critical role in the energy profile of the Pacific Northwest. Reliable electricity at nationally low prices, half a century of management for the prevention of flood damage, and the capacity to invest in energy efficiency are among the benefits the region has received from the shared management decisions of Bonneville and the Northwest Power and Conservation Council. Mitigation, however, is just one side of the coin of climate change, and the need to adapt promises to stretch hydroelectric operations further than ever.

The U.S. Department of State is currently renegotiating the Columbia River Treaty with Canada. The recommendations of the region to the State Department are emblematic of the shared concern for the impacts and uncertainty brought by climate change. In their recommendation, the administrator of Bonneville and regional division commander of the U.S. Army Corps of Engineers explain that the goals of hydropower and flood risk management need to be joined with the goal of providing a more comprehensive approach, based on the functions of the ecosystem for fish, other wildlife, and the cultural resource interests of the tribes. Perhaps most importantly, the recommendation states that each and every element of a new treaty should consider the impacts of climate change. As they say, current uses of the system will be affected in ways that may not be adequately predicted today. Under such circumstances, the only conceivable way for operations to proceed is to allow for adaptive management as time goes on.

Lights on or off?

CHAPTER 30

Planning for Greenhouse Gas Reduction: An Oregon Perspective

Anne Russett, AICP, and Amanda Joy Pietz

In 2007, the Oregon legislature declared that the impacts of climate change pose a serious threat to the economic well-being, health, and environmental resources of the state (Chapter 907, Oregon Laws 2007). The legislature's greenhouse gas emissions reduction goals were to halt increases in emissions by 2010, and reduce those emissions to 10 percent below 1990 levels by 2020 and to 75 percent below 1990 levels by 2050.

To meet these ambitious policy goals, the state needed to act. In part through the recognition that emissions from the transportation sector account for approximately 30 percent of all greenhouse gas emissions in the state (Oregon Department of Transportation 2009), the legislature passed Senate Bill (SB) 1059 (Chapter 85, Oregon Laws 2010, Special Session). SB 1059 directed the Oregon Transportation Commission (by proxy the Oregon Department of Transportation) to develop a statewide transportation strategy to aid the state in reaching its greenhouse gas emissions reduction goals.

The Planning Process

In response to SB 1059, the Oregon Department of Transportation (2013) initiated a two-year planning process to develop the *Oregon Statewide Transportation Strategy: A 2050 Vision for Greenhouse Gas Emissions Reduction* (Oregon 2013b). At the time, no blueprint or guide existed to inform the process. The Oregon Department of Transportation decided to design the process with flexibility in mind, incorporating stakeholder outreach and utilizing advanced modeling tools to inform the policy direction (Pietz and Gregor 2014).

A team of consultants, agency managers, planners, economists, and technical staff collaborated with a policy and technical advisory committee to develop the Statewide Transportation Strategy. The advisory committees were comprised of elected officials, agency commissioners, regional and local jurisdiction staff, freight and aviation industry representatives, special interest groups, and others from across urban and rural Oregon representing a variety of fields and interests. To identify potential strategies, the Oregon Department of Transportation built a model called GreenSTEP (Greenhouse Gas Strategic Transportation Energy Planning Model)[1] for analyzing the effects of a variety of factors on greenhouse gas emissions, and used the model to evaluate nearly 200 different scenarios, each representing unique policy combinations. Factors included, for instance, the amount of light- and heavy-duty vehicle travel, public transportation service levels, parking pricing, and land-use patterns. In addition to estimating greenhouse emissions, GreenSTEP estimated other evaluation measures such as vehicle miles traveled, energy consumption, travel delay, and household transportation costs.

A Vision for Reduced Emissions from the Transportation Sector

The Statewide Transportation Strategy is not a regulatory document; it charts a potential path forward. Despite the aggressive assumptions made, the experts and policy makers involved in the process considered the mix of strategies plausible. In this vision, total transportation sector emissions will be reduced by 60 percent from 1990 levels, which equates to an 80 percent reduction in per capita transportation sector emissions. To reach this level would require aggressive action from federal, state, and local governments, and the private sector on a broad range of strategies, including:

- Cleaner vehicles, engines, and fuels
- Enhanced operational efficiency through technology, infrastructure investment, and operations management
- Greater transportation options that produce fewer emissions and provide more efficient movement of people and goods
- Land-use planning that supports the transportation network through location proximity, compact growth, and development
- Pricing mechanisms that support more sustainable funding and provide market incentives for developing and implementing ways to reduce emissions

Relationship to Transportation Planning in Oregon

As shown in Figure 30.1, the Oregon Transportation Plan sets the foundation for transportation planning and influences the policy direction for other state modal

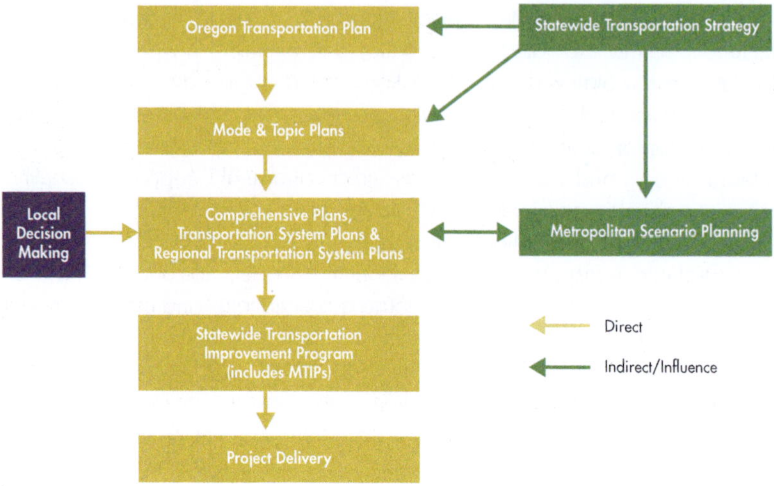

Figure 30.1. The Statewide Transportation Strategy in context

and topic plans, as well as local transportation system plans. The Statewide Transportation Strategy plays a different role in the transportation planning process. It functions as an aspirational document that points to promising approaches for policymakers and planners to consider at the state, regional, and local level.

Moving Forward

The Oregon Transportation Commission accepted the strategy in March 2013, and the Oregon Department of Transportation is moving forward with implementation. The Statewide Transportation Strategy does not identify which specific strategies to pursue or when to pursue them. Commitments to actions will be an important next step in achieving the targets set by the state and the benefits that accompany emission reductions, such as improved health, cleaner air, and a more efficient transportation system.

The Oregon Department of Transportation has completed the first of three implementation plans. Recognizing that the agency already engages in many efforts that help to advance the Statewide Transportation Strategy, such as the development of a road user charge program and the pursuit of expanded passenger rail service, the first implementation plan focused on new or expanded efforts to implement within five years. This plan includes actions with a relatively high degree of political acceptance and low cost that the agency expects will produce fairly rapid greenhouse gas reductions. Furthermore, the short-term plan only includes initiatives within the Oregon Department of Transportation's authority.

The actions in the short-term implementation plan include, for example:

- **Electric Vehicle and Low Emission Fuels**. Expand ongoing work around electric vehicles in the state through such actions as the development of communication materials that highlight the benefits of alternative fuel vehicles and the creation of maps and other resources that identify the state's existing vehicle charging network.[2]
- **Eco-Driving**. Promote eco-driving or fuel-efficient driving, through public educational materials and an eco-driving certification program for transit operators (Oregon 2014a).
- **Metropolitan Area Strategic Assessments**. Work in partnership with Oregon's Department of Land Conservation and Development to negotiate technical and financial assistance with metropolitan planning organizations interested in a strategic assessment. Strategic assessments evaluate how a region's transportation system would likely perform in the future, assuming that adopted plans are implemented and current trends continue. This is one of the first steps in a scenario planning process, which includes the use of models and other analysis tools that allow metropolitan areas to ascertain whether they are on track to meet regional goals, including greenhouse gas emission targets and community visions.
- **Intelligent Transportation Systems**. Use technology and software to improve system operations and management. Deploy variable speed limit projects, plan for the expansion of adaptive signal control technologies, strengthen interagency coordination related to incident management, and develop a TripCheck Smartphone application that provides travelers with improved access to traveler information, such as roadway conditions, route information, and modal options (Oregon 2014e).
- **Transportation Options**. Develop an employee Transportation Options Plan that focuses on internal agency operations and developing opportunities, such as carpooling and telecommuting, and a topic plan for policy direction on transportation options statewide (Oregon 2014c).
- **Statewide Transportation Planning**. Incorporate the Statewide Transportation Strategy into everyday planning practices. Planners and policy makers should consider greenhouse gas reduction and work to move in the direction of the vision set by the strategy in all statewide plans, plan updates, and guidance documents.

The Oregon Department of Transportation has committed to the preparation of a biennial progress report for the Oregon Transportation Commission. This report is intended to update state officials and others on the status of implementation programs, as well as the cumulative statewide change in greenhouse gas emissions in the transportation sector.

CHAPTER 31

Shifting Baselines: Dam Removal and the Evolution of Environmental Ethics in the Pacific Northwest

Ken Yocom

The Last Dam Summer

In 2011, the U.S. National Park Service and the Olympic National Park distributed more than 5,000 buttons and other promotional materials emblazoned with their new marketing platform, "The Last Dam Summer." The promotional campaign celebrated the removal of two hydropower dams on the Elwha River, the largest dam removal project in U.S. history and the second largest ecological restoration project in the United States, behind only that of the Everglades. While the summer represented a remarkable moment for the Elwha and the surrounding communities, its greater significance rests as a moment of transition, the overlap between the end of an era in which the river had been contained, controlled, and harvested and a new beginning. For nearly 100 years the Elwha Dam and the Glines Canyon Dam transformed the community, ecology, and economy of the river and surrounding area. After more than 25 years of negotiation and debate, the new beginning and the return of a free-flowing river was about to take place.

This inherently local story rapidly began receiving national and even global attention from news outlets and media productions, capturing the imagination of many about the opportunity dam removal would present for restoring anadromous salmon runs and the return of an ecology that had been lost for so long. In many ways the story of the Elwha River and the removal of the two dams represent a distinct shift in the policy and ethics that have, for such a long time, reflected a utilitarian and progressive perspective toward nature (Figure 31.1). Yet it is also a reminder of the important role these perspectives, particularly on dam construction and riverine management, have had in shaping our contemporary environment and communities.

Figure 31.1. The Elwha River above the dam sites

Hydropower and Economic Growth

On a national scale, the construction and use of dams over the past 150 years to harness the power of free-flowing rivers has been closely linked to the settlement of vast regions of the United States and its rise as a global economic power (Billington, Jackson, and Melosi 2005, White 1995). Ranging in scale from small, privately owned water impoundments to the massive Hoover and Grand Coulee, dams were constructed across the United States during the 20th century as a legacy of Progressive Era water policy, focused on maximizing the efficient use of a hydrological resources (Billington, Jackson, and Melosi 2005). Peaking in the decades between the 1930s to the 1960s, dam construction was viewed as a technological achievement, an extension of a utilitarian perspective for controlling and utilizing the resources provided by nature in service of American society and economy (Sowards 2007). As historian Mark Harvey observed, "Dams [. . .] harnessed 'wild' and 'untamed' rivers and transformed them into docile waterways" (Harvey 1998, 3 as cited in Billington, Jackson, and Melosi 2005).

As the rivers were transformed, so too was the American landscape. In some cases the damming of rivers improved access and navigation and controlled flooding, resulting in agricultural and urban development in floodplains. In other cases dams had more far-reaching impacts on the landscape, as irrigation sources for once arid lands, as sources for municipal water supplies, and to produce electricity. The realization of such great economic potential drove this extended era of dam building and settlement resulting in, according to some estimates, more than two million dams of all sizes across the United States and the impoundment of more than 60,000 miles of rivers.

In the Pacific Northwest, the largest scale landscape transformation of its time was the construction of the Grand Coulee Dam on the Columbia River. Completed in 1941, the Grand Coulee provides irrigation for more than a half-million acres in the arid Columbia Basin of eastern Washington, and for a period it was the world's largest hydroelectric power generator. Coupled with other hydroelectric dams in the Pacific Northwest—in Washington, Oregon, and Idaho—hydroelectricity production meets more than half of the energy demands in the region and supports the lowest energy costs per household of any region in the United States (Northwest Power and Conservation Council 2013a). According to the National Inventory of Dams (NID) produced by the U.S. Army Corps of Engineers, in Washington alone, there are 798 dams listed in the NID, 83 of which are for hydroelectric production (U. S. Army Corps of Engineers 2014).

Competing Values

While the positive impact of dams to the economy of the region and nation is readily apparent, they come with high environmental and sociocultural costs in the form of community dislocation and compromised landscapes, ecosystems, and fisheries (Pizzuto 2002). Yet it wasn't until the 1960s and early 1970s that incidents such as the Teton Dam failure in southeastern Idaho and a growing debate over the effects of dams on migratory fish populations began to coalesce on regional and national scales. forcing agencies such as the Bureau of Reclamation and the Federal Energy Regulatory Commission (FERC) to reevaluate their processes and management practices regarding dam safety and environmental mitigation strategies (Billington, Jackson, and Melosi 2005).

In the following decades, petitions, filings, and lawsuits regarding dam safety and their ecological impacts increased, and trends in dam oversight and management began to reveal an effort to seek new alternatives, provide mitigation for lost resources, and in some instances remove the dams altogether. Since the middle decades of the 20th century, the rate of new dam construction at the regional and national scale has subsided considerably, and in some instances where the use or economics of small dam operations and maintenance are no longer viable, they have been removed (Poff and Hart 2002).

Placed squarely in the midst of these larger debates are the Elwha River and the Elwha and Glines Canyon dams. Located on the Olympic Peninsula of Washington, the Elwha River draws water from the peaks of the Olympic Mountains in the Olympic National Park and flows north before releasing

Figure 31.2. The Elwha River watershed

into the Straits of Juan de Fuca. Once one of the most productive rivers in the Puget Sound region, supporting six species of Pacific salmon and steelhead (*Oncorhynchus spp.*), it was dammed in the early 20th century to produce electricity and support the growth of the nearby city of Port Angeles and the surrounding region. Never constructed to provide passage for migrating fish despite a state of Washington mandate even during those times, the ecological and cultural impacts to the communities that relied on the fish and river system were immediate. Further, over time the dams no longer generated enough power to remain economically viable (Figure 31.2).

While the physical event of the dam removals highlights an important period in this project, the convolution of ethics, politics, and economics that lead to the event and the projections and expectations for what are to come reveal the complex issues engaged by contemporary approaches to natural resource use, energy production, and environmental planning.

The Elwha

While the narrative history of the Elwha system reaches back centuries, intrinsically tied to the community, culture, and economy of the Klallam people, the role of the dams in transforming the biological and physical processes of the river system begins with Euro-American settlement in the region. Specifically, it dates to 1890, when a young Canadian emigrant named Thomas Aldwell arrived on the Olympic Peninsula. At the time Port Angeles was a small, yet burgeoning frontier town ripe with rumors of a railroad and filled with high expectations for future industry, development, and prosperity (Hult 1954). Described as "an idealist of the industrial capitalist stripe," Aldwell wholeheartedly took up the banner for progress, proclaiming himself a "conquerer" of the wilderness (Crane 2011, 41). Author Jeff Crane wrote that Aldwell cast "himself in the image of the heroic pioneer, he saw or portrayed himself as playing a critical role in transforming raw wilderness, as he understood it, into a thriving urban community, not merely a domesticated landscape of welcoming hearths but one of production and wealth" (Crane 2011, 42). He found this opportunity with the Elwha.

Aldwell's perspective toward the environment and broader concepts of nature was common in his time. Like many other settlers of European descent, he embraced a utilitarian perspective of nature in which the water, wildlife, and forests were present for their value and use in the economy (Nash 1989). Seeking to harness its power to provide electricity and support growth in Port Angeles and the surrounding region, Aldwell gathered investors, formed the Olympic Power Company, and shortly thereafter began construction on the Elwha Dam, five miles up from the mouth of the river. After an initial attempt failed, the earthen dam was constructed and began operations in 1913. Almost immediately it was realized that the single dam would be insufficient to meet the energy demands of the growing region and plans were initiated to construct a second hydropower project on the river. Located eight miles upstream from the Elwha Dam at the head of a steep and narrow canyon, the Glines Canyon Dam was built, licensed by the Federal Power Administration (now FERC), and began operations in 1927.

While the two dams supplied a reliable source of power for the region and fostered growth and development during the early decades of the 20th century, they also significantly altered the established ecology and culture of the watershed. For centuries the Klallam people of the Lower Elwha lived in the valley and near the mouth of the river along the shores of the Straits of Juan de Fuca. Their community, spiritual beliefs, and economy were deeply embedded in the watershed and with the river and the salmon it produced. While state law at the time required design considerations for fish access on salmon and steelhead streams, the dams were both constructed without consideration for fish passage, effectively plugging the river and stopping the ability for native fish populations to complete their anadromous life history, thus decimating the population and reducing the return of fish from an estimated 392,000 annually to less than 3,000 (National Park Service 2005). With their decline, the community of the Lower Elwha Klallam people struggled to maintain their identity through, as author Lynda Mapes (2009, 74) describes, "[. . .] the sacrifice of their food, their homeland, even their very lives."

Although financial concessions were made to the people of the Lower Elwha Klallam and efforts to restore fish stocks through hatchery control and fish plantings were attempted, these had little noticeable impact. In the decades following the construction of the dams, the ecological health of the river, as well as the quality of life for the Klallam, continued to worsen. It wasn't until 1968, when the Crown Zellerbach Company, then owners of the dams, attempted to gain a federal license for the Elwha Dam and a relicensing of the Glines Canyon Dam in 1976, that conversations regarding dam safety, the financial viability of the dams, and social and ecological impacts were renewed. In 1986, backed by conservation groups such as the Seattle Audubon Society and the Sierra Club, the Klallam filed motion to FERC questioning the legality of the dams and seeking remuneration and a restoration plan for the depleted fishery as well as an order to provide for the phasing out and removal of the two dams.

Federal Action

The motion set forth a barrage of pleadings, petitions, and requests for further information from conservationists, the Klallam, and state and federal agencies until, in 1992, President George H.W. Bush signed the Elwha River Ecosystem and Fisheries Restoration Act (Public Law No. 102-495), mandating the full restoration of the river and directing the Department of the Interior to assess a range of alternatives that would enable the recovery of the river's ecological health and fish populations. A little more than a year later, the *Elwha Report* was submitted to Congress, addressing the costs and benefits associated with four alternatives for fully or partially removing the dams in comparison to the no-action alternative of retaining both dams without fish passage. Requests from Congress and federal and state agencies for more information resulted in a series of environmental impact studies (EIS) assessing programmatic and implementation issues. The 1995 Final Programmatic EIS concluded that the removal of both dams was the only way to meet the mandate for full restoration, and the Implementation EIS released in 1996 identified that the most feasible and cost-effective approach to managing the estimated 34 million yards of accumulated sediment (enough to fill more than 11 baseball stadiums) in the two reservoirs behind the dams was to have the free-flowing river erode buildup over time (Mapes 2013a).

No longer was it a question of *if* the dams were going to be removed, but *when* (Wunderlich, Winter, and Meyer 1994). For much of the next two decades, stakeholder groups including conservationists, tribal leaders, and local, state, and federal policy makers negotiated the removal of the Elwha and Glines Canyon dams. Discussions and disagreements initially centered upon if and how it should be done, then focused on who should pay for the project and what compensations were needed (Duda et al. 2008).

As part of these negotiations a robust research agenda was established to assess the baseline conditions of the physical, chemical, and biological properties of the river system and watershed, including the nearshore areas of the Straits of Juan de Fuca near the mouth of the Elwha (Duda, Freilich, and Schereiner 2008). The river processes had long been altered, and researchers and policy makers wanted to assess not only how the river had changed over the period since the dams were constructed, but to understand how quickly and to what extent the conditions of the watershed and river system will adjust once the dams have been completely removed.

In the end, the project is estimated to cost $325 million including the purchase of the dams, their removal, and the construction of flood protection infrastructure and two water treatment plants. Economic evaluations conducted as part of the 2005 Supplemental EIS estimate a return in value from dam removal and fisheries enhancement of more than $350 million over the next century.

Conclusion

On September 17, 2011, a large gathering of stakeholders and local dignitaries converged on the banks of the Elwha River above the Elwha Dam as a ceremonial, gold-painted excavator took the first scoop to remove the dams. Within months, the Elwha Dam was removed, and the deconstruction of the Glines Canyon Dam was well under way. Immediately, restoration began, reestablishing native plant communities on the now exposed lands that were once submerged by the waters of the reservoirs behind the dams, and within the first year, salmon and steelhead were sighted well above the lower dam site. Even greater numbers of returning fish were recorded spawning in the main channel and tributaries between the dams in 2012 (Figure 31.3).

Yet, as with any project of this magnitude, the removal of the dams has presented difficulties. Removing the dams has reengaged the transport of a cen-

Figure 31.3. Glines Canyon Dam

tury of sediment built up behind the dams. Although this was fully anticipated, several large storms in the fall of 2012 made the waters so turbid that they clogged the filtration screens at the newly constructed treatment plants. Deconstruction of the Glines Canyon Dam was halted for a year as adjustments were made. Merely a pause in the process, the dams were finally removed entirely by August 2014, and once again the river flows free.

Just as the dams had played a dominant role in the development of Port Angeles and the region, removing them will create new opportunities for growth and vitality in the region. As author Jeff Crane (2011, 4) writes, "The story of the Elwha River reveals a great deal about this relationship, tying together river ecosystems and human communities and fueling discourse over environmental issues, economics and government power." He adds, "Our evolving views and uses of the Elwha River reflect the very values and debates that define our culture."

Once cultural symbols of progress, removing the dams in order to improve ecological conditions on the Elwha River represents a shift in the ethical baselines of society and the relationship to our surroundings. The case argues that—despite often overwhelming odds and competing constituencies—we can effectively negotiate our policies and perspectives to improve relations, ecology, and the economy. Reflecting on a visit to the Elwha Dam site shortly after its removal, author Lynda Mapes wrote, "The future here had yet to take root. But the river was already back—roaring through its native channel plugged by the dam for a century, as if nothing had ever been amiss" (Mapes 2013b, 8).

CHAPTER 32

InterAction!

David Cutler

'WHAT IS THE CITY BUT [CONNECTIONS BETWEEN] THE PEOPLE?'
(WILLIAM SHAKESPEARE, *THE TRAGEDY OF CORIOLANUS*)

In Seattle, three independent yet interrelated outcome-based planning efforts—the Seattle Climate Action Plan (CAP), the Seattle 2030 District, and the Capitol Hill EcoDistrict—are prioritizing direct, tactical engagement with the connective networks between people and organizations to bridge the distance between planning and action. The goal is to effect rapid progress toward deeply sustainable urbanism.

Despite each effort's unique physical boundaries, assets and points of leverage, and actors and audiences, three common themes are contributing to project uptake: an acute understanding of the needs of constituents, direct contact with decision makers, and an ability to continuously adapt both process and outcomes to project goals.

The Seattle Climate Action Plan

In 2013, Mayor Mike McGinn, a former community organizer and Sierra Club state chair, presided over the first major overhaul of the CAP, shifting the overall emphasis from deep-green urban policy toward an earnest call to act (Seattle 2013d).

With action as the goal, planners at the city's Office of Sustainability and the Environment (OSE) sought to reframe the immense scale and complexity of citywide sustainability planning in terms that were clear, comprehensible, and personally relevant to the public. The intent was to build a "climate-friendly" constituency by communicating that the character and basic functionalities of low-carbon neighborhoods were consistent with long-standing community values, and that the CAP could help fulfill familiar needs, such as stable business districts, frequent transit service, and lower energy costs.

OSE enlisted professional design and media firms to provide photo-realistic visualizations of prototypical Seattle neighborhoods before and after the implementation of potential CAP-related policies; it collaborated with musician Chris Ballew to create a web-friendly *We're So Green* music video and infographic slide deck; and it recruited local citizen leaders as Planning Outreach and Engagement Liaisons (POELs) to organize and conduct events in their own neighborhoods on the city's behalf.

The initial public response was positive, but limited. Open houses reached nine underrepresented communities, online surveys garnered hundreds of responses, and in early 2014, CAP outreach expanded to grassroots sustainability organizations through Community Climate Forums at city hall. But even taken together, these groups represented only a fraction of the city. Legislation reached somewhat farther. With the support of the Seattle Planning Commission, the city council passed a "Transit Communities" amendment to the Comprehensive Plan, deploying new climate-friendly policy tools to areas within a 10-minute walkshed of high-frequency transit service, despite opposition from single-family neighborhood groups, the traditionally untouchable third rail of Seattle politics.

Capitol Hill EcoDistrict

The Capitol Hill EcoDistrict was initiated in 2011 by Capitol Hill Housing (CHH) to investigate how sustainability at the neighborhood scale could be engendered though public engagement. Notwithstanding its diverse and mobile population, the Capitol Hill neighborhood presented significant physical obstacles to building a coalition for coordinated projects. The development pattern consisted of more than 1,500 unique structures with fragmented ownership, comprising 70 percent of the EcoDistrict's total building area. CHH began the project by embracing this structural granularity, soliciting actionable strategies, plan directives, and communication tools directly from the community.

Visioning and coordination workshops generated grassroots visualizations and a consensus-based final report that, at the early planning stages, resonated as locally authentic (Figure 32.1). A series of CHH-led one-on-one meetings with nearby institutions, stakeholders, and potential funders, as well as a Community Forum, spawned an all-volunteer Steering Committee, chaired by Seattle University and a prominent neighborhood developer. Within a year, CHH garnered funding to hire a full-time EcoDistrict director.

Despite early organizational successes, maintaining momentum proved challenging. The EcoDistrict report had evaluated and catalogued 64 unique,

Figure 32.1. EcoDistrict visualizations reimagined Dick's Drive-In, a local neighborhood icon, as a "Bike-In," where burgers are grilled with solar energy and garnishes are harvested from rooftop gardens.

outcome-oriented strategies that EcoDistrict Director Joel Sisolak describes as suited to "a point in time." As the effort's emphasis naturally shifted from planning to implementation and as the leadership structure matured, the mechanics of consensus building, project prioritization, and measurement shifted as well. Sisolak says "visibility" (in addition to sustainability and near- or long-term impact) arose as a key driver in choosing what to undertake first, in part because "seeing" physical progress could garner public interest in a way that plan documents and analytics could not.

In 2014, the EcoDistrict successfully lobbied the city council for funding for on-the-ground pilot projects, (Seattle 2014a) and as Sisolak describes, it began working with local partners to implement high-visibility projects such as "Community Solar," district-wide shared parking, and new "Pollinator Pathways" along neighborhood Greenstreets. It also signed on to the Seattle 2030 District (detailed below), allowing access to the 2030 District's membership base, discounts on high-efficiency building energy systems, and other financial tools and resources.

Seattle 2030 District

The Seattle 2030 District began in 2009 with an audacious charge: establish a high-performance building district in the city's commercial core, halving

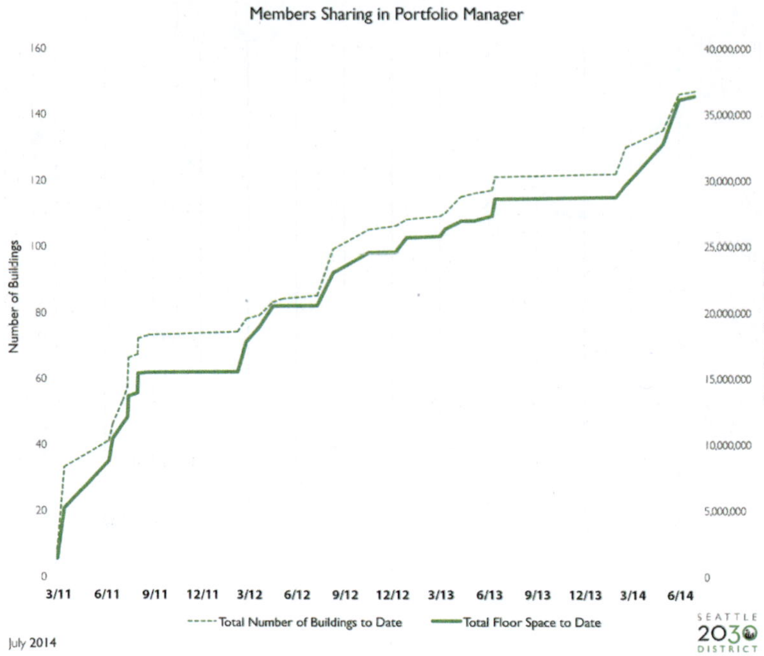

Figure 32.2. The Seattle 2030 District's membership growth was leveraged by direct peer-to-peer connections among building owners and managers able to communicate the competitive advantage of a downtown core with an advanced, deep-green building stock.

energy and water consumption and transportation emissions among existing buildings and achieving net-zero energy use for new construction by 2030. Two dozen local leaders in government, real estate, construction, and design initiated the effort by personally lobbying their organizations for in-kind contributions to the project. They amassed donations of $225,000, which leveraged a $450,000 EPA Climate Showcase Communities grant to support administration and start-up costs. If there was a coordinated engagement strategy, it was to maintain what 2014 Board Chair Brett Phillips calls a "bias toward action."

From the outset, the district's board structure required a majority membership of building owners and property managers. This helped place project planning decisions directly in the hands of those who would bear the risk of implementation. It reduced much of the initial member outreach to peer-to-peer conversations, and with nearly five million square feet of the district's building area controlled by the board alone, it helped establish an early foundation of organizational credibility.

To demonstrate that the district's goals were achievable across the breadth of building types, the group established district-wide baselines for energy and water consumption and commute-related transportation emissions by tuning national averages to local conditions using members' aggregated building performance information. In the district's first three years, fully 38 million square feet of building area signed on, representing over one third of the 96 million total square feet within the district's boundaries (Figure 32.2).

As of 2014, district members' buildings were beating the district's 2015 targets for energy and water twofold. However, the performance of the district as a whole lags behind. Like the EcoDistrict, most buildings in the 2030 District are small in building area, controlled by unique ownership, and have older, low-efficiency building systems.

Making Connections

The CAP, the EcoDistrict, and the 2030 District may be best understood as organizations in process, working actively to connect people to deeply sustainable outcomes. Their achievements and shortcomings suggest that progress can be incremental and as much the result of thoughtful, tactical interactions with people as advance strategy and planning.

When viewed together, the CAP's top-down climate messaging operation, the EcoDistrict's bottom-up visioning process, and the 2030 District's lateral membership drive reveal three basic contributors to forward progress:

- **Understand the audience**. Early on, OSE recognized that even in Seattle, where politics are progressive and educational attainment high (U.S. Census Bureau 2004), the public perception remained that sustainability planning was indecipherably complex and of limited personal relevance. CAP outreach was tailored to instill the political confidence to enact new climate-friendly legislation and programs. Similarly, the EcoDistrict built a constituency by reflecting community diversity in its myriad outcome-based strategies and visualizations. The 2030 District's property owner board could credibly make the business case for district membership.
- **Involve decision makers**. CAP's messaging to neighborhoods helped build political comfort with highly impactful climate-friendly legislation. The EcoDistrict's involvement of the city and local institutions on its steering committee helped address barriers to supportive investments and legislative actions. Likewise, the Seattle 2030 District's decision to place real estate entities at the center of the process removed the traditional separation between planning and action, allowing projects to be conceived and implemented simultaneously.

- **Adapt tactically, with goals in mind**. After CAP adoption, OSE shifted its focus from engagement to interdepartmental coordination and management, shepherding CAP-supportive implementation projects. To strengthen the organization, EcoDistrict projects were reprioritized to build public momentum. Despite heavy interest and involvement from design and planning professionals, the 2030 District deferred the development of detailed analytics to focus on membership growth.

Taking a step back even further, viewing these projects' focus on engagement against the backdrop of the "Seattle Process"—that is, perpetual debate, introspection, slow decision making, and revisionism (Moody 2003)—it is not hard to imagine that Seattle itself is simultaneously the thing that each effort is looking to overcome, to embrace, and ultimately to transform. It appears that the job of urbanism is never complete.

CHAPTER 33

Portland's Artisan Economy—Beyond the Myth of Romantic Localism

Charles Heying

Ah, the artisan economy! Such an evocative ideal, expressing the hope, in this time of deep concern over rapacious global capitalism, of a return to a local economy of self-sufficient yeoman entrepreneurs. In the misty haze of our imaginings, we see bearded brewers quaffing pints of a super-hoppy IPA, hipster moms draining raw cheese through pristine white muslin, urban farmers selling dahlias from their front doorstep, and chocolatiers individually wrapping one-off batches made from cacao grown in remote and exotic places.

Such images have sparked both parody (*Portlandia*) and adulation (*Those Who Make*—Vimeo Channel). In my book, *Brew to Bikes: Portland's Artisan Economy* (Heying 2010), I also celebrate artisans and their embrace of self-reliance. But since its publication, I have become concerned that the myth of romantic localism is distracting and inaccurate. It distorts the economic significance of artisan enterprise and stifles the discussion of artisans as exemplars of a new way of working and living in the postindustrial economy. Consider these challenges to the romantic image of small-scale artisans selling handmade goods to appreciative local patrons. Where in this image do we place Portland artisan Ken Wheeler whose Renovo Hardwood Bicycles will now carry the Audi brand and be sold in their auto showrooms throughout the world (Brettman 2011)? And how do we think about Jeanne and Dan Carver, who started an artisan yarn business to help save their high desert sheep ranch and now partner with New York-based Ralph Lauren to provide the yarn for U.S. Olympic Team apparel (Brettman 2011)? As romantic localists, should we feel incensed with Duane Sorensen, founder of Portland's iconic Stumptown Coffee, when he quietly sold out to TSG Consumer Partners, a San Francisco equity firm known for flipping fast-growing small companies (Brown 2011)? Has Sorensen abandoned his dedication to meticulously sourced, quality roasted, precisely brewed artisanal coffees that put Portland on the map as a world-class coffee town? Finally, should we be puzzled or fascinated that Portlander Steve Smith is obsessively working his way down to an ever smaller world of gourmet tea lovers with his new company, Smith Teamaker, after having founded and sold both Tazo and Stash tea companies (Cole 2009)?

These examples show that artisans can grow substantial enterprises with national and even global reach, but they do present a paradox. Why, now, is the artisan imaginary of locally based, personally crafted, small-scale enterprise so attractive to a global audience, and how do artisans manage the cognitive dissonance of these seemingly contradictory local DIY/global entrepreneur identities? It's a paradox I frame in my public presentations as "localism without parochialism" and attempt to illustrate with a discovery I made while writing *Brew to Bikes*. On a website describing life in the Victorian era, I found a list of "200 artisan skills required to make a Victorian town functional" (Hopkins 2009). To my surprise, I was able to count at least 112 of these skills being practiced in contemporary Portland—everything from milliners and dry stone wallers to beekeepers, brewers, and cheese makers. While this observation seems to link contemporary artisan enterprise to the romantic self-sufficiency of village life, it elides differences that define artisanship in these two eras. Contemporary artisans share with their Victorian counterparts many work/life characteristics such as autonomy, adaptive design, skill mastery, and responsiveness to local conditions, but they are not limited by the parochial and technological boundaries of the Victorian village. The materials, tools, transport, communications, and knowledge infrastructure of our era allows contemporary artisans to operate in villages of their own design. Most importantly, that transformative tool, loosely called the Internet, has become the on-ramp for artisans to find communities of interest, access specialized tools and services, and reach audiences that can grow quickly from local niche to global hit. The paradox of local artisans in a global era is that the reach of technologies that connect us to an unlimited network of possibilities, both push and pull us toward our particular place and passion, and encourage us to appreciate the same in others.

Consider the following. Several years ago, Claudia Lucero was that romantic hipster mom described in the opening paragraph. She was literally making cheese in her kitchen. She began, as many artisans do, with a DIY impulse. As she noted, "cheese is something that locals have been making for thousands of years, how hard could it be?" The few tools she needed, she found online from specialty suppliers. Soon she was selling her cheeses at Montavilla Farmers Market, a community project recently launched in her neighborhood. Her enthusiasm for home cheese making was infectious and friends encouraged her to offer classes. They filled up, and soon she was the local authority on homemade cheese. To expand her community, she launched her *Urban Cheesecraft* blog, and to bridge the gap between the complex professional trade and the novice cheese maker, she developed a simple DIY Cheese Kit.

The starter kit was a hit on her Etsy site. Local press loved the story of the cheese-making mom-turned-entrepreneur and so did the expanding network of foodie media. *Urban Cheesecraft* was profiled in the new *Home Dairy* book, and Daily Grommet, a website that shares unique products through video and blogs, also featured her kit. Etsy, the eBay for crafters, sent their video team to Portland and Lucero and her DIY Cheese Kit were the feature video on the Etsy home page. Her Etsy video caught the attention of Willams-Sonoma, which began offering her goat cheese and mozzarella/ricotta kits starting in the spring of 2012 (Lucero 2011a, 2011b, 2011c, 2012).

Beginning with intuitive sense of possibilities, Lucero capped her adventure with a marketing triple play. Etsy gave her shelf space in its department store in the Cloud, Williams-Sonoma promoted her kit in their brick-and-mortar stores, and she continued her local connections through direct sales at the farmers market. But unlike the parochial Victorian artisans whose domain was limited to the physical needs of their local village, Claudia Lucero, the intentional localist, served the specialized tastes and psychic needs for connection, meaning, and self-reliance in her found village.

What lessons can be learned from these vignettes that might be useful for urban planners in the Northwest? The first and most obvious lesson is that the lens of romantic localism distorts what is happening in the artisan economy. Some, perhaps many, planners dismiss artisans as a cute sideshow to the real economy. Artisans are those folks who run craft festivals for tourists and do nifty things in their garages that end up on knickknack shelves. From the stories presented here, it becomes evident that artisan production can be significant not only for its impact on the economy (craft brewing in Oregon is a $500 million business) (Oregon Brewers Guild 2014), but more importantly because artisans are modeling the way to work and live in the postindustrial economy. The mass-production economy is the mature forest that is being overtaken by age and events. Artisans are the pioneering species building the understory of the new economy.

Beyond this, I would argue that planners could learn from the challenge that the artisan economy represents to traditional models of economic development. While most people are employed in the service economy, economic development planners have focused nearly exclusively on the production economy. The dismissal of what is inadequately called the service economy is a legacy of industrial-era thinking, where economies seemed to have boundaries, where wealth was built by producing goods for export, and where the service economy was imagined as circular (taking in each other's wash) and nonproductive because "no area can reasonably expect to expand its economy by developing a higher than average number of grocery stores" (Cortright 2006, 39).

The story of Claudia Lucero suggests that in the postindustrial era you can grow an economy by "developing a higher than average number of grocery stores" or at least by creating alternatives to the traditional production/distribution models that rearticulate where and how food is made and sold. She disrupts that industrial model by selling her homemade cheese directly to her customers at a farmers market. She creates a new set of niche products too specialized to find shelf space in a chain supermarket. Through her classes she opens the black box of a processed food and shows how to make cheese for home consumption. She builds a community of interest as well as customers through her classes and blog. And the blog connects her globally to a community of DIY foodies and like-minded entrepreneurs such as the people at the Daily Grommet. She follows these expansions into the producer realm by making a DIY Cheese Kit.

Lucero's direct marketing, new services, and innovative DIY Cheese Kit have been disruptive innovations that do not fit well into the notion that you can't grow an economy by "developing a higher than average number of grocery stores." She is growing the economy. From her point of view, it has been a natural, if rather rapid, progression from local niche to global hit. But all of the disruptive innovation of Lucero and other artisans is generally dismissed as trivial or is only seen obliquely by economic development planners because the intellectual blinders of their economic training does not prepare them to recognize its meaning or value.

It is my sense that artisans are modeling the product qualities, organizational structures, work life, and outlook of our emerging economy. Urban economies in the early part of the 21st century will look a lot more like an artisan economy than they will the industrial economy of the century past. And while most artisan enterprises will remain part of the essential understory, some few will find the light and become the vigorous stands of a renewed economy. So nourish the understory, the old trees are falling.

CHAPTER 34

A Decade of Food Systems Planning in the Central Puget Sound

Branden Born and Megan Horst, AICP

For the past decade the Central Puget Sound region has been a national leader in community food systems planning. Notable elements have included data and assessment efforts, programs, policy change, food-specific plans, and new staff positions, partnerships, and collaborations. This chapter highlights that history, discusses impacts and policy gaps, and concludes with suggestions on future opportunities. To collect information for this chapter, we used as primary methods literature review and participant observation, augmented by focus groups.[1] We argue that food systems planning has become institutionalized, albeit unevenly and incompletely, in the region. It has raised the prominence of food systems issues, contributed to important issues such as food production and fighting obesity, and developed new mechanisms for regional collaboration around common planning goals including community, sustainability, and equity.

The central Puget Sound region is comprised of King, Kitsap, Pierce, and Snohomish Counties and over 80 cities and towns, tribes, port districts, and defined regional growth centers (Figure 34.1). These four counties form the boundary for the region's metropolitan planning organization, the Puget Sound Regional Council (PSRC). The diverse landscape supports a wide range of food production. Rivers are home to native salmon runs, which have been a food source for people in the Pacific Northwest for 10,000 years. The river valleys offer fertile farmland, and the estuaries provide rich shellfish grounds. Agriculture in this region is generally small scale, with farms from one to a few hundred acres, in contrast to the large commodity crop agriculture of eastern Washington (Canty and Wiley 2012). Food items commonly raised or grown include dairy, berries, herbs, shellfish, and vegetables (Puget Sound Fresh 2014).

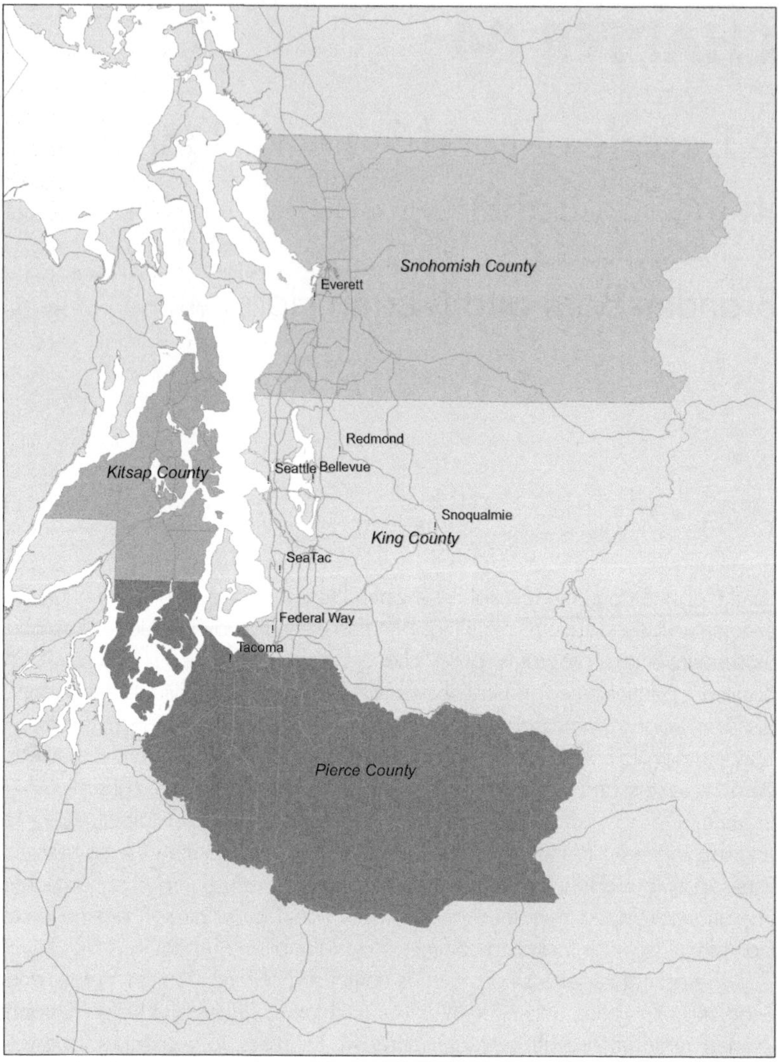

Figure 34.1. Central Puget Sound region (Source: GIS files from the state of Washington and city of Seattle, accessed via Washington State Geospatial Data Archive)

Influences on food systems planning in the Central Puget Sound region are similar to those across the country. The region's 3.7 million residents (Puget Sound Regional Council 2014b) rely largely on food imported from outside the region (American Farmland Trust 2012). While there is rich farmland, there is also pressure from development. In some places farmland is protected, but an aging farming population and a loss of agricultural infrastructure indicates that agriculture, as an industry, is not. Fisheries are threatened, as are the native salmon and the animals, cultures, and businesses that depend on them. Ocean acidification and water pollution in the Puget Sound threaten the important shellfish industry (Welch 2014) and endanger health. There are diet-related health disparities that hew closely to lines of race and socioeconomic status (Communities Count 2013). As is the case elsewhere, broader issues related to poverty and income inequity present major challenges to ending hunger. The region's food system is ultimately embedded within and influenced by the global, industrial capitalist food system—critiqued for its negative environmental and social impacts, consolidation of power and wealth, and lack of transparency and democracy (Koc and Dahlberg 1999). In this complex context, local governments have begun formalizing food systems planning.

The growth in food systems planning in the region has both influenced and been influenced by academic and professional literature. In a 1999 study, Potchukuchi and Kaufmann (2000) declared an absence of planner engagement in food systems work, citing food's low visibility, a perception of no problems, and its association with rural rather than urban policy. Since that article, scholars, conference organizers, academic journals, and the American Planning Association have brought visibility to food issues and firmly established food systems planning as a subfield. There is also evidence of a rising prominence of food systems planning practice across the country. Cities including Seattle, San Francisco, and New York have hired food systems planners. Regional planning authorities including the Delaware Regional Valley Planning Commission and the Chicago Metropolitan Agency for Planning have established food systems plans. There are nearly 200 Food Policy Councils across North America (Burgan and Winne 2013).

History of Food System Planning in the Central Puget Sound Region

Contemporary food system planning in the region has roots at least back to the 1950s. Diverse organizations were founded to address issues including healthy food retail (Puget Sound Consumers Cooperative, founded in 1953), urban agriculture (Seattle Tilth, founded in 1977), local food and farming (Cascade Harvest Coalition, founded in 1997), and hunger (Northwest Harvest Coalition in the late 1970s). These and other organizations have been responding to problems in the food system and gaps in service provision, and advocating for policy changes, many for decades. Their activity in the region has burgeoned, in terms of geographic range and level of activity, in the past 10 years. Their leadership has been an important influence on local government.

Efforts by government in the 1970s provided a base for a more comprehensive approach to food systems planning. In Seattle, government support for urban agriculture was formalized with its community garden program in 1974. The program is now one of the largest in the county, with more than 80 gardens and 6,100 gardeners. It is expanding to include food forests and community-supported agriculture. Many of the community gardeners have subsequently gone on to become active leaders in community food systems issues. Seattle also started funding emergency food programs in the 1980s, and other cities across the region now invest in similar programs.

In terms of agricultural preservation, King County became a national leader by establishing one of the first Purchase of Development Rights programs for farmland preservation. The King County Farmland Preservation Program was funded by bond measure in 1979, and has protected some 13,000 acres of farmland from development. In 1985 the county designated specific Agricultural Production Districts, which now consist of 42,000 acres (King County 2013a). Prompted by the state's Growth Management Act (GMA), other counties have followed. All four counties are part of a Regional Transfer of Development Rights alliance, although it has had minimal impact on agricultural land to date.

The Washington legislature adopted the GMA in 1990. It created urban growth boundaries for cities and required counties to preserve agricultural lands. While King County was an early adopter, others responded only after legal action by a nonprofit statewide watchdog organization, now called Futurewise. These includePierce County, for failing to identify and protect agricultural land and Snohomish County for allowing development on identified agricultural lands. While difficult to assess, many planners believe that the GMA has ultimately led to better planning for agriculture. In addition to land classification, the GMA requires jurisdictions to prepare comprehensive plans, something food systems planners see as potential vehicles for implementing new food policy.

By 2000, many actors were already working on various food systems issues, although often in disparate fashion. When the national conference of the Community Food Security Coalition was held in Seattle in 2002, it served as a catalyst for coordinated action. The conference spurred subsequent local meetings and yielded new organizations and outputs, including the impetus for a regional food policy council to be discussed later.

Building on these activities, Seattle has implemented numerous policies centered on the food system. These include loosening restrictions on urban agriculture and direct market sales in the zoning code, passing the Local Food Action Initiative, and developing the Seattle Farm Bill Principles (subsequently adopted by the National League of Cities as NLC Resolution #2012-16). The city declared 2010 to be a year of urban agriculture, and in 2011 hired a food policy advisor. In 2012, Seattle released a Food Action Plan and contracted with the Regional Food Policy Council to identify food policies for its forthcoming comprehensive plan update. Seattle also has an Interdepartmental Team on food issues that has survived several mayoral terms, engaging staff members from multiple departments in regular conversations around food issues. Attention to food system issues in the city has spread beyond the core advocates. For example, a 2008 Parks and Greens Spaces levy included significant funding for the expansion of community gardens. The Parks Department also included a focus on food issues such as gardening and cooking to achieve their goal of "Healthy Parks, Healthy You."

Other cities in the region have also been engaging in food systems work. For example, Tacoma, a city of approximately 200,000 people, has prioritized urban agriculture. Supportive policies were added to the city's Comprehensive Plan and staff are working with the Pierce Conservation District to expand the community gardening program. A proposal to develop a food forest in a city park has drawn support from the city council.

Six suburban cities (Des Moines, Federal Way, SeaTac, Snoqualmie, Redmond, and Renton) were part of a "Communities Putting Prevention to Work" grant through the Centers for Disease Control and Public Health, which was led locally by Public Health—Seattle and King County. The cities assessed their food environments and reviewed their current policies and ordinances. Subsequently, planners in each city took action. Des Moines added elements about increasing access to healthy food in city facilities and programs, while Federal Way added policies supportive of community gardening and direct farm sales. Snoqualmie adopted an Open Space, Parks and Recreation Plan containing policies supporting edible landscaping and community gardens, as well as a level of service standard for community garden plots (King County 2013b).

At the county level, King County has long been a strong supporter of agriculture. The county has a robust agricultural program and is nationally and locally recognized for its Purchase and Transfer of Development Rights programs (Canty, Martinsons, and Kumar 2012). In 2012, the county adopted a set of new policies to foster local food systems, including local production, economic development, and food access in its Countywide Planning Policies. County leadership and staff are pursuing strategies to foster the agricultural economy. Two new staff positions have been created, including a food economy program manager. The county has been collaborating with partners including Pike Place Market, PCC Farmland Trust, and the city of Seattle about connecting farmland preservation to marketing and distribution efforts, and working with farmers and environmental advocates to develop policies and practices around flood mitigation and response that are less restrictive for farmers. Apart from farmland issues, King County has also prioritized healthy eating as part of its public health approach, including initiatives for obesity prevention in local schools throughout the county. One King County employee said they are working to find a balance between flexibility and security in regulatory structures around public health—for example, in regulations on grocery stores, restaurants, and mobile vendors.

Snohomish County established a Focus on Farming program in its Economic Development Department, with the goals of increasing county farmland and improving farm productivity and profitability.[1] One action has been to streamline planning and permitting processes for farming. The county has also created an Agriculture Action Plan and an Agricultural Sustainability Project Report. In addition, it has led a consensus-based process with the intent to resolve a long-standing conflict among the agriculture industry, tribes, and environmentalists. While the process is still under way, the effort has resulted in an agreement that increases both restoration efforts and farmland. Snohomish County is also working with the Snohomish County Growers Alliance and other partners to establish a year-round farmers market and food hub in downtown Everett.

Pierce County established a Farm Advisory Commission and in 2006 released an Agriculture Strategic Plan, which describes a strategy to reinforce the agriculture sector's competitiveness in Pierce County. In 2012, a new Agriculture Roundtable, a coalition of organizations, individuals, and farmers dedicated to the conservation of productive agriculture, was formed. In 2014, Pierce County hosted a Farm Forum to facilitate discussions that would help expand local agricultural markets. There is also robust activity around healthy eating, particularly through the MultiCare Center for Healthy Living, which collaborates with the Tacoma-Pierce County Public Health department on nutrition education and healthy food access. Local community food systems leaders are in discussions about developing a forum for more coordinated policy and planning, with likely financial support from a local grant-giving organization.

In Kitsap County, a Food Policy Council was established by resolution to advise the board of commissioners on improving and maintaining a sustainable food system. The county also released a Strategic Agricultural Plan and Inventory in 2011, which identified follow-up actions and policies to protect and promote agriculture in its Comprehensive Plan.

The Puget Sound Regional Council's Regional Food Policy Council

In response to local governmental and nonprofit sector activity, the PSRC established the Regional Food Policy Council in 2010. It grew out of the Seattle/King County Acting Food Policy Council (AFPC), which met regularly from 2006 to 2009. The AFPC produced a series of briefing papers and an early regional food system assessment, and succeeded in getting food and agriculture included in the 2007 King County Climate Action Plan. Leaders of the AFPC worked with local and county elected officials and staff to formalize their organization as an advisory body to local government, which occurred in 2010 with the formation of the Regional Food Policy Council (RFPC). As a metropolitan planning organization, PSRC is well positioned as a connector of numerous urban and rural jurisdictions and has leverage over regional land-use planning and regional economic development. The organization's limitations include the inability for PSRC to lobby for state or federal policy change, differing priorities across the region, a relative lack of authority over local policies, and an absence of historic engagement on food issues beyond agricultural preservation.

In its first three years, the RFPC has provided technical advice to the city of Seattle about Comprehensive Plan policies and on assessing urban agriculture activity. Under a contract with the state of Washington, the RFPC developed a set of policy blueprints and is serving as technical adviser to other jurisdictions on issues including farmers markets, urban agriculture, local food procurement, and rural farmland preservation. While the RFPC has brought jurisdictional attention to food systems, it still struggles with its role and purpose, a concern expressed by members at its monthly meetings.

In short, food systems planning has become increasingly institutionalized in the region in the past decade. Evidence includes assessments, funding decisions, programs, plans, policies, staff, and collaborations. However, the process has been uneven. A scan conducted by PSRC staff of local policies across the region's cities and counties revealed stark differences, with many jurisdictions having no policies directly fostering community food systems and some even presenting barriers (Horst 2011). While some issues, like farming, are relatively well addressed in local policy, other issues including climate change, equity, and nutrition remain largely unmentioned. Local government's commitment to food issues via funding is also not conclusively supportive. For example, funding for anti-hunger programs is relatively minor and increasingly insecure. Meanwhile, food issues often receive lower priority than other traditional planning areas. It is unclear whether food systems planning has become institutionalized in a way that guarantees attention and resources when current leaders step away. Still, food systems planning has had noteworthy impacts.

Food Systems Planning Impacts

While it is premature to see major impacts, we briefly reflect on whether the first wave of community food systems planning is meeting its own goals. The American Planning Association's 2007 *Policy Guide on Food Systems Planning* established two overarching goals for planners: to help build stronger, sustainable, and more self-reliant community and regional food systems, and to suggest ways the industrial food system may interact with communities and regions to enhance benefits such as economic vitality, public health, ecological sustainability, social equity, and cultural diversity.

The Central Puget Sound region has made progress toward both goals. The past decade of food systems planning has corrected the misconception that there are no problems in the food system and has demonstrated that food issues are deeply connected to other planning activities. According to one interviewee, the impact has been "a sea change . . . more people get it. Food is not questioned. There has been a significant cultural shift." Even given the short history, there is some evidence of impact. Community food systems planners and collaborators have developed innovative ways to foster local food production and consumption, address environmental concerns, and encourage healthy eating. There is increased infrastructure for local food production, with over 81 community gardens in Seattle (up from 16 in 1980) and 66 in Pierce County. Local food purchasing has increased, with direct-to-consumer sales in King County (farmers markets, farmstands, CSAs) up 15 percent per year from 2002 to 2007 (U.S. Department of Agriculture 2002, 2007). Less food waste in Seattle goes to the landfill, from around 45 thousand tons in 2006 to 33 thousand tons in 2010 (Seattle Public Utilities 2010). There was a 17 percent decline in youth obesity in participating schools (from 9.5 percent to 7.9 percent) after Public Health—Seattle and King County partnered with communities to implement obesity prevention initiatives (King County 2014).

Still, policy and programmatic gaps remain. While significant amounts of farmland have been protected, much remains at risk of development, and more may be needed to ensure a sufficient agricultural base to feed the population if that became a regional goal (American Farmland Trust 2012; Canty, Martinsons, and Kumar 2012). Meanwhile, otherwise successful farmland protection programs have not solved the challenges of insecure land tenure or the tenuous economic viability of farming. And despite innovation within the anti-hunger network, food insecurity levels have actually risen and local government funding to counter hunger is limited and not guaranteed.

A big challenge is that gains in the food system are not shared by all residents. While local food purchasing has increased, much of it remains out of reach for poor residents. One interviewee reflected: "I used to talk that we need to build an alternative food system—and now I know there is one—but look at all the people who don't have the alternative. It's not about creating an alternative—but making it equitable."

Attention to local food systems issues has often missed the justice or sustainability implications of the food system. For example, food system planning is only just beginning to consider the system's reliance on low paid food systems employees, including restaurant workers and immigrant farm labor. Current socioeconomic and political economic realities create challenges that are difficult to address at the local level. For example, rising income disparities exacerbate uneven access to healthy foods. Lastly, while there are many discussions about food systems, they rarely consider the diverse and historic Native American food systems that existed in the region and are still important to local tribes. Ironically, the tribes might be the strongest actors legally, as they have significant claims on resources through treaty rights.

Food systems actors understand that to address these deeper problems, they must collaborate across jurisdictions and interests to address bigger issues, including federal policy and social inequalities. One way local efforts have attempted to address federal policy gaps is through Farm Bill advocacy, although to many this seems an unwinnable battle. One interviewee commented on the high subsidies for commodity agriculture, noting that "the reality is that we have this highly subsidized system—and how do we create something to compete with that? Building a food system that works—and yet we don't have that subsidy—that is something that has to be called out . . . there is $22 million going to marketplace right now, none of which is supporting the work we do." Another interviewee reflected, "It is tough, we need to take on the whole economic system. Our failure is that we haven't been able to reform our economic system." While food system planners generally recognize the problem, no one is quite sure how local community food systems planning can combat it.

Conclusion

The experience in the Central Puget Sound region—a longtime leader in food systems planning—provides an example for food systems planning across the country. While the evidence of increased food systems planning activity is to be celebrated, its relative prominence is low and it warrants further development. To ensure its growth locally and across the county, critical needs are: adequate funding for staff positions and programs, attention from policy makers and senior decision makers, integration of food systems goals into other planning activities ranging from parks and recreation to health and transportation, and coordinated pressure and advocacy from citizens and activists.

Going forward, there is a need in Central Puget Sound regional food systems planning to find more common ground among the goals of protecting farmland, fostering environmental sustainability, promoting economic development, and fostering equity and social justice. One way to foster shared commitment is via new and enhanced collaborations among government, the private sector, farmers, nonprofits, and community groups—for example, in getting more fresh, local food into the emergency food system and in providing incentives for fruit and vegetable consumption as part of public health programming.

The early gains and success of food systems planning in the Central Puget Sound region provides an important baseline for ongoing efforts. One direction for future work is in more critical reflection and community engagement. This means paying attention to broader discussions among food systems activists, participants, and researchers. An important consideration for planners should be the critiques of alternative food projects (Hope-Alkon and

Mares 2012), as many ideas in food planning come from this arena. Alternative food systems efforts, including farmers markets, community supported agriculture, farm-to-school, and food labeling have potentially positive and negative aspects. If implemented uncritically, they can represent simply a reformist approach to an unsustainable and inequitable food system. These efforts can easily perpetuate existing inequities. Critiques of these projects are that they focus on highly individualized purchasing decisions in lieu of political action (Allen 2008) and that they continue a paternalistic, color-blind approach that assumes a universal ethic (generally that of a white middle class) around food (Guthman 2008). Central Puget Sound region food systems planners can respond to this critique by more intentionally engaging diverse groups (for example, as members on the Puget Sound Regional Food Policy Council) and more explicitly prioritizing social justice.

A second area for critical reflection is whether community food systems planning should be seeking incremental reform or a more radical food systems transformation. Thus far, community food systems planning has tended more toward the former, and this is probably where most planners feel comfortable. As noted by food systems scholars, reformist approaches to food systems work can perpetuate existing political economic relationships (currently, neoliberal and capitalist) and thus offer little hope for significant systemic change (Holt-Gimenez and Shattuck 2011). At the same time, incremental social reform may be exactly what is needed to build food democracy and lead to greater local autonomy in food systems decision making and even a radical transformation (Hassaenein 2003). The role of planners in fostering incremental reform and structural transformation is a part of a much larger discussion about the role of planning, and worthy of consideration in future food systems planning and research.

CHAPTER 35

Cart Blanche: Pacific Northwest Street Food

Sarah Mooney

Much has been written up about the food cart scene in the Pacific Northwest. However, television programs like *The Great Food Truck Race* on the Food Network understandably gloss over the greasy underbelly of this amusing and delicious aspect of the food world. Local regulations vary widely for these businesses and can be daunting for small businesses trying to get started with limited budgets.

While mobile street food vendors have a long-standing tradition in major cities like New York, Bangkok, and Berlin, the movement did not exist with much interest in the Northwest until the last decade. One of the major differences between the Portland and Seattle food cart scenes is the permanence of food cart locales. Unlike the tradition of mobile food carts temporarily set up on a street corner for the lunch hour rush, Portland has found economic resurgence by creating food pods. These pods often include between eight to 20 food trucks, are located in privately owned lots, and are regulated by the city. Many of these pods also contain picnic tables, restroom facilities, and heated tent areas for year-round use (Figure 35.1).

Today in Portland you can find more than 600 hundred food carts in about 40 pods. Vendors offer services from coffee and breakfast for early-morning commuting professionals to crepes and gravy-covered fried food with 4:00 a.m. closing times for the late-night crowd. Some of the landlords who own the land simply want to maximize their profits, while others manage their pods more closely, creating a strong sense of community among the businesses and patrons. Because of low operating costs and the interest in self-employment, Portland's food cart scene is successfully surviving the eco-

Figure 35.1. Portland food pod on SE 27th and Burnside

nomic recession. According to *Yes!* magazine and OregonBusinness.com, a successful vendor can support a family, bringing in as much as $50,000 a year (Burningham 2009; Quillen 2014). Several highly successful food carts, like Salt and Straw, Pok Pok, and Whole Bowl, have even transitioned from this start-up business model to create brick-and-mortar restaurants. Although the initial hype has diminished since the 2010 waiting list for a pod spot, the food cart industry in Portland continues to see a massive interest by both locals and tourists.

Heading north, you won't find food pods in Seattle, where efforts to activate the public realm downtown have only recently led planners to rewrite the regulations that previously limited street food to hot dogs and coffee. The Seattle departments of planning, parks, and transportation are now working together to make it easier for vendors to operate in parks, plazas, parking lots, sidewalks, and designated locations in the right-of-way. Lunchtime around Amazon's campus in South Lake Union swarms with food trucks that roll in to feed the thousands of employees who now work in the neighborhood. These carts then roll out after the lunchtime rush (Figure 35.2).

While the street food scene has gotten much more vibrant in both cities, the challenge for people trying to start a business is the dizzying array of regulations from a variety of agencies and departments within those agencies. These business newcomers deal with how to dispose of graywater and grease, provide access to bathroom facilities, and locate sufficient power to

Figure 35.2. A Seattle food truck serving customers

operate. Seattle's Office of Economic Development has created a checklist with the list of requirements for those looking to start a food truck in Seattle (Seattle, n.d.). As planners continue working with street food vendors, Seattle is developing more opportunities for these small, delicious businesses to thrive.

Today, the street food scene is picking up momentum across the country. As every state has its own regulations and restrictions, some areas show greater success rates. Planners can help the process by creating checklists as Seattle had done or streamlining the process into a one-stop review. In the Northwest, Portland and Seattle has a dedicated consumer base that enjoys great food while supporting workforce jobs and local community businesses.

CHAPTER 36

Growing Transit Communities

Ben Bakkenta, AICP; Mary Pat Lawlor;
Amanda Roberts, AICP;
and Miranda Redinger

The central Puget Sound region plans to invest an estimated $25 billion in high-capacity transit in the coming decades, expanding the region's light rail, bus rapid transit (BRT), express bus, streetcar, and commuter rail services. This chapter describes the Growing Transit Communities Partnership (GTC Partnership) and the planning process that is designed to support this substantial investment by creating vibrant, equitable communities oriented around high-capacity transit.

The region's voters have approved a series of funding initiatives (Sound Move in 1996 and ST2 in 2008, and Community Transit's and King County Metro's BRT services) to build high-capacity transit systems to serve the central Puget Sound region's most densely populated and diverse communities. Over the next 10 to 20 years, 100 new transit stations are scheduled to be constructed throughout all parts of the region, in 25 high-capacity transit corridors. These systems are intended to improve regional mobility and reduce environmental impacts attributed to traffic congestion and vehicle miles traveled. Together, all of these investments represent a generational opportunity to shape the region's urban form toward more sustainable development, improve the quality of life, and foster vibrant, healthy neighborhoods.

What are Equitable Transit Communities?

Equitable transit communities are transit-served neighborhoods that provide housing and transportation choices, a mix of services, amenities, and businesses, and greater social and economic opportunity for current and future residents. Successful communities are created through inclusive planning and decision making, resulting in development that accommodates future residents and jobs, increases opportunity for existing communities, and enhances public health.

Regional Planning

The GTC Partnership is a regionwide coalition of businesses, developers, local governments, transit agencies, and nonprofit organizations. It developed the "GTC Strategy" through a collaborative, regionwide planning process. The strategy includes a framework of actions, tools, and projects that are intended to create equitable transit communities throughout the region. The work is consistent with VISION 2040, central Puget Sound's long-range vision for maintaining a healthy region—promoting the well-being of people and communities, economic vitality, and a healthy environment. Under Washington's growth management planning framework, VISION 2040 guides the development of regional implementation plans, local comprehensive plans, and development regulations.

The Challenges

Despite the strong planning framework that Vision 2040 provides, the central Puget Sound region was challenged to effectively implement many aspects of its vision. A fast-growing region, an additional 1.5 million residents are expected in the metropolitan area over the next 30 years.

With nearly 90 separate jurisdictions with land-use and transportation implementation authority, six different transit agencies, and a long, linear urban form constrained by geography, it was challenging to effectively coordinate decision making about growth and identify immediate local priorities across jurisdictional lines. Even though development of high-capacity transit was funded by voter-approved initiatives, the region lacked a coordinating vision for the future development of the areas near transit.

Regional leaders recognized the need for robust participation of these neighborhoods surrounding transit stations and along high-capacity transit corridors to ensure they benefit from—and are not harmed by—critical regional transportation investments. Regional researchers and institutions agreed on a single key objective: to create the sustainable, equitable communities envisioned at the state, regional, and local levels. Barriers to transit-oriented development and concentrated growth in regional transit station areas must be overcome. Several foundational reports and publications emphasized the need to develop new strategies and partnerships to address the issue of how to coordinate and effectively plan for equitable development in the region's high capacity transit station areas.(see Cascade Land Conservancy 2005; Nikolic et al. 2009; Puget Sound Partnership 2008; Quality Growth Alliance 2009).

How to Create Equitable Transit Communities

The GTC Partnership was initiated to implement regional and local actions that respond to these challenges, within the framework for growth in VISION 2040. The region was awarded a $5 million regional planning grant from the U.S. Department of Housing and Urban Development Office of Sustainable Housing and Communities. The grant funds supported the GTC Partnership's three-year (2011–2014) work program, which began with a foundational commitment to three key goals:

- To attract more of the region's housing and job growth near high-capacity transit
- To provide housing choices affordable to a full range of incomes near high-capacity transit
- To increase access to opportunities for existing and future community members in transit communities

To do so, they developed the GTC Strategy, an action framework for partners across the region, using a corridor-based planning approach. Corridor task forces for three new light-rail corridors (North LINK, East LINK, and South LINK) guided collaborative planning efforts that engaged partners and citizens. GTC partners developed a toolkit of 24 actions and strategies based on current needs and opportunities. This framework of strategies is designed to coordinate development, housing, jobs, and community amenities, and to attract transit-oriented development (TOD) along the three corridors. Strategies include:

- Establish a regional program to support thriving and equitable transit communities
- Build partnerships and promote collaboration
- Engage effectively with community stakeholders
- Build capacity for community engagement
- Evaluate and monitor impacts and outcomes
- Conduct station area planning
- Use land efficiently in transit communities
- Locate, design, and provide access to transit stations to support TOD
- Adopt innovative parking tools
- Invest in infrastructure and public realm improvements
- Assess current and future housing needs in transit communities
- Minimize displacement through preservation and replacement
- Increase housing support transit-dependent populations
- Implement a TOD property acquisition fund

- Expand value-capture financing as a tool for infrastructure and affordable housing
- Make surplus public lands available for affordable housing
- Leverage market value through incentives
- Implement regional fair housing assessment
- Assess community needs
- Invest in environmental and public health
- Invest in economic vitality and opportunity
- Invest in equitable mobility options
- Invest in equitable access to high-quality education
- Invest in public safety in transit communities

In addition, the GTC Partnership's work program included the following complementary efforts to guide the creation of equitable transit communities:

- **A regional equity network** to promote equitable community planning and mobilize residents and community groups representing diverse populations to participate in local planning and decision making and providing a forum for collaboration and discussion, along with expertise focused on equitable development principles and strategies
- **Affordable housing tools**, including local policies and financial tools to encourage and facilitate a wide variety of housing choices along high-capacity transit corridors, such as white papers and plans for a fund to encourage affordable housing preservation, a regional assessment of barriers to fair housing choice, a white paper to support legislation for a financing tool, an inventory of public lands, and a database mapping subsidized housing
- **Opportunity mapping**, a comprehensive, regional map of equity, opportunity, and sustainability in the Central Puget Sound Region
- **Capacity-building grants**, 67 grants totaling $525,000 to 43 community-based organizations to support engagement, outreach, organizing, and research
- **Puget Sound Equity Summit**, a two-day event that brought together more than 400 community members, activists, and representatives of the public and private sector focused on the mission of creating equitable transit communities

GTC Partners also developed other innovative tools and demonstration projects, including tools and resources to bridge the gap from goals and

Figure 36.1. Eight implementation approaches of the Growing Transit Communities strategy

policies to specific actions and steps to assist local communities in planning, decision making, and building local support for sustainable development. Catalyst demonstration projects and case studies in high-capacity transit neighborhoods serve as templates for sustainable development. Products included an Area-wide Environmental Impact Statement and Subarea Plan for Tacoma's South Downtown neighborhood, Urban Design Framework and Healthy Transit Communities Principles for Seattle's Northgate station area and urban center, and best practices research and implementation support activities for East Link station areas in Bellevue and Redmond.

The Next Steps

A three-part framework for action is envisioned to support the Growing Transit Communities Strategy moving forward:

- **The Pledge**—The Growing Transit Communities Compact affirms the support of a variety of partners for the partnership's work and a commitment to work toward regional goals by implementing the strategy. The compact includes numerous goals for growth and affordability in transit station areas and calls for ongoing collaboration and action.
- **The Playbook**—A Toolkit of Actions and Strategies with 24 recommended actions and strategies and eight Implementation Approaches (Figure 36.1), along with corridor specific priorities, designed to guide an evolving approach to implementing transit communities throughout the region.
- **The Plans**—Individual Work Plans set the stage for local governments, agencies, and organizations to develop individual work

> plans defining short- and medium-term actions for implementing the strategy. Successful implementation will require a shared commitment and collaboration among governments, major stakeholders, and community members. There are roles for many different regional and local partners, each with a distinct jurisdiction, authority, and mission. The nature and format of the individual work plans will vary to reflect the diversity of public and private partners, legislative and decision-making processes, and actions adopted.

Examples of these plans for the East Corridor and the City of Shoreline are shown below.

East Corridor Implementation, Washington

This GTC Partnership assignment advanced the work of locally adopted station area plans along the proposed East LINK light-rail corridor. A consultant team supported East Corridor Task Force members from the cities of Bellevue and Redmond, King County Metro, Sound Transit, A Regional Coalition for Housing, the Housing Development Consortium of Seattle-King County, Impact Capital, and other partners to complete several products focused on affordable housing, business retention and attraction, partnerships, and transportation. From research on the qualities that contribute to vibrant urban neighborhoods, to evaluation of potential for district energy and EcoDistrict implementation in the station areas, the work furthered community plans for implementing equitable transit-oriented communities to fit each station area context.[1]

The Case of Shoreline, Washington

The city of Shoreline is working on creating vibrant, equitable neighborhoods around high-capacity transit through station subarea plans for two North LINK stations. In developing its toolkit of actions and strategies, the GTC Partnership categorized station areas by typology of people and place, designating the 185th Street station as "Build Urban Places" and 145th as "Protect and Grow." For "Build Urban Places," the typology suggests that Shoreline intensify activity with infill development, fund capital investments, pursue a range of new affordable housing options, and address community needs through targeted investments. The report also recommended preserving existing affordable housing, adopting development regulations, making capital facility investments, and providing small business support for the "Protect and Grow" typology (Figure 36.2).

According to these plans, Shoreline would ensure that its subarea plans support redevelopment of equitable transit communities through comprehensive plan and zoning amendments, code regulations with design and transition standards, and incentives for affordable housing and green building. The subarea

Figure 36.2. City of Shoreline, 185th Street Transit Corridor concept

plans would identify capital improvements that encourage innovative engineering solutions, such as green streets and district energy. The planned action process, allowed by Washington's State Environmental Policy Act, would streamline future project approvals, reducing costs to facilitate affordable housing and greater investments in infrastructure and community amenities.

Conclusion: Realizing the Vision

The idea behind the GTC Strategy is to make the most of the region's major investment in high-capacity transit by encouraging redevelopment in station areas that locates housing, jobs, and services close to transit. The strategies, actions, and tools developed as a result of the GTC Partnership's work program are intended to support local jurisdictions, developers, and nonprofit organizations in creating vibrant, equitable transit communities throughout the region. Catalyst demonstration projects, case studies, and best practices highlighted in the work products are meant to serve as templates for sustainable, transit-oriented development. By working together, GTC partners from the central Puget Sound region believe they can achieve the vision for a sustainable future that advances our people, our prosperity, and our region.

CHAPTER 37

The Happiness Factor

Seth Geiser, Betsy Jacobson, AICP, and Mary Fialko

There is a confounding question that confronts planners and designers of urban space: Why do some urban spaces designed to meet traditional "good" design metrics (e.g., street trees, open space, resting places) fail in terms of activation, while some spaces with traditionally "bad" design qualities thrive?

The concept of using happiness to measure success is gaining traction globally, including a United Nations General Assembly (2011) resolution asking all governments to acknowledge "the pursuit of happiness and well-being in development with a view to guiding their public policies." As happiness initiatives are cropping up internationally, advances are also being made in the Cascadia region with policies including the Oregon's Genuine Progress Indicator (Graves 2012) and Seattle's Happiness Initiative (Sustainable Seattle 2014).

Given the reflexive relationship of inhabiting the city, shaped by and for each other, it is no coincidence that the prime factors in promoting active urban spaces match those that promote long-term happiness, including foremost:

1. Free-flowing and convivial connection between people
2. Direct and sensorial interaction with nature
3. Sense of control in one's place and actions

Happiness, then, is not some feel-good frivolity or mere distraction from the troubles of our time. Instead, happiness can be a seen as a foundational concept to reframe how we design space, how we think about space, and how we think about each other.

15TH

AVENUE EAST, CAPITOL H

On an overcast Sunday morning in November, we went to 15th Ave East in Capitol Hill, to linger, people watch, take photos, and

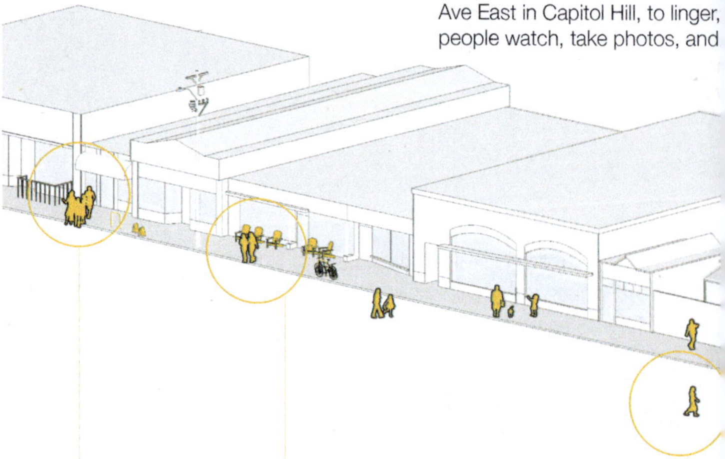

LINGERABILITY

This is the concept of "hanging out" or staying to be near the activity, the people, and the action without feeling forced into consumerism. Many of the businesses on 15th Ave E encourage window shopping, chatting, and staying without exerting pressure on their customers. Lingerability reveals a sens e of community, a sense of belonging to a place by the people who use it.

INTERACTION

The interaction created on this strip is why many are drawn here. The sidewalks are not particularly easy to navigate, since signs, chairs, bike lanes, and trees occupy space. However, a slow stroll involves the serendipitous meetings of many people up and down the street - friends meet friends, acquaintances and neighbors stop for a chat.

PEDESTRIAN

Two friends noticed each other from across the street, one slowly walked across 15th in front of traffic. Jaywalking acros 15th is fairly common despite heavy vehicle an bus traffic. Pedestrians will sometimes wait for a opening in traffic before crossing while others wil make eye contact with a motorist, expecting them to stop - knowing that pedestrians take priority this environment.

Figure 37.1. Happiness and urban design on 15th Avenue East in the Capitol Hill neighborhood of Seattle

ık coffee. This is what we saw - happy people, ;pite the rough and cluttered sidewalks, people) owned the city and felt comfortable crossing the ›et whenever they wanted, people who came on a ıday morning just to be around other people. We / people who were happy together and allowed to be.

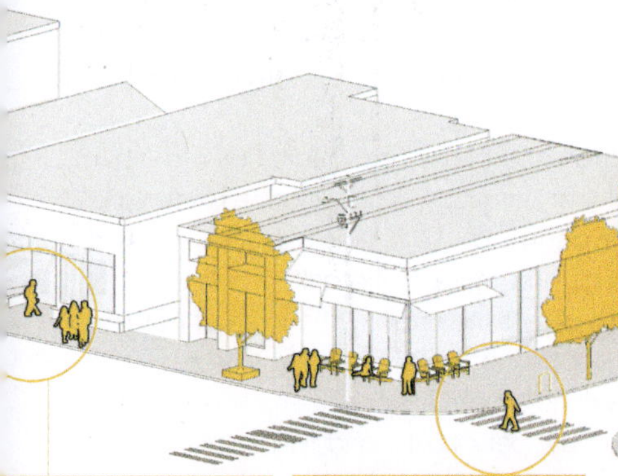

)WNERSHIP

eaving or creating a ›ersonal mark shows ıe ownership taken by ›eople in the community ›ver the street. While not pecial in terms of public pace design, neighbors nd vendors have taken upon themselves to reate art, leave chairs nd dog bowls out, add ılanters, write poems, nd display collections f art and toys in the /indows, making the treet truly one-of-a-kind.

INCLUSIVITY

This area of Seattle is not known for its ethnic diversity but it is home for a variety of different age and income groups and the small businesses along 15th cater to this diverse population. Nearby is a children's game store and we noticed a girl holding a balloon initiate a conversation with an older gentleman in the chair. Both started giggling before the traffic signal turned green.

That is nice and all, but how can a focus on happiness deal with problems in our urban spaces?

We can all think of designed public spaces that discourage physical activity, force people into uncomfortable and dangerous situations, and limit mobility. Focusing on happiness can open up new solutions to fixing our failed spaces. We also know that there are spaces that succeed under various traditional design criteria but still fail to be active and lively places. Think of your nearest dead plaza that has not adequately considered the needs of potential users or opportunities to bring about more happiness in everyday experiences.

So How Do We Approach Happiness in Urban Design?

On a cold and rainy Sunday morning, the three of us went for a walk along 15th Avenue East, in the Capitol Hill neighborhood of Seattle. There, we noticed a large concentration of people on the street that simply looked happy to be out in the public realm—a group of friends hugged as they met, a girl carried a balloon across the street, and an older man drinking a coffee was talking to a woman at the stoplight. At one particular moment, we counted more than 50 people within one block.

While the street is served by transit and dense, proximate housing, nothing about 15th is especially beautiful or unique. With its cracked sidewalks and hodgepodge of buildings, the design of 15th is less of the polished visions that make for magazine covers and more of the gritty functionality of main streets found in cities and towns across the region. The three of us were left wondering: Why did so many people choose to spend this time on 15th?

In observing this vibrant street, we noted a number of behaviors reflected a sense of comfort, interaction, inclusivity, personality, and lingerability. These qualities, shown in Figure 37.1, are the sort of behaviors that should be encouraged and promoted elsewhere to foster happiness-generating public spaces.

What Can Planners and Designers Actually Do?

It's curious that, in this time of broken budgets and diminishing resources, the notion of happiness should be resurgent. One might expect calls for austerity and pragmatism in the face of scarcity, but the true luxury would be to continue ignoring the perceptual and human component of spatial design. Without a focus on the happiness dimension, planners, designers, and users will simply continue to tolerate the development and continued existence of underutilized, joyless spaces.

Policy makers are calling for a reorientation toward the promotion of happiness, not simply as a means of coping with hard times, but as the best solution to rebuilding and revitalizing our cities and societies. This pursuit of happiness is not new, but shifting the concept to the forefront of design is needed. As our urban design seeks to promote the long-term vitality of our public spaces, so too should we focus on the promotion of long-term human happiness.

To the planning and design professions, we propose the following:

- As a baseline, we should no longer tolerate the creation of urban "blandscapes" that sap, diminish, and deter happiness.
- As a goal, we should design public spaces that foster the factors of happiness to evolve and grow over time.
- As a hope, we should design with expressed intent of creating spaces that intrinsically generate happiness.

We have the means to build a happier future in our cities; we just need to design for it.

CHAPTER 38

Green Infrastructure Mashup in the Emerald City

Mary Roderick

Green infrastructure has evolved as an umbrella solution to improve the sustainability and resilience of metropolitan regions. It is utilized for everything from habitat and resource provisioning and protection; growth management; and climate change mitigation and adaptation at regional scales to stormwater and flood management; landslide, erosion, and sediment control; urban heat island mitigation; brownfield remediation; and mobility, recreation, education, and public health provision at city, community and site scales. But how do we plan to achieve these multiple benefits? How do we reconcile green infrastructure as conservation with retrofit and restoration, as cultural artifact versus accident? A multi-scalar, multifunctional perspective creates stronger interrelationships and investment opportunities, but requires strategic planning and advanced decision support to realize synergies and manage trade-offs.

Landscape, "the visible expression of natural and human ecosystem processes that work across scales and contexts to provide multiple benefits for people and their environments" (Rouse and Bunster-Ossa 2013), may be one approach that helps planners think in terms of an integrated whole rather than through the piecemeal lens of "green" site improvements to address specific issues. In practice, however, city agencies are responsible for discrete networks of infrastructure. The challenge is to harmonize these networks with the four-dimensional landscape structure and function—the horizontal, lateral, and vertical axis of space combined with the continuum of time, in which they are embedded.

Seattle branded Metronatural™ (from 2006 to 2013) by the Seattle Convention and Visitors Bureau to express "having the characteristics of a world-class metropolis within wild, beautiful natural surroundings" and "one who respects the environment and lives a balanced lifestyle of urban and natural experiences" (Visit Seattle 2014). It provides fertile ground for examining the opportunities for synergistic green infrastructure planning at multiple scales and for multiple benefits. Nestled between the Cascade and Olympic Mountains, draped in evergreens and surrounded by water, it is also known as the Emerald City, a metaphor that pervades the city's planning ethos. This chapter highlights how the city's agencies are planning and implementing green infrastructure to augment their infrastructure networks within the landscape context, and where actual and potential synergies and trade-offs among these efforts may be found.

The City Green

Seattle's 2014–19 Capital Improvement Program (CIP) is a good departure point for examining the city's commitment to green infrastructure. It includes 625 individual projects and totals $5.2 billion, 84 percent of which is allocated for utilities and transportation through which much of the city's green infrastructure is realized (Seattle 2013a). Four out of six policy drivers for the CIP are related to green infrastructure, which reinforces its importance to the city:

- 2011 Sustainable Building and Sites Policy
- 2014 Comprehensive Plan Update (which includes open space, environmentally critical area and low-impact development requirements)
- 2013 NPDES stormwater discharge permits and Combined Sewer Overflow (CSO) Consent Decree
- Endangered Species Act (driven primarily by the listing of Chinook salmon) and resulting 50-year Cedar River Watershed Habitat Conservation Plan (2000–2050).

The following sections illustrate the breadth of green infrastructure planning and implementation within and across key city departments.

Utilities

Seattle Public Utilities (SPU) oversees the most common and usual suspects of green infrastructure: water supply; combined sewer, stormwater, and flood management; and habitat provision and restoration. At the regional scale, two protected municipal watersheds, the Cedar River and South Fork Tolt River, provide water to 1.4 million people in the Seattle area. Seattle was an early adopter of municipally owned utilities and watershed acquisition after the Great Fire in 1889, when the private supplier failed to deliver. The city began to acquire the Cedar River Watershed in 1890 and the water rights to the South Fork Tolt River Watershed in 1936 (Seattle 2014g).

A 50-year Habitat Conservation Plan (HCP) (Seattle 2000), developed under the auspices of the Endangered Species Act to address incidental takes of several fish species and to comply with the Muckleshoot Indian Tribe's fishing rights, guides management and restoration activities in the Cedar River Watershed and serves as the model for similar activities in the Tolt (Seattle 2011c), where commercial timber harvest degraded the watershed until the mid-1990s. Congruent with a landscape perspective, the HCP covers five geographic areas linking the municipal watershed to the Puget Sound. While watershed protection is often touted for its multiple benefits, water supply was at odds with habitat provision and species protection for more than a century due to a diversion dam and water supply aqueduct. Through the integrated approach of the HCP, fish passage to upstream spawning grounds was restored in 2003, just three years after plan implementation began. Both municipal watersheds, important nodes in Seattle's infrastructure network, demonstrate that the range of benefits provided have to be carefully balanced, and that some, like water source protection and commercial timber harvest, are at odds with each other.

At the city scale, SPU's Restore Our Waters strategy is being relaunched within the context of SPU's Protecting Seattle's Waterways Plan (Seattle 2014f) to integrate urban creek watersheds and manufactured drainage basins, which better capture the synthetic nature of the urban landscape. Two plan alternatives are under development to meet the requirements of Seattle's CSO Consent Decree, the first to allow stormwater projects to be prioritized ahead of CSO projects. Both alternatives include natural drainage as a part of the solution to reduce and improve the quality of stormwater runoff. Seattle pioneered the use of natural drainage in the right-of-way to address runoff with the Street Edge Alternative Street project in 2001, and has since completed five natural drainage system (NDS) projects that have been scaled up from a few blocks to entire neighborhoods (the largest is Seattle Housing Authority's High Point neighborhood redevelopment with 34 blocks and 129 acres). Four more neighborhood-scale projects are currently underway (Seattle 2014c).

SPU has moved the NDS from projects to policy through green stormwater infrastructure (GSI) requirements in the Seattle Stormwater Code for sites with greater than 2,000 square feet of new or replaced impervious surfaces. The city also adopted a Green Stormwater Infrastructure Goal of managing 700 million gallons of stormwater through GSI by 2025 (Seattle 2013c).The city's Office of Sustainability and Environment (OSE) is leading the development of the GSI Implementation Plan. As part of the plan SPU, Seattle Department of Transportation (SDOT), and the Department of Planning and Development will develop a coordinated approach to the integration of GSI in the right-of-way. These agencies, plus Seattle Parks and Recreation

(SPR), Seattle City Light, and the Department of Finance and Administration, are also tasked with ensuring that their development-related codes, rules, and standards remove barriers to GSI and prioritize its use in capital projects. While the city's GSI Goal and Implementation Plan is critical for formalizing and synergizing GSI efforts across city departments, it addresses only one type of green infrastructure for one main outcome.

Forests and Farms

A review of the Seattle's 2013 Urban Forestry Stewardship Plan (Seattle 2013g), also prepared by the OSE, indicates that the proposed ecological approach to tree management is congruent with GSI since it seeks to improve forest function and not just expand canopy cover. The forestry plan also highlights a wide range of other functions provided by trees. However, the plan does not address trade-offs between tree species. Some are likely to provide multiple benefits, but those that are optimal for air and stormwater pollutant removal are probably not fit, for example, for food production.

Urban agriculture is experiencing a revival through the local food movement, and should also be included in the green infrastructure portfolio, rather than treated as a limited benefit of certain types of GSI (i.e., green roofs and trees) as it is in the Center for Neighborhood Technology's *The Value of Green Infrastructure* guide. The 2012 Seattle Food Action Plan, prepared by the OSE, seeks to increase food production in the city right-of-way and on city-owned property, which is incompatible with stormwater management and may conflict with forestry goals due to shading (with the exception of orchards). With 14,682 acres of right-of-way in the city (27 percent of the land area), it's likely that conflict can be avoided; however, a mechanism to identify parcel suitability for different green infrastructure options is needed. GSI and forestry will need to make room for gardens, and the Food Action Plan will need to address the impacts of gardening on water quality and water consumption (Seattle 2012a).

Transportation

As the purveyor of the transportation network, SDOT is also an important partner and provider of green infrastructure in all three areas already mentioned: drainage, forestry, and urban agriculture. SDOT manages more than 35,000 street trees, plants approximately 800 new ones per year, and collaborates with SPU to develop NDS in the right-of way and to retrofit road culverts for fish passage and sediment control. Its Complete Streets Checklist (Seattle 2011a) includes options for GSI and forestry, and its right-of-way management also allows gardens and orchards. SDOT also maintains 47 miles of multiuse trails with plans for expansion in fulfillment of the Bicycle and Pedestrian Master Plans. The vegetation along these trails, while perhaps not optimized for green infrastructure benefits (e.g., drainage, food production, canopy), still contributes to Seattle's green infrastructure, as do the landscaping features in their ongoing sidewalk improvements.

Parks

Parks provide the final key piece of Seattle's green infrastructure, and are inherently a multifunctional landscape and network. Seattle Parks and Recreation's (SPR's) system includes more than 500 recreation and community facilities, 465 parks and natural areas, 25 miles of park boulevards, and 120 miles of trails that total 6,200 acres—11 percent of Seattle's land area. By 1937, the city had 37 Olmsted parks and boulevards, which were designed with the landscape and ecological function at the fore and set the tone for the future. Today, the Parks Legacy Plan (2014d) emphasizes recreation and community services, while still continuing the tradition of environmental stewardship. In addition to managing an estimated 600,000 trees, 20 percent of Seattle's canopy, SPR works on wetland restoration, creek daylighting, habitat protection, and beach renourishment and nearshore habitat improvements. The Green Seattle Partnership, a public-private collaboration between SPR, SPU, OSE, nonprofits, and individuals, is also working to r-establish 2,500 acres of healthy forested parkland by 2025.

Realizing Synergies, Managing Trade-Offs

Although this snapshot of Seattle's green infrastructure is far from complete and other agencies and plans should be considered in a full account of green infrastructure, it lays the groundwork for imagining a strategic approach to green infrastructure planning that helps the city realize synergies and manage trade-offs among the diverse efforts of multiple city agencies. While collaboration occurs among agencies for specific types of green infrastructure (e.g., GSI, forestry), and most agencies provide multiple types of green infrastructure at multiple scales, there is no shared "big picture" for green infrastructure of all types, at all scales. Imagine trying to do transportation planning without a comprehensive understanding and representation of transportation networks.

Both a broader conceptualization of green infrastructure beyond GSI and an explicit mapping to on-going agency activities, similar to Figure 38.1 and Figure 38.2, are the foundation of shared understanding that can guide strategic planning. The Capital Improvement Program is a tangible starting point to document which funded activities are related to green infrastructure and these should be connected to the conceptual map of the city's green infrastructure.

The Office of Sustainability and Environment, the lead agency on the interdepartmental GSI Implementation Plan as well as the forestry and food plans, is uniquely positioned to coordinate across their own initiatives as well as those of other agencies. Similar to the analysis undertaken for the

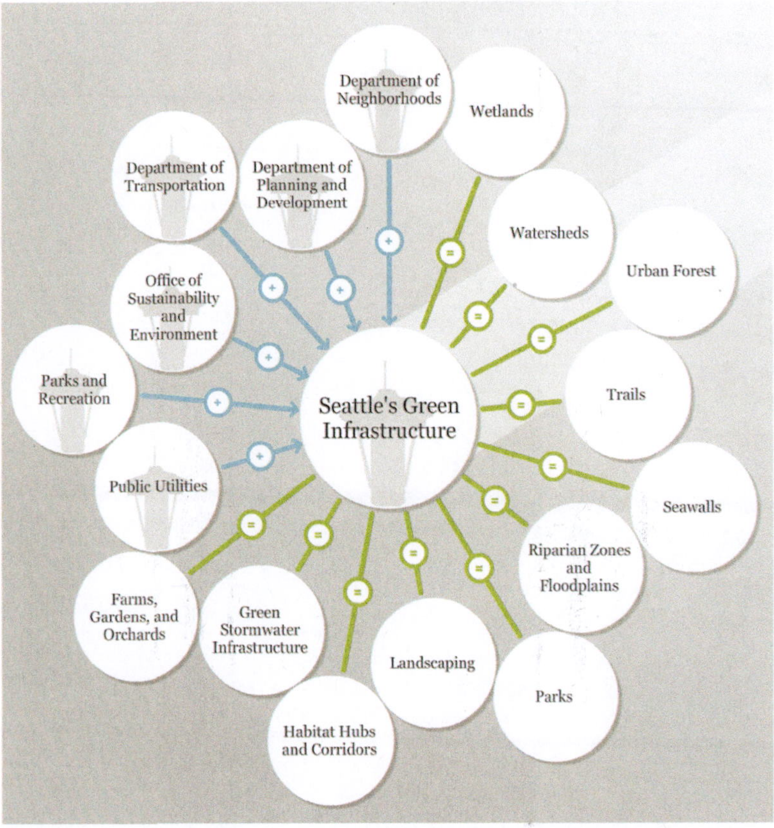

Figure 38.1. Concept map of Seattle's green (green) infrastructure and responsible agencies (blue)

forestry plan of Seattle departments' existing programs and policies related to tree management (eight have been identified) (Seattle 2014g), and the establishment of the Urban Forest Interdepartmental Team, the OSE could facilitate comprehensive planning and implementation of green infrastructure. To support the effort, each project in the CIP, together with existing green infrastructure and related networks, should be made spatially and temporally explicit using a geographic information system (GIS).

All of the agencies reviewed already use GIS. A multicriteria analysis framework can be developed that includes each agency's decision factors for prioritizing and funding projects to check for both spatial-temporal and fiscal-objective compatibility (see McElvaney 2012; Steinitz 2012). Of course, technology alone will not result in strategic planning. However, a cyber-enabled, geographic mapping environment augmented by a multicri-

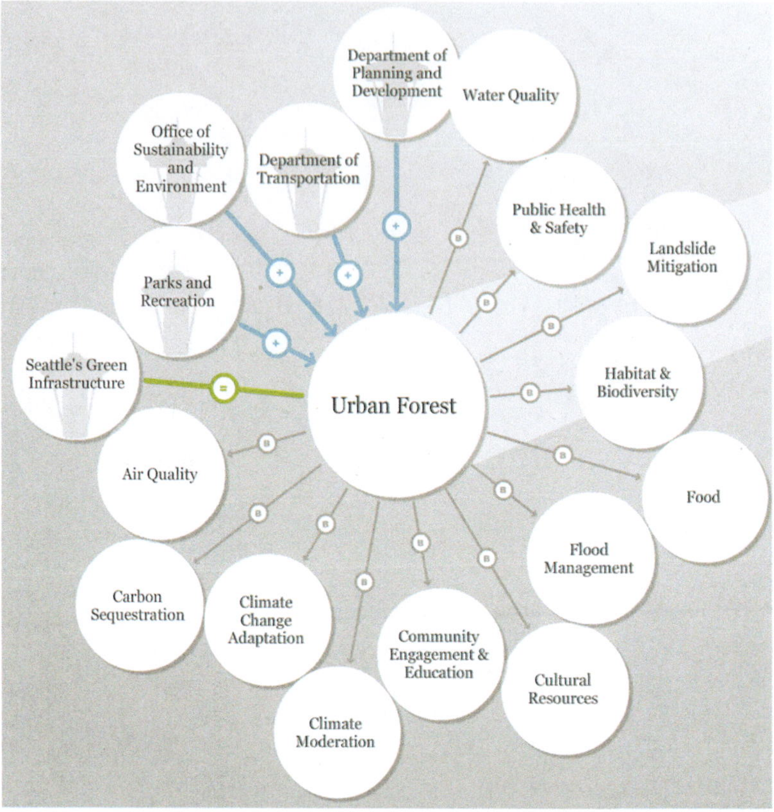

Figure 38.2. Concept map for a specific type of green infrastructure, responsible agencies, and benefits

teria analysis framework and a comprehensive green infrastructure concept map, can go a long way in facilitating dialog in and between agencies to identify shared investment opportunities, functional synergies among types of green infrastructure, and potential trade-offs.

CHAPTER 39

Solar in the Rainy City

Michele Hill, Kristen Gelino, Lydia Fulton, Stefanie Young, and Jan Whittington

'Solar Doesn't Work in Seattle'

Seattle: The Rainy City. Why not Seattle: The Solar City? Thoughts of Seattle generally evoke gray skies and drizzle—not what one typically envisions as an ideal place for solar power production. Photovoltaic (PV) resource maps created by the National Renewable Energy Laboratory further reinforce this characterization as a solar-challenged area: Some of the lowest PV resource levels in the contiguous United States are found in the Puget Sound region. While it is true that Seattle has, on average, 226 cloudy days per year, this fact alone does not preclude PV systems as a viable option for the Pacific Northwest.

In this chapter we challenge common assumptions regarding the feasibility of solar power production in the Pacific Northwest, discuss general advantages and disadvantages of solar power, provide an overview of the Pacific Northwest energy policy context, and explore the wider implications of lessons learned from one student-led project to bring solar power to the University of Washington (UW) campus.

In March 2008, the U.S. Department of Energy designated Seattle as one of its 25 Solar American Cities. At that time, the city had approximately 400 kilowatts (kW) of installed PV systems within its borders. By 2011, there were closer to 1,100 kW installed, the majority on residential structures (U.S. Department of Energy 2011). Interest in solar power and the expansion of PV capacity has continued in Seattle and the surrounding region over the last several years.

- Seattle City Light has initiated two successful Community Solar programs, allowing residents to help finance solar arrays that are not located on their properties.

- The Bullitt Center, designed to meet the Living Building Challenge, has a solar array sized to produce as much electricity from solar resources as the building uses (Bullitt Center 2014).
- A newly designed neighborhood on nearby Bainbridge Island has homes that have been designed to run entirely on solar power (Peters 2013).
- The King County Housing Authority installed an array on a mixed income housing development in White Center. This system was the largest residential array in the state at the time of installation (King County Housing Authority 2013).

The average Washington resident uses 1,037 kW of electricity per month (U.S. Energy Information Administration 2014b). According to Seattle City Light, a properly positioned and installed 1 kW system in Seattle produces between 900 and 1,000 kW hours (kWh) per year (Seattle City Light 2013). Although this production skews heavily toward the summer months, a 100-square-foot PV system has the potential to offset seven to eight percent of the annual electric usage of a typical single-family residence.

Seattle, like most of the Pacific Northwest, sources its electricity predominantly from hydroelectric dams. In 2010, hydroelectric power comprised 66 percent of the net generation of electric power in the state (U.S. Energy Information Administration 2012c). Hydroelectricity is a renewable energy source that boasts a very low price point. In fact, national rankings in 2010 ranked Washington State 49th in both average retail price per kWh and pounds of carbon dioxide emissions produced per megawatt-hour (MWh)[1,2] So why would Seattleites want to invest in additional (and expensive!) renewable energy infrastructure when the predominant power source is already so cheap and so green?

Why Choose Solar Power?

Advantages

Solar power offers advantages in terms of resilience, local power production, and financial savings.

Resilience

Finding alternate sources of power can boost a community's resilience in the face of both short- and long-term hazards. Resilience is "a measure of the ability of these systems to absorb changes . . . and still persist (Holling 1973, 17)." By becoming less dependent upon the grid, a community with local, renewable, and redundant energy sources will still have access to electricity in case of grid failure.

Local Power Production

Most power in the electrical grid is centralized and produced at great distances from where it is consumed. To avoid the significant problems of line loss (the amount of electrical power lost along power lines), power is transmitted with high voltage, which suffers much less line loss than low-voltage power (Hokin 2014). High-voltage power requires additional infrastructure (electrical substations) to step down the power to a voltage usable in buildings. Producing power locally means power is consumed much closer to where it is produced, reducing or even eliminating the need for high-voltage transmission lines and substations. Over the long term, reducing the need for constructing new (or replacing aging) electrical infrastructure will result in financial savings at the federal, state, and local levels.

Financial Savings

The entire financial commitment in solar power is the equipment and installation; once this cost is recouped, the energy produced is free to the user. In addition, the equipment used to produce solar power, as opposed to wind or hydroelectric power, has no moving parts and, therefore, tends to have fewer associated maintenance costs (Home Power 2014). This keeps the long-term maintenance costs low. Also, while the cost of solar equipment historically has been high, costs continue to decrease as technology improves.

Disadvantages

Solar power does have some disadvantages: production versus consumption timing, connections to existing infrastructure, and dependence on sunlight.

Peak Production versus Consumption Timing

Depending on a region's climate characteristics, peak production capability may not match peak consumption times. Seattle is an example of this problem. Seattle's climate consists of overcast and rainy days throughout the fall, winter, and spring, and clear and sunny days in the summer. While solar power can be produced all year, peak production occurs during the summer when solar systems benefit from the combination of longer daylight hours and more sunshine. However, peak power consumption occurs during the winter's cooler temperatures and shorter daylight hours. Building heating and lighting loads increase power demand during the cooler seasons. The potential to produce electricity from solar in the summer does not match well with peak power consumption in the winter.

Connections to Existing Infrastructure

The electrical grid relies on real-time matching between power demand and supply and is not designed to store electricity for future use. Intermittent sources of power, like solar, can pose difficulties for grid connection because production potential does not relate to demand patterns.

Dependence on Sunlight

Obviously, solar power production depends on sunlight. As such, solar is an intermittent source of power, not producing any electricity at night.

Current Energy Policy Context in the Pacific Northwest

Oregon and Washington are the top two hydroelectric-producing states in the nation. Washington alone produces 29 percent of the nation's net hydroelectricity. Its largest dam, the Grand Coulee, has a total generating capacity of 6,809 MW. Washington and Oregon are ranked first and second in the nation in hydroelectric production (U.S. Energy Information Administration 2012b, 2012d). At the same time, Oregon and Washington have been leaders in pursuing solar energy opportunities. If these two Pacific Northwest states already have a reliable, clean source of electricity, why are they investing in solar energy?

Climate change impacts in the Pacific Northwest are likely to alter the timing, frequency, and duration of precipitation. Winters in the Puget Sound region are likely to become wetter and summers are likely to become drier. These changes may affect hydroelectric power production in the region. Some studies have estimated that power production due to the effects of climate change may decrease between 12 and 15 percent in the summer months by the 2040s.[3] This decrease in production capacity, coupled with increases in population, may create power supply problems. Increasing solar capacity in the Pacific Northwest will add to the power production capacity of the region in the months when utilities are projected to experience scarce supplies in hydroelectric power and in the months when solar power will be most effective.

Washington and Oregon have been investing in solar-electric projects at local levels for over 30 years. In particular, both states are creating incentives for small-scale, close-to-home solar energy systems. For example, Ashland, Oregon, located near the California border, was one of the first cities to promote solar power with solar rights ordinances, starting as early as the 1980s (DSIRE 2014a). In Washington, community solar projects, loosely defined as projects producing less than 75 kWh per year and owned by nonutility companies, are eligible for more tax incentives.[4]

Actions initiated at a local level have begun to spread statewide. Washington has created tax credit incentive programs to encourage solar production and purchase within the state, with higher credits available for projects using locally produced panels and inverters (DSIRE 2014b). Solar manufacturers are being incentivized as well, with a Tax Abatement for Solar

Manufacturers reducing the building and operations taxes for the producers of Washington PV modules and their parts (DSIRE 2014c). After Washington voters passed Initiative 937 in 2006, which requires 15 percent of the electricity produced by electric utility companies be from renewables by 2020, the Bonneville Power Association (BPA) took quick action (DSIRE 2014c). BPA runs 31 federal hydroelectricity projects in the Columbia River Basin, and is now investing in increasing the solar capacity in the region (Bonneville Power Administration 2014).[5]

One Small Project, Many Big Ideas: UW-Solar

In the winter of 2012, a dynamic group of University of Washington students from five colleges came together to form UW-Solar. Our students came from various departments—urban planning, architecture, public policy, real estate, the information school, computer science, and electrical engineering. This interdisciplinary team identified two main objectives: 1) to promote the use of clean and sustainable power production in order to reduce reliance on outside energy resources, improve the resilience of power systems to outages, and reduce the overall carbon footprint of the university; and 2) to provide an opportunity for students to lead a project that develops and studies a smart solar energy industrial control system.

UW-Solar chose to pursue these objectives through a student-led demonstration project that partnered with the Seattle campus Department of Housing and Food Services (HFS), the group responsible for the development of six new dorm and apartment buildings over the past three years. The team secured initial funding from the Campus Sustainability Fund, a program created and managed by students that uses student tuition dollars to support student-led sustainability efforts on campus.

After completing a feasibility study, the team secured two additional sources of funding: funds from HFS and a grant awarded by Bonneville Environmental Foundation. In addition, the team coordinated with the UW Alumni Association to set up a long-term funding source based on alumni donations. In the future, we anticipate that alumni contributions should be able to fund additional solar arrays on campus.

Next, the UW-Solar team partnered with HFS on a request for proposals for a solar-electric system to be installed on a recently completed student housing complex overlooking Portage Bay. In the spring of 2014, a 35 kW system with an integrated industrial control system and weather station was installed. The industrial control system remotely monitors and controls the solar-electric system, along with collecting real-time weather and performance data.

The body of data collected by the industrial control system provides ongoing opportunities for analysis by academics and professionals.

Lessons for Planners

While the feasibility study, design, and build phases of this project presented myriad opportunities for student learning, we have also identified lessons learned that are applicable for practicing planners.

We recommend that practicing planners partner with universities to take advantage of the fertile learning climate, freedom to fail, and expanded opportunities to succeed that our higher education system offers. Student projects are often the perfect place to test new ideas or to challenge the pervasive status quo. While the consequences of failure are not so dire, successes can challenge institutional barriers.

The UW-Solar team strove to deepen the body of evidence that solar does work in Seattle and to break down some of the real and perceived barriers of installing PV systems in the unique confines of a publicly funded university. Our hope was that through our pilot project, solar panels would more readily disperse across the rainy roofs of campus. The University of Washington will become more resilient for these efforts.

Beyond the immediate educational goals of our group, our work will have a life beyond our time at UW. Undergraduate and graduate researchers, along with professors, will have access to the body of data collected by the industrial control system. Collecting weather data along with performance data provides new opportunities for analysis by researchers studying climatology, meteorology, energy, and engineering. The virtual industrial control lab allows for continuing studies in cybersecurity, an issue that will only become more important at the local, state, and federal levels as details about energy systems and other critical infrastructures become accessible through the Internet. Such visions underlie notions of planning for "smart" cities. Learning begets learning.

Planning is a spectacularly broad and challengingly diverse field, and we believe that this is why many of us are drawn to it. This process highlighted for us the importance of bringing different fields to the table. While we enjoyed learning about electrical engineering, equity flips, and cybersecurity, we relied on the expertise and knowledge of other members of the team to bring valid and overlooked perspectives to the table. This was a great experience in planning as facilitating—not necessarily facilitating for the general public, but for identifying the technical knowledge that needs inclusion in the discussion.

Planners are used to looking into the future and helping others envision a better world. As facilitators, we can ensure relationships are built between disciplines in order to build smart, sustainable, and equitable communities. As planning students, we learn the role of visioning, of comprehensive plans, of inspiring the public with new ideas. But it is perhaps even more important to remain inspired ourselves. We need to continue to think about what will be in the future, rather than being limited by what is now.

Ideas are too commonly discounted because they are not a one-stop fix for a problem or issue. Is solar power a magic bullet for powering the Pacific Northwest? Put simply: No. But we do not live in a simple world. Just because solar power is not a panacea does not mean that we should not pursue it. Dealing with complexity in an uncertain world requires a range of options and ample redundancy. Rather than accepting the common notion that solar won't work in Seattle, we explored how solar can be integrated as a part of a sustainable city—even if it is a sustainable city that has cloud cover 226 days per year. The idea is not to discount solar because it doesn't solve every problem, but to embrace its potential contribution for solving a small part of a large problem. As students, we hope to take this message with us into our professional lives: every "no" and "does not" is a simple answer to a complex problem. Stay curious. "Why not?" is just as important as "will not."

CHAPTER 40

Game-Changing Perspectives on Planning

Jill Sterrett, FAICP, and Brian Campbell, FAICP

Since early 2011, Washington and Oregon planners have been collaborating on a unique regional effort that steps out of our traditional planning roles. This effort, started by a few people, has led to some big results. It is, perhaps, indicative of a planning approach that may typify the planning profession in the Pacific Northwest. This group perceived a set of problems that no one constituent group has been willing to own or address, organized across state lines, and harnessed powers of organizing and practice through process (for which we are so famous in the Northwest). This article tells the story of how the collaboration started and what it is trying to achieve.

Early in 2010 there was a small gathering of Oregon Fellows[1] from the three design and planning professions—the American Planning Association (APA), the American Institute of Architects (AIA), and the American Society of Landscape Architects (ASLA) at a Portland brewpub (where else?) to discuss our duty as senior professionals to "give something back to our profession and communities" and to address the huge challenges confronting society. What to do about these challenges was further discussed at a meeting with the national presidents of APA, AIA, and ASLA at a conference later that year in Portland, resulting in a white paper focusing on improving the quality of life through design.

Meanwhile, planning leaders in Washington were focusing on the problems of climate change. A team of 30 planners prepared a 100-page online guidebook to provide Washington planners the tools they needed to get started: *Sustainable Washington 2009: Planning for Climate Change* (American Planning Association 2009).

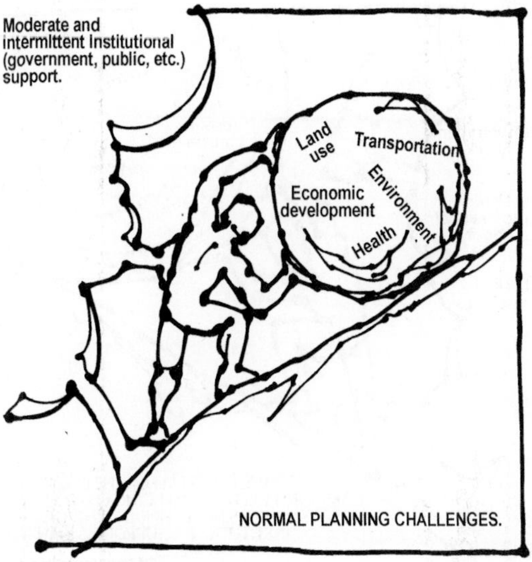

By early 2011, as the Oregon and Washington chapters of APA began preparations for a joint fall planning conference, the leadership of the two chapters realized they had identified a similar set of challenges and that regional collaboration could bring new ideas to the table and new results.

In the Don Quixote style of the best visionaries of our profession, the group decided not that *someone* should take action but that *we* should do something about these challenges. The idea was born to organize a symposium that would gather experts from many fields to bring different perspectives to this set of global challenges (or "wicked problems") (Rittel and Webber 1973) that we had identified, specifically:

- The economic recession, with a "new normal" that is likely to be slow growth for years to come
- Increasing economic inequities and demographic changes that undermine a strong middle class with shared values
- Accelerating degradation of our natural resources due to population growth and unsustainable rates of consumption
- Global climate change that will further stress natural systems and cause severe effects on our cities

The symposium brought together 50 distinguished leaders from Oregon and Washington, including elected officials, journalists, scientists, econo-

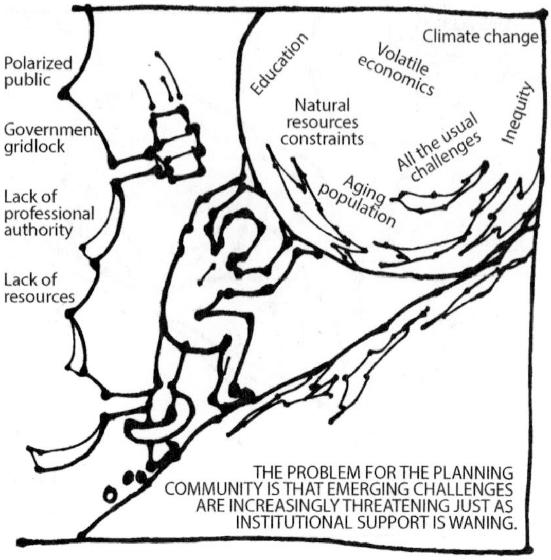

mists, real estate professionals, academics, social equity organizations, and our professions (planning, landscape architecture, and architecture). This half-day symposium, called Moving Forward: Game Changing Initiatives, and the accompanying planning conference session, resulted in an Action Agenda built around five basic concepts:

- Create a vision of livable cities, towns and rural places to inspire action.
- Build alliances with other professions and organizations working on similar issues.
- Develop a communications strategy to build public support and influence decision makers.
- Conduct needed research and trial studies.
- Foster political, legislative, and institutional change.

Our basic message from this work was this: The critical issues of our times call for a complete rethinking of how planners and allied professions engage our communities. We would like our organizations to address these issues in terms of setting clear policy agendas, increasing communication with the public and other organizations, and expanding advocacy roles to achieve social and political change. As planners, we need to make use of our unique training and abilities to bring together disparate views and find equitable solutions.

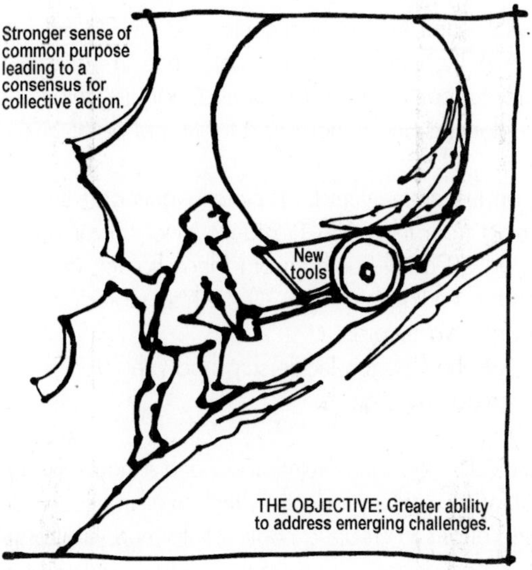

In short, this effort was no longer about simply providing new tools for planners to do their work in light of these challenges. Now it was about creating social and political change. It was about fostering a civil society that engages in public issues, educating public officials on potential solutions, and about promoting a legislative framework that recognizes and responds to these 21st century "wicked problems."

> GOING INTO THE SYMPOSIUM, I HAD HOPED FOR A GOOD EXCHANGE OF IDEAS AND SOME SPECIFIC ACTIONS THAT WE MIGHT TAKE AS PART OF OUR STATE APA CHAPTERS. WHAT REALLY SURPRISED ME WAS THE ENERGY AROUND THESE CONCERNS AND THE STRONG SENSE FROM THE WHOLE GROUP THAT COLLECTIVE ACTION FROM A LARGER GROUP WAS POSSIBLE—EVEN ESSENTIAL."
>
> —JILL STERRETT, FAICP

After that seminal event, our joint-state organizing committee took our message on the road to gain further exposure nationally and expand on the original ideas with the input of others. Principal stops in this "road show" included:

- The APA Chapter Presidents Council and the College of Fellows at the April 2012 leadership meetings in Los Angeles

- The ASLA and AIA national conferences in 2012
- The APA National Planning Conference in Chicago in 2013, where our panel session on Game-Changing Initiatives attracted 120 planners and generated a lively and productive discussion

Building on the momentum from these events and inspired by a similar message coming from then APA President Mitch Silver, FAICP, our joint-state group organized a Daniel Burnham Big Ideas Forum, cosponsored by APA. This event, held in Portland in May 2013, had more than 160 participants from Oregon and Washington.

By this point, the Oregon leadership had prepared a draft vision document with five overarching goals:

1. Reduce climate change vulnerability and enhance natural system health.
2. Progress toward a productive, inclusive and sustainable economy.
3. Extend efforts to create a healthy, informed, and equitable society.
4. Renew and deepen efforts to make vibrant cities and towns.
5. Reinvigorate and reshape our systems for increasing civic engagement and cultivating leadership and effective governance.

Discussion groups at the forum discussed these goals and generated a host of ideas for implementing actions.

Following the Big Ideas Forum, the two states decided to move in separate directions. In Washington, task force groups were created to further the ideas of the forum and recommend potential actions. Their results were prioritized by chapter members' votes, combined to form the basis of a white paper called "Ten Big Ideas for Washington's Future," which was endorsed by the chapter board. These ten ideas are highlighted below:

1. **Address climate change**: Step up to address climate change mitigation and adaptation at state, regional and local levels.
2. **Enhance regional decision making**: Strengthen regional decision making to address regional problems.
3. **Restore and protect ecosystems**: Restore and protect healthy natural systems and incorporate the value of ecosystem services in decision making.
4. **Link health and urban planning**: Plan communities to combat the growing epidemic of obesity.
5. **Increase local government capacity**: Provide local governments the capacity to do the job and educate the public on local fiscal constraints.
6. **Support economic development**: Empower sustainable economic development and incentivize local business growth.

7. **Foster social equity**: Incorporate issues of mental health, displacement, and affordable housing in planning for local communities.
8. **Support sustainable agriculture**: Address sustainable agriculture and healthy food systems in both rural and urban areas.
9. **Build social capital**: Build social capital by increasing civic engagement, supporting a culture of education, and fostering leadership and entrepreneurship.
10. **Rebuild infrastructure**: Plan and fund updates to infrastructure (water, roads, transport, energy, stormwater, communications) to create sustainable, smart, and energy-efficient systems.

For each of the 10 ideas, working groups are moving this effort from big ideas into actions, such as:

- Creating specific tools for planners to deal more effectively with these issues
- Identifying needed legislative changes and crafting proposed legislation
- Generating public support through media outreach
- Building support for planning through public officials outreach

In contrast to this action-oriented planning focused approach, the Oregon organizing committee decided to take a broader visionary, multiorganizational approach. They developed a vision statement: Oregon 2050/ A Vision for Oregon—Healthy, Vibrant, Resilient (Oregon 2050 Alliance 2014), building upon the vision articulated for the Big Ideas Forum. Oregon then created the Oregon 2050 Declaration and began circulating both documents among interested organizations with the intent of creating an effective, interdisciplinary Oregon 2050 Alliance.

Building the Oregon 2050 Alliance is seen as the key to creating a movement that will be an effective player in helping set the agenda for the future of the state. The intent is to use the power of this alliance to change the "public will" and to shape the opinions and priorities of the state's leaders to achieve the outcomes laid out in the vision. The expectation is that this will happen through alliance members adjusting their own programs, taking collaborative action with other members to accomplish those outcomes, and working in concert with one another to change the political landscape. Through that work, the alliance will promote genuine institutional change and policy reform to make Oregon a more livable place for all.

Leaders in both states agree that a single effort combining both the visionary, alliance-building and the grassroots, action-oriented approaches would be ideal. However, one of the lessons learned from this effort is the need to fit the approach within a framework that best fits the planning culture and the unique circumstances of each state. Oregon's organizing committee was composed of architects and landscape architects as well as planners from the outset, and it has always intended to create a broad effort that would appeal to a large spectrum of organizations. Without an alliance that could collaborate, reinforce one another, and work together on various programs, projects and legislative efforts, there appeared to be very limited ability to succeed in achieving the vision and goals that have been set for Oregon 2050. It was felt that the momentum from a large alliance was necessary for long-term success.

In contrast, Washington's effort has stayed mostly within the planning community. Instead of broad alliances, Washington's "bottom-up" approach is getting many planners involved. This effort seeks is looking to create more immediate change, albeit in smaller ways, while legislative change in Washington appears blocked by a divided legislature.

Regardless of our specific results in the Northwest, if our efforts are replicated in other parts of the country, this small beginning could create the momentum at a national level for lasting change. Some of the lessons learned from our process may help others in this effort:

1. Active collaboration between the two states provided a regional perspective and gave both momentum to the initial effort and legitimacy to the work.
2. The interactive interdisciplinary effort brought together professionals from multiple fields in a collaborative process that fostered new ideas and added strength to the effort.
3. Hosting a large event (the Big Ideas Forum with 160 participants) allowed us to gain followers and allies in both states. Subsequently, more than100 planners in Washington volunteered to participate in the action teams. Working with allied organizations in Oregon allows us to spread the ideas, gain momentum, and make change happen.
4. Seeking funding from APA helped us host the Big Ideas Forum in Portland and support from the Chapter Presidents Council allowed us to reach a broader audience and to document our process for other APA chapters to follow. We are now in the process of seeking longer term funding to take this work to the next level—making the institutional and political changes necessary to address the great challenges of our times.
5. Details of this process and various interim products are available to the APA Chapter Presidents Council and on the website for the Washington Chapter of APA and the Oregon 2050 Alliance.

This initiative is born of the belief that it is incumbent upon the professionals who plan and design our cities and communities to lead the way. Our purpose is to reinvent approaches to problem solving in this new context, reaching beyond established methods and conventions to identify initiatives that the design professions can together implement consistently and effectively.

There is a historical precedent for this effort. A 2013 article in the *New Yorker* explored the origins of the environmental movement, starting in Seattle with the 1969 speech by Wisconsin Sen. Gaylord Nelson announcing a national "teach-in" that became the first Earth Day, held on April 22, 1970 (Lemann 2013). On that first Earth Day, Congress took the day off and two-thirds of its members spoke at many of the 12,000 events held across the country.

Most of the environmental legislation we value today dates from the years around that event: the National Environmental Policy Act (1969), the Clean Air Act (1970), the Clean Water Act (1972), and the Endangered Species Act (1973). In this organic model, grassroots efforts sprouted repeatedly and in so many locations that the national leaders could not fail to take notice. Ultimately they provided the leadership that created lasting change.

What we aspire to do is nothing less than launching a similar movement focused on social change and addressing our 21st century challenges that will achieve equally impressive results.

What can planners do in your state?

CONCLUSION

Planning in the Pacific Northwest

Jill Sterrett, FAICP; Connie Ozawa; Dennis Ryan; Ethan Selzer; and Jan Whittington

Is There a Brand?

Is planning in the Pacific Northwest distinctive from planning in other parts of North America? Would a call for chapters from other parts of the United States yield a similar variety of topics, actors, and perspectives?

This is not an easy set of questions to answer. On the one hand, planning is taught, practiced, and accredited based on the assumption that it rolls out the same pretty much everywhere. On the other hand, we know that context is profoundly important for our work and that location matters much more than just for real estate value. Ecology, culture, history, and more combine distinctly in places, big and little. Still, distilling a "cause-and-effect" set of relationships between place and planning styles, issues, and outcomes is no simple task.

While it is up to others to decide the extent to which what we do here is similar or different from practice in their own part of the country, our experience and these chapters suggest that there are indeed particular characteristics that bind together planning in the Pacific Northwest. Careful attention to the movement and ecological function of water in the natural landscape is a strong theme from the rivers crisscrossing the Portland and Seattle metropolitan areas to the fragile coastlines. Creating space for the people who live in a place, whether they are the descendants of the first human settlers or newly arrived Millennials, is important here. Adherence to a legal framework set up to conserve land is an absolute given, especially in Oregon.

Although distinctiveness may only be a matter of opinion, we think that the dialogue created by the preceding chapters brings more than a little substance to bear on the questions we started with. And yes, we do think that place—our region—has made a difference in what we plan, why we plan, and how we plan:

- The region takes planning seriously and both states have created institutions to define the role of planning in protecting resources, preserving farms and forest lands, and limiting the sprawl of urban places. Institutions of state planning laws demand local attention and draw planners together into dialog.
- Landscape means a lot to this region, the people who have chosen to make it their home, and the planners who take on the job of protecting it. Ever a focus, the majestic landscape inspires action—whether that is taming the rivers with dams to provide power, adapting to changing seasonal flows due to climate change, or removing the dams to restore salmon, a cultural icon of the First People (in chapters by Whittington and Young and by Yocom). Or, sometimes, it is simply what keeps a planner at her job when the political and public wills collide (Lyons's chapter).
- Public engagement is a fundamental part of planning here—sometimes to the point that the outcomes are difficult to reach, as in the infamous "Seattle process" in Nunley's chapter on replacing the viaduct. The fundamental notion that those affected by the planning ought to be actively engaged in making the plans is expected, valued, and integrated in the way we plan.
- Here in the Northwest, planning is both a process of social learning, where planners facilitate a free flow of information, and also planning is about outcomes. Plan making and implementation are important because they present opportunities for ongoing conversations. We measure whether the rate of farmland conversion has slowed (Daniels chapter), whether new development is within the urban growth boundary (Tovar and McCormick chapter), and even whether the measurement systems for green development are effective (Faghin chapter).
- We expect planning to make change. Planners, architects, landscape architects, and urban designers have all been deeply engaged in the major social movements of this region in the last 50 years. Today, many are engaged in issues of climate change, alternative energy, social equity, healthy built environments, food systems, and green infrastructure, as we saw in section 3.

Recent Successes & Current Issues in the Puget Sound Region

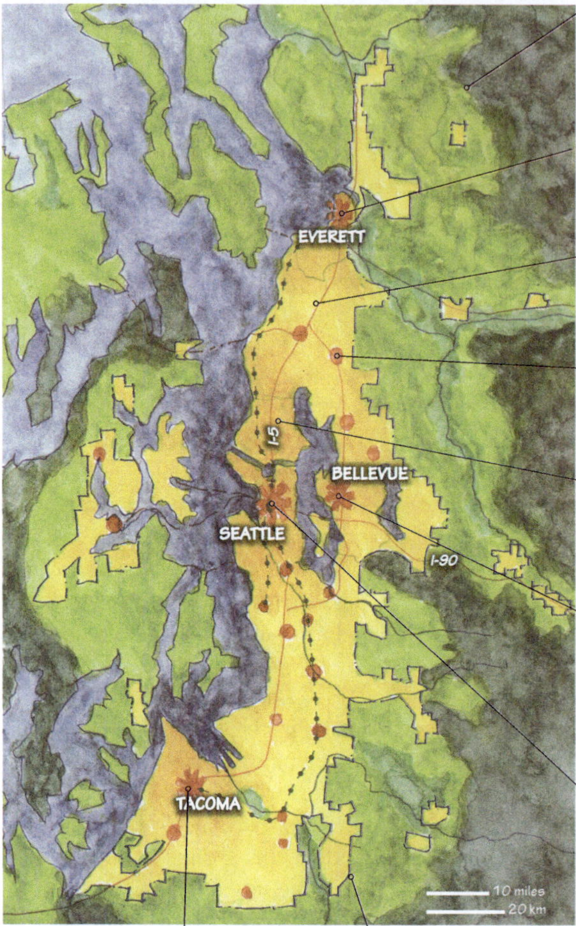

Salmon recovery efforts are underway with new shoreline regulations & restoration projects.

Downtown Everett is being transformed from a mill town into a metropolitan center.

Snohomish County is building "linear communities" along Bus Rapid Transit

A constellation of vibrant, pedestrian-friendly centers has been developed.

Seattle's neighborhoods are lively & livable but housing affordability is a vexing challenge.

Bellevue & Redmond are creating a metropolitan complex along a proposed light rail link line that promises to alter the region's focus.

Seattle's downtown is one of the nation's most attractive & economically successful.

Non-governmental organizations are leading conservation & wilderness protection efforts.

Communities are working on sustainability issues but without a much needed regional strategy.

With its cleaned-up & redeveloped Foss Waterway, museums, light rail link, convention center, & UW satellite campus, Tacoma has achieved the state's most ambitious downtown urban design transformation.

Growth boundaries have mostly curtailed sprawl but farmland is still threatened. Planners are working on tools such as TDR's to save open space.

- Metropolitan centers
- Urban centers
- Urbanized areas
- Rural areas
- Agricultural lands
- Forest lands
- Major highways
- Rail transit
- Urban growth boundaries (UGB)

Recent Successes & Current Issues in the Portland/Vancouver Region

Downtown's Pearl District demonstrates how an old industrial area can be transformed into a thriving mixed-use community.

A new I-5 bridge over the Columbia River is needed but the project is now tied up by political controversies.

Typical suburban sprawl in many parts of the region present significant redevelopment challenges.

The Columbia River Gorge Commission is a model for achieving environmental, aesthetic, recreational & community development objectives.

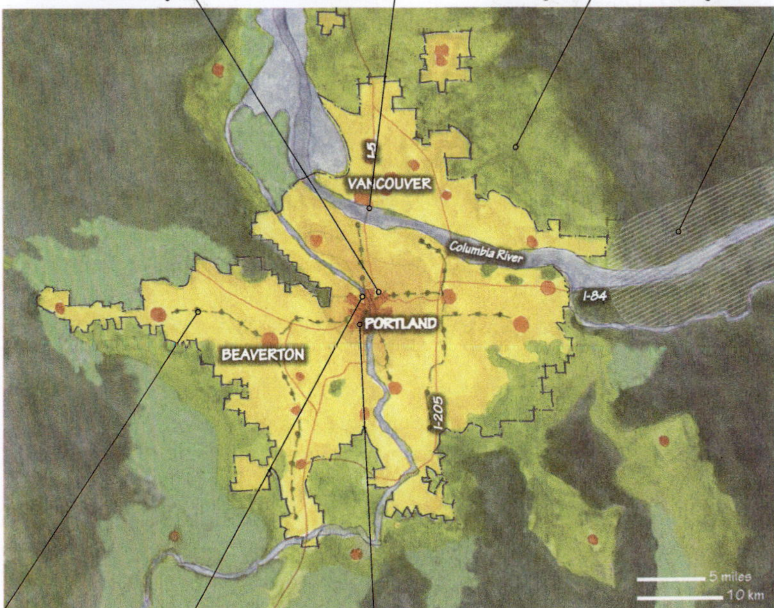

The "Silicon Forest" in Beaverton - Hillsboro area is the heart of the Metro area economy.

Portland Harbor has significant Superfund & EPA challenges but the Riverfront is a wonderful civic amenity.

Portland's central city & inner neighborhoods - a renowned planning success with a thriving service economy & high livability factors.

The major regional challenge is to improve opportunities for 'affordable living' throughout Metro area.

Challenge for the Planning Field

> ONE OF THE KEY CHARACTERISTICS THAT MAKES US HUMAN APPEARS TO BE THAT WE CAN THINK ABOUT ALTERNATIVE FUTURES AND MAKE DELIBERATE CHOICES ACCORDINGLY. CREATURES WITHOUT SUCH A CAPACITY CANNOT BE BOUND INTO A SOCIAL CONTRACT AND TAKE MORAL RESPONSIBILITY. . . . WE ARE THE ONLY SPECIES ON THIS PLANET WITH THE FORESIGHT CAPABLE OF DELIBERATELY PLOTTING A PATH TOWARD A DESIRABLE LONG-TERM FUTURE. PLAN IT FOR THE APES; BECAUSE THEY CAN'T
>
> —THOMAS SUDDENDORF (2013), PROFESSOR OF PSYCHOLOGY, UNIVERSITY OF QUEENSLAND, AUSTRALIA

Because we can think ahead, we bear moral responsibility to do so. In the face of today's "wicked problems" with their social, technical, and political complexities—along with our local contributions to the global threats to survival of the human species (not just climate change but also diminishing species and genetic diversity, etc.)—are the tools we have sufficient to plan for an unknown and rapidly changing future?

The work of planners has been discussed and debated for decades, and the role has been described in many ways, ranging from an idealized "planner as analyst" to the "planner as mediator" (both literally and figuratively). These roles have been defined within institutional structures that no longer seem adequate for addressing today's problems. Although we shouldn't engage lightly in institutional overhauls or begin discarding tools that have worked well in the past with superficial consideration of their pros and cons, it may indeed be time to reconsider both our tools and institutions with a critical eye to how they can and must help us to move forward.

Moreover, we should ask: Do the many activities carried out by planners add up to a grand conceptualization of planning as a field? Fifty years ago, the United States was immersed in the giddy boom of post-World War II recovery. The economy was spinning forward with technological advances that in many cases were destroying the global environment. We noticed the degradation close to home, and put in place laws to keep most of the biggest offenders in check on U.S. soil. Meanwhile, the same activities were simply exported to foreign lands and we tried to keep our heads in the sand.

Today, economic prosperity is far more complicated. More than ever, we can feel the reality of that lovely image of our small blue planet taken from space in the 1960s. Coal mined from the interior West, shipped to China and burned as fuel, returns on the wings of the global wind currents and rains down upon the Pacific Northwest in the form of deadly pollutants.

Exporting raw materials improves the country's trade balance and some local economies, but at a cost to the interests of future generations that planning serves.

We are connected through social media on a global level to an extent unfathomable even a couple of decades ago. Information about almost any topic is disseminated at lightning speed without screening or checks on technical accuracy or political correctness. The amount and types of information, the sources, and the linkages between grassroots entities and individuals are beyond comprehension, much less organization.

How does planning today fit into this picture? Do planners continue to keep their heads in zoning books and plans, or is there another role for this field that prides itself on thinking ahead and orchestrating actions to optimize moral behavior? Do regions matter anymore or should they?

Planning in the Pacific Northwest has been fortunate. The demographic and economic shifts, noted in the book's Introduction and section 1 Introduction, brought a level of receptivity to planning that were important in establishing how the field is known here. And the fundamental given—the region's environmental conditions and values—offered an opportunity at all scales to plan with the environment in mind.

Planning will continue to build on this legacy, but it cannot settle into roles shaped by yesterday's context. The challenges ahead, while similar in some respects to the past, are in fact questions presented and understood in completely new ways by a whole range of societal expertise. The context is shifting dramatically. For planning to be an effective source of leadership and interpretation for citizens, it must conceptualize and define itself in ways that differ from the past. Building on the confidence evidenced by the articles in this collection, the field will have to take risks. It will need to be bold as well as ambitious, leaning into limitations in knowledge with courage and doing so with others. The work will be about framing appropriate questions and shaping the ways to engage them with others, more than about finding solutions.

The methods in tomorrow's planning will need to fit the broad and complex issues we face. Central for the field at this moment is a methods question with two parts; what methods does planning have that it can continue to count on and what does it need to have in order to lead, articulate societal values, and to be a source for guidance that citizens have come to expect from this profession?

In the Spirit of the Unknowable: Working Together Matters

One of the joys of working together on this book has been the opportunity for the editors to share ideas on these issues—the role of planners and the future of planning as a profession. And as educators, we have also talked about the future of planning education.

The conversation started with climate change and how to present such a large, intractable "wicked" problem to students in our undergraduate and graduate programs without so dispiriting them that they no longer choose to get involved or take action. The question led to a discussion of, as Howell Baum put it, the "organization of hope." After all, whether as citizen or planner, planning for a future that you may personally never experience, never know, is a profoundly optimistic, hopeful act. Plans are pledges for a more hopeful future, one certainly on a better path than the one we'd get if we just put our feet up and changed the channel.

Are the problems we know about big and scary, some even wicked? Yes. Even more, complexity is another way to describe a lack of knowledge. Perfect knowledge, an unraveling of complexity into its component and manipulable parts, would be tantamount to knowing the outcome before it occurred, to know the future. As practitioners, we know that this will never be the frame for our actions as planners, and to promise it only enables the kind of disassociation and inaction that we're witnessing on so many issues, even those where our knowledge outshines our will to act.

But our response to a challenging future is to do what planners do: We plan, and in this case, in this region, we act. Planning is fundamentally a hopeful enterprise. We have skills and insights to begin addressing the wicked problems—not just the social problems of the 1970s where the term originated, but also the complex, multifaceted "unknowable" super-wicked problems of today. Addressing those wicked problems means we have to take action, not wait for the problems get any less wicked.

The methods question posed above is also about the future of planning education and research. What needs to be learned and how should this educational process happen for the next generation of planners who will deal directly with the wicked problems we leave behind?

To initiate discussion on these questions, several broad areas emerged from our work that should be included:

- Emphasize creativity, divergent thinking and innovation—they are essential qualities for the challenging processes ahead. The art and creative energy of planning are as critical as the science of this field and where discovery of the possible—"the mysteries of the spaces between things," as graphic design legend Milton Glaser puts it, will always be of value.
- Draw on the new knowledge of the roles and processes of communications in addressing complex social problems and strengthen the field's capacities across the increasingly rich range of forms.
- Deepen the understanding of the social and human behavioral dimensions of what goes on in planning as well as in the dy-

namic social physics of our changing communities.

- Support learning with more voices present, with different values and backgrounds, and different methods and visions. Value more vertical education experiences that integrate educational generations and span academic and professional contexts.
- Foster open dialogue and debate about the field and the boundaries of the institutional frames we work with, push on what it might be like to alter structures or equally, to appreciate limitations.
- Expand and deepen interdisciplinary learning. The current brevity of experiences only permits a light film of understanding. Support coordinated collaborative activities including new processes to share in knowledge creation, innovation, and in working together. Export education in planning beyond professional programs—it's too important to keep confined.
- Double-down on two qualities of critical value in planning—leadership and confidence. Manifest these throughout the educational process by teachers and learners alike. Foster educational environments that mimic planning itself—integrate teaching and learning together, flattening the traditional structures and raising the bar of mutual achievement and discovery.
- Impart a deep knowledge and appreciation for place—the complexities of the ecological, cultural, and ontological realities at this intersection of change and potential.

We, as practicing professionals and educators, can expand our concept of planning to be able to link, integrate, and orchestrate a multiplicity of disciplines into a unified whole. We can recognize and be willing to tackle the super-wicked problems. We can bring to the table a set of values that both reflect and enlarge upon the public values in our communities.

Moreover, we can reassert what planners have been asked to do on behalf of their communities since the planning profession emerged in the United States about 100 years ago: Plans and planning are what we develop to truly care for the places we live, and the landscapes and people we—all of us—affect. This remains our challenge in these challenging times.

We may not have all the answers to the "wicked problems" we face or the impending challenges of tomorrow. However, we do have the knowledge to take an approach that is interdisciplinary, comprehensive, and integrative. We do have the ability to facilitate a process that is open, collaborative, and consensus building. Planners have the skills to create a long-range view of the future and the ability to define how it may be achieved. We can be leaders. Why not?

ENDNOTES

CHAPTER 8

1 For more information about neighborhood planning in the Pacific Northwest, see Portland (2014a), Seattle (2010), Spokane (2010), Tacoma (2008), and UDistrict Livability Partnership (2013).

CHAPTER 14

1 The primary planning and regulatory laws for shorelines in Washington State are the Washington Shoreline Management Act (RCW 90.58) and the Growth Management Act (RCW 36.70A). Other relevant state and federal regulations include: for contaminated sites, the Comprehensive Environmental Response, Compensation and Liability Act (42 U.S.C. §9601 *et seq.*, 1980) at the federal level and the Model Toxics Control Act (RCW 70.105D) at the state level, and more generally the Hydraulic Project Approval (RCW 77.55), Section 10 of the Rivers and Harbors Act of 1899 (33 U.S.C. §103), and the Section 404 permit under the Clean Water Act (33 U.S.C. §1344). In British Columbia the primary regulatory driver is the federal Fisheries Act, administered by the Department of Fisheries and Oceans and Environment Canada. The primary purpose of the Fisheries Act is to protect fish and fish habitat in coastal and inland waters.

2 Extensive information about this pilot project can be found at: https://sites.google.com/a/uw.edu/seattle-seawall-project/home.

CHAPTER 16

1 This ethos and way of life was perhaps most famously described by Ernest Callenbach (1975) in *Ecotopia*.

2 In British Columbia, the Local Government Act (LGA) passed in 1996 requires a regional growth strategy (RGS) to include a plan for providing adequate, affordable and appropriate housing (British Columbia 1996). This commitment is similarly reflected in Oregon's landmark Land Conservation Act,

passed in 1973 (Oregon 2014b), and Washington's Growth Management Act, passed in 1990 (Washington 2014).

3 As demand for housing in central city locations continues to exceed supply in all three metro regions, lower-income households find it increasingly difficult to compete for affordable housing opportunities. This phenomenon has resulted in lower-income households paying in excess of 45 percent of total household income toward the combined costs of housing and transportation in the Portland and Seattle Metropolitan regions as documented by the Center for Neighborhood Technology and others (Center for Neighborhood Technology 2014; Vancouver 2014).

4 Created by the Tax Reform Act of 1986, the Low-Income Housing Tax Credit (LIHTC) is the most important resource for creating affordable housing in the United States today. According to the LIHTC database, created by the US Department of Housing and Urban Development, there were 37,506 housing projects and almost 2,318,000 housing units placed in service between 1987 and 2011 across the United States (U.S. Department of Housing and Urban Development 2014).

5 For low-income housing tax credits, "lower income" is defined as 60 percent or less of the Area Median Income (U.S. Department of Housing and Urban Development 2014).

CHAPTER 18

1 In the Upper Columbia Watershed, restoration efforts are guided by the Upper Columbia Spring Chinook Salmon and Steelhead Recovery Plan.

2 Formally, the Confederated Tribes and Bands of the Yakama Nation.

3 In addition, in four of the five river studies, at least 45 percent of respondents (and as many as 62.5 percent) expressed opposition to requiring that boaters self-register before floating the river; the majority of these individuals "strongly" opposed.

CHAPTER 26

1 For more information about the trail, see Portland's Springwater Corridor website at www.portlandoregon.gov/parks/finder/index.cfm?action=ViewPark&PropertyID=679.

2 For more information about the Pre-Disaster MitigationGrant Program, see the program site at www.fema.gov/pre-disaster-mitigation-grant-program.

3 For more information about World Environment Day, see the event website at www.portlandoregon.gov/WED.

4 For more information about the Foster Floodplain Natural Area, see the "Foster Floodplain Natural Area Celebration" video at www.portlandoregon.gov/bes/article/467038.

CHAPTER 30

1 The national version of GreenSTEP was called the Energy and Emissions Reduction Policy Analysis Tool (EERPAT).

2 For more information, see the state's Electric Vehicles and Infrastructure Program website at www.oregon.gov/ODOT/HWY/OIPP/Pages/inn_ev-charging.aspx.

CHAPTER 34

1 Three focus groups were held in fall 2013, with representatives from local government, agriculture, and organizations focused on social justice and anti-hunger issues. Perspectives and quotes from the focus group participants are referenced throughout this chapter. The participants are kept anonymous.

CHAPTER 36

1 To access the work products developed, see Puget Sound Regional Council (2014a).

CHAPTER 39

1 Idaho ranks 50th in both categories. See U.S. Energy Information Administration (2012b).

2 Washington State rates were listed as 6.66 cents per kWh and 298 pounds carbon dioxide emissions per MWh. See U.S. Energy Information Administration (2014c).

3 For example, see Hamlet et al. (2010).

4 Revised Code of Washington (RCW) § 82.16.110.

5 Full disclosure: The authors of this chapter were members of UW-Solar, which was awarded a grant by the Bonneville Environmental Foundation in October 2013.

CHAPTER 40

1 Original group of fellows from the American Planning Association, the American Institute of Architects, and the American Society of Landscape Architects: Brian Campbell, FAICP; Arnold Cogan, FAICP; Carol Mayer-Reed; Dave Siegel, FAICP; and Paddy Tillett, FAICP.

REFERENCES

Abbott, Carl, Sy Adler, and Margery Post Abbott. 1997. *Planning A New West: The Columbia River Gorge National Scenic Area*. Corvallis, Ore.: Oregon State University Press.

Alesko, Michael. 1979. "Growth Boundary Debate Aired: MSD vs. 1000 Friends." *The Oregonian*, September 15.

Allen, John Eliot, Marjorie Burns, and Scott Burns. 2009. *Cataclysms on the Columbia: The Great Missoula Floods*, rev. 2nd ed. Portland, Ore.: Ooligan Press.

Allen, Patricia. 2008. "Mining for Justice in the Food System: Perceptions, Practices, and Possibilities."*Agriculture and Human Values* 25 (2): 157–161.

American Farmland Trust. 2012. *Western Washington Foodshed Study*. Available at http://wafoodshed.wix.com/western-wa-foodshed.

American Friends Service Committee. 1970. *Uncommon Controversy: Fishing Rights of the Muckleshoot, Puyallup, and Nisqually Indians*. Seattle: University of Washington Press.

American Planning Association. 2009. *Sustainable Washington 2009: Planning for Climate Change*. Available at www.washington-apa.org/sustainable_washington.

Azhar, Salman, Wade Carlton, Darren Olsen, and Irtishad Ahmad. 2011. "Building Information Modeling for Sustainable Design and LEED Rating Analysis." *Automation in Construction* 20 (2): 217–224.

Bain, Lesley, Barbara Gray, and Dave Rodgers. 2012. *Living Streets: Strategies for Crafting Public Space*. Hoboken, N.J.: John Wiley & Sons.

Bainbridge (Washington), City of. 2009. *Ordinance 2009-06*. Available at www.ci.bainbridge-isl.wa.us/DocumentCenter/View/41.

________. 2013. *Ordinance 2013-25*. Available at http://wa-bainbridgeisland.civicplus.com/DocumentCenter/View/2298.

Bard, Marylin. 2011. "Remembering the Paddle to Seattle: 'Their Shoulders Bore the Traditions of Eight Millennia.'" *North Kitsap Herald*, July 12. Available at www.northkitsapherald.com/opinion/125424683.html.

Barnett, Erica C. 2006a. "The Death of Pike/Pine." *The Stranger*, November 30. Available at www.thestranger.com/seattle/Content?oid=111746.

________. 2006b. "Requiem for a Block." *The Stranger*, June 20. Available at http://slog.thestranger.com/2007/06/requiem_for_a_block.

Bean, Karen, and Kathryn H. Krafft. 1988. "The Preservation Ethic: Public Roles/Private Efforts." *ARCADE* 8 (5).

Bellingham (Washington), City of. 2005. "Waterfront Advisory Group Minutes." 2005. Available at www.cob.org/cob/wagmin.nsf/50999134738287ed8825733200620fb5/895f675eda6135828825724b00833c53!OpenDocument.

Bend (Oregon), City of. 2014. "Plans and Programs." January 1, 2014. Available at http://bendoregon.gov/index.aspx?page=115.

Berger, Knute. 2008. "Saving the Lesser Seattle Landmarks: Laws Alone Aren't Enough to Preserve Our Urban Heritage." *Crosscut.com*, February 23. Available at http://crosscut.com/2008/02/23/mossback/11839/Saving-lesser-Seattle-landmarks.

________. 2012. "U.S. Approves Salish Sea Name." *Crosscut.com*, November 12. Available at http://crosscut.com/2009/11/12/crosscut-blog/19183/US-approves-Salish-Sea-name.

________. 2013. "How Gas Works Park Shapes the Northwest Today." *Crosscut.com*, February 1. Available at http://crosscut.com/2013/02/01/mossback/112765/gasworks-park-historical-landmark.

Billington, David P., Donald C. Jackson, and Martin V. Melosi. 2005. *The History of Large Federal Dams: Planning, Design, and Construction in the Era of Big Dams*. Washington, D.C.: U.S. Department of the Interior. Available at www.cr.nps.gov/history/online_books/dams/federal_dams.pdf.

Blair Jr., Bowen. 1987. "The Columbia River Gorge National Scenic Area: The Act, Its Genesis, and Legislative History." *Environmental Law* 17: 863–970.

Bonneville Power Administration. 2014. "About Us." Available at www.bpa.gov/news/AboutUs/Pages/default.aspx.

Bonneville Power Administration, U.S. Bureau of Reclamation, and U.S. Army Corps of Engineers. 2001. *The Columbia River System Inside Story*, Second Edition. Available at www.bpa.gov/power/pg/columbia_river_inside_story.pdf.

Bratt, Rachel. 2007. *Should We Foster the Nonprofit Housing Sector as Developers and Owners of Subsidized Rental Housing?* Cambridge, Mass.: Joint Center for Housing Studies of Harvard University. Available at www.jchs.harvard.edu/research/publications/should-we-foster-nonprofit-housing-sector-developers-and-owners-subsidized.

Brettman, Allan. 2011. "Portland Bikes Earn Audi Insignia." *The Oregonian*, March 31.

________. 2014. "Imperial Stock Ranch Ready to Enter Apparel Field, Boosted by Ralph Lauren U.S. Winter Olympics Sweater." *OregonLive.com*, January 25. Available at www.oregonlive.com/playbooks-profits/index.ssf/2014/01/post_27.html.

British Columbia, Province of. 1996. *Local Government Act*. Available at www.bclaws.ca/Recon/document/ID/freeside/96323_00.

Brotherton, Barbara, ed. 2008. *S'abadeb, The Gifts*. Seattle: University of Washington Press.

Brown, Ruth. 2011. "The Selling of Stumptown." *Willamette Week*, June 8. Available at www.wweek.com/portland/article-17590-the_selling_of_stumptown.html.

Bullitt Center. 2014. "Building Features: Solar District #1." Available at www.bullittcenter.org/building/building-features/solar-district-1.

Burgan, Michael, and Mark Winne. 2013. *Doing Food Policy Councils Right: A Guide to Development and Action*. Available at www.markwinne.com/wp-content/uploads/2012/09/FPC-manual.pdf.

Burningham, Lucy. 2009. "Portland Food Carts Push through Recession." *Oregon Business*, December 17. Available at www.oregonbusiness.com/articles/78-january-2010/2775-cash-and-carry.

Callenbach, Ernest. 1975. *Ecotopia*. Berkeley, Calif.: Banyan Tree Books.

Canizaro, Vincent. 2007. *Architectural Regionalism*. New York: Princeton Architectural Press.

Cannady, Dale. 1970. Letter to Columbia Region Association of Governments Executive Committee, December 17.

Canty, Dennis, Alex Martinsons, and Anshika Kumar. 2012. *Losing Ground: Farmland Protection in the Puget Sound Regions*. Seattle: American Farmland Trust. Available at www.farmland.org/documents/aftlosinggroundreportweb.pdf.

Canty, Dennis, and Helena Wiley. 2004. *A Characterization of Puget Sound Agriculture: A Report to the Puget Sound Shared Strategy*. Seattle: Shared Strategy.

Carder, Justin. 2009. "Cap Hill Bloggers to Throw $10,000 Party Resurrecting Legendary Pine." *Capitol Hill Seattle* blog, July 19. Available at www.capitolhillseattle.com/2009/07/cap-hill-bloggers-to-throw-10000-party-resurrecting-legendary-pine.

_________. 2013."Travelers Making Way for Gaming Cafe on E Pine." *Capitol Hill Seattle* blog, June 6. Available at www.capitolhillseattle.com/2012/06/travelers-making-way-for-gaming-cafe-on-e-pine.

Cascade Business News. 2012. "Facebook Unveils Economic Impact Study." January 24. Available at www.cascadebusnews.com/news-pages/e-headlines/1814-facebook-unveils-economic-impact-study.

Cascade Land Conservancy. 2005. *The Cascade Agenda: 100 Years Forward*. Available at www.forterra.org/files/1.1_Cascade_Agenda_Summary.pdf.

Casola, Joseph H., Jennifer E. Kay, Amy K. Snover, Robert A. Norheim, Lara C. Whitely Binder, and the Climate Impacts Group. 2005. *Climate Impacts on Washington's Hydropower, Water Supply, Forests, Fish, and Agriculture*. Available at http://cses.washington.edu/db/pdf/kc05whitepaper459.pdf.

Center for Columbia River History. 2014. "Columbia River History." Available at www.ccrh.org/river/history.php. (2014)

Center for Neighborhood Technology. 2014. "H+T Affordability Index" Available at http://htaindex.cnt.org.

Chandler, Homer. 1970. Memorandum to Columbia Region Association of Governments Executive Committee, December 21.

Chapman, Roger. 2010. *Culture Wars: An Encyclopedia of Issues, Viewpoints, and Voices*. Armonk, N.Y.: M.E. Sharpe.

Climate Impacts Group. 2014a. "Climate Impact Group: Welcome." Available at http://cses.washington.edu/cig.

________. 2014b. "Climate Change." Available at http://cses.washington.edu/cig/pnwc/cc.shtml.

Cohen, Bryan. 2013. "Pike/Pine Preservation Showdown: Developers Oppose Hurdles to Building Bigger on Capitol Hill." *Capitol Hill Seattle* blog, August 15. Available at www.capitolhillseattle.com/2013/08/pikepine-preservation-showdown-developers-oppose-raising-hurdles-to-build-bigger.

Cohen, Rebecca. 2011. *The Impacts of Affordable Housing on Health: A Research Summary.* Washington D.C.: Center for Housing Policy and National Housing Conference. Available at www.nhc.org/media/files/Insights_HousingAndHealthBrief.pdf.

Colburn, Kevin. 2001. "How Much Wood does a Paddler Chuck?" *American Whitewater Journal,* March/April, 57–59.

Cole, Leslie. 2009. "Haute Tea." *The Oregonian*, October 20.

Columbia Gorge Future Forum. 2008. *Envisioning Our Future: Building a Vibrant, Sustainable Future for the Gorge.* Available at www.gorgecommission.org/client/FF_Final_Report_complete.pdf.

Columbia Region Association of Governments. 1970. Interim Regional Land Use Plan.

________. 1972. *Planning in the CRAG Region: An Appraisal & New Direction.*

________. 1976. *Land Use Framework Element of the CRAG Regional Plan.*

________. 1978. *Urban Growth Boundary Findings.*

Columbia River Gorge Commission. 2012. *Collaborative Engagement Assessment: Columbia River Gorge National Scenic Area, Assessment Report.* Prepared by the Oregon Consensus National Policy Center. Available at www.gorgecommission.org/client/pdfs/projects/GorgeNSACollaborativeAssessmentReport.pdf.

Columbia River Gorge Commission and U.S. Department of Agriculture. 2009. *Vital Signs Indicators Project: State of the Gorge 2009.* Available at www.fs.usda.gov/Internet/FSE_DOCUMENTS/stelprdb5182173.pdf.

Colwell, Shanti, and Tracy Tackett. 2011. *Ballard Roadside Raingardens, Phase I—Lessons Learned.* Available at: http://water.epa.gov/infrastructure/greeninfrastructure/upload/gi_ballardproject.pdf.

Commoner, Barry. 1971. *The Closing Circle: Nature, Man, and Technology.* New York: Knopf.

Communities Count. 2013. "Disparities in Teen Obesity by Race/Ethnicity Foreshadow Adult Disparities." Available at www.communitiescount.org/index.php?page=grade.

Cook, John. 2012. "Seattle Ranks 4th as Global Startup Hub, Edges Out NYC." *Geekwire*, November 20. Available at www.geekwire.com/2012/seattle-ranks-4th-global-startup-hub-edges-nyc.

Cortright, Joseph. 2006. *Making Sense of Clusters: Regional Competitiveness and Economic Development.* Washington, D.C.: The Brookings Institution. Available at http://www.brookings.edu/~/media/research/files/reports/2006/3/cities%20cortright/20060313_clusters.pdf.

Coughlin, Robert E., John C. Keene, and J. Dixon Esseks. 1981. *National Agricultural Lands Study.* Washington, D.C.: U.S. Department of Agriculture.

Crane, Jeff. 2011. *Finding the River: An Environmental History of the Elwha.* Corvallis, Ore.: Oregon State University Press.

Cronin, Kevin (senior business development coordinator, Portland Development Commission). 2014. Personal communication with author, February.

Crowley, Walt. 1998. *National Trust Guide: Seattle.* New York: National Trust for Historic Preservation.

Data Center Knowledge. 2014. "Inside Microsoft's New Quincy Cloud Farm." Available at www.datacenterknowledge.com/inside-microsofts-new-quincy-cloud-farm.

Davidson, Nestor M. 2007. "Cooperative Localism: Federal-Local Collaboration in an Era of State Sovereignty." *Virginia Law Review* 93: 959–1034.

Deloria, Philip J. 2004. *Indians in Unexpected Places*. Lawrence, Kans.: University of Kansas Press.

Desbois, Martine. 2006. *The Green Shores Project: A Review of Green Building Assessment and Rating Tools and their Applicability to a Green Shores Rating System*. Vancouver, B.C.: Green Shores Technical Working Group.

Dibenedetto, Bill. 2008. "Three-Way Deal in Tacoma." *Journal of Commerce*, February 24. Available at www.joc.com/maritime-news/three-way-deal-tacoma_20080224.html.

Donohue, Patrick. 2013. Telephone interview with Alyse Nelson, November 15.

Downtown Seattle Association. 2012. "Belltown: 2012 Neighborhood Profile." Available at http://downtownseattle.com/files/file/Belltown.pdf.

DSIRE (Database of State Incentives for Renewables and Efficiency). 2014a. "Oregon: City of Ashland—Solar Rights Ordinance." Available at http://dsireusa.org/incentives/incentive.cfm?Incentive_Code=OR06R&re=0&ee=0.

________. 2014b. "Washington: Renewable Energy Cost Recovery Incentive Payment Program." Available at www.dsireusa.org/incentives/incentive.cfm?Incentive_Code=WA27F.

________. 2014c. "Washington: Tax Abatement for Solar Manufacturers." Available at www.dsireusa.org/incentives/incentive.cfm?Incentive_Code=WA28F.

Duda, Jeffrey J., Jerry E. Freilich, and Edward G. Schreiner. 2008. "Baseline Studies in the Elwha River Ecosystem Prior to Dam Removal: Introduction to the Special Issue." *Northwest Science* 82 (Special Issue): 1–12.

Elazar, Daniel. 1972. *American Federalism: A View from the States,* 2d ed. New York: Thomas Y. Crowell Co.

Elefante, Carl. 2007. "The Greenest Building Is . . . One That Is Already Built." *National Trust for Historic Preservation Forum Journal* 21 (4): 62–72.

Elsner, Marketa McGuire, Jeremy Littell, and Lara Whitely Binder, eds. *The Washington Climate Change Impacts Assessments: Evaluating Washington's Future in a Changing Climate*. Available at http://cses.washington.edu/db/pdf/wacciareport681.pdf.

Emery, John. 1977. *Why Nothing Has Happened: A Case Study of Johnson Creek*. Boulder, Co: Western Interstate Commission for Higher Education.

Encinar, José M., Juan F. González, and Antonio Rodriguez-Reinares. 2005. *Biodiesel from Used Frying Oil Variables Affecting the Yields and Characteristics of the Biodiesel. Industrial & Engineering Chemical Research* 44 (15): 5491–5499.

Facebook. 2011. Press Release. "Facebook Opens First Data Center in Prineville, Oregon." Available at www.facebook.com/note.php?note_id=10150150581753133.

Farley, Kristi Langlow. 1977. *A Primer: Preservation in Seattle*. City of Seattle.

Farmland Information Center. 2014. "2010 National Resources Inventory." Available at www.farmlandinfo.org/2010-national-resources-inventory.

Follansbee, Joe. 2012. "Is Seattle Its Own Greatest Roadblock?" *Seattle Magazine*, March. Available at www.seattlemag.com/article/seattle-its-own-greatest-road-block.

Foster Green EcoDistrict. 2014. "Welcome to Foster Green!" Available at www.fostergreenecodistrict.org.

Garde, A. 2009. "Sustainable by Design?: Insights from U.S. LEED-ND Pilot Projects." *Journal of the American Planning Association* 75 (4): 424–440.

Goff, Maureen. 2010. "Evaluating Habitat Enhancements of an Urban Intertidal Seawall: Ecological Responses and Management Implications." Masters thesis, University of Washington.

Gonzales, Angela A., and Timothy Q. Evans. 2013. "The Imposition of Law: The Federal Acknowledgement Process and the Legal De/Construction of Tribal Identity." In *Recognition, Sovereignty Struggles, and Indigenous Rights in the United States: A Sourcebook*, ed. Amy E. Den Ouden and Jean M. O'Brien, 37–64. Chapel Hill, N.C.: University of North Carolina Press.

Google. 2014. "The Dalles, Oregon." Available at www.google.com/about/datacenters/inside/locations/the-dalles.

Graves, Bill. 2012. "How Happy is Oregon? Governor Kitzhaber Joins Portland State University Class That Aims to Find Out." *The Oregonian*, April 16. Available at www.oregonlive.com/education/index.ssf/2012/04/how_happy_is_oregon_governor_k.html.

Green Futures Lab. 2010. *Westgate Special District Form Based Code Recommendations*. Seattle: University of Washington.

________. 2014. *Burlington at the Crossroads Recommendations*. Seattle: University of Washington.

Green Lents. 2014. "Welcome Neighbor!" Available at www.greenlents.org.

Green Shores. 2014. "Coastal Development Rating System." Available at http://stewardshipcentrebc.ca/Green_shores/cdrs.

Guthman, Julie. 2008. "Bringing Good Food to Others: Investigating the Subjects of Alternative Food Practice." *Cultural Geographies* 15 (4): 431–447.

Hajbabaei, Maryam, Kent C. Johnson, Robert A. Okamoto, Alexander Mitchell, Marcie Pullman, and Thomas D. Durbin. 2012. "Evaluation of the Impacts of Biodiesel and Second Generation Biofuels on NO_x Emissions for CARB Diesel Fuels." *Environmental Science & Technology* 46 (16): 9163-9173.

Hamlet, Alan F., Se-Yeun Lee, Kristian E.B. Mickelson, and Marketa M. Elsner. 2010. "Effects of Projected Climate Change on Energy Supply and Demand in the Pacific Northwest and Washington State." *Climatic Change* 102 1–2: 103–128.

Harris, Keith. 2010. "Park(ing) Day Press." *People's Parking Lot* blog, September 21. Available at http://peoplesparkinglot.blogspot.in/2010/09/parking-day-press.html.

Harrison, John. 2008a. "Columbia River: Description, Creating, and Discovery." *Columbia River History Project*, October 31. Available at www.nwcouncil.org/history/ColumbiaRiver.

________. 2008b. "Hydropower." *Columbia River History Project*, October 31. Available at www.nwcouncil.org/history/hydropower.

________. 2008c. "Indian Fishing." *Columbia River History Project*, October 31. Available at www.nwcouncil.org/history/IndianFishing.

________. 2008d. "Megawatt." Available at www.nwcouncil.org/history/megawatt.

________. 2011. "Endangered Species Act and Columbia River Salmon and Steelhead." Available at www.nwcouncil.org/history/endangeredspeciesact.

Harvey, Mark. 1998. "Symbols from the Big Dam Era in the American West." Paper presented at the American Society for Environmental History Conference, San Antonio, Tex.

Hassanein, Neva. 2003. "Practicing Food Democracy: A Pragmatic Politics of Transformation." *Journal of Rural Studies* 19 (1):77–86.

Hawkins III, William. 2011. "Colonel L. L. Hawkins and His Early Role in the Establishment of Portland Parks." In *Wild in the City, Exploring the Intertwine*, edited by Michael C. Houck and M.J. Cody. Portland, Ore.: Oregon State University Press.

Henderson, Theresa, Andi VanderWal, and the Squaxin Island Heritage and Culture Committee. 2002. "Squaxin Island." In *Native Peoples of the Olympic Peninsula: Who We Are* by Jacilee Wray, ed., 83–98. Norman, Okla.: University of Oklahoma Press.

Hernandez, Pedro. 2013. "Microsoft Buys Land for Massive Data Center Expansion in Quincy, Wash. *eWeek*, December 26. Available at www.eweek.com/cloud/microsoft-buys-land-for-massive-data-center-expansion-in-quincy-wash.html.

Heying, Charles. 2010. *Brew to Bikes: Portland's Artisan Economy*. Portland, Ore.: Ooligan Press.

Hockaday, Joan. 2009. *Greenscapes: Olmsted's Pacific Northwest*. Pullman, Wash.: WSU Press.

Hokin, Samuel. 2014. "Transmission Lines." Available at www.bsharp.org/physics/transmission.

Holden, Dominic. 2011. "Stop The Insanity." *The Stranger*, March 16. Available at www.thestranger.com/seattle/stop-the-insanity/Content?oid=7200124.

Holling, C.S. 1973. "Resilience and Stability of Ecological Systems." *Annual Review of Ecology and Systematics* 4 (1): 1-23.

Holt, Gimenez E., and Annie Shattuck. 2011. "Food Crises, Food Regimes and Food Movements: Rumblings of Reform or Tides of Transformation?" *The Journal of Peasant Studies* 38 (1): 109–144.

Home Power. 2014. "Solar Electricity Basics: Why Use Solar Electricity?" Available at www.homepower.com/articles/solar-electricity/basics/why-use-solar-electricity.

Hope-Alkon, Alison and Teresa Marie Mares. 2012. "Food Sovereignty in US Food Movements: Radical Visions and Neoliberal Constraints." *Agriculture and Human Values* 29 (3): 347–359.

Hopkins, Rob. 2009. "The 200 Artisan Skills Required to Make a Victorian Town Functional." *Transition Culture* blog, January 22. Available at http://transitionculture.org/2009/01/22/the-200-artisan-skills-required-to-make-a-victorian-town-functional.

Horner, Richard, Heungkook Lim, and Stephen J. Burges. 2002. *Hydrologic Monitoring of the Seattle Ultra-Urban Stormwater Management Projects*. Available at: www.seattle.gov/util/groups/public/@spu/@usm/documents/webcontent/spu02_020016.pdf.

Horst, Megan. 2011. "A Scan of Existing City and County Policies and Plans." Paper presented at Puget Sound Regional Food Policy Council meeting, Seattle, November 8.

Houck, Michael C., and Jim Labbe. 2007. *Ecological Landscapes: Connecting Neighborhood to City and City to Region*. Portland, Ore.: Institute of Portland Metropolitan Studies. Available at http://pdxscholar.library.pdx.edu/cgi/viewcontent.cgi?article=1052&context=metropolitianstudies.

Hult, Ruby. 1954. *The Untamed Olympics: The Story of a Peninsula*. Portland, Ore: Binford & Mort.

Huxtable, Ada Louise. 2008. *On Architecture: Collected Reflections on a Century of Change*. New York: Walker & Company.

Initiative for Bicycle & Pedestrian Innovation. 2010. *The Portland Bicycle Story*. Available at www.pdx.edu/ibpi/sites/www.pdx.edu.ibpi/files/portlandbikestory_1.pdf.

IPCC (Intergovernmental Panel on Climate Change). 2013. "Summary for Policymakers." In *Climate Change 2013: The Physical Science Basis*, Thomas F. Stocker, Dahe Qin, Gian-Kasper Plattner, Melinda M.B. Tignor, Simon K. Allen, Judith Boschung, Alexander Nauels, Yu Xia, Vincent Bex, and Pauline M. Midgley, eds. 3–32. Cambridge, U.K.: Cambridge University Press. Available at www.climatechange2013.org/images/report/WG1AR5_SPM_FINAL.pdf.

Jacobs, Jane. 1992. *The Death and Life of Great American Cities*. New York: Vintage Books.

James, Philip A., Luk M. St. Onge, Mark E. van Voorst, and Matthew P. Walker 2006. "Cypress Street Viaducts." Available at www.engineering.com/Library/ArticlesPage/tabid/85/ArticleID/73/Cypress-Street-Viaducts.aspx.

Johnson Creek Corridor Committee. 1992. *Johnson Creek Vision: A Look at the Future of the Johnson Creek Watershed*. Portland, Ore.: Johnson Creek Corridor Committee.

_________. 1995. *Johnson Creek Resource Management Plan*. Portland, Ore.: Johnson Creek Corridor Committee.

Johnson, Kirk. 2013. "Voters in SeaTac, Wash., Back $15 Minimum Wage." The *New York Times*, November 26. Available at www.nytimes.com/2013/11/27/us/voters-in-seatac-wash-back-15-minimum-wage.html.

Jurjevich, Jason, and Greg and Schrock. 2012. *Is Portland Really the Place Where Young People Go To Retire? Migration Patterns of Portland's Young and College-Educated, 1980–2010*. Portland, Ore.: Nohad A. Toulan School of Urban Studies & Planning, Portland State University. Available at http://mkn.research.pdx.edu/wp-content/uploads/2012/09/JurjevichSchrockMigrationReport1.pdf.

Kania, John, and Mark Kramer. 2011. "Collective Impact." *Stanford Social Innovation Review*, Winter. Available at www.ssireview.org/articles/entry/collective_impact.

King County (Washington). 2009. *Large Wood Stakeholder Committee: Final Report and Recommendations*. Available at http://your.kingcounty.gov/dnrp/library/water-and-land/flooding/0912-large-wood-safety-rule/Large_Wood_Stakeholder_Committee_Final_Transmittal.pdf.

_________. 2013a. "Agriculture Program." Available at www.kingcounty.gov/environment/wlr/sections-programs/rural-regional-services-section/agriculture-program.aspx.

_________. 2013b. "City of Snoqualmie." Available at www.kingcounty.gov/healthservices/health/partnerships/CPPW/whosinvolved/snoqualmie.aspx.

_________. 2014. "Drop in Youth Obesity Epidemic Tied to Public Health Investments." Available at www.kingcounty.gov/healthservices/health/news/2014/14022001.aspx.

King County Housing Authority (Washington). 2013. "Greenbridge." Available at www.kcha.org/development/greenbridge.

Klingle, Matthew. 2007. *Emerald City: An Environmental History of Seattle*. New Haven, Conn.: Yale University Press.

Knothe, Gerhard, Jon Van Gerpen, and Jürgen Krahl, eds. 2005. *The Biodiesel Handbook*. Champaign, Ill.: AOCS Press.

Koc, Mustafa, and Kenneth A. Dahlberg. 1999. "The Restructuring of Food Systems: Trends, Research, and Policy Issues." *Agriculture and Human Values* 16 (2): 109–116.

Konrad, Alex. 2012. "America's 50 Best Cities." *Bloomberg Businessweek*, September 28. Available at http://images.businessweek.com/slideshows/2012-09-26/americas-50-best-cities?cmpid=msn.

Kramer, Steven L., and Marc O. Eberhard. 1995. *Seismic Vulnerability of the Alaskan Way Viaduct: Summary Report.* Seattle: Washington State Transportation Center, University of Washington. Available at www.wsdot.wa.gov/research/reports/fullreports/363.4.pdf.

Kreisman, Lawrence. 1988. "Preservation in Seattle: A Personal View," *ARCADE* 8(5).

Kreisman, Lawrence. 1999. *Made to Last: Historic Preservation in Seattle and King County*. Seattle: University of Washington Press.

Kueter, Vince. 2001. "Seattle through the Years." *Seattle Times*, November 13. Available at http://seattletimes.com/news/local/seattle_history/articles/timeline.html.

Kuipers, Dean. 2011. "Last Coal Plant in Pacific Northwest to Shut Down Starting in 2020." *Los Angeles Times*, March 6. Available at http://latimesblogs.latimes.com/greenspace/2011/03/last-coal-plant-in-pacific-northwest-to-shut-beginning-2020.html.

Kurtz, Tim. 2012. "Green Infrastructure in the City of Portland." Presentation to Danish stormwater professionals, Portland, Ore., October.

Lanier, Jaron. 2013. *Who Owns the Future?* New York: Simon & Schuster.

Larson, Matt (Mayor of Snoqualmie). 2014. Telephone interview with Jill Sterrett, October 28.

League of American Bicyclists. 2013a. *Bicycle Friendly Business Report.* Washington, D.C.: League of American Bicyclists.

________.2013b. *Where We Ride: An Analysis of Bicycling in American Cities.* Available at http://bikeleague.org/content/new-report-where-we-ride.

________. 2014. "2014 Bicycle Friendly State Ranking." Available at http://bikeleague.org/content/ranking.

Lee, Mark, Eric Villagomez, Penny Gurstein, David Eby, and Elvin Wyly. 2008. *Affordable EcoDensity: Making Affordable Housing a Core Principle of Vancouver's EcoDensity Charter* Vancouver, B.C.: Canadian Centre for Policy Alternatives. Available at www.policyalternatives.ca/sites/default/files/uploads/publications/BC_Office_Pubs/bc_2008/affordable_ecodensity.pdf.

Lemann, Nicholas. 2013. "When the Earth Moved: What Happened to the Environmental Movement." *The New Yorker,* April 15.

Lettman, Gary, Andrew A. Herstrom, Darla R. Hiebenthal, Neil McKay, and Tyler J. Robinson. 2011. *Forests, Farms and People: Land Use Change on Non-Federal Land in Oregon 1974–2009*. Salem, Ore: Oregon Department of Forestry.

Levin, Kelly, Benjamin Cashore, Steven Bernstein, and Graeme Auld. 2012. "Overcoming the Tragedy of Super Wicked Problems: Constraining Our Future Selves to Ameliorate Global Climate Change." *Policy Sciences* 45 (2): 123–152.

Levitt, Julia. 2011. "Preservation Green Lab's Liz Dunn on the Economics of Urban Grain." *The Atlantic*, December 1. Available at www.theatlantic.com/national/archive/2011/12/preservation-green-labs-liz-dunn-on-the-economics-of-urban-grain/248190.

Liptan, Tom, and Robert Murase. 2002. "Water Gardens as Stormwater Infrastructure." In *Handbook of Water Sensitive Planning and Design*, Robert L. France, ed., 125–154. Boca Raton, Fla.: CRC Press.

Litman, Todd. 2014. *Evaluating Transportation Equity: Guidance for Incorporating Distributional Impacts in Transportation Planning*. Victoria, B.C.: Victoria Transport Policy Institute. Available at www.vtpi.org/equity.pdf.

Lowe, Don, and Roberta Lowe. 1980. *35 Hiking Trails in the Columbia River Gorge*. Beaverton, Ore.: The Touchstone Press.

Lubell, Jeffrey, Rosalyn Crain, and Maya Brenna. 2007. *Framing the Issues—The Positive Impacts of Affordable Housing on Education*. Washington D.C.: Center for Housing Policy and National Housing Conference. Available at www.nhc.org/media/documents/FramingIssues_Heath.pdf.

Lucero, Claudia. 2011a. "New Home Dairy Book and We're in It!" *Urban Cheesecraft* blog, April 4. Available at www.urbancheesecraft.com/cheesy-adventures/new-home-dairy-book-and-were-in-it.

________. 2011b. "DIY Cheese Kits on Daily Grommet—Inventions, Innovative Products, Good Gifts . . . " *Urban Cheesecraft* blog, April 13. Available at http://urbancheesecraft.wordpress.com/2011/04/13/diy-cheese-kits-on-daily-grommet-inventions-innovative-products-good-gifts.

________. 2011c. "Playing Around with Vegan Cheeses . . . " *Urban Cheesecraft* blog, July 10. Available at www.urbancheesecraft.com/cheese-recipes/playing-around-with-vegan-cheeses.

________. 2012. "Urban Cheesecraft Kits Launch at Williams-Sonoma Today!" *Urban Cheesecraft* blog, April 10. Available at www.urbancheesecraft.com/cheesy-adventures/urban-cheesecraft-kits-launch-at-williams-sonoma-today.

Mapes, Jennifer, and Jennifer Wolch. 2011. "'Living Green': The Promise and Pitfalls of New Sustainable Communities." *Journal of Urban Design* 16 (1): 105–126.

Mapes, Lynda V. 2009. *Breaking Ground: The Lower Elwha Klallam Tribe and the Unearthing of the Tse-whit-zen Village*. Seattle: University of Washington Press.

________. 2013a. "Elwha Dam-Removal Project Held Back as Silt Estimate Too Low." *The Seattle Times*, January 3. Available at: http://seattletimes.com/html/localnews/2020045074_elwha03m.html.

________. 2013b. *Elwha: A River Reborn*. Seattle: The Mountaineers Books.

Marine View Ventures. 2014. "Portfolio." Available at www.marineviewventures.com/page.php?id=31.

Mason, Randall. 2006. "Theoretical and Practical Arguments for Values-Centered Preservation." *CRM: The Journal of Heritage Stewardship* 3 (2): 21–48.

Mays, Wanda. 1972. Letter to the Columbia Region Association of Governments Executive Board about the work of the Action and Direction Committee, October 26.

McCormick, R. L., A. Williams, J. Ireland, M. Brimhall, and R.R. Hayes. 2006. *Effects of Biodiesel Blends on Vehicle Emissions: Fiscal Year 2006 Annual Operating Plan Milestone 10.4*. Golden, Colo.: National Renewable Energy Laboratory. Available at www.nrel.gov/docs/fy07osti/40554.pdf.

McDonnell, Janet A. 1991. *The Dispossession of the American Indian, 1887–1934*. Bloomington, Ind.: Indiana University Press.

McElvaney, Shannon. 2012. *Geodesign: Case Studies in Urban and Regional Planning*. Redlands, Calif.: Esri Press.

McGann, Chris. 2008. "Gregoire: 'Watch Me Tear down the Viaduct.'" *Seattle Post-Intelligencer*, January 3. Available at www.seattlepi.com/local/transportation/article/Gregoire-Watch-me-tear-down-the-viaduct-1260638.php.

Meadows, Donella H., Dennis L. Meadows, Jorgen Randers, and William W. Behrens III. 1972. *The Limits to Growth: A Report for the Club of Rome's Project on the Predicament of Mankind*. New York: Universe Books. Available at www.donellameadows.org/wp-content/userfiles/Limits-to-Growth-digital-scan-version.pdf.

Methow Conservancy. 2005. *Economic Impacts of Land Resources in the Methow Valley: Executive Summary.* Prepared by Resource Dimensions. Available at www.methowconservancy.org/survey_summary.pdf.

Metro (Portland, Oregon). 2012. *Title 7: Housing Choice. Metro Code Chapter 3.07: Urban Growth Management Functional Plan.* Available at www.oregonmetro.gov/sites/default/files/0307_eff_011812_including_maps_for_title_4_6_and_14_updated_010814_ord_13-1316final.pdf.

Metro (Portland, Oregon). 1996. *How Should Our Community Grow.*

Metta, Jessica (former Gorge commission planner). 2013. Discussion with author, October 12.

Miller, Julia. 2004. *Protecting Older Neighborhoods through Conservation District Programs.* Washington, D.C.: National Trust for Historic Preservation.

Miller, Rich. 2011. "Amazon's Cloud Goes Modular in Oregon." *Data Center Knowledge*, March 28. Available at www.datacenterknowledge.com/archives/2011/03/28/amazons-cloud-goes-modular-in-oregon.

________. 2012. "Facebook Has Spent $210 Million on Oregon Data Center". *Data Center Knowledge*, January 30. Available at www.datacenterknowledge.com/archives/2012/01/30/facebook-has-spent-210-million-on-oregon-data-center.

Moody, Fred. 2003. *Seattle and the Demons of Ambition: From Boom to Bust in the Number One City of the Future.* New York: Macmillan.

Mumford, Lewis. 1939. *Regional Planning in the Pacific Northwest: A Memorandum.* Portland, Ore.: Northwest Regional Council.

Nash, Roderick. 1989. *The Rights of Nature: A History of Environmental Ethics.* Madison, Wis: The University of Wisconsin Press.

National Biodiesel Board. 2014. "Biodiesel Retailer Listings." Available at www.biodiesel.org/using-biodiesel/finding-biodiesel/retail-locations/biodiesel-retailer-listings.

National Oceanic and Atmospheric Administration. 2014. "Federal Columbia River Power System Biological Opinion." Available at www.westcoast.fisheries.noaa.gov/fish_passage/fcrps_opinion/federal_columbia_river_power_system.html.

National Park Service. 2005. *Final Supplement to the Final Environmental Impact Statement: Elwha River Ecosystem Restoration Implementation.* Available at www.nps.gov/olym/naturescience/loader.cfm?csModule=security/getfile&PageID=136240.

Nelson, Katherine. 1994. "Resolving Native American Land Claims and the Eleventh Amendment: Changing the Balance of Power." *Villanova Law Review* 39: 525–626.

Nikolic, Sara, Dan Bertolet, Peter Dane, David Cutler, Don Vehige, Tim Trohimovich, and Bill La Borde. 2009. *Transit-Oriented Communities: A Blueprint for Washington State.* Available at www.gglo.com/files/Downloads/Our%20Insight/Blueprint_for_Transit-Oriented_Communities.pdf.

Northwest Power and Conservation Council. 2012. *Council Brief.* Available at www.nwcouncil.org/media/30086/2012_04.pdf.

________. 2013a. "Power Supply: Adequacy and Reliability." Available at www.nwcouncil.org/energy/powersupply.

________. 2013b. *Sixth Power Plan: Mid-Term Assessment Report.* Available at www.nwcouncil.org/media/6391355/2013-01.pdf.

________. 2013c. *The State of the Columbia River Basin: Fiscal Year 2013, Annual Report*. Available at www.nwcouncil.org/media/6877852/2013-07.pdf.

O'Connell, Lenahan. 2009 "The Impact of Local Support on Smart Growth Policy Adoption." *Journal of the American Planning Association* 75 (3): 281–291.

Ochsner, Jeffrey Karl. 2008. "Victor Steinbrueck Finds His Voice: From the *Argus* to *Seattle Cityscape*." *Pacific Northwest Quarterly* 99(3): 122–133.

Ochsner, Jeffrey Karl, ed. 2014. *Shaping Seattle Architecture*, Second Edition. Seattle: University of Washington Press.

Oliver, Emmett. 1991. "Reminiscences of a Canoe Puller." In *A Time of Gathering, Native Heritage in Washington State* edited by Robin Wright. Seattle: University of Washington Press.

Olmsted, John Charles, Portland Park Board, Olmstead Brothers Landscape Architects, and Frederick Law Olmsted. 1903. *Portland: Report of the Park Board, Portland Oregon*. Portland, Ore.: City of Portland.

Oregon 2050 Alliance. 2014. *Oregon 2050/A Vision for Oregon—Healthy, Vibrant, Resilient*. Available at www.aslaoregon.org/assets/blog/2014-05-27/OREGON%202050,%20Final%20Vision%20Statement%20Working%20Draft_%20GK_2-7-14.pdf.

Oregon Brewers Guild. 2014. "Oregon Craft Brew Facts." Available at http://oregoncraftbeer.org/facts.

Oregon, State of. 1969. *Senate Bill 10*. Available at www.oregon.gov/LCD/docs/bills/sb10.pdf.

________. 1974. *State-Wide Planning Goals and Guidelines*. Salem: Ore.: Oregon Land Conservation and Development Commission.

________. 1977. *Report and Recommendation of Hearings Officer*. Salem: Ore.: Oregon Land Conservation and Development Commission.

________. 1979. Acknowledgement of Compliance Reports to Land Conservation and Development Commission, June 28 and December 10.

________. 1980. *Compliance Acknowledgement Order In the Matter of the Metropolitan Service District's Regional Urban Growth Boundary*. Salem: Oregon Land Conservation and Development Commission.

________. 2006. *Oregon Administrative Rule 660-012-0035, Evaluation and Selection of Transportation System Alternatives*. Available at http://arcweb.sos.state.or.us/pages/rules/oars_600/oar_660/660_012.html.

________. 2009. *Background Report: The Status of Oregon Greenhouse Gas Emissions and Analysis*. Available at www.oregon.egov.com/ODOT/TD/OSTI/docs/hb2186/background.pdf.

________. 2010a. *Executive Order No. 10-07: Rebuilding Vernonia's Schools and the Surrounding Community in the Wake of the December 2007 Storm*. Available at www.oregon.gov/gov/pdf/eo_1007.pdf.

________. 2010b. *Oregon's Statewide Planning Goals & Guidelines*. Available at www.oregon.gov/LCD/docs/goals/compilation_of_statewide_planning_goals.pdf.

________. 2012a. *Oregon Administrative Rules, 660-007-0030, New Construction Mix*. Available at www. arcweb.sos.state.or.us/pages/rules/oars_600/oar_660/660_007 .html.

________. 2012b. Oregon Administrative Rules, 660-007-0035, Minimum Residential Density Allocation for New Construction. Available at http://arcweb.sos.state.or.us/pages/rules/oars_600/oar_660/660_007.html.

________. 2012c. *Oregon's Statewide Planning Goals & Guidelines, Goal 10: Housing*. Available at www.oregon.gov/LCD/docs/goals/goal10.pdf.

________. 2013a. *Oregon Revised Statute 426.508, Sale of F. H. Dammasch State Hospital; Fair Market Value; Redevelopment of Property; Property Reserved for Community Housing*. Available at www.oregonlegislature.gov/bills_laws/lawsstatutes/2013ors426.html.

________. 2013b. *Oregon Statewide Transportation Strategy: A 2050 Vision for Greenhouse Gas Emissions Reduction*. Available at www.oregon.gov/ODOT/TD/OSTI/Pages/STS.aspx.

________. 2014a. "EcoDrive." Available at www.oregon.gov/ODOT/TD/TP/pages/ecodrive.aspx.

________. 2014b. "Oregon Department of Land Conservation and Development: Statewide Planning Goals." Available at www.oregon.gov/LCD/Pages/goals.aspx.

________. 2014c. "Oregon Transportation Options Plan." Available at www.oregon.gov/ODOT/TD/TP/Pages/toplan.aspx.

________. 2014d. "Transportation Planning Rule (TPR)." Available at www.oregon.gov/LCD/Pages/Rulemaking_TPR_2011.aspx.

________. 2014e. "Welcome to TripCheck." Available at www.tripcheck.com/Pages/RCMap.asp?curRegion=0.

Oregonian Editorial Board, The. 1979. "Don't Foster Urban Sprawl." *The Oregonian*, July 22.

Orloff, Chet. 2004. "If Zealously Promoted by All: The Push and Pull of Portland Park History." In *The Portland Edge: Challenges and Successes in Growing Communities*, ed. Connie P. Ozawa, 140–163. Washington, D. C.: Island Press.

Ott, Jennifer. 2011a. "Alaskan Way Viaduct, Part 1: Early Transportation Planning." Available at www.historylink.org/index.cfm?DisplayPage=output.cfm&file_id=9925.

________. 2011b. "Alaskan Way Viaduct, Part 2: Planning and Design." Available at www.historylink.org/index.cfm?DisplayPage=output.cfm&file_id=9951.

________. 2011c. "Alaskan Way Viaduct, Part 3: Building the Viaduct." Available at www.historylink.org/index.cfm?DisplayPage=output.cfm&file_id=9978.

________. 2011d. "Alaskan Way Viaduct, Part 4: Replacing the Viaduct." Available at www.historylink.org/index.cfm?DisplayPage=output.cfm&file_id=9983.

Outdoor Industry Association. 2012. *The Outdoor Recreation Economy*. Available at https://outdoorindustry.org/pdf/OIA_OutdoorRecEconomyReport2012.pdf.

Outdoor Industry Foundation. 2006. *The Economic Contribution of Active Outdoor Recreation—Technical Report on Methods and Findings*. Prepared by Southwick Associates, Inc. Available at www.outdoorfoundation.org/pdf/ResearchRecreationEconomyTechnicalReport.pdf.

Oxford Martin Commission. 2013. *Now for the Long Term: The Report of the Oxford Martin Commission for Future Generations*. Oxford: Oxford Martin School, University of Oxford. Available at www.oxfordmartin.ox.ac.uk/downloads/commission/Oxford_Martin_Now_for_the_Long_Term.pdf.

Paanenen, Ron. 2010. "Tunnel Construction: Subterranean in Seattle." *Roads & Bridges*, December 17. Available at www.roadsbridges.com/tunnel-construction-subterranean-seattle.

Packwood, Bob. 1984. "The Columbia River Gorge Needs Federal Protection." *Environmental Law* 15: 67–70.

Peters, Adele. 2013. "Is This the Most Sustainable Neighborhood in the U.S.?" *Fast Company Co.EXIST*, November 13. Available at www.fastcoexist.com/3021385/is-this-the-most-sustainable-neighborhood-in-the-us.

Pietz, Amanda Joy, and Brian J. Gregor. 2014. "Oregon Statewide Transportation Strategy: A 2050 Vision for Greenhouse Gas Emission Reduction." Transportation Research Board 93rd Annual Meeting Compendium of Papers, Transportation Research Board, Washington, D.C.

Pizzuto, Jim. 2002. "Effects of Dam Removal on River Form and Process." *Bioscience* 52 (8): 683–691.

Poff, N. Leroy, and David D. Hart. 2002. "How Dams Vary and Why It Matters for the Emerging Science of Dam Removal." *BioScience*. 52 (8): 659–668.

Pollack, Melinda, and Bryan Prater. 2013. *Filling the Financing Gap for Equitable Transit-Oriented Development*. New York: Living Cities. Available at www.liifund.org/wp-content/uploads/2013/04/TOD-Report-03-26-13-FINAL.pdf.

Population Research Center. 2013. "Certified Population Estimates 2013." Available at http://www.pdx.edu/prc/population-estimates-0.

Port of Bellingham. 2004. *Waterfront Vision & Framework Plan: Connecting Bellingham with the Bay*. Available at www.portofbellingham.com/DocumentCenter/View/2336.

________. 2008. *Draft Environmental Impact Statement*. Available at http://portofbellingham.com/424/Draft-Environmental-Impact-Statement.

Portland (Oregon), City of. 1996. *Bicycle Master Plan*. Available at www.portlandonline.com/shared/cfm/image.cfm?id=40414.

________. 2001a. *Johnson Creek Restoration Plan*. Available at www.portlandoregon.gov/bes/article/214367.

________. 2001b. *Parks 2020 Vision*. Available at www.portlandoregon.gov/parks/40182.

________. 2005. *Actions for Watershed Health: 2005 Portland Watershed Management Plan*. Available at www.portlandoregon.gov/bes/article/107808.

________. 2007. *Cultural Resource Management Plan: Planning Framework and Implementation*. Available at www.portlandoregon.gov/parks/article/165571.

________. 2008. *Portland Ecoroof Guide*. Available at: www.portlandoregon.gov/bes/article/53988.

________. 2010a. *Portland's Bicycle Plan for 2030*. Available at www.portlandoregon.gov/transportation/article/289122.

________. 2010b. *Portland's Green Infrastructure: Quantifying the Health, Energy, and Community Livability Benefits*. Prepared by Entrix, Inc. Available at: www.portlandoregon.gov/bes/article/298042.

________. 2011. *Legislative Report*. Available at www.portlandoregon.gov/ogr/article/372406.

________. 2012. *Actions for Watershed Health: Portland Watershed Management Plan. Five Year Implementation Strategy, 2012–2017*. Available at www.portlandoregon.gov/bes/article/394563.

________. 2013a. *City of Portland Comprehensive Plan Working Draft*. Available at https://www.portlandoregon.gov/bps/60986.

________. 2013b. "Community Watershed Stewardship Program (CWSP)." Available at www.portlandoregon.gov/bes/43077.

________. 2013c. "Fact Sheet." Available at www.portlandoregon.gov/transportation/article/407660.

________. 2013d. "Green Investment Fund (GIF) Grant." Available at www.portlandoregon.gov/bps/42134.

_____. 2013e. "Grey to Green Accomplishments." Available at www.portlandoregon.gov/bes/article/321331.

________. 2013f. "Tabor to the River." Available at www.portlandoregon.gov/bes/47591.

________. 2014a. *Comprehensive Plan Update (Portland Plan Implementation)*. Available at www.portlandoregon.gov/bps/57352.

________. 2014b. "Rollin' Tire Site (2008)." Available at www.portlandoregon.gov/bes/article/425969.

________. 2014c. "Salmon in Portland." Available at www.portlandoregon.gov/bes/51048.

________. 2014d. "Watershed Revegetation Program." Available at www.portlandoregon.gov/bes/article/394076.

________. 2014e. "Willing Seller Program." Available at www.portlandoregon.gov/bes/article/106234.

Pothukuchi, Kameshwari, and Jerome L. Kaufman. 2000. "The Food System: A Stranger to the Planning Field." *Journal of the American Planning Association* 66 (2): 113–124.

Puget Sound Fresh. 2014. "Harvest Schedule." Available at www.pugetsoundfresh.org/harvest-schedule.

Puget Sound Partnership. 2008. *Puget Sound Action Agenda*. Available at www.mypugetsound.net/index.php?option=com_docman&task=doc_download&gid=97&Itemid=172.

Puget Sound Regional Council. 2014a. "East Corridor Implementation Support Project." Available at www.psrc.org/about/advisory/gtc-committees/corridor-task-forces/east-corridor-task-force/east-corridor-implementation-support-project.

________. 2014b. "Population and Housing Estimates." Available at www.psrc.org/data/pophousing/pophousing-estimates.

Putnam, Robert D., and Lewis M. Feldstein. 2003. *Better Together: Restoring the American Community*. New York: Simon & Schuster.

Puyallup Tribe of Indians. 2014. "Treaty of Medicine Creek." Available at www.puyallup-tribe.com/history/treaty_of_medicine_creek/.

Quality Growth Alliance. 2009. *From Barriers to Solutions and Best Practices: Urban Centers and TOD in Washington*. Prepared by Charles R. Wolfe and Paul Symington, The Runstad Center for Real Estate Studies, University of Washington. Available at www.qualitygrowthalliance.org/SEA/wp-content/uploads/2010/01/Urban_Centers_and-TOD.Analysis_of_Barriers_and_Solutions.UW_September_2009.pdf.

Quil Ceda Village. 2014. "About Us." Available at www.quilcedavillage.com/info_about.asp.

Quillen, Abby. 2014. "Portland's Food Truck Heaven: How a New Kind of Fast Food Brings Jobs, Flavor, and Walkability." *Yes!*, January 17. Available at www.yesmagazine.org/issues/how-to-eat-like-our-lives-depend-on-it/portland-s-food-truck-heaven.

Real Estate Research Corporation. 1974. *The Costs of Sprawl: Environmental and Economic Costs of Alternative Residential Development Patterns at the Urban Fringe*. Washington, D.C: U.S. Government Printing Office.

Richmond, Henry, and Timothy G. Houchen. 2007. *Oregon's Public Investment in Conservation, Prosperity and Fairness: Reduced Taxation of Farmland and Forestland, 1974–2004*. Portland, Ore.: American Land Institute. Available at http://ir.library.oregonstate.edu/xmlui/bitstream/handle/1957/5503/Property_Tax_Report.pdf;jsessionid=111E6F12C0E3B480F7547402E730762E?sequence=4.

Rittel, Horst W.J., and Melvin M. Webber. 1973. "Dilemmas in a General Theory of Planning." *Policy Sciences* 4 (2): 155–169.

Romano, Craig. 2011. *Day Hiking: Columbia River Gorge.* Seattle: The Mountaineers Books.

Rottle, Nancy. 2005. "Factors in the Landscape-Based Greenway: A Mountains to Sound Case Study." *Landscape and Urban* Planning 76 (1): 134–171.

Rouse, David C., and Ignacio F. Bunster-Ossa. 2013. *Green Infrastructure: A Landscape Approach*, Planning Advisory Service Report no. 571. Chicago: American Planning Association.

Sager, Tore. 1995. "Teaching Planning Theory as Order or Fragments?" *Journal of Planning Education and Research* 14 (3): 166–73.

Seaside (Oregon), City of. *Seaside Transportation System Plan, Volume I: Plan.* Available at www.seasidetsp.org/ProjectLibrary/Seaside%20TSP_Final.pdf.

Seattle (Washington), City of. 1998. *Belltown Neighborhood Plan.* Available at www.seattle.gov/neighborhoods/npi/plans/belltown.

________. 2000. *Cedar River Watershed Habitat Conservation Plan.* Available at www.seattle.gov/util/EnvironmentConservation/OurWatersheds/Habitat_Conservation_Plan/AbouttheHCP/Documents/index.htm.

________. 2001a. *Neighborhood Plan Stewardship Survey: A Snapshot of Plan Stewardship in Seattle.* Available at www.seattle.gov/Documents/Departments/SeattlePlanningCommission/stewardship-survey.pdf.

________. 2001b. *Seattle's Neighborhood Planning Program 1995–1999: Documenting the Process.* Available at www.seattle.gov/Documents/Departments/SeattlePlanningCommission/finalreport.pdf.

________. 2004. *Historic Resources Plan.* Available at www.seattle.gov/parks/publications/HistoricResourcesPlan.htm.

________. 2007. *Seattle Bicycle Master Plan.* Available at www.seattle.gov/transportation/bikemaster07.htm.

________. 2008. *Pike/Pine Neighborhood Conservation Study, Phase 1 Report: Neighborhood Character and Recommendations.* Prepared by Lund Consulting, Inc. Available at www.seattle.gov/dpd/cs/groups/pan/@pan/documents/web_informational/dpdd016691.pdf.

________. 2009. *Ordinance Number 123020.* Available at http://clerk.seattle.gov/~scripts/nph-brs.exe?s3=&s4=123020&s5=&s1=&s2=&S6=&Sect4=AND&l=0&Sect2=THESON&Sect3=PLURON&Sect5=CBORY&Sect6=HITOFF&d=ORDF&p=1&u=%2F~public%2Fcbor1.htm&r=1&f=G.

________. 2010a. *Green Roofs in Seattle: A Survey of Vegetated Roofs and Rooftop Gardens.* Prepared by Annika McIntosh, University of Washington, Green Futures Lab. Available at www.seattle.gov/dpd/GreenBuilding/docs/dpdp020213.pdf.

________. 2010b. *Ordinance Number 123392.* Available at http://clerk.seattle.gov/~scripts/nph-brs.exe?s3=&s4=123392&s5=&s1=&s2=&S6=&Sect4=AND&l=0&Sect2=THESON&Sect3=PLURON&Sect5=CBORY&Sect6=HITOFF&d=ORDF&p=1&u=%2F~public%2Fcbor1.htm&r=1&f=G.

________. 2011a. "Complete Streets Checklist." Available at www.seattle.gov/transportation/docs/UPDATED_CompleteStreetsChecklistfinaldraft51914.pdf.

________. 2011b. *Ordinance Number 123776.* Available at http://clerk.seattle.gov/~scripts/nph-brs.exe?s3=&s4=123776&s5=&s1=&s2=&S6=&Sect4=AND&l=0&Sect2=THESON&Sect3=PLURON&Sect5=CBORY&Sect6=HITOFF&d=ORDF&p=1&u=%2F~public%2Fcbor1.htm&r=1&f=G.

________. 2011c. *South Fork Tolt Watershed Management Plan.* Available at www.seattle.gov/util/groups/public/@spu/@conservation/documents/webcontent/01_012728.pdf.

________. 2011d. "Sustainable Building Policy RES ATT." Available at www.seattle.gov/Documents/Departments/OSE/dpdp021677.pdf.

________. 2012a. *Food Action Plan.* Available at www.seattle.gov/Documents/Departments/OSE/Seattle_Food_Action_Plan_10-24-12.pdf.

________. 2012b. *Olympic Sculpture Park: Year 5 Monitoring of Shoreline Enhancements.* Prepared by Jason Toft, Andrea Ogston, Jeffrey Cordell, Elizabeth Armbrust, Claire Levy, and Erin Morgan. Seattle: School of Aquatic and Fishery Sciences and School of Oceanography, University of Washington.

________. 2013a. *2014–2019 Proposed Capital Improvement Program.* Available at www.seattle.gov/financedepartment/1419proposedcip/documents/2014-2019ProposedCIP-BOOK.pdf.

________. 2013b. *City of Seattle: Analysis and Decision of the Director of the Department of Planning and Development.* Available at www.seattle.gov/council/rasmussen/attachments/Pike-Pine%20SEPA%20DNS%20decision%20v2.pdf.

________. 2013c. *Executive Order: 2013-01 Citywide Green Stormwater Infrastructure Goal and Implementation Strategy.* Available at: www.seattle.gov/Documents/Departments/OSE/GSI-exec-order.pdf.

________. 2013d. *Seattle Climate Action Plan.* Available at www.seattle.gov/Documents/Departments/OSE/2013_CAP_20130612.pdf.

________. 2013e. "Seattle Green Factor." Available at: www.seattle.gov/dpd/cityplanning/completeprojectslist/greenfactor/whatwhy.

________. 2013f. *Seattle Bicycle Master Plan: Draft June 2013.* Available at www.seattle.gov/transportation/docs/bmp/2013/SBMP%20Complete%206%205%202013%202%20pm.pdf.

________. 2013g. *Urban Forestry Stewardship Plan.* Available at www.seattle.gov/trees/docs/2013%20Urban%20Fores%20Stewardship%20Plan%2009111 3.pdf.

________. 2014a. "2014 Seattle City Council Green Sheet: Add $45,000 of GSF to the OSE BCL for the Capitol Hill EcoDistrict, and Impose a Proviso." Available at http://clerk.seattle.gov/public/meetingrecords/2013/budget/26-1-A-1-2013.pdf.

________. 2014b. "Bell Street Park Parks and Green Spaces Levy Project Information." Available at www.seattle.gov/parks/projects/bell_street/boulevard_park.htm.

________. 2014c. "Current Projects." Available at www.seattle.gov/util/EnvironmentConservation/Projects/DrainageSystem/GreenStormwaterInfrastructure/CurrentGSIProjects/index.htm.

________. 2014d. "Seattle Parks and Recreation Legacy Plan." Available www.seattle.gov/parks/legacy.

________. 2014e. "Seattle Parks Foundation." Available at www.seattle.gov/parks/getinvolved/.

________. 2014f. "Sewage Overflow Prevention." Available at www.seattle.gov/util/EnvironmentConservation/Projects/DrainageSystem/SewageOverflowPrevention/index.htm.

________. 2014g. "Our Watersheds." Available at www.seattle.gov/util/EnvironmentConservation/OurWatersheds/index.htm.

_________. n.d. "Seattle Street-Food Vending Checklist." Available at www.seattle.gov/ECONOMICDEVELOPMENT/mobilefood/PDF%20FILES/Street_Food_Checklist.pdf.

Seattle City Council. 2006. *Alaskan Way Viaduct: Review of the Transportation Factors Associated with a Surface Roadway*. Prepared by DKS Associates. Available at www.seattle.gov/council/attachments/06awv_transportation_factors.pdf.

Seattle City Light. 2013. *Guide to Installing a Solar Electric System*. Available at www.seattle.gov/light/conserve/cgen/docs/SCL_ElectricSolarGuide.pdf.

Seattle Public Utilities. 2004. *Seattle's Natural Drainage Systems*. Available at www.seattle.gov/util/groups/public/@spu/@usm/documents/webcontent/spu02_019984.pdf.

_________. 2007. *NW 110th Street Natural Drainage System Performance Monitoring*. Prepared by Richard Horner and Cameron Chapman, Department of Civil and Environmental Engineering, University of Washington. Available at: www.swrcb.ca.gov/rwqcb4/water_issues/programs/stormwater/municipal/ventura_ms4/CommentLetters/AttachNRC/Chapman%20and%20Horner%20-%20110th%20monitoring%20report.pdf.

_________. 2008. *Restore Our Waters Status Report 2004–2008*. Available at www.seattle.gov/util/groups/public/@spu/@conservation/documents/webcontent/spu01_006037.pdf.

_________. 2009. *Thornton Creek Water Quality Channel: Final Report*. Available at www.seattle.gov/util/groups/public/documents/webcontent/spu01_006146.pdf.

_________. 2010. *2010 Residential Waste Stream Composition Study Final Report*. Available at www.seattle.gov/util/groups/public/@spu/@garbage/documents/webcontent/01_014338.pdf.

_________. 2013a. "Project Details." Available at: www.seattle.gov/util/EnvironmentConservation/Projects/DrainageSystem/SwaleonYale/ProjectDetails/index.htm.

_________. 2013b. *Protecting Seattle's Waterways: Community Guide to the Plan*. Available at www.seattle.gov/util/groups/public/@spu/@drainsew/documents/webcontent/01_026050.pdf.

_________. 2013c. "RainWise Program." Available at www.seattle.gov/util/MyServices/DrainageSewer/Projects/GreenStormwaterInfrastructure/RainWise/index.htm.

Shrank, David, Bill Eisele, and Tim Lomax. 2012. *TTI's Urban Mobility Report*. College Station, Tex.: Texas A&M Transportation Institute. Available at http://d2dtl5nnlpfr0r.cloudfront.net/tti.tamu.edu/documents/mobility-report-2012.pdf.

Sirianni, Carmen. 2007. "Neighborhood Planning as Collaborative Democratic Design." *Journal of the American Planning Association* 73 (4): 373–387.

Slovic, Beth. 2011. "Portland's $1.4 Billion Big Pipe Project Comes to an End after 20 Years." *OregonLive*, November 25. Available at www.oregonlive.com/portland/index.ssf/2011/11/portlands_14_billion_big_pipe.html.

Smith, Stephen. 2012. "Architecture & Design: 6 Horrible Facadist Renovations, from Auckland to Yekaterinburg." *International Business Times*, February 7. Available at www.ibtimes.com/architecture-design-6-horrible-facadist-renovations-auckland-yekaterinburg-slideshow-554043.

Snoqualmie (Washington), City of. "City Development Past and Present." Available at www.ci.snoqualmie.wa.us/EconomicDevelopment/CityDevelopment.aspx.

Sowards, Adam M. 2007. *United States West Coast: An Environmental History*. Santa Barbara, Calif.: ABC-CLIO.

Spirn, Anne Whiston. 1984. *The Granite Garden: Urban Nature and Human Design*. New York: Basic Books, Inc.

Spokane (Washington), City of. 2010. "Neighborhood Planning." White paper, Planning Services Department, City of Spokane. Available at https://static.spokanecity.org/documents/business/planning/neighborhood/2010-planning-development-services-white-paper.pdf.

Stacey, Robert. 1976. Letter to Larry Rice on behalf of 1000 Friends of Oregon, January 20.

Stacey, Robert. 1977. Memoranda to Henry Richmond on behalf of 1000 Friends of Oregon, February 4 and 8.

Statistics Canada. 2014a. *Focus on Geography Series, 2011 Census: Census Metropolitan Area of Surrey, CY-British Columbia*. Available at www12.statcan.gc.ca/census-recensement/2011/as-sa/fogs-spg/Facts-csd-eng.cfm?LANG=Eng&GK=CSD&GC=5915004.

________. 2014b. *Focus on Geography Series, 2011 Census: Census Metropolitan Area of Vancouver, British Columbia*. Available at www12.statcan.gc.ca/census-recensement/2011/as-sa/fogs-spg/Facts-cma-eng.cfm?LANG=Eng&GK=CMA&GC=933.

Steinberg, Ari. 2013. Telephone interview by Jennifer Gerend, October 9.

Steinitz, Carl. 2012. *A Framework for Geodesign*. Redlands, Calif.: Esri Press.

Suddendorf, Thomas. 2013. "What Makes Us Human?" *Huffington Post* blog, December 9. Available at www.huffingtonpost.com/thomas-suddendorf/what-makes-us-human_b_4414357.html?utm_hp_ref=animals.

Sustainable Seattle. 2014. "The Seattle Area Happiness Initiative." Available at http://sustainableseattle.org/sahi.

Sutor, Julie. 2012. "Partnerships Spark Biodiesel Success for Essential Baking Co." *Clean Cities Now* 16 (2): 4–5.

Tackett, Tracy. 2012. "Green Stormwater Infrastructure to the Maximum Extent Feasible." Presentation, Seattle Public Utilities. Available at www.ecy.wa.gov/programs/wq/stormwater/municipal/LID/May12SPUppLIDcommittees.pdf.

Tacoma (Washington), City of. 2008. *Comprehensive Plan: Neighborhood Element*. Available at http://cms.cityoftacoma.org/Planning/Comprehensive%20Plan/13%20-%20Neighborhood%206-30-09.pdf.

Terravita. 2014 "Community Map." Available at http://terravitaseattle.com/community.aspx.

Thrush, Coll. 2008. *Native Seattle: Histories from the Crossing-Over Place*. Seattle: University of Washington Press.

Toft, Jason. 2013. "Nearshore Monitoring in Puget Sound." Presentation at the Salish Sea Shoreline Forum, Edmonds, Wash., September 30. Available at www.youtube.com/watch?v=p_rqWg_f1Kc (2:30:00).

Toft, Jason D., Jeffery R. Cordell, Sarah M. Heerhartz, Elizabeth A. Armbrust, and Charles A. Simenstad. 2010. "Fish and Invertebrate Response to Shoreline Armoring and Restoration in Puget Sound." In *Puget Sound Shorelines and the Impacts of Armoring—Proceedings of a State of the Science Workshop May 2009*, Hugh Shipman, Megan N. Dethier, Guy Gelfenbaum, Kurt L. Fresh, and Richard S. Dinicola, eds., 161–170. Washington, D.C.: U.S. Department of the Interior.

Tramutola, Chris. 2013. "Making Peace with Mother Nature." *Planning*, August/September 2013, 24–29.

Travel Oregon. 2013. *The Economic Significance of Bicycle-Related Travel in Oregon: Detailed State and Travel Region Estimates.* Prepared by Dean Runyun Associates. Available at www.deanrunyan.com/doc_library/bicycletravel.pdf.

Travel Oregon Network. 2014. "Oregon Scenic Bikeways." Available at http://rideoregonride.com/rides/scenic-bikeways.

Trust for Public Land. 2014. "ParkScore Index." Available at http://parkscore.tpl.org.

Tulalip Tribes. 2009. *2009 Tulalip Comprehensive Land Use Plan.* Available at www.tulaliptribes-nsn.gov/Home/Government/Departments/CommunityDevelopment/PlanningandPermitting/ComprehensivePlan.aspx.

U.S. Army Corps of Engineers. 2014. "CorpsMap: National Inventory of Dams." Available at http://geo.usace.army.mil/pgis/f?p=397:12.

U.S. Army Corps of Engineers and Bonneville Power Administration. 2014. "Columbia River Treaty, 2014/2024 Review: Overview and History." Available at www.crt2014-2024review.gov/History.aspx.

U.S. Bureau of Economic Analysis. 2013. "Local Area Personal Income: New Estimates for 2012; Comprehensive Revisions for 2001–2011." Available at www.bea.gov/newsreleases/regional/lapi/lapi_newsrelease.htm.

U.S. Bureau of Indian Affairs. 2013. *Indian Entities Recognized and Eligible to Receive Services from the United States Bureau of Indian Affairs.* 78 Fed. Reg. 26384, May 6. Available at www.gpo.gov/fdsys/pkg/FR-2013-05-06/pdf/2013-10649.pdf.

U.S. Bureau of Labor Statistics. 2014. "Quarterly Census of Employment and Wages." Available at www.bls.gov/cew/dataguide.htm.

U.S. Census Bureau. 2004. "Seattle Residents among Nation's Most Educated." Available at http://web.archive.org/web/20071005192642/http://www.census.gov/Press-Release/www/releases/archives/american_community_survey_acs/001802.html.

________. 2010a. "2010 Census Summary File 1." Available at http://factfinder2.census.gov/faces/tableservices/jsf/pages/productview.xhtml?pid=DEC_10_SF1_SF1DP1&prodType=table.

________. 2010b. *The American Indian and Alaska Native Population: 2010.* Available at http://www.census.gov/prod/cen2010/briefs/c2010br-10.pdf.

________. 2012. "2012 American Community Survey 1-Year Summary File." Available at http://factfinder2.census.gov/faces/tableservices/jsf/pages/productview.xhtml?pid=ACS_sumfile_2012&prodType=document.

U.S. Congress. 1887. *Allotment of Indian Lands.* 25 U.S. Code, Chapter 9. Available at www.law.cornell.edu/uscode/text/25/chapter-9.

________. 1989. *Puyallup Tribe of Indians Settlement Act of 1989.* 101st Cong., S. 402. Available at www.govtrack.us/congress/bills/101/s402.

U.S. Department of Agriculture. 2002. *County Summary Highlights.* Available at www.agcensus.usda.gov/Publications/2002/Volume_1,_Chapter_2_County_Level/Washington/st53_2_001_001.pdf.

________. 2007. *County Summary Highlights*. Available at www.agcensus.usda.gov/Publications/2007/Full_Report/Volume_1,_Chapter_2_County_Level/Washington/st53_2_001_001.pdf.

U.S. Department of Energy. 2004. *Hydropower: Setting a Course for Our Energy Future*. Available at www.nrel.gov/docs/fy04osti/34916.pdf.

________. 2011. *Challenges and Successes on the Path toward a Solar Powered Community: Solar in Action*. Available at www1.eere.energy.gov/solar/pdfs/51061_seattle.pdf.

________. 2014a. "Alternative Fuel Use Requirement." Available at www.afdc.energy.gov/laws/6214.

________. 2014b. "Biodiesel Feedstock Tax Exemption." Available at www.afdc.energy.gov/laws/8261.

________. 2014c. "Fishes of the Columbia River." Available at http://ecology.pnnl.gov/Fishes_Columbia_River.asp.

________. 2014d. "Washington Laws and Incentives." Available at www.afdc.energy.gov/laws/state_summary?state=WA.

U.S. Department of Housing and Urban Development. 2014. "Low-Income Housing Tax Credits Data Sets." Available at www.huduser.org/portal/datasets/lihtc.html.

U.S. Department of Transportation, Washington State Department of Transportation, King County, and City of Seattle. 2009. *Alaskan Way Viaduct Replacement Project History Report*. Available at www.wsdot.wa.gov/projects/viaduct/Media/Default/Documents/Reports/AWVProjectHistoryReport_Sept09.pdf.

________. 2011. *Alaskan Way Viaduct Replacement Project Final Environmental Impact Statement, Appendix A: Public Involvement Discipline Report*. Prepared by Enviroisues, Inc. Available at http://data.wsdot.wa.gov/publications/viaduct/AWVFEIS-AppendixA.pdf.

U.S. Energy Information Administration. 2012a. *Annual Energy Review 2011*. Available at www.eia.gov/totalenergy/data/annual/pdf/aer.pdf.

________. 2012b. "Oregon: Profile Overview." Available at www.eia.gov/state/?sid=OR.

________. 2012c. "State Electricity Profile 2010." Available at www.eia.gov/electricity/state/pdf/sep2010.pdf.

________. 2012d. "Washington: Profile Overview." Available at www.eia.gov/state/?sid=WA.

________. 2014a. *Annual Energy Review, Table 10.4: Biodisel Overview*. Available at www.eia.gov/totalenergy/data/monthly/pdf/sec10_8.pdf.

________. 2014b. "Frequently Asked Questions: Average Monthly Residential Electricity Consumption, Prices, and Bills by State (Excel)." Available at www.eia.gov/tools/faqs/faq.cfm?id=97&t=3.

________. 2014c. "State Electricity Profiles: Washington Electricity Profile 2012." Available at www.eia.gov/electricity/state/Washington.

U.S. Environmental Protection Agency. 2010. *Green Infrastructure Case Studies: Municipal Policies for Managing Stormwater with Green Infrastructure*. Available at http://water.epa.gov/polwaste/green/upload/gi_case_studies_2010.pdf.

________. 2014. "Climate Change Impacts and Adapting to Change." Available at www.epa.gov/climatechange/impacts-adaptation.

UDistrict Livability Partnership. 2013. *A Strategic Plan for Seattle's University District*. Available at www.seattle.gov/economicdevelopment/pdf_files/UDistStrategicPlan-Final-20130128-small.pdf.

United Nations General Assembly. 2011. *Happiness: Towards a Holistic Approach to Development*, Resolution 65/309). Available at www.un.org/ga/search/view_doc.asp?symbol=A/RES/65/309.

Upper Columbia Salmon Recovery Board. 2007. *Upper Columbia Spring Chinook Salmon and Steelhead Recovery Plan*. Available at www.ucsrb.org/Assets/Documents/Library/Plans/UCSRP/UCSRP%20 Final%209-13-2007.pdf.

Van Meter, Mia. 2013. E-mail interview with Alyse Nelson, October 12.

Vancouver (British Columbia), City of. 1999. *Southeast False Creek Policy Statement: Toward a Sustainable Urban Neighbourhood and a Major Park in Southeast False Creek*. Available at http://vancouver .ca/docs/sefc/policy-statement-1999.pdf.

_________. 2006. "Southeast False Creek." Available at http://web.archive.org/web/20061007005900 /http://www.vancouver.ca/commsvcs/southeast.

_________. 2012. *Transportation 2040*. Available at http://vancouver.ca/files/cov/Transportation_2040_Plan_as_adopted_by_Council.pdf.

_________. 2014. "Mayor's Task Force on Housing Affordability." Available at http://vancouver.ca/your-government/mayors-task-force-on-housing-affordability.aspx.

Vernonia (Oregon), City of. "Transportation Plan Documents." Available at www.vernonia-or.gov/TSP /index.asp.

Visit Seattle. 2014. "How is Metronatural Defined?" Available at http://visitseattle.org/Articles/Features-and-Latest-News/How-is-metronatural-defined-.aspx.

Walker, Richard. 2011. "Reclaiming the Duwamish River: A Conversation with James Rasmussen." *Indian Country Today Media Network*. November 23. Available at http://indiancountrytodaymedianetwork.com/2011/11/23/reclaiming-duwamish-river-conversation-james-rasmussen-64439.

Washington Department of Fish and Wildlife. 2014. "Hatcheries: Salmon Hatcheries Overview." Available http://wdfw.wa.gov/hatcheries/overview.html.

Washington State Department of Transportation. 2006. *Supplemental Draft Environmental Impact Statement*. Available at www.wsdot.wa.gov/Projects/Viaduct/Library/Environmental#SDEIS 2006.

_________. 2011a. "Seattle's Past." Available at http://viaducthistory.com/timeline.htm.

_________. 2011b. "Viaduct Beginnings: Planning." Available at http://viaducthistory.com/history.htm.

_________. 2012. "Tolling the SR 99 Tunnel." Available at www.wsdot.wa.gov/Projects/Viaduct/SR-99Tolling.

Washington State Department of Transportation, King County, and City of Seattle. 2009. *Alaskan Way Viaduct & Seawall Replacement Program, Central Waterfront Tri-Agency Partnership: Executives' Recommendation*. Available at www.wsdot.wa.gov/NR/rdonlyres/93710132-0DD1-4A3E-A9D4-6EB325007C65/0/ExecutivesRecommendationReport_Aug09.pdf.

Washington State Local Governance Study Commission. 1988. *The Quiet Crisis of Local Governance in Washington: Final Report of the Local Governance Study Commission*. Olympia, Wash.: Institute for Public Policy, The Evergreen State College. Available at www.leg.wa.gov/JointCommittees /JSCJTD/Documents/1988QuietCrisisofLocalGovernanceInWA.pdf.

Washington, State of. 1999. "Institutionalizing the Government-to- Government Relationship in Preparation for the New Millennium." Available at www.goia.wa.gov/government-to-government/data /agreement.htm.

________. 2002. "Sixteen Critical Basins: Basins with Shortage of Water for Fish." Available at www.ecy.wa.gov/programs/wr/instream-flows/Images/pdfs/16basinsmap.pdf.

________. 2013. *House Bill 1194*. Available at http://apps.leg.wa.gov/documents/billdocs/2013-14/Pdf/Bills/House%20Passed%20Legislature/1194.PL.pdf.

________. 2014. *Chapter 36.70A RCW, Growth Management*. Available at http://app.leg.wa.gov/rcw/default.aspx?cite=36.70A.

"Waterfront Design Honored for a Huge Scale That 'Still Feels Soft.'" 2013. *Seattle Daily Journal of Commerce*, October 7. Available at www.djc.com/news/ae/12057999.html.

Waycott, Michelle, Carlos M. Duarte, Tim. J.B. Carruthers, Robert Orth, William C. Dennison, Suzanne Olyarnik, Ainsley Calladine, James W. Fourqurean, Kenneth Heck Jr., A. Randall Hughes, Gary A. Kendrick, W. Judson Kenworthy, Frederick T. Short, and Susan L. Williams. 2009. "Accelerating Loss of Seagrasses across the Globe Threatens Coastal Ecosystems." *Proceedings of the National Academy of Sciences* 106 (30): 12377–12381.

Welch, Craig. "Sea Change: Oysters Dying as Coast Hit Hard." *Seattle Times*, September 12, Available at http://apps.seattletimes.com/reports/sea-change/2013/sep/11/oysters-hit-hard.

White, Richard. 1995. *The Organic Machine: The Remaking of the Columbia River*. New York: Hill and Wang.

Whyte, William H. 1968. *The Last Landscape*. Garden City, N.Y.: Doubleday.

Wiley, Pam. 2001. *No Place for Nature, The Limits of Oregon's Land Use Program in Protecting Fish and Wildlife Habitat in the Willamette Valley*. Washington D.C.: Defenders of Wildlife.

Wilkinson, Charles F. 2006. *Blood Struggle: The Rise of Modern Indian Nations*. New York: W. W. Norton & Company.

Williams, Alex. 2010. "From the Old to the New: Data Centers Rise Along the Columbia River." *Readwrite*, November 1. Available at http://readwrite.com/2010/11/01/from-the-old-economy-to-the-ne#awesm=~ond0FS7AEYeHUp.

Wilsonville (Oregon), City of. 2013a. *City of Wilsonville Comprehensive Plan*. Available at www.ci.wilsonville.or.us/DocumentCenter/View/ 553.

________. 2013b. *Section 4.008.02, Unique Features of Wilsonville's Development Review Process*. Available at www.ci.wilsonville.or.us/DocumentCenter/View/687.

________. 2013c. *Villebois Village Master Plan, Figure 1: Land Use Plan*. Available at www.ci.wilsonville.or.us/DocumentCenter/Home/View/939.

________. 2014. *Wilsonville Residential Land Study*. Prepared by ECONorthwest. Available at www.ci.wilsonville.or.us/DocumentCenter/View/6311.

World Resources Institute. 2014. "Infographic: The Global Carbon Budget." Available at www.wri.org/ipcc-infographics.

Wunderlich, Robert C., Brian D. Winter, and John H. Meyer. 1994. "Restoration of the Elwha River Ecosystem." *Fisheries*. 19 (8): 11–19.

Yakama Nation. 2013. "Chewuch River Recreation and Large Wood Assessment." Comments from online questionnaire.

Zaferatos, Nicholas Christos. 2004. "Tribal Nations, Local Governments, and Regional Pluralism in Washington State: The Swinomish Approach in the Skagit Valley." *Journal of the American Planning Association* 70 (Winter): 81–95.

CONTRIBUTORS

Kristina Ackley is a member of the faculty in Native American Studies at The Evergreen State College.

Sy Adler is professor of Urban Studies and Planning and associate dean of the College of Urban and Public Affairs at Portland State University.

Ben Bakkenta, AICP, is a program manager in the Puget Sound Regional Council's Growth Management Department.

Branden Born is an associate professor in the Department of Urban Design and Planning at the University of Washington.

Angie Brewer, AICP, is a senior regional planner for the Columbia River Gorge Commission.

Brian Campbell, FAICP, is a retired planner and urban designer in Portland, and represents District 5 on the American Planning Association's Board of Directors.

Manish Chalana is an associate professor in the Department of Urban Design and Planning at the University of Washington.

Kurt Creager is director of Housing & Community Development at Otak, Inc., a Portland, Oregon, design firm.

Marty Curry, AICP, worked for the city of Seattle for 25 years, including a role as planning commission director, and for 10 years as an affiliate faculty member in the Department of Urban Design and Planning at the University of Washington.

David Cutler is a principal and director of planning and urban design at GGLO and cochair of the Seattle Planning Commission.

Katherine Daniels, AICP, is the farm and forest lands specialist for the Oregon Department of Land Conservation and Development.

Karen Dyson is a candidate in the University of Washington Interdisciplinary PhD Program in Urban Design and Planning, and a member of the Urban Ecology Research Laboratory.

Ronald Eber was the farm and forest land specialist for the Oregon Department of Land Conservation and Development from 1976 until he retired in 2008.

Nicole Faghin is the coastal management specialist for Washington Sea Grant based at the University of Washington in Seattle.

Mary Fialko is a development manager at Tarragon in Seattle.

Lydia Fulton is in the last year of the bachelor's degree program in Architecture at the University of Washington.

Seth Geiser is the media and content coordinator for Happy City and is a 2014 Presidential Management Fellow.

Kristen Gelino is a student in the Master of Urban Design and Planning program at the University of Washington and has worked as a consultant in hazard mitigation planning for the past year.

Jennifer Gerend, AICP, is a member of the faculty in urban planning at The Evergreen State College.

Charles Heying is an associate professor at the Nohad A. Toulan School of Urban Studies and Planning at Portland State University.

Michele Hill is a recent graduate of the Master of Urban Planning program at the University of Washington and is a founding principal of Xylo Hill Design, a design and planning firm in Seattle.

Megan Horst, AICP, is a PhD candidate in Urban Design and Planning at the University of Washington.

Michael Houck is executive director of the Urban Greenspaces Institute, cofounder of The Intertwine Alliance, and a member of the Planning and Sustainability Commission in Portland, Oregon.

Eric J. Howard is a student in the Interdisciplinary PhD Program in Urban Design and Planning and a research assistant with the Urban Form Lab at the University of Washington.

Betsy Jacobson, AICP, is an urban designer at MAKERS Architecture and Urban Design LLP in Seattle.

Cayce James is a candidate in the Master of Landscape Architecture program at the University of Washington and manager of the Green Futures Research and Design Lab.

Julie Kriegh, an international passive-house consultant, is principal of Kriegh Architecture Studios in Seattle and an AIA 2014 Upjohn Fellow.

Mary Pat Lawlor is a program manager in the Puget Sound Regional Council's Administrative Services Department.

Gary Lettman is the former principal forest economist for the Oregon Department of Forestry.

Nicole Lewis, AICP, is a Portland, Oregon, native and professional planner with MIG, Inc., a multidisciplinary planning firm with offices in Oregon, California, and Colorado.

Terra Lingley, AICP, is a project manager and transportation planner at CH2M HILL in Portland, Oregon.

Jeffrey B. Litwak is legal counsel for the Columbia River Gorge Commission and an adjunct professor of law at Lewis And Clark Law School In Portland, Oregon.

Salina Lyons, AICP, is the principal planner in the Community Development Department of Covington, Washington.

Michael J. McCormick, FAICP, has served state and local government and residents of Washington State for over 45 years as a planner, administrator of the state Growth Management Act office, and as a planning consultant.

Sheila Martin is a professor in the Nohad A. Toulan School of Urban Studies and Planning and director of the Institute of Portland Metropolitan Studies and the Population Research Center at Portland State University.

Sarah Mooney splits her time between her home in Portland, Oregon, and Black Sheep Creamery in Adna, Washington, where she makes cheese and plays with lambs.

Chris Neamtzu, AICP, is the planning director of Wilsonville, Oregon.

Alyse Nelson, AICP, works as a Public Space Management Permit Reviewer in the Seattle Department of Transportation and as a Sightline Institute Writing Fellow.

Ian Nunley is a candidate in the Master of Urban Design and Planning program at the University of Washington.

John Owen is a partner at MAKERS architecture and urban design, a consulting firm in Seattle.

Connie Ozawa is director of and professor at the School of Urban Studies and Planning at Portland State University and director of the PSU-China Innovations in Urbanization Program.

Valerie Pacino is a climate protection planning specialist in Seattle's Office of Sustainability and Environment.

Daniel Pauly, AICP, is an associate planner in the Wilsonville, Oregon's Planning Division.

Paul Peninger is an independent housing and urban economics consultant based in San Francisco.

Andrea Petzel, AICP, the former project manager for Community Power Works for Home, is the principal of Broadview Planning.

Amanda Joy Pietz is the transportation planning unit manager for the Oregon Department of Transportation.

Hillary Pritchett is a candidate in the Master of Architecture and the Master of Landscape Architecture programs at the University of Washington.

Miranda Redinger is a senior planner in Shoreline, Washington. She co-manages the city's station-area planning work.

Paula Reeves, AICP CTP, is manager of community design for the Washington Department of Transportation's Local Programs Division.

Amanda Roberts, AICP, is a principal, urban planner, and community design specialist with Otak, Inc. She assisted the Growing Transit Communities Partnership with support on the projects highlighted.

Mary Roderick is a candidate in the Interdisciplinary PhD in Urban Design and Planning program at the University of Washington.

Nancy Rottle is an associate professor at the University of Washington in the departments of Landscape Architecture, Architecture, and Urban Planning and Design, and director of the Green Futures Research and Design Lab.

Anne Russett, AICP, is a senior planner for the Oregon Department of Transportation.

Dennis Ryan was the founding director of the Urban Design Program at the University of Washington. He continues to teach part time and also practices environmental design in the San Juan Islands.

Ethan Seltzer is a professor in the Nohad A. Toulan School of Urban Studies and Planning at Portland State University, and was the school's former director. He was also the founding director of Portland State's Institute of Portland Metropolitan Studies.

Jill Sterrett, FAICP, is an affiliate instructor with the Department of Urban Design and Planning at the University of Washington and principal of Sterrett Consulting, LLC.

Ed Sullivan has practiced land-use law in Oregon for 45 years and has written extensively on the Oregon planning system.

Holly Taylor is principal of Past Forward Northwest Cultural Services and a student in the University of Washington's PhD program in the Built Environment, where she studies historic preservation policy.

Joseph Tovar, FAICP, is a consultant, former city planning director, past chair of the Growth Management Hearings Board, and an affiliate associate professor at the University of Washington.

Paddy Tillett, FAICP, who began his career in the United Kingdom, is a principal planner and urban designer with ZGF Architects LLP in Portland, Oregon.

Tim Trohimovich, AICP, is director of planning and law for Futurewise in Seattle.

Kristen A. Vitro is a graduate of the Masters of Urban Planning program at the University of Washington, and a PhD student in the Department of City and Regional Planning at the University of North Carolina.

Roger Wagoner, FAICP, is a former Seattle planning commissioner. He is now a consultant on neighborhood plans, and volunteers in his own neighborhood planning process. He continues to be active in the implementation of neighborhood plans.

Marie Walkiewicz is an environmental program coordinator at Portland, Oregon's Bureau of Environmental Services on the Johnson Creek Watershed Team.

Jan Whittington is an assistant professor in the Department of Urban Design and Planning at the University of Washington, Seattle.

Ken Yocom is an assistant professor in Landscape Architecture and the graduate program coordinator at the University of Washington.

Stefanie Young is a PhD student in Urban Design and Planning at the University of Washington and has worked for the past five years as an urban planner and architecture designer focusing on sustainability.

CREDITS

Pages xvi–xvii	John Owen and Betsy Jacobson, MAKERS architecture and urban design, LLP, and Brian Campbell, FAICP
Page xxii	Seattle Art Museum
Figure 1.1	John Owen and Betsy Jacobson, MAKERS Architecture and Urban Design, LLP
Figure 2.1	Joseph W. Tovar
Figure 2.2	Joseph W. Tovar
Figure 2.3	Washington Department of Commerce
Figure 4.1	Sy Adler
Figure 4.2	Meg Merrick
Figure 4.3	C. Bruce Forster
Figure 5.1	Gary Lettman, Oregon Department of Forestry
Figure 5.2	Gary Lettman, Oregon Department of Forestry
Figure 5.3	Gary Lettman, Oregon Department of Forestry
Figure 5.4	Gary Lettman, Oregon Department of Forestry
Figure 5.5	Gary Lettman, Oregon Department of Forestry
Figure 5.6	Gary Lettman, Oregon Department of Forestry
Figure 6.3	Daniel Pauly
Page 76	Growth Strategy map, from Puget Sound Regional Council VISION 2020 rendering: Puget Sound Regional Council. Reprinted with permission.
Page 77	Market Street Improvements Plan schematic: City of Seattle
Page 78	Planning for Downtown Seattle: City of Seattle
Page 78	Pioneer Square Plan map: City of Seattle
Page 79	Denny Regrade Development Plan schematic: City of Seattle
Page 79	South Lake Union Urban Design Framework schematic: City of Seattle

Page 80	Overlake Village Final Phase Visualization: City of Redmond/Crandall Arambula
Page 81	Central Waterfront Plan Vision Looking South photo: City of Seattle
Figure 10.1	University of Washington Libraries, Special Collections, UW36289
Figure 10.2	Tim Thompson
Figure 10.3	Holly Taylor
Figure 11.1	City of Portland Archives and Records Management
Figure 11.2	Metro Sustainability Center, 2014
Figure 11.3	Courtesy of Seattle Parks and Recreation
Figure 11.4	Open Space Seattle 2100
Page 110	Artist, Robert Connell; image, Davidson Galleries
Figure 13.1	Map by Arlen Speights
Figure 13.2	Laura Grabhorn
Figure 13.3	Arlen Speights
Figure 14.1	Port of Bellingham
Figure 14.2	Port of Bellingham
Figure 14.3	PWL Partnership Landscape Architects Inc.
Figure 14.4	PWL Partnership Landscape Architects Inc.
Figure 14.5	Karen Dyson
Figure 14.6	Karen Dyson
Figure 15.1	Photo from the Oregon Department of Transportation archives
Figure 15.2	Columbia River Gorge Commission
Figure 16.1	Seattle Housing Authority
Figure 16.2	REACH
Figure 17.1	Nancy Rottle
Figure 17.2	City of Portland, Environmental Services
Figure 17.3	Nancy Rottle
Figure 17.4	Nancy Rottle
Figure 17.5	Downspout Disconnect Program photo: Ecoroof; Infiltration Gardens photo, Tabor to the River map: Portland Bureau of Environmental Services; Swale on Yale photo: Seattle Public Utilities; all other photos: Nancy Rottle; graphic layout: Cayce James
Figure 18.1	Teresa M. Fish
Figure 21.1	City of Seattle, Community Power Works
Figure 21.2	Clean Energy Works
Figure 23.1	Courtesy Seattle Municipal Archives, Item number 4313
Figure 23.2	"The Alaskan Way Viaduct" by Rootology—Own work. August 8, 2008. Licensed under Creative Commons Attribution-Share Alike 3.0 via Wikimedia Commons, http://commons.wikimedia.org/wiki/File:The_Alaskan_Way_Viaduct.jpg
Figure 24.1	Manish Chalana
Figure 24.2	Keith Harris/People's Parking Lot
Figure 24.3	Manish Chalana
Figure 25.1	Courtesy of Kriegh Architecture Studios, Seattle, Washington
Figure 25.2	Courtesy of Green Futures Lab, University of Washington, Seattle, Washington

Figure 25.3	Courtesy of Green Futures Lab, University of Washington, Seattle, Washington
Figure 26.1	© City of Portland, courtesy Bureau of Environmental Services
Figure 26.2	© City of Portland, courtesy Bureau of Environmental Services
Figure 26.3	© City of Portland, courtesy Bureau of Environmental Services
Figure 26.4	© City of Portland, courtesy Bureau of Environmental Services
Figure 26.5	© City of Portland, courtesy Bureau of Environmental Services
Page 230	Courtesy of PDX Contemporary Art and James Lavadour
Figure 27.1	Courtesy of ZGF Architects LLP; © Bruce Forster Photography, Inc.
Figure 27.2	Paddy Tillett
Figure 28.1	Alyse Nelson
Figure 28.2	Alyse Nelson
Figure 28.3	Greg Raisman/Portland Bureau of Transportation
Figure 28.4	Alyse Nelson
Figure 28.5	Nathaniel S. Cormier, ASLA, PLA, LEED AP
Figure 29.1	U.S. Army Corps of Engineers (http://commons.wikimedia.org/wiki /File:Corps-engineers-archives_celilo_falls_color.jpg)
Figure 30.1	Oregon Department of Transportation
Figure 31.1	Ken Yokom
Figure 31.2	U.S. National Park Service
Figure 31.3	Brian Cluer Photography
Figure 32.1	Courtesy GGLO
Figure 32.2	Courtesy Seattle 2030 District
Figure 34.1	Map created by Megan Horst
Figure 35.1	Sarah Mooney
Figure 35.2	Sarah Mooney
Figure 36.1	Puget Sound Regional Council
Figure 36.2	Otak, Incorporated
Figure 37.1	Seth Geiser, Betsy Jacobson, and Mary Fialko
Figure 38.1	Mary Roderick
Figure 38.2	Mary Roderick
Page 321	John Owen, MAKERS architecture and urban design, LLP
Page 322	John Owen, MAKERS architecture and urban design, LLP
Page 323	John Owen, MAKERS architecture and urban design, LLP
Pages 330–331	John Owen and Betsy Jacobson, MAKERS architecture and urban design, LLP, and Brian Campbell, FAICP

9781611901283